I0117770

CENTERFIRE RIFLES:

A BUYER'S AND

SHOOTER'S GUIDE

SPECIAL AR-15 SECTION INCLUDED

by

STEVE MARKWITH

Part of the *Survival Guns* series of books
published by:

Prepper Press
Your Survival Library

PrepperPress.com/SurvivalGuns

Centerfire Rifles: A Buyer's and Shooter's Guide

Special AR-15 Section Included

ISBN 13: 978-1-939473-48-6

Copyright © 2016 by Steve Markwith

All rights reserved.

Printed in the United States of America.

Prepper Press Trade Paperback Edition: November 2017

Prepper Press is a division of Kennebec Publishing, LLC

No part of this book may be reproduced or utilized in any form or by any means, electronic or me-chanical, including photocopying, recording, or by any information storage or retrieval system, with-out permission in writing from Kennebec Publishing, LLC.

Photos and illustrations used throughout the book are privately owned, public domain, or licensed under the Creative Commons Attributions-Share Alike or GNU Free Documentation License, except where credits are otherwise noted.

Disclaimer. This book is intended to offer general guidance relating to firearms. It is sold with the understanding that every effort was made to provide accurate information; however, errors are still possible. The author and publisher make no warrantees or claims as to the truth or validity of the information. The author and publisher shall have neither liability nor responsibility to any person or entity over any loss or damage caused, or alleged to have been caused, directly or indirectly, by the information contained within this book.

ABOUT THE AUTHOR

Steve has a lifelong interest in just about all things that shoot including rifles, shotguns, revolvers, pistols, airguns, and black powder guns, as well as vertical or horizontal bows.

He began formal firearms training at age 11 during NRA-sanctioned small-bore target rifle events, and was an active hunter by the age of 12. He began reloading shotgun shells at 14, using a handheld Lee Loader to feed his addiction.

After joining the U.S. Army, he served two combat tours in Vietnam, gaining experience with numerous military firearms during Air Cavalry helicopter operations and ground-based reconnaissance missions.

Upon returning to civilian life, Steve resumed shooting, participating in NRA bullseye, combat pistol, and trap events. These activities expanded his reloading experience to metallic ammunition and bullet casting. Steve eventually became an NRA-certified pistol, rifle & shotgun instructor, as well as a certifying official for state firearms permit applicants. He also worked for a well-known gunsmith and PO Ackley disciple, until an untimely death forced a career change.

Joining a major state correctional agency, Steve was soon appointed as a firearms instructor, eventually assuming control of all state correctional firearms operations. He's still working, and holds a master instructor rating, plus numerous other federal, state, and industry certifications. He has over 25 years of full-time firearms training experience, and many industry connections.

Steve also has extensive hunting experience in the Northeast, and at other locations throughout the United States. He holds an archery deer record, and actively remains afield on a year-round basis, whether chasing spring turkeys or winter coyotes with night-vision equipped AR-15s. He also writes when time permits, and has had numerous articles published about firearms and the great outdoors.

PREFACE

The birds were singing and the sun was shining. Our Firearms Training Unit members all agreed it was a good day to be on the range and, before long a shiny new SUV pulled in. Out came an intriguing gun case, so we gathered around a bench as a very tactical new rifle emerged. It was time for a pitch from an equally "tactical" salesman. Afterward, our FTU instructors assembled on the firing line for a turn behind the trigger. I was up first, so I corked off a few rounds. Mr. Tactical was into volume and urged me on as the other instructors eagerly awaited their chance. That's when a technical difficulty arose. Upon my next volley a major structural part fell off, thus ending the demonstration and any sales prospects. The newer cadre members had been mesmerized by this blaster, and now appeared crushed. Others, not so much...

While shiny new toys are nice, a few of us had been here before with things like supposedly high-end firearms that wound up going full-auto. There was the massive large-caliber bolt-gun that gutted its scope on the third shot. Another military-type rifle fired out of battery when the bolt went home, spraying brass shrapnel in all directions. We've also had a few pistols blow up for no apparent reason. These episodes illustrate why we do "testing and evaluation" prior to embracing the latest marvel. For that matter, T&E never really stops. A few decades behind a firing line present further opportunities to see what works – as well as what doesn't. "Works" by the way, means more than reliable function. Ergonomics, control, and ease of operation also count, as does requisite training. The last factor is often overlooked, and accounts for a recurring KISS theme throughout the entire Survival Guns series.

Once again, In keeping with the other editions, I've tried to stick with firearms, ammunition, and equipment with which we've had the most experience. The "we" refers to not only me, but also a well-seasoned group of firearms cadre, and other trusted contacts from the fascinating world of shooting.

THE SURVIVAL GUNS FIREARMS SERIES

This book is one of several Survival Guns firearm publications. The first lays out some basic principles, while the others deal with specific firearm systems. It should be noted that a "system" consists not only of a gun, but also its ammunition, and related equipment. The complexity of each further relates to training and practice needs, which are part of its true bottom line. A thorough understanding of each system can fully exploit its capabilities without undue expense. A planned procurement strategy is of further benefit, since firearms with similar function can improve overall proficiency. The upcoming selection guidelines govern the whole process, and the series runs as follows:

Practice, training and fun made possible by planned procurement: This rimfire/centerfire shares common function.

SURVIVAL GUNS: A BEGINNER'S GUIDE

In the first publication we laid out some groundwork for a practical collection of firearms. Each was geared toward "Prepper" use, and chosen from key requirements. Widespread use; dependability; ease of operation; availability of parts, accessories, and ammunition were thrown in the mix. Also covered was a hard look at firearms safety and responsible firearms ownership. Part of that process involved secure storage methods. We procured a gun safe and then framed up a small but practical inventory of firearms based on these requirements, adding a shotgun, rimfire rifle, centerfire rifle, and a handgun. The idea was to choose, when possible, types with similar function. Use of each would thus promote skills with another to improve overall proficiency. Toward that goal, our initial selections were based on the K.I.S.S. principle. We had to start somewhere, and most of us don't have deep enough pockets to rush headlong into the nearest Guns –R-Us for an arm load of shootin' irons. We needed something to cover the basics while developing resources to fund other items. That's where the second book began….

SHOTGUNS: A COMPREHENSIVE GUIDE

The second edition served as a specific firearms starting point, and examined this versatile but often misunderstood firearm. You'll sometimes hear it called a "scattergun" in reference to its multiple-projectile payload. However, pellet distribution is based on a number of factors ranging from gauges through chokes. A carefully selected shotgun can also utilize single projectiles to extend its range or tackle the largest North American game animals. From birds to defense, a shotgun offers many useful options, making it a good first choice for our safe. The right shotgun also makes a great foundation for future acquisitions, which leads us to the next edition…

RIMFIRE RIFLES: A BUYER'S AND SHOOTER'S GUIDE

Several different calibers are classified as rimfires, beginning with the well-known .22 Long Rifle. The venerable "twenty-two" hosts a wide array of interesting loads, including some ultra-quiet choices and fairly nasty high-speed rounds. Even hotter rimfire calibers include the .22 Winchester Magnum Rimfire; plus three small-bore derivatives, the .17 Mach II; .17 Hornady Rimfire Magnum;; and Winchester's high velocity.17 Super Magnum. Careful shopping can provide a useful rimfire (or maybe even two), with which to quietly harvest small game or eliminate pests. An economical .22 LR firearm can also serve as a great high powered rifle trainer if similar function is considered beforehand. A rimfire can't do *everything*, but it can do a lot once fully understood.

AIR RIFLES: A BUYER'S AND SHOOTER'S GUIDE

Air-powered guns offer a number of useful advantages. For starters, they are unregulated by BATF, meaning they have non-firearm status. Some state and local restrictions exist but, in most municipalities, you can order one by mail. Many airguns are also very quiet - a useful advantage if low-impact hunting is necessary. Uninformed people will lump them all together as simple BB guns, but the field has greatly evolved. The general lack of knowledge does provide an additional benefit. An airgun tends to be publicly more acceptable in areas that would raise firearm concerns. Not everyone will need or want an air-powered system, choosing low-powered .22 loads instead. Confusion can play a role in this decision due to the various power-plants and types. Performance and pricing varies widely, from garden-variety pellet guns, through precise examples of airgun manufacturing. Some of are even available in head-turning calibers like 9mm, .45, or .50! The airgun is an interesting specialty tool for clandestine subsistence, quiet practice, and all around fun.

SELECTION GUIDELINES

Let's examine the key requirements referenced in the previous editions. With apologies to those readers who already labored through them, the criteria laid out here may avoid future headaches.

Whatever we're looking at must be in widespread use: An established design is reassuring. It takes time for a system to gain recognition and grow in numbers. Well-established firearms have plenty of history behind them, and will hold few surprises. Widespread use is an indicator of numerous desirable traits.

Whatever we choose should be something with a solid reputation for dependability: It's comforting to have confidence in a chosen tool. As explained in Survival Guns, there are teething pains with many new products and firearms are no exception. It's not uncommon to run into issues ranging from function through ergonomics. Anecdotal experience based on one or two examples can give you a false read and, more often than not, seems to be the basis for unswerving opinions. A well-established track record is the better bet.

It must be easy to operate: Disparate function is never a good thing during stressful circumstances, and operational proficiency is commensurate with training. The more complicated something is, the more training will be necessary. If time and range access are issues, simple is better. Also, simpler designs normally offer less opportunity for breakage. But, even the simplest systems can quit working at some point, so...

Parts must be readily available: *During Shotguns: A Comprehensive Guide,* we held up the Remington Model 870 as an example of 10 million-plus firearms that have been in continuous production since 1950. In other words, plenty of spare parts abound. The same is true of heavily produced military systems like the U.S. M-16/AR-15 rifle. Other firearms like Marlin's line of lever-actions span a century of continuous production. Using a proven system, you can predict which parts are likely to fail and stock up on spares.

Ammunition must be widely available: You can't go wrong with an established military caliber like the 5.56 mm (.223 Remington); or 7.62x51 NATO (.308 Winchester). Just about any hardware store with an FFL will have .30/06 cartridges on hand. When you're buying, mainstream choices will just about always be cheaper and if you're scrounging, the odds will tip in your favor. You can also benefit from a much wider selection of loads to match individual requirements.

It must be easy to maintain: In a survival situation function is crucial. At some point, even the best-designed firearms will quit without cleaning. Simpler designs facilitate the process, which will also prolong the life of your investment. Good walnut and polished bluing may be esthetically pleasing, but synthetic stocks and stainless-steel are better in rough weather. Even stainless can rust though, so attention will still be necessary. Captive parts and easy disassembly also help when on the go.

It should accommodate practical accessories:

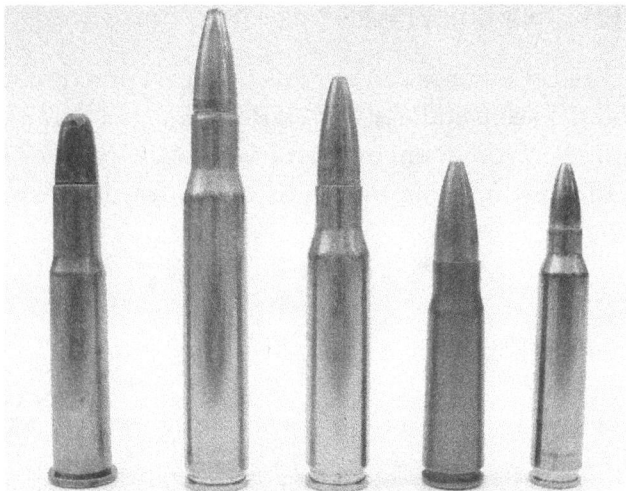

Common cartridges are good insurance if scarcity is a concern. L-R: .30/30; .30/06; .308; 7.62x39 Russian; 5.56 NATO (.223).

It's easy to overlook some simple necessities, one good example being a sling. QD sling swivel mounts help, whether offered from the factory, or fitted later. Scope mounts are important, too. By sticking with the most popular guns, availability of such accessories is assured. You'll have little trouble equipping a Remington Model 700 rifle, thanks to 50+ years of steady sales. The AR-15 rifle offers possibilities never imagined by its designers. Nowadays, a real concern involves knowing where to draw the line. We needn't go overboard, but it's nice to have some practical options.

Complexity should not be ignored and some prospective owners would be well-served by a simpler firearm. However, due to its long service life, millions of veterans can operate an M-16 variant on demand. Training is a major component of a system's cost.

It must represent good value: The well-known rule of thumb is to buy the best equipment you can afford.

However, when it comes to firearms, "equipment" means more than just a gun. Looking at a rifle some basics extras like a scope, mounts, sling, case, ammo, and a few spare magazines may be needed. Adding up the essentials (with extra room for training), creates a real bottom line. We call this our "system cost." An honest rifle at a fair price can help keep a lid on expense.

THE NEXT STEPS

These guidelines can steer us toward a practical firearms battery, but where do we start? The possibilities seem endless! For starters, why not break the whole rifle subject down into more manageable pieces? From there, we can more easily examine the finer points. In keeping with the above tenets, our primary focus will be directed toward firearms and gear with established track records.

TABLE OF CONTENTS

ADDENDUM

CENTERFIRE RIFLES: A BUYER'S AND SHOOTER'S GUIDE.

SECTION ONE: GENERAL PURPOSE RIFLES

CHAPTER 1

INTRODUCTION

With a shotgun on hand, we'll be well-equipped to defend our premises, harvest waterfowl, or even tackle big game. Our rimfire rifle can put meat in the pot and sharpen our skills without shaking up the countryside. An air rifle also makes a nice addition for practice or clandestine critter operations. While the first two firearms constitute essential systems, neither has the reach to cover every circumstance. We could just ditch the rimfire in favor of a bigger rifle, but everyone within two miles will know when you touch it off. If your target is small game you'll probably wind up hungry, too.

On the other hand, when bigger game or longer ranges are called for, a dependable high power rifle is just the ticket. If ducking incoming fire from distances beyond 125 yards, neither the shotgun nor rimfire is likely to save the day. Instead, a rifle with adequate range and power is called for. It will hopefully be chambered for a commonly available caliber without excessive recoil, at a reasonable-cost. Here's a problem though: There are lots of choices!

The British .303 SMLE soldiered through two world wars and can still be found in far corners of the globe.

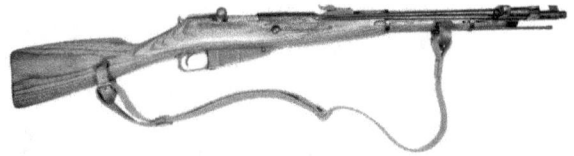

The 7.62x54 circa 1891 Mosin-Nagant was Russia's flagship battle rifle for decades. It's still common for good reason. Like other principle military bolt-actions, it works.

It boils down to an appropriate system, whether bolt-action, lever, pump or self-loading. Perhaps, if you've labored through the previous editions, you have one in mind. If you can match it up with a centerfire version, so much the better. We'll also need to choose a caliber suitable for our needs. The rifle I have in mind would be comfortable to carry for extended periods, on the move. It would also fire a full-power cartridge. By that I mean one of the many similar rounds fielded by various military forces during the early 1900s. A few that come to mind are the famous and still very popular: U.S. Army .30/06, the German 8mm Mauser, Soviet 7.62x54mm, and .303 British. I'm not necessarily advocating for one of these specific rounds so much as I am something of their equivalent power. The exception is the immortal .30/06 Springfield which, although adopted in 1906, is still the American benchmark when comparing relative power.

U.S. Military cartridges, shown in chronological order of development (R-L): 9mm Luger; .45 ACP; .30/06 Springfield; .30 Carbine; 7.62x51 NATO (.308); 5.56x45 NATO (.223). Although the 9mm was fielded by Germany in 1908, it didn't see widespread NATO/U.S. use until the 1980s.

Flashing back in time, the various ordnance boards from the early 20th century were probably composed of experienced officers who had a firm grasp of so-called "stopping power." The new generation of military bolt-action rifles fielded during that period were designed to handle a revolutionary series of high velocity, flat-shooting calibers. The prospect of long-range engagements was now a reality and every army wanted in. The United States Army learned a bitter lesson about such performance during the Spanish American War. Seriously out-ranged by Spanish 7x57mm Mausers, it wasn't long before the .30/06 Springfield arrived on the scene. It's probably no coincidence that the equally famous .45 ACP was adopted shortly thereafter. To this day both remain gold standards despite pre-dating World War I.

During World War II, the revolutionary German STG 44 arrived, along with its shortened 8mm "assault rifle" cartridge. Power was less than a traditional battle rifle, but the diminished recoil improved control during full-auto fire. Today's military cartridges, the 5.56mm NATO and 7.62x39mm Russian, owe their lineage to this concept. They represent a series of shorter and less powerful cartridges that fire lighter bullets. Interestingly, they see only limited use in the game fields of America. Those who stalk deer, bear, elk, and moose continue to use cartridges approximating World War I performance. As often as not, the rifle they carry is chambered for a .30/06, or even a more powerful magnum caliber.

The WWII German STG-44 assault rifle strikes a familiar profile. Is the resemblance to an AK-47 more than coincidence?

However, interest in the 5.56mm is now huge. The civilian version is known as the .223 Remington, which can be fired in a NATO chamber. The lion's share of this ammunition is fired through M-16 and AR-15 type rifles, used by military, law enforcement, and civilian shooters. Much of the interest is geared toward defensive roles, but sporting use is on the rise. You'll see such rifles referred to as MSRs, which stands for "Modern Sporting Rifles." Varmint shooters embraced the .223 early on, but its popularity has spurred the development of .223 loads designed for bigger animals—within limits.

Then there's long-range mania, which has recently set in, driven by accurate rifles, high-performance loads, laser range finders, and trajectory-compensating scopes. A new wave of shooters feels woefully inadequate unless equipped to engage targets beyond 500 yards. This is great in principle, but there is also reality. Somewhere between the extremes lies a viable choice with adequate range, moderate recoil, portability, and widespread ammunition availability—all for reasonable cost. For many, but not all of us, that choice will be a U.S. military caliber—the 7.62x 51 NATO. You may better recognize it as the .308 Winchester. It's a widely distributed, well-proven, and shorter Cold War version of the .30/06 (with nearly

After five decades of strong interest, the Cold War M-16 has evolved to its hugely popular MSR format. A pistol grip remains but the semi-auto AR-15 is NOT an "assault rifle."

Precise long-range capability comes at a price beyond dollars. Don't forget weight.

the same punch). For close-to-medium range defense, the .223 fills a low-recoil, high capacity niche.

Let's jump off the cartridge bandwagon for a moment and look at rifles. Ideally, we'll own something relatively portable. Unless you're built like Attila the Hun, a super-sized rifle with a 26-inch barrel won't be much fun to lug around. Most magnums use bigger actions with longer barrels to help burn extra powder. A .300 Winchester Magnum can charitably be called a "man-sized rifle.." Velocity will increase over a .30/06 by around 200 fps, boosting performance to a whole new level. Recoil will increase as well, and a fairly light rifle won't be much fun to shoot. Based on our experience running daily firearms programs, recoil is a major problem for many shooters—including a bunch of seasoned sportsmen built like Paul Bunyan. Their reaction to recoil is often a flinch, accompanied by downward muzzle movement in anticipation of the bang. This action is, obviously, undesirable. Since a lighter rifle in a given caliber generally has greater kick, the more potent calibers benefit from the added weight associated with their construction.

Newer cartridges like the .300 Winchester Short Magnum (.300 WSM) have the overall length of a .308, but use a fatter case that holds more powder. Feeding can be balky but they'll fit in a short action receiver to help reduce rifle size. Velocity will be close to a .300 Win Magnum. The concept is clever, providing magnum power in a short action rifle, good for long distance treks in rough country. It'll also kick more than a plain old .308. Jumping on that bandwagon early on, I picked up a highly customized, lightweight Remington Model Seven bolt-action chambered for the similar .300 SAUM. SAUM stands for "Short Action Ultra Mag," which is a bit of a mouthful. Two points I'll note about this combination are:

The .300 Short Action Ultra Mag and .308 share the same case length, but the SAUM holds more powder. Good luck finding ammo on the fly!

1. It kicks like a mule.

2. Factory ammo is drying up.

I fixed the recoil problem by installing a muzzle brake. The reduction was dramatic, and it now kicks more like a .243! On the downside, its report can be heard in Ecuador.

The Remington .300 SAUM actually pre-dates the .300 WSM and both are very similar but, for whatever reason, the Remington offering is fading away. When I bought the rifle I also invested in 500 new cartridge cases, which are still hand-loaded in small increments. I'm not worried about running out of bullets since it shares the same .30 caliber projectiles used in other calibers. As long as I'm close to home life is good; but, I'd hate to evacuate without that brass, or the dies to reload it with. In the unlikely event .300 SAUM ammo was found, price would be off the charts.

Had I stayed with a good old .308, I could've used the same size rifle, which would've kicked significantly less, providing a very useful level of performance with a readily available cartridge. Indeed, there is something to be said for "widely available" and "well-established.." The .223/5.56 easily meets these criteria but, as a hunter, I'd like more punch. Still, I'd hate to be without this caliber, which we'll explore more thoroughly in the AR-15 section.

Many diehard firearm enthusiasts tend to shun more common cartridges for more exotic chamberings. The approach is somewhat elitist but, admittedly, it's also fun to play with new toys. I'm guilty of this but not at the expense of forgetting my roots. Our family guns bear markings like .308 and .30/06 for good reasons. Others will swear by a .270, .280, 7mm Remington Magnum, or any one of dozens of other great cartridges. More than one heated campfire debate has centered on the virtues of one caliber versus another. Truth be told, most such calibers work pretty well. The challenge may involve wrapping a useful rifle around the caliber of your preference. By sticking to common ground the odds for success improve.

CHAPTER 2

GUIDELINES

We examined the various action types in the rimfire edition of this series. Essentially, they boil down to bolt-actions, lever gun-actions; pump-actions; and semi-automatics. We can throw single-shot rifles and combination guns in as well, although more as ala carte servings.

Among the four main types many good choices exist (although the pump gun field is admittedly narrow). Instead of endorsing one type as the best, why not look at several good candidates? The bolt-action probably reigns supreme with precision marksmen and big game hunters, but plenty of good woodsmen cut their teeth on lever-actions. Some of these folks can make one sing like a semi-auto; another popular choice. The pump or slide-action is hugely popular among shotgunners but, for some strange reason, less so with the rifle crowd. However, it's nearly as fast as a self-loading rifle, making a good smoothbore companion. One thing all may share is hard use. If so, there are desirable traits to consider before narrowing down the field.

PRACTICAL CONSIDERATIONS

Some folks have guns they call "safe queens," which generally dwell securely within the confines of a stable environment, protected from bumps and falls. Even serious outdoorsmen often own a showpiece firearm, which will have little chance of seeing a snowflake or raindrop. When the going gets tough you can bet they'll reach for a simpler but well-tested alternative, complete with dings and accompanying stories.

Real world factors: While a rimfire may not see much use during extreme conditions, a shotgun and centerfire rifle more than likely will. At such times, a durable and weather-resistant firearm will be a desirable commodity. Things can also go to hell in a hurry. A horse could fall on your rifle scabbard or you could flip an ATV. I snapped a custom $2,000 rifle in half at the wrist of its stock after getting tangled up with a barb wire strand before dawn (yes, it was sickening). A bad fall may not always wreck a rifle but it can unravel a scope. It's often worth having an alternate sighting system, along with some means to make the switch.

Scopes have come a long way, and even our traditionally-minded military has acquiesced to optics. A dependable and accurate rifle will benefit greatly from a weatherproof aiming system capable of resolving difficult targets. Conventional iron sights lack the precision for surgical shot placement and don't work well in low light. A decent scope solves these problems nicely and, since most modern rifles are now designed to accommodate optics, it's easy to assemble a practical combination. One potential problem for a prepper is that many rifles now lack any other aiming system. Although iron sights have limitations, it's reassuring to know they are available for backup use. Carefully chosen scope mounting systems can permit toolless detachment on the spot. When shopping for a rifle it's worth at least considering those models with backup sights.

Some level of useful accuracy also helps. Nowadays, every rifle crank (including me) obsesses over the "minute of angle" (MOA) bar.

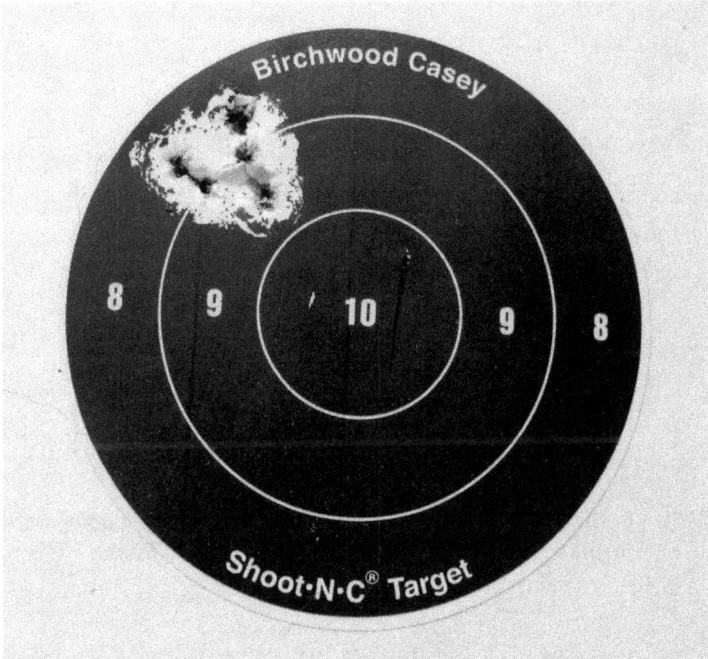

This 5-shot, sub-MOA group was fired from a solid rest at 100 yards. It's pretty but we could survive with more generous standards.

MOA defined: An MOA is an angular measurement equaling 1/60th of a degree, which translates into roughly one inch at 100 yards (1.047" to be exact). A field grade rifle that can place three consecutive shots within this space is considered "accurate.." A heavier-barreled tactical rifle will be expected to deliver five such rounds within one MOA, although many can do better. This level of accuracy will be tested off a solid rest with as much of the human factor eliminated as possible. There's also practical accuracy, influenced by numerous factors from weather to individual ability. For our purposes, a sturdy but portable general purpose rifle should do the job. Truthfully, although an MOA rifle is nice, we could live with a bit less.

DESIREABLE TRAITS

First off, it's not a perfect world, so there is seldom "the perfect choice.." Even if the ideal pick does magically appear, money plays a key role. If we can wrap in some key features, we might do worse than settle for a solid meat and potatoes compromise.

Practical accuracy: Most of today's bolt-actions will do 1.5 MOA without any trouble. Plenty of other types including plain lever-actions will put three shots inside 2 MOA. In the latter case, the rifle will be mechanically capable of putting a bullet within one inch of its sights at 100 yards. Using a garden-variety .30/30 and the right loads, maximum useful range will probably stretch to 200 yards. That's still a fair poke. At that distance, even the 'ol lever gun will tag a four-inch target in the hands of a good shot.

A plain 1.5 MOA bolt-action gun will shoot within three inches of the crosshairs at 400 yards—sufficient accuracy for most endeavors. Many shooters probably lack the experience to reliably judge range, wind, and hold allowance anyway. Without these skills, shooting to the far side of 200 yards is iffy at best. Assuming better than 1.5 MOA is possible there are still other things to fuss over.

Metal work: Tough use calls for a durable rifle, which should also include its finish. Some people worry about the reflective aspect of stainless steel. I once picked up on a blinding flash from several hundred yards, which turned out to be another hunter equipped with bright, stainless rifle. I'll concede this concern may have validity in some environments. Much of my hunting is in thick places at close range and, so far, I'm not aware of any game-spooking episodes. Because deer season in northern New England can involve harsh weather, I'll gladly go with stainless whenever I can. Some of the bead-blasted finishes are fairly dull, which helps. The latest advances include rust-resistant finishes, which are sometimes applied to bare stainless surfaces. Since stainless steel can still rust over time with neglect, the extra coating pro-

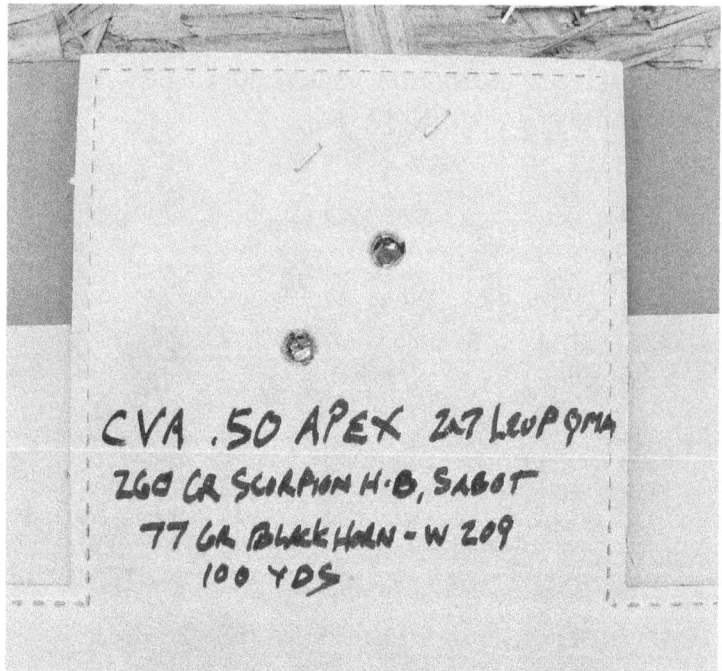

Match grade accuracy? No, but this .50-caliber muzzle-loading performance is obviously "good enough" to fill a freezer.

vides even more corrosion resistance. I still wipe all metal surfaces down with a lightly oiled rag after every handling. It doesn't take long and has worked so far.

Stocks: Although classic walnut is a feast for the eyes, I much prefer a more water-resistant material. Two main alternatives are laminated wood and the various synthetics. Not everyone likes laminated stocks, but I find them visually appealing. They tend to be heavier than plain wood but provide additional stability. The latter trait should help maintain consistent bedding during exposure to the elements. While this is generally true, I've still seen problems. During a prairie dog shoot several years back the weather closed in and a light drizzle began. It lasted all morning, but wasn't bad enough to drive our gophers underground. We were using heavy-barreled Remington bolt-action varmint rifles with synthetic or laminated stocks. The synthetic rifles stayed on target, whereas my laminated rig gradually changed zero. Soon, I was over-shooting varmints. Constant corrections were necessary and the situation only got worse. Later, I discovered a dollar bill would no longer slip between the supposedly free-floated barrel and stock. It dried out overnight but the original zero didn't return. I fixed it 2,100 miles later, back home. One thing I do like about laminated stocks is their lack of noise in the bush. Synthetics are just about weather-proof, but can be very noisy. A zipper tab, branch, or sling swivel making contact with a hollow stock can sound like a band saw cutting sheet metal at the worse moment. In tight hunting spots I'll dress carefully for noise and remove the sling. None of this would be a huge concern beyond 100 yards but, at closer range, it's the kiss of death. Safety buttons also tend to make more noise in synthetic stocked rifles. I've learned how to carefully manipulate mine for silent operation.

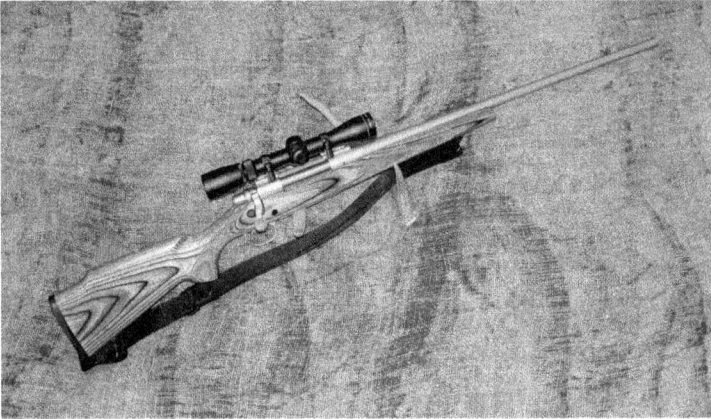

This .30/06 Remington M-700 sports a laminated stock. It's quiet in the woods, but heavier than many walnut or synthetic stock alternatives.

A working rifle: Considering all the pros and cons, I keep going back to stainless rifles with synthetic stocks. I generally give them the same type of care any other type of finish would receive, but I'm less inclined to fret before doing so. Many times I'll return from a hunt chilled to the bone and soaking wet. I give the rifle a quick wipe, pull the bolt out, lay it upside down across the arms of a chair near the woodstove, throw in more firewood, and then get changed. Proceeding with caution, I might even blow out the barrel channel and action with a hair dryer. Later, the rifle will get a good wipe down with an oily rag. I'll probably run a patch through the bore, too. Peace of mind is improved not only in the woods, but at the home front. Without power or a ready source of heat, such attributes will be even more important.

Stainless and synthetic construction helps during tough weather, at the possible expense of a noisier stock.

The search for stainless and synthetic rifles can narrow your options. Although it's not too difficult to track down a bolt-gun with these features, it can be a challenge with other action types. I was interested in a beater semi-auto .308 for use on late season running deer. Nothing was really jumping off the page so I settled for a matte-blued, synthetic stocked Remington Model 7400. The metal surfaces have enough tooth to hold oil, which helps to some extent. Ideally, a bad-weather rifle will also be easy to disassemble so hidden water won't cause problems. Since an M-7400 is tough to completely take apart, I settle for in-between maintenance. The techniques described above suffice, but only after the forend is removed. Regardless of your firearm's construction, don't put it away wet and expect it to last. You'll still need to perform regular maintenance.

OPERATION

Stress is a factor worth considering since one immediate effect will be a decrease in manual dexterity. At some point nearly every hunter has experienced some degree of knee-knocking "buck fever," and an adrenaline charged defensive scenario will only be worse. A complex firearm, combined with marginal training, is a recipe for failure. Most of us think we're better than we actually are, gauging proficiency off static, low-stress range environments in full daylight. Factoring in Murphy's Law, true proficiency will constitute the ability to effectively employ a firearm in any light, with either hand, and from any position. That's easier said than done, requiring proper training and lots of practice!

Familiar function: For many shooters, limited range access and financial constraints may impose a compromise strategy. In such cases, simplicity is good! In fact, coordinated purchases can pay further dividends. Again, if you can match a rimfire selection to your centerfire choice you'll reap extra training-based rewards. You may not always achieve an exact match but you may be able to get fairly close. If your centerfire rifle is a bolt-action, a similar functioning rimfire makes sense. This principle can extend to all of the action types for increased proficiency. Familiar operation can reinforce skills using cheaper rimfire ammunition.

Ambidextrous features: The ability to run a rifle off either shoulder is a good skill to possess. As mentioned above, defensive skills should even include single-handed use (supported by formal training). However, a more mundane issue may arise with shared users such as family members. Although a left-handed shooter can cycle a right-handed bolt-action, port side versions are sold for a reason. Within the upcoming Training Chapter, you'll see emphasis placed on cycling an action with the rifle remaining on the shoulder. This useful skill takes practice, but will ensure a fast follow-up shot. Unfortunately, some shared users will be cut out of this loop. While a bolt-gun is a depend-

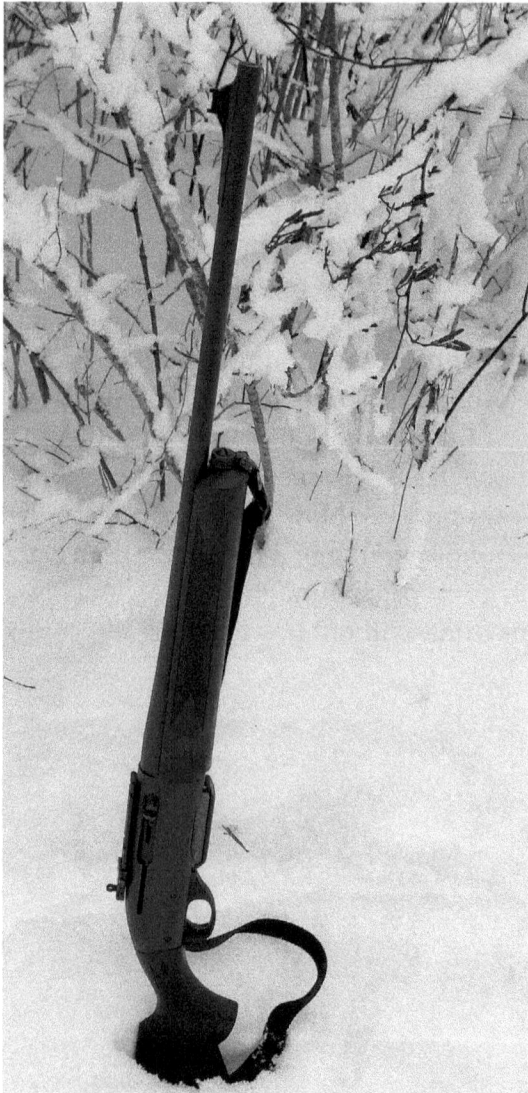

This .308 Remington M-7400 is set up for tough conditions. Its matte steel finish helps hold oil and the synthetic stock is weatherproof.

A recent rendition is the "modern sporting rifle" (MSR) with a bit of extra punch. This all-weather AR-15 will be effective in the hands of many veterans. The caliber is .300 Blackout.

able and operator-friendly choice, a fully ambidextrous Browning BLR lever-action might make more sense. Essentially, it's a lever-powered bolt-action, complete with a detachable magazine. Once more, pump shotgun fanciers may want to think about a slide-action rifle. Semi-auto systems are another possibility, although increased complexity and ejected brass become concerns.

Some careful shopping can provide a centerfire and rimfire system with common function. Familiarity helps – especially during stress!

Other limitations: Prospective buyers should also consider their anticipated interests and likely rifle uses. Some shooters may envision a possible drift toward longer-range shooting involving high-end scopes, flat-shooting cartridges, and bipods. Such a "tactical" package will often be used from prone, limiting the practicality of lever-actions and pumps. On the other hand, those on the fly won't appreciate a fully decked out twelve-pound tactical rifle. People operating in areas where bad weather is common will also be better served with a firearm permitting quick disassembly.

These factors are best considered prior to a purchase! What's best for me may not be best for you. It's time to sort out some details by taking a closer look at the predominant action types…

CHAPTER 3

BOLT-ACTION RIFLES

This type of centerfire rifle is pretty much a no-brainer. For starters, it's a straight-forward design. On top of that, just about all of the major manufacturers produce a decent rifle which will shoot well to boot. Much to-do is made over the classic Mauser action with its rugged parts, giant claw-extractor, and controlled feed design. Cartridge rims slip up under the extractor jaw as they rise from the magazine, remaining in full breech bolt contact during the feed-fire-extract process. Double-feeding is thus prevented during tense situations. The system works exceedingly well and is embodied by the German 8mm K-98, which saw action in two world wars. The U.S. Springfield Rifle, which fires the .30/06 Springfield cartridge, was finalized in 1906. It is closely based on the Mauser design, and many sporterized examples of either system are still in use today. A controlled-feed system is often preferred in a dangerous game rifle for the same reasons it was used by the military. I also think it's somewhat overblown in sporting print.

The U.S. Springfield .30/06 faced off against the Mauser 98 in World War I. The Springfield is a close enough evolution that the U.S. paid royalty fees to Germany. Note the pair of 5-round stripper clips permitting quick reloads.

Other less elaborate push-feed systems, which just shove rounds forward from a magazine, have been used successfully for years. Most of today's bolt-action rifles employ this design. Truthfully, a good many outdoor folks probably don't know the difference between a controlled-feed or push-feed action. All that really matters for them is whether their rifle works or not. Either system should suffice.

A bigger problem for some will involve locating a left-handed rifle. I've tried shooting a right-handed bolt-action as a lefty and it wasn't pretty. The first thing I did was run over my left thumb with the bolt. While it can (and should) be done with practice, fortunately, some great rifles are available in either persuasion.

The classic German 8mm Mauser 98 remains a benchmark bolt-action design after well over a century.

The classic Mauser bolt designs employ two opposing integral steel lugs, which engage corresponding mortises machined into the receiver. Most cock upon opening after 90 degrees of upward handle rotation. This system applies plenty of leverage, but can result in bolt handle contact with some low-mounted scopes. More recently, three-lug designs have appeared, a forerunner

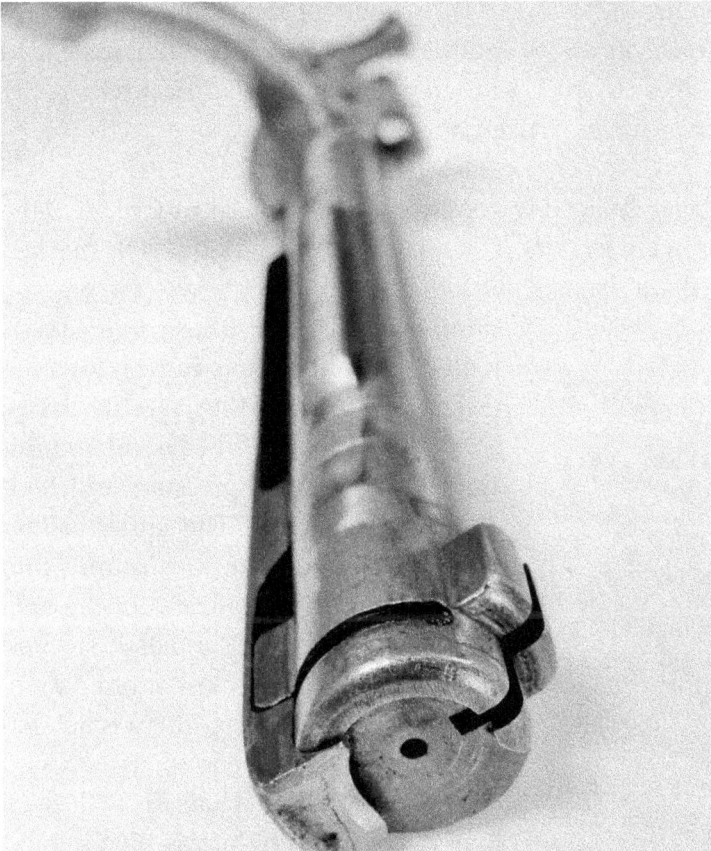

Mauser controlled-feed bolt, with two locking lugs and a strong, rotating extractor claw that can rip out stubborn cartridge cases. The ejector is a separate blade located within the receiver.

being Weatherby's famous ultra-strong Mark-V action (which used a series of smaller lugs). Browning adopted a three-lug pattern with their excellent A-Bolt line, and Ruger now markets a smooth-stroking "American" variant. Some amount of additional lift effort is required to open and cock the three-lug actions, but it's not excessive, and the handle's 60 degree rotation is less likely to interfere with scopes. Either bolt design should work just fine for our purposes.

MAJOR PLAYERS

Since listing everything would be a daunting task I've focused on a few widely used brands. All have been around for 50 years, meaning they're known quantities. There are certainly others worth a look within the crowded bolt-action field. Among the top four, first up is a hugely popular rifle...

Remington Model 700-series: Dating back to 1962, the Model 700 instantly became a major hit. It's a handsome rifle available in a large assortment of calibers and variations. All share the common push-feed, two-lug action of my department Model 700 Police rifle. The U.S. Military employs the same system for purpose-built sniper rifles, indicating that such a design is a viable choice in dangerous situations.

Despite a crowded bolt-action marketplace, the Model 700 remains widely successful in terms of sales. It was designed for mass-production with a tubular receiver to help maintain competitive pricing. Today you can buy a Model 700-type rifle in two action sizes. The long action version handles magnum calibers, as well as the stalwart rounds like .30/06 or .270. A short action receiver is scaled for .308-length rounds and the newer "Short-mag" offerings. An even smaller variant is the Model Seven, which is a different but similar rifle using a shortened receiver.

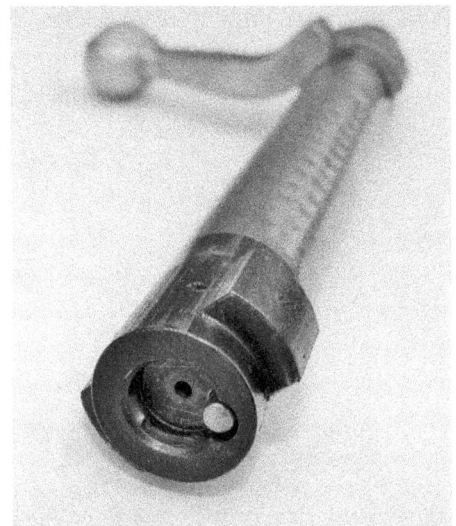

Remington's push-feed bolt employs two lugs, a clip extractor, and spring-loaded ejector button.

Remington also utilizes their short, .308- length M-700 and M-7 actions for the smallest cartridges like .223 Rem. Too bad they don't scale the receiver down another notch like CZ or Sako. Instead, a magazine spacer is employed to take up the excess room. Positioning the smallest cartridges correctly is a nuisance, but I gladly pay this price in trade for great accuracy.

In fact, one of the rifle's greatest selling points is predictably good-to-outstanding accuracy. All of the small caliber .222 and .223 versions I've shot were ringers. The heavy-barreled Model 700s marked close to ½ MOA without much effort. The Model Sevens, which are built for light weight, employ

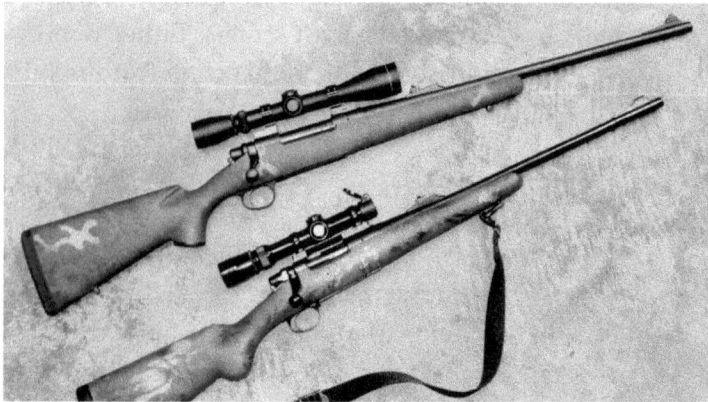

A pair of Remington bolt-actions, based on two similar but different receivers. The long action M-700 is shown above a compact Model Seven.

skinny barrels. Still, those I've played with could put 5 shots in roughly one-inch groups (one MOA) at 100 yards. Sometimes, but not always, minor tinkering with forend pressure and bedding was necessary. The larger caliber M-700s will often put three rounds into one-MOA groups, right out of the box. I had one bad shooter, a plastic stocked .30/06, M-700. Upon close examination, the forend appeared a bit twisted. Although not recommended, I managed to straighten it with a hair dryer. Presto: It shot 1.25 MOA, which is plenty good for just about any big game rifle.

Another nice feature is the factory-supplied, adjustable trigger. Most are okay right out of the box but, if not, they can be tweaked. A recurring topic is the accidental discharge controversy aired by NBC. I'm not sure if anyone has a definitive answer on this one, but the theme is common. In rare

Remington employs a tubular action with a separate recoil lug. The bolt-release tab is ahead of the trigger. Two of the three adjustment screws are visible (the sealant has been removed).

instances, upon closing the bolt, the rifle discharges. If we recall Rule #2, we won't point our firearm in the direction of another person. Here is a classic example of why we always observe that rule. It's easy to replicate this problem through incorrect trigger tuning, which may be a contributing cause. Remington began coating the three trigger adjustment screws with an unobtrusive layer of sealant for good reason. In 2009, they began offering a new "X Mark Pro" user-adjustable trigger. On the old design removal of the barreled action from the stock was necessary. The latest version

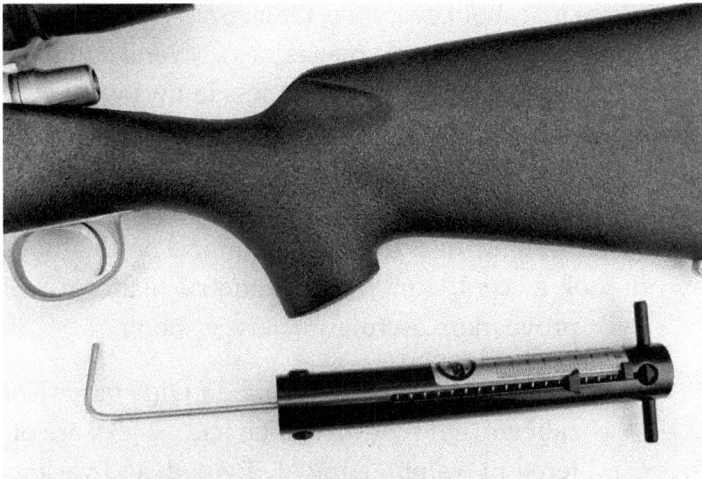

Trigger tinkering requires knowledge and a scale. In this case, the trigger broke at a bit above three pounds.

can be accessed with the rifle assembled, through the trigger blade. While a useful pull-weight is supposedly attainable, some have complained about inconsistency. On top of that, an X Mark factory trigger recall was necessary. Having not had the chance to shoot one extensively, I'll reserve judgment. My one post-09 Compact Tactical has a factory-issue 40-X, match trigger normally supplied on Custom Shop rifles. It was good enough out of the box, so I haven't touched it. We still use a pile of rifles with the older design and they've see hard use in bad weather, while working dependably.

For anyone wanting a premium trigger, after-market units are readily available. Trigger pulls measured in ounces are possible with some benchrest versions. For field use I wouldn't go below 3 pounds, which is plenty light. Timney is a well-known source for reliable, aftermarket trigger assemblies that can be user-installed. The original Model 700's safety locked the bolt in its closed position in the "on" setting. This might seem contrary to true safety since the lever had to be moved forward to "fire" for unloading; however, it did keep the bolt handle fully locked down. The newer Remington design omits this feature. While one can unload the chamber with the safety applied, it is also possible to bump the bolt knob and raise it just enough to get a misfire. Awareness is the cure but, for those seeking an alternate solution, we arrive at the next big selling point for Remington's Model 700: A large assortment of after-market parts.

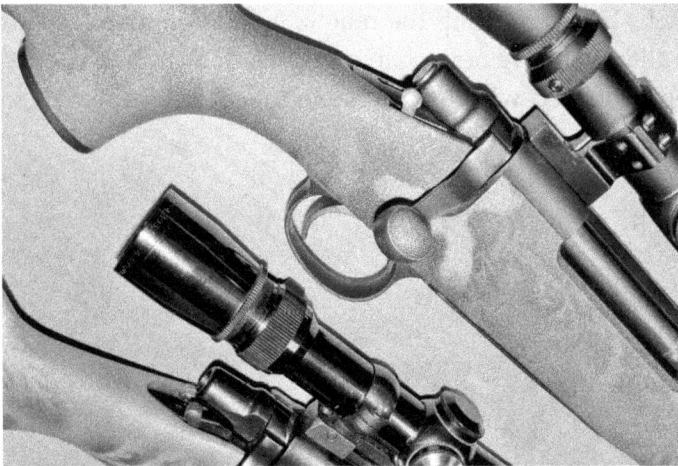

Remington's safety-tabs are quick, positive, and easy to access. They can also be quietly manipulated with a bit of practice.

I really like the Remington safety location, which is simple and positive. It blocks both the sear and the trigger. So far, the factory triggers and safeties have done the job for me. But, you can purchase an interesting three-position bolt shroud assembly which works like Winchester Model 70. Other neat accessories include a lightweight aluminum bolt shroud that replaces the steel unit, including those made with a J-Lock. Remington made a run of rifles with a "J-Lock" feature, which locates a small locking nub on the bolt shroud. I have a custom Model Seven with one, but I never use it. Internet gossip indicates J-Lock rifles may not shoot as accurately, but you can't prove it by my mine. For some, the locking feature may even be desirable.

With the Model 700, there's bound to be something for just about everyone. Other accessories include custom stocks, custom bottom metal (including some with detachable magazines), several complete and radical-looking rifle chassis, a huge assortment of scope bases, and goodness knows what else. Long range shooting has become popular thanks to laser rangefinders, great scopes, and ballistic programs. Some of the latest so-called "tactical" conversions are built for this field. A few resemble an AR-15 with pistol grips, adjustable stocks, and accessory rails. One thing to keep in mind is that long range work occurs from prone. Another is increased weight. Add these together and on-the-move shooting becomes difficult. Although it may not look as cool, a more conventional platform will prove more useful for average shooters.

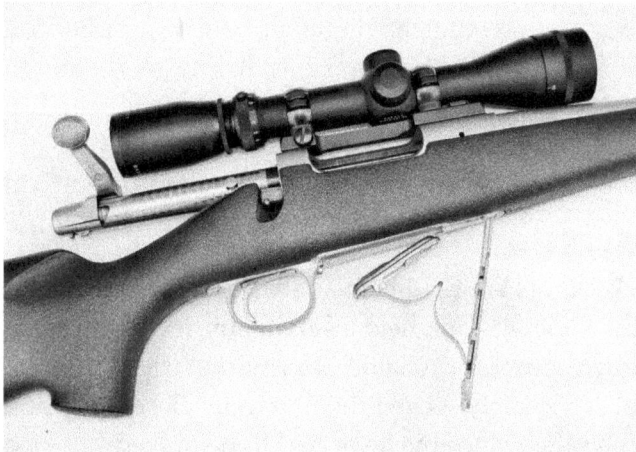

The M-700 BDL and M-7s employ a hinged floor plate for easy unloading. The release is the small button located on the front of the trigger guard.

Fortunately, in factory form, a wide variety of calibers and models can be had. Stocks are offered in walnut, laminated wood, and various synthetics. Metal can be polished blue, matte, or stainless. Barrels run the full gamut, from lightweight mountain rifles to heavy-barreled designs. The Remington Custom Shop has other options. The M-700 action is also the preferred foundation for many other custom rifle builders—a good indication of its intrinsically sound design.

The basic M-700 ADL series omits a hinged magazine floor plate. It's the simplest and lightest production version, but rounds need to be manually cycled at least part way through the action during unloading. The BDL series have hinged bottoms, which are secured with a latch. You can dump the magazine's contents into your palm and, as long as the process is intentional, all is well. I've never had one unlatch by accident, even with some fairly stout calibers. A DM version is offered with a detachable magazine. I was hot to have one shortly after the design appeared, since it seemed like just the ticket for loading on the fly. In cold weather and low light individual cartridges can be tricky to handle. The system worked well and latched positively with opposing release tabs. When fully loaded the magazine was quiet and I never felt overly concerned about losing it in the woods. One thing I hadn't planned on was leaving it at home. Nowadays I'm back to the BDL design. I have considered an after-market bottom-metal / detachable magazine kit for a .223 short-barreled varmint rifle. Lately, a number of systems have evolved, driven by strong tactical shooter interest. Some boost capacity to 10 rounds, incorporating

This 7mm Remington Magnum is the M-700 DBM offering. Squeezing two checkered tabs permits removal of its magazine.

reinforced trigger guard assemblies. Most can be user-installed, too. The latest Howa units are down-right affordable. Magpul probably just broke major new ground with an affordable semi-tactical stock and magazine assembly. Although the trigger guard and magazine well is polymer, it works much like costlier metal versions. Magpul will probably have a hard time keeping up on orders with this innovative upgrade!

The Remington series are the rifle of choice in our family of hunters. We've used them hard for decades without problem. My sons grew up shooting .30/06 versions, and have lots of experience with running deer. They were trained to run their bolt guns while mounted on their shoulders. When the heat is on, they can spit out a serious volley of lead and, from a distance, you'd have hard time believing you were hearing bolt-actions at work.

The supposed Achilles' heel is the somewhat weird spring-clip extractor, which lacks the inspiring massive claw of a Mauser design. Some folks pay good money for a custom, gunsmith installed, Sako-type claw conversion; but overall, the Remington system works. The one failure I experienced involved a brand new .350 Model Seven from, of all places, the Remington Custom Shop. I discovered the problem right of the box before firing a shot. The rifle was returned and has been going strong ever since 1989.

A Mannlicher-stocked .350 Remington Magnum M-7 accounted for this buck.

Unlike some other designs, disassembling an M-700 bolt will require more than fingers. Removal of the bolt itself is as easy as depressing a catch ahead of the trigger; however, removal of the spring-loaded firing pin assembly is more involved. Some folks use the edge of a quarter, clamping it in a vise. The coin's edge is then hooked within a disassembly notch located on the bolt shroud. A stiff pull rearward will relieve enough spring pressure for the shroud/firing pin assembly to be unscrewed from the bolt body. Snagging a section of boot lace can even work in a bind, but reasonably priced, specialized tools are also available. I have a small, self-contained Kleinendorst unit that makes this job a breeze. Sinclair sells a different type that does the same thing, and either will stow in a kit. Plenty of hunters skip this chore and some no doubt have stories involving clicks instead of bangs. Annual bolt servicing may suffice, but hard use or bad weather will increase the necessary frequency.

Remington's M-700/M-7 bolt release is a small tab, located inside the trigger guard, just ahead of the trigger.

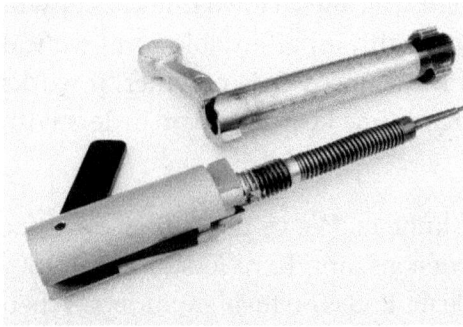

A disassembled Remington bolt shows the striker and Kleinendorst tool.

No design is perfect. Nowadays one can see lower-cost rifle brands, which look suspiciously similar to a Remington. Imitation, as we know, is a sincere form of flattery.

Savage Model 110: While we're on the push-feed theme we need to discuss a design known for its simple construction and exceptional accuracy. The M-110 has actually been around a year longer than the Remington Model 700. It's a direct competitor but for a long time it lacked some of the glitz. That's because the 110 – a number that matched its original price – was designed as an affordable alternative to the big-name Remington and Winchester rifles.

Bringing the Savage to fruition required some innovative engineering. Along the way a simple but highly effective barrel-mounting system was perfected. Barrels are fitted to the tubular receivers with a large threaded collar. It provides a very rigid connection, and also permits precise head-space tuning. The chamber, bolt face and cartridge must all fall within precise tolerances for safe containment of pressure. The Savage system simplifies the process, and its floating bolt head has enough movement to self-correct for full locking lug engagement. The result is good alignment that typically requires gunsmith fitting with other designs. These features explain the inherent accuracy of a Model 110.

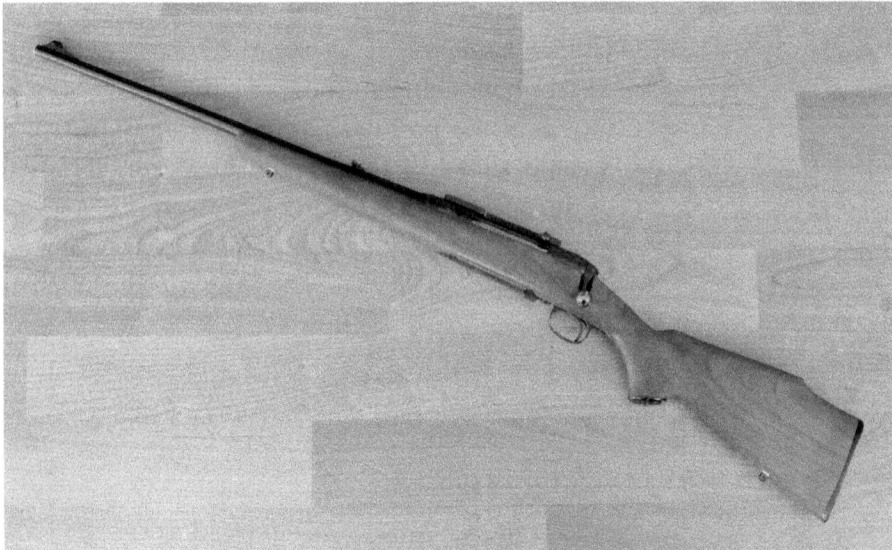

A vintage Savage 110 in left-handed persuasion.

Savage is an old school company that had a diverse but not very profitable line of firearms. After falling on hard times a decision was made to dump everything except the Model 110 and focus on product improvements. The plan paid off and Savage is back with a vengeance. Even from the beginning useful improvements appeared. They were the first to offer a true left-handed rifle. A subsequent redesign resulted in a detachable magazine model. The safety is a well-thought-out tang design located behind the bolt. It has three positions and the middle permits bolt operation while still on "safe.."

But what really kicked the Savage into high gear was a major trigger improvement: the "Accu-Trigger.." It's user-adjustable and safely permits good pull-weights. You'll know when you're looking at an Accu-Trigger because it has a Glock-like inner blade protruding through the trigger's face. Not only did Savage solve one of its biggest detractions, but it also caused an industry shake-up. All of the heavy lawyer-proof triggers were rendered obsolete by Savage's innovative design, causing the other manufacturers to play a hasty game of catch-up.

Today, Savage has a dizzying array of 110-series rifles, from a lightweight lady's gun to heavy-barreled tactical canons used by serious long-range competitors. A lower-priced Stevens line sticks to the basics, and pre-scoped "package" rifles are offered. You'll get an honest rifle for a fair price, and after-market parts are now more common.

Ruger Model 77: For those controlled-feed diehards, a Ruger Model 77 is really a modernized Mauser. Since its creation in 1968 some changes have been made, but the M-77 is still a tough rifle. The giant extractor claw will rip out just about anything, and its hook has been modified to snap over pre-chambered rounds (handy for single loading). Ejection is accomplished through a robust fixed-blade system, rather than a small, spring-loaded plunger within the bolt face. Running the bolt with enthusiasm will ensure extremely reliable function.

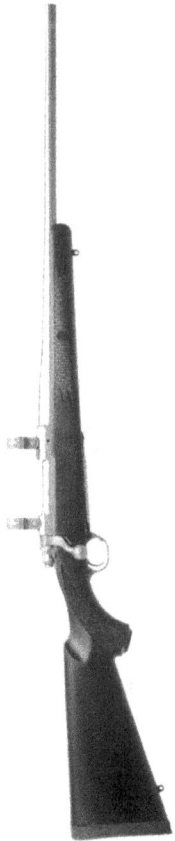

Ruger's Model 77 Hawkeye in stainless steel and synthetic dress.

The original design had a tang safety, a sliding button located directly behind the bolt. The rifle was redesigned in 1991. The safety was relocated and it now resembles a Winchester Model 70. It employs a horizontal, three-position swinging lever which, in its rearward position, locks the trigger and bolt. The trigger remains blocked in the safety's middle location, but the bolt can still be operated. You push it all the way forward to fire a shot. The new system is no doubt safer than the old one. I've owned several of each, and I much prefer the sliding tang system for its speed.

The scope mounting system remains unchanged and is among the strongest on the market. Ruger's proprietary rings clamp to integral receiver bases for a bank vault-style connection. Although each rifle is an individual, I'll go out on a limb by saying the odds of getting a real tack driver are possibly less with a Model 77; however, it should still deliver a useful degree of accuracy. A redesigned trigger helps and, unlike many other types, it's easily accessible for maintenance. The bolt is also simple to service.

The hot-selling Gunsight Scout Rifle is too good to ignore, and deserves serious consideration. It's based on a concept espoused by the late Jeff Cooper, who was a well-respected firearms authority, dean of modern pistol-craft, and founder of the Gunsight shooting school. In a nutshell, the "Scout Rifle" is a short and handy bolt-action rifle, chambered for a full-power cartridge with the means to mount

CR-3 Rifle Ruger 7744: The smallest Ruger 77s are available in 357 and .44 Magnum. They're logical choices for revolver owners.

Winchester 's Model 70 Featherweight is another American classic.

a low-powered, long eye relief scope forward of its receiver. The primary advantages include rapid sighting and fast handling qualities. Ruger has done their homework, capturing all of the key design elements in one useful package. We'll give it another look later on.

Their latest Hawkeye models have very nice lines. A long action variant is the "Guide Gun" with a laminated stock and 20-inch barrel. Another really neat idea is the Ruger .357 Magnum bolt-action, which is built on the smaller .22 hornet action. It seems contradictory to pitch full-power cartridges while touting a pistol round, but for any revolver-toting preppers, a common-caliber system makes lots of sense. It's certainly not a new idea, dating back to the 1800s. The .357 really gathers steam in a rifle-length barrel. The rifle is constructed of stainless steel, has a flush-mounted rotary magazine, and a synthetic stock. Add a stainless .357 revolver and you'll gain a light and handy bad-weather combination capable of handling deer-sized game inside 100 yards. For anyone contemplating a rimfire companion, the Rugers are worth a look.

Winchester's famous Model 70: Otherwise known as "The Rifleman's Rifle," the Model 70 arrived in 1936. It was designed with a controlled-feed bolt, but was simplified (some would say cheapened) in 1964, along with many other Winchester products, creating an infamous "pre-64" classification.

Quality declined but gradually turned around, and a second generation of controlled-fed rifles resumed production in 1992. Production of all New Haven-produced Winchesters ceased during 2006, but it's hard to keep a good thing down. The Model 70 is back, produced by the parent company, FN, in South Carolina. Quality is supposedly better than ever.

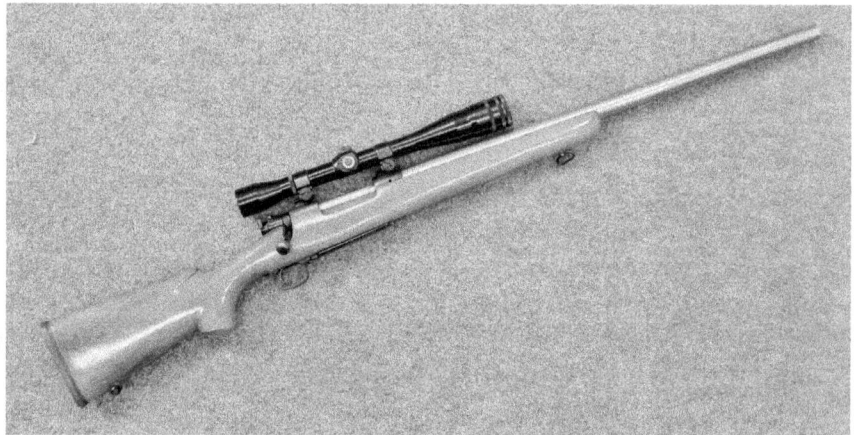

The Model 70 is a time-tested design which, like the M-700, has seen much customization.

Like the Remington Model 700, the Winchester Model 70 has been offered in a wide assortment of calibers. It was only available as a long action rifle for many years. That finally changed, and the short action "Featherweight" is a joy to handle. As a close competitor to the Model 700, a number of Model 70 variations appeared. They have been sold in several finishes with a full menu of stock choices. Lest anyone think the Model 70 isn't worthy, the famous Marine Corps sniper, Carlos Hathcock, used one to great effect during the Vietnam War.

One signature Model 70 feature is its three-position swinging safety lever. It's quite similar to the latest Rugers. Located on the right side of the bolt's shroud, a generous tab offers plenty of engagement surface. With it swung fully rearward, the firing pin will be secured and the bolt will be locked down. By pushing the lever forward one click the bolt will be unlocked for safe unloading. In the tab's most forward position, the rifle can be fired. It's a well-proven system with strong tactile and visual cues. However, swinging the safety through its full arc does require more movement than Remington's M-700 design.

For reasons still unclear, I've never spent much time with the M-70. One reason may be the safety. It's certainly "safe," but I just prefer the ergonomics of a Remington. The one rifle I owned was a .30/06. I sold it in unfired condition after failing to find a satisfactory scope mounting solution. As it

Model 70-type striker showing the three-position safety tab.

turns out, a long action Winchester is aptly named. I was bound and determined to mount a Leupold 2x7 scope, but couldn't acquire the necessary eye relief. The scope's ocular bell hit the forward base, preventing further rearward adjustment. I could've switched to higher offset rings, but the scope would have been too high for a proper cheek weld. I've used 2x7 Leupolds on a number of other rifles without any difficulty. For most folks it would be a non-issue but, because I shoot with my scopes further rearward than most, it was a major irritation.

That said, the Model 70 is an extremely popular rifle. It and the Remington Model 700 probably are at the top of the list. Anyone who already owns a Winchester can't go wrong by keeping it. The latest FN-built rifles will meet all expectations.

OTHER DOMESTIC BOLT-ACTION RIFLES

The well-established big-name rifles we just covered are only the tip of the iceberg. There are plenty more…

Kimber builds a series of classy rifles with Winchester Model 70-type safety levers. Models are available in classic walnut with blued steel or in lightweight synthetic/stainless versions. Some just

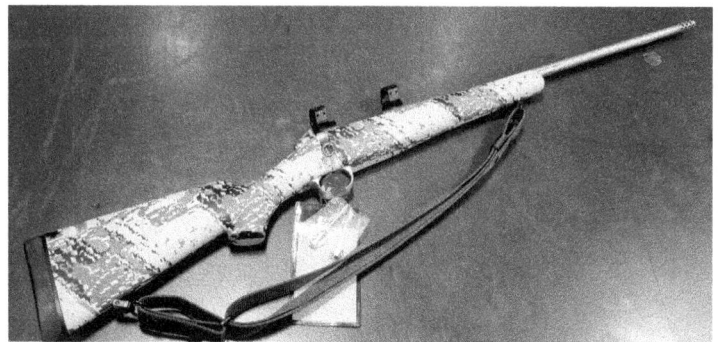

After spying this Kimber .308 "Mountain Ascent," my son plunked down a deposit. Since muzzle brakes are loud, an accessory collar is provided. The "blind magazine" lacks a floor plate.

beg to be slung over a shoulder in high places where wild sheep and goats reside. Being a nut over common function, I've so far resisted owning a Kimber centerfire, strictly because of its safety. Years of Remington M-700 use have ingrained its location. Too bad for me!

Mossberg is a well-established U.S. firm with an interesting new line of bolt guns. Some offer modular adaptations to user-specific requirements (more on this soon). Others, in the Patriot line, are more conventional. Some variants are even sold as package guns with mounted Vortex scopes. The Mossbergs are all affordable—and rugged to boot!

Thompson/Center sells an affordable Venture series, plus a novel interchangeable-caliber "Dimension.." Extra barrels, bolts, and magazines all connect to the Dimension's standard receiver. Some disassembly is required, but a change only takes a few minutes. Parts are coded to ensure correct matchups, and supplied torque wrenches ensure consistent installation. The newest introduction is the T/C Compass, which looks like one heck of a rifle for $400.

OFFSHORE BRANDS

There are plenty of great rifles to choose from, which are built abroad, but sold by well-established USA firms.

Browning is a brand synonymous with quality and includes a line of great-handling rifles. Their hugely popular A-Bolt series has recently advanced to a trim line of X-Bolt rifles, which are built by Miroku in Japan, a factory known for well-built firearms. Among their many nice features is a well-positioned safety. A more affordable offshoot has also appeared. Rimfire versions further support the overall system.

Be sure to check out Browning's "Hell's Canyon" X-Bolt which is chock-full of great features. Detachable magazines are standard.

Sako: This brand is a good example of the import and marketing process. Sako is an internationally prized rifle maker with roots going back to World War II. As their product line grew, it evolved to an elegant series of actions scaled for .222/.223, .308, and .30/06/magnum-class cartridges. Rimfire actions further rounded out the line. Various importers sold them in the U.S. until Beretta bought the company, improving distribution. Through Beretta USA, the general line continues with plenty of interesting choices. Buyers should be aware that the centerfire actions incorporate proprietary, integral scope bases. Instead of drilled holes, tapered dovetails are used for a very strong mounting system. Ring choices are thus somewhat diminished but, after owning a modest Sako collection, I consider this a fair trade-off. All were great shooters, and I still view them as the Mercedes of the rifle field.

Tikka: Here is another well-regarded Finish rifle builder, closely wedded to Sako. In fact, both brands are now owned by Beretta. Again, quality is the by-word. The actions are simple and slick. The receivers are grooved for scope mounting in a manner reminiscent of rimfire rifles, but most are shipped with very strong rings. You can link into both brands through Beretta USA.

CZ's scaled down M-527 is a natural host for smaller cartridges like the .223 and 7.62x39 Russian.

CZ: This Czech-based company sells a diverse line of rifles sold through CZ USA. Like Sako, they build scaled actions, including really neat, miniature-Mauser versions chambered for .223-sized rounds. These M-527 models are also sold as 7.62x39 carbines with detachable magazines. The receivers incorporate a dovetail-type scope mounting system which is superficially similar to Sako's. My 7.62x39 shot cheap Russian ammo with MOA accuracy! One thing to be aware of is its safety, which works in the reverse of most others. It drove me nuts until I thought of it as a hammer, drawing it rearward to fire.

Weatherby & Howa: The Japanese Howa factory builds a very nice line of well established rifles, once sold in the U.S. by S&W and Mossberg. Marketing continues through Weatherby and Legacy Sports. The actions are based on the Sako design, with Remington M-700 scope-base patterns. Weatherby's versions are sold as "Vanguards," offering a somewhat lower-priced alternative to their high-end Mark-V rifles. Those sold by Legacy Sports are branded as "Howa.." They represent good value, and the product line is huge. One recent addition is their scaled down, .223-sized "Mini Action," which will also be available in 7.62x39 Russian chambering. Like some of the larger-action Howas, the Minis run off detachable, proprietary magazines. In fact, an affordable aftermarket Remington M-700 conversion system is also available.

ECONOMY RIFLES

I'm probably doing the latest generation of affordable bolt-action rifles a major disservice by not giving them more attention. But, for starters, this can't be "The Bolt-action Rifle Book.." Secondly, they are new and completely different designs. The major gun makers like Browning, Remington, Ruger, T/C, and Winchester have been forced to come out with lower price-point products. Simple construction and synthetic stocks are the basis of their designs. Many of the latest iterations appear to be delivering respectable accuracy despite their lower costs. But, one thing they all share is their newness. The first four rifles we reviewed have been around for half a century, meaning they are well-proven designs. New offerings come and go. Such was the case with Smith & Wesson's most recent attempt. Marlin came out with a nice line of bolt-action centerfires but they've disappeared from the 2015 catalog. We need ready service, parts, and a proven track record, hence the strong emphasis on longstanding models.

More on Mossberg: Still, I feel compelled to mention one new rifle that has piqued my curiosity. It's a novel design from an older company that has rocked the industry with some innovative concepts. Check out Mossberg's new MVP line. First out were rifles with actions scaled to .223-size that accept M-16 magazines. This feature requires some clever engineering since most conventional bolt-actions aren't compatible with GI magazines. Mossberg added a small hinged steel flap to the bottom of the bolt. It pops downward under spring pressure to scoop the top round from the magazine. With a shorter barrel and laminated stock we have a very useful package. The newest "Flex" addition permits interesting stock modifications. Most recently, a series of similar but scaled up 7.62 NATO/.308 rifles has appeared. They feed from detachable AR-10 and M-14 magazines, and among them is a Mossberg .308 "Scout Rifle.." To me, an MVP sounds like a dandy truck gun or on-the-move choice. New for 2015 is their very tactical-looking Light Chassis Gun with a Magpul AR butt and pistol grip connected to an aluminum stock. Mossberg has certainly managed to find the pulse of current shooting interests.

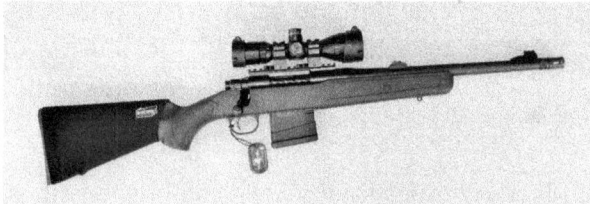

Mossberg's MVP rifles accept AR magazines. This one is a factory package gun chambered in .308.

More Ruger: Last but not least is Ruger's latest "American" line of affordable bolt-action rifles. They're selling well enough that the line is quickly expanding, with several interesting variations. They have synthetic stocks with innovative, accuracy-improving bedding, detachable magazines, and a tang safety. Among them is a fully set up "package gun" that includes a decent Redfield scope. Moving in the opposite direction, Ruger was watching the long-range market blossom.

Some very clever engineering morphed the American into a nearly unrecognizable chassis-type "Precision Rifle." Considering its numerous features, the $1,400 price tag is one heck of a bargain. Just about everything is adjustable and it shoots like the Dickens while running off of common AR-10 magazines. Like other similar so-called tactical rifles, it's no flyweight. The lightest version is a 20-inch .308 that scales nearly 10 pounds sans optics or ammo. Ruger also sells matching conventional American rimfire rifles ideal for small game or practice. The .22 LR version even uses Ruger's 10/22

Believe it or not, this chassis-type rifle is a bolt-action. It'll fit in small spaces, but the weight will be obvious when you pick it up.

This chassis-type stock can accommodate nearly anyone – for a price. The latest tactical rifles are feature-intensive.

magazines. Considering the prices of these rifles, things don't get much better. The whole American line is worth a serious look, whether on a budget or not!

THE CHASSIS AND TACTICAL RIFLE CRAZE

Many of the major bolt-gun players are now launching re-stocked versions of their popular rifles. These "chassis rifles" typically use some sort of aluminum/synthetic stock, which may resemble the general outline of an AR-15. Features often include adjustable cheek pieces and butts, or even folding stocks. Most also are fitted for a detachable magazine. Like the latest AR-15 forends, some of the newest bolt-action chassis-stocks are trending toward less mass. Meanwhile, it's worth thinking about portability. A big tactical-type rifle is intriguing, but it won't be fun to lug around. Metal stocks are also tough on fingers during extreme cold, and noise may be a concern. Positives include individualized adjustments, accessory rails, and detachable magazines. An additional advantage of some involves their V-block action-bedding surfaces, which can improve accuracy.

CLOSING BOLT-GUN COMMENTS

A very light rifle will exaggerate recoil, and may be harder to shoot. Some "ultra-light" rifles are the product of a pencil-weight barrel on a standard-weight action. The result can be a very muzzle-light feel which is less steady from off-hand. The latest heavy-barreled tactical rifles are just too heavy for most of us in field conditions. Besides weight, barrel length can also affect velocity, balance, and handiness. In other words, extremes are seldom optimum when choosing one general purpose rifle. A rifle with a 20-22-inch barrel, weighing somewhere around 6 ½ - 7 pounds, makes a practical starting point with non-magnum calibers. Don't forget! A scope, mounts, sling, and ammo will quickly add additional weight.

Beyond these standard items, we should think about future accessories. By starting with a basic but popular model, easy upgrades will be feasible. Meanwhile, money saved by a more pedestrian rifle can be directed toward essential extras.

As for defense, it's easy to forget that many of the 20th century's major conflicts were fought with bolt-action rifles. In the hands of a skilled user, such a rifle can still be a formidable tool. If just one is planned for all centerfire rolls, some sort of detachable magazine system may be advised. Spares will permit faster reloads, improving its fighting capabilities.

Chapter 4

SEMI-AUTOS

Sometimes it truly is hard to have your cake and eat it too. If long-term production, ready access to parts, extreme durability AND ease of disassembly are important, some great military choices exist. If we add the requirement of a full-sized round like the .308, the field narrows somewhat. Adding portability and the ability to easily handle optics, the prospects grow shorter. Then, there's cost.

Remember, a rifle is but part of an overall system that also includes optics, magazines, ammunition, and other accessories. Mounting a scope to some military rifles can be challenging and expensive. The finished product may also be less than satisfactory due to excess weight and poor ergonomics. Many rifles like the M-14, FAL, G-3, and AK-47 are Cold War concepts designed for iron sights. The M-16 and its civilian AR-15 counterpart were in the same boat, but they have undergone a remarkable metamorphosis. Optics can now be easily accommodated without excessive weight but, compared to a .308, the system's smaller 5.56 NATO round gives up some terminal punch. We can't fit the former round into this smaller-sized platform, so a larger variant is needed. Round and round we go!

Steyer's 5.56 AUG was a revolutionary concept with a bull-pup design and integral optics. Although it disappeared from U.S. markets, the AUG has made a recent comeback.

This rack of military-based semi-autos covers everything from buzz guns to battle rifles. They share easy maintenance, but some become ungainly when decked out with optics and extras.

As for reliability, most semi-automatic firearms will run with proper servicing. Here we have a problem. Many users just don't clean them or replace springs. Later, when these rifles quit working, we hear about their poor reliability. Most of them are gas-operated and need regular maintenance. Knowing that, it's helpful to choose a system which will promote the process. Not all of the civilian rifles are as accommodating as the military designs.

MILTARY DESIGNS

First on the list is an easily serviceable rifle, familiar to many folks with military experience.

The iconic Vietnam era M-16 was the predecessor of today's "modern sporting rifle."

The AR system: Anyone who has seen footage of the Vietnam conflict should recognize this platform. Despite some early shortcomings, the M-16 probably helped save the day early on, during the 1965 Battle of the Ia Drang. Later evolutions are still going strong. Magazines have grown in capacity from 20 rounds up to 30 (or more), but the basic design remains intact. The civilian version of the select-fire M-16 is a semi-auto AR-15 (and a larger AR-10). The AR-15 fires a small-caliber 5.56 x 45 NATO (or .223 Remington) cartridge. The AR-10 shoots 7.62 x 51 NATO (.308 Winchester) ammunition.

In fact, the Stoner-designed Armalite Rifle (or AR) was originally built to fire the 7.62 round from 20-round magazines. It's the same cartridge used by the post-war U.S. M-14 rifle. The whole system was soon shrunk around the smaller and more portable 5.56x45 NATO cartridge, subsequently adopted by the U.S. military. As a result, you can't fit a .308 in a standard AR-15 platform. It needs to be scaled back up to AR-10 size, which is charitably "large.." Granted, some reductions have been recently made to .308 platforms. Colt recently introduced an AR-type rifle capable of adapting to both 5.56mm and 7.62 cartridges, but it's scaled to the larger round. The 7.62 DPMS Generation II uses trimmer components, resulting in a smaller rifle. Other manufacturers have slimmed down barrels to save weight. These ideas help, but as is the case with AR-10 systems in general, proprietary parts come into play. Heavier recoil and additional bolt carrier mass can also stress the weapon's internals. Unlike an AR-15, there really isn't a standard AR-10 parts list.

How about a 5.56/.223 AR-15? The original direct-impingement gas-operated design has been well-proven through five decades of steady use, but so-called piston guns are gaining traction. Instead of ducting high-pressure gas directly to the bolt assembly, a forward-mounted piston and connecting rod is used. The concept results in a cooler and cleaner action, although like the AR-10, there are a number of proprietary designs.

An AR chambered for 7.62x51 NATO (.308 Winchester) will generally be much larger. This Patriot Ordnance is a piston design, accounting for its greater forend height.

To ensure availability of parts, a system based on the original design makes sense. It will also bias an AR choice toward the smaller and basic 5.56mm AR-15 gas impingement design. Regardless of the AR type, it won't be as cheap as many other rifles—although prices have come down. As a whole, ARs are surprisingly accurate, sometimes rivaling bolt-action varmint rifles. A drawback is their small .22 caliber projectiles, which lack the power of full-size battle rounds. Those planning on owning only one centerfire might want something with more terminal performance.

I have a very long-standing relationship with this system. I'd shoot a deer with a carefully chosen .223 bullet, but it wouldn't be my first pick. Larger game like elk or moose would be off the list and, in fact, the .223 would be illegal for big game in some states. There's a reason our military people have been kicking tires on alternate calibers. You can stuff an interesting assortment of other cartridges in an AR-15 platform and, although some offer extra punch, most will be harder to find.

One possible strategy involves the use of two upper receivers. Thanks to the design of the AR-15, they could be quickly switched out without tools in less than a minute. Suddenly, the option of using a 5.56 AR in conjunction with a larger, mid-size caliber becomes practical. Out of dozens available, excluding less powerful pistol rounds, the 6.8 SPC and .300 Blackout are probably the most common. As a handloader, I manufacture my own .300 Blkt brass from fired 5.56 cases. Standard G.I. magazines will work to a point, but neither cartridge is likely to be found lurking in a hardware store or basement. Anyone going this route had better stock up on ammo. If the supply dwindles you can just pop two pins and slap on that 5.56/.223 upper.

A great sounding AR option is the 7.62x39 Russian, most commonly associated with the AK-47. Although uppers are available, this caliber can be problematic. Lately, dedicated rifles are appearing. They run more reliably due to major redesigns of the whole rifle, including its magazine well. The ta-

An AR-15 is the ultimate transformer. Shown here is a .300 Blackout carbine with a switch-top precision .223 upper.

A clever 7.62x39 Russian AR-15 adaption is Windham Weaponry's modular magazine well system. The upper module accepts standard AK magazines.

pered cartridges really need the classic "banana" type Soviet magazines that won't fit a standard AR lower. Unfortunately, these modifications preclude the use of most upper receivers. Windham Weaponry now sells an MGI designed multi-caliber caliber system that solves this problem through interchangeable magazine well modules. A 9mm option is even part of their system.

There is just so much involved with the AR system that one chapter won't do it justice. Instead, an entire section of this book has been reserved for the design. It's certainly a viable choice, but it's also not the only game in town...

The U.S. M-14 rifle: One choice jumping off the page is a rifle I carried through Basic Training many years ago. In this age of stamped parts and plastic stocks, there is something reassuring about the robust steel and walnut construction of an M-14. Its ability to fire a full-size .308 rifle cartridge is also comforting. A supply of 20-round magazines seals the deal, although the total system won't be light. Springfield Armory still sells civilian examples, branded as M1As. Available in several configurations, their shortest SOCOM or Scout models may meet the needs of some.

We still inventory an armory full of military-grade surplus rifles, so the M-14 is not a stranger. While it's certainly reliable, it's also big and heavy — something those of us in OD Green quickly figured out. We were recently presented with the requirement for a .308 semi-automatic system, capable of meet-

21st century M-14 cosmetics — lots of rails and, of course, a telescoping AR-type stock.

Steel and walnut Cold War technology: The U.S. 7.62x51 NATO (.308) M-14 rifle.

ing law enforcement "designated marksman" needs. After reviewing our options, we spent money accurizing a couple of M-14s. Next we added good scope mounts, Leupold 1.75x5 scopes, and cheek pads. The resulting packages shoot pretty well, but they're now really big. Even with free rifles we still have a substantial investment in them.

Springfield's SOCOM and Scout M1As are shorter-barreled versions with scope bases ahead of their receivers. The result is a simple, strong and low-profile system which, with a small, forward-mounted "scout scope" or dot sight, would be more portable. The shorter barrels shave some weight but these models still weigh 8.8 pounds without optics. Their synthetic stocks offer improved weather resistance.

Efforts to field a designated marksman M-14 resulted in a large rifle.

Other versions of the M-14 could be similarly equipped, using an after-market base. Amega Mounts and UltiMAK sell Picatinny rail systems that replace the upper handguard. Some of the latest dot sights are extremely compact. Using this system, they'll also sit lower than a conventionally mounted scope. You'll sacrifice some precision for a more manageable system.

For an on-the-run, battle-proven rifle, an M-14-based system is a solid choice. Magazines and parts are readily available. Assuming the overall rifle package is tolerable, its downside will be cost. Don't forget the extra weight of loaded spare magazines.

Russian systems: The AK-47 fires a smaller round, the 7.62x39 Russian, which has terminal effect similar to a .30/30. It works, but lacks long-range capability. Like other Cold War systems, satisfactory optical arrangements can present challenges. The slightly older and simpler, semi-automatic 7.62x39 Soviet SKS is another utilitarian but robust firearm, designed for conscript soldiers. Although quickly replaced by the AK-47 "assault rifle," millions were built.

The select-fire (semi and full-auto) AK-47 is as iconic as an M-16, but is oriented toward massed-fire tactics over accuracy. The Soviet systems have been produced on a huge global scale and the AK variants are probably the most widely distributed weapons, period. A smaller-caliber AK-74 fires the 5.45x39 cartridge. It shares many, but not all parts. Different barrel lengths and stocks are part of the entire Kalashnikov family, which entered large-scale Soviet service in 1949.

Most sold domestically are semi-auto imports, although some well-built U.S. copies are now appearing. The result is an abundant supply of similar weapons which all get lumped in as "AKs" regardless of their origins or fine points. Quality and tolerances of firearms, magazines, and ammunition can vary but, as a general rule, the weapons are built to function in terrible conditions. They are assembled with ample clearances to shrug off mud and neglect, so stellar accuracy is an unreasonable expectation.

The Soviet designed AK-47 embodies "assault rifle" perception. Despite its late 1940s heritage, the AK remains a global staple within firearm markets.

Having never been designed with optics in mind, an AK may serve best by relying on its iron sights; although it can be scoped. For on-the-fly defensive use an AK may has merit, especially if combined with a supply of 30-round magazines. One thing an AK won't do is lock open on the last shot—a feature I greatly dislike. A heavy trigger and mediocre accuracy exclude it from a well-rounded role that covers hunting and precision work. Accessories abound, so customization is easy. Kalashnikov USA has set up a factory to beat recent Russian import sanctions and during the

The time-tested AK-47 sighting system, around which the rifle is configured.

Note the extreme height of the scope above this AK's stock.

process they made improvements such as CNC machined parts instead of castings. The AK has been modernized to offer rails and collapsible stocks more common to the AR-15. Their US132SS model is especially intriguing. Unfortunately, its general profile sets off the alarm bells of liberal politicians, so an AK is no longer legal everywhere.

Lacking a signature "assault rifle" pistol grip and large magazine, the SKS is perhaps a tad more politically correct, although its folding spike bayonet is certainly imposing! It fires the same 7.62x39 cartridge from an integral 10-shot magazine, which can be quickly reloaded using stripper clips. Weight, size, recoil, and cost are not excessive, making an SKS a possible choice for smaller shooters, or those on a tight budget. Some people accessorize it for rudimentary sporting purposes. Common additions include a basic low-powered scope and an aftermarket stock. Conversion to a detachable magazine system is also possible. It can be disassembled without tools so modifications are easy. More than one SKS is no doubt cached in a bug-out location.

The semi-auto Russian SKS preceded the AK, but fired the same 7.62x39 round. It's simple and it works.

Regarding AK and SKS rifles, the above comments serve only as a basic guide due to the many variants. An in-depth examination would fill many pages and, while I do have some experience with these weapons, most has been on the receiving end. While some preppers will legitimately focus on them, I'm leaning toward other systems.

A decidedly non-Keep It Simple Stupid (KISS) bull-pup example of an SKS gone wild. You almost need three hands to change magazines.

This modified SKS is set up to use AK-type detachable magazines.

The M-1 Carbine: I almost skipped this neat little rifle, but feel compelled to throw it in. Having been around since World War II, the GI Carbine is certainly established. It fires is a straight-walled (or nearly so) .30 caliber cartridge, which launches a light 110-grain bullet at just below 2000 fps. Compared to the much larger .30/06 M-1 Garand, it's no powerhouse. The M-1 Carbine does, however, offer a compact package with little recoil. In my Air Cav outfit, select-fire M-2 Paratrooper versions were popular helicopter crew weapons. My captured wood-stocked M-2 fit me to a tee, and was easy to shoot during nighttime engagements.

Sometimes a good idea refuses to die. The WW II M-1 Carbine has made a recent comeback thanks to its handy attributes.

An M-1 Carbine is still a good choice for defensive purposes. With good expanding bullets, although light for deer, I'd use it in a bind (in fact, I have). Detachable 15 or 30-shot magazines feed it, and the controls are well laid out. Disassembly and maintenance are simple. Thanks to a huge production run, parts remain available. Accessories are not a problem.

Due to its design, equipping a carbine with an optical sight can pose challenges similar to an M-14. Mounts are available from S&K, Weaver, and others. One neat fix is a forward-mounted scope base that replaces the handguard. UltiMAK and Amega Mounts sell these units and their Picatinny rails provide a great spot for a long eye relief handgun scope or small dot sight. I'd opt for the latter arrangement.

The military-surplus carbines are now assuming collector-price status. A few civilian clones are of questionable quality, but Kahr Arms makes a decent repro-model. Others like the new Inland M-1 are suddenly appearing. Sometimes it's hard to keep a good idea down. Anyone who already has an M-1 Carbine in their household should hang onto it. Smaller-statured shooters will no doubt take a shine to this rifle.

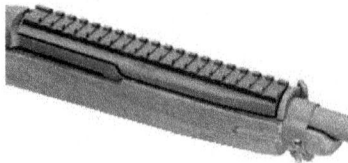

This aftermarket M-1 Carbine forend system is an optical-sight solution.

Other military systems: The FAL and G-3 are both full-size, .7.62/.308 battle rifles. The FN SCAR is no flyweight despite its compact size. Bull-pup designs like the Tavor and Steyr AUG offer a more compact package, due to rearward action designs. All have their devotees, some of whom have put effort into modifying these weapons. In many cases, a significant factor is cost. Spare parts can also be a concern, depending on what corner of the globe you live in. Here in the USA, an M-16 based rifle is wildly popular but in some countries an FAL-pattern rifle will be more familiar. It was produced by several nations and fielded in large numbers, meaning magazines and parts may be more common. In the United States, DSA Inc. has an interesting line of FAL rifles and parts.

CIVILIAN DESIGNS

The more popular civilian semi-autos are generally easier to scope and lighter to tote. They're typically marketed toward sporting use like deer hunting. The average hunter might fire a few shots just prior to opening day, and then roam the woods. In many cases a 20-round box of cartridges will last several years. Lower cost will be traded for battlefield-tough durability, although a possible exception is a hybrid military/civilian design...

The FAL was produced in large numbers and adopted by numerous nations. It still has devotees and DSA sells modernized versions of this great 7.62 NATO rifle.

Another Cold War relic is the German G-3, along with its derivatives. Typical of this era, the system is large, and designed primarily for the use of iron sights.

Ruger's Mini-14 & Mini-30: These rifles have been around for years, and are popular among civilians and some law enforcement users. Several variations are available, including the Ranch Rifles with integral scope bases for Ruger rings. Although they closely resemble the U.S. M-14, Mini-14s are different. The Mini-30 version is chambered for the Russian 7.62x39 AK-47 round, whereas the Mini-14 shoots 5.56mm or .223 ammo. Recently, a .300 Blackout appeared.

Ruger's Mini-14 continues to sell well. This one is equipped with a non-magnifying, battery-powered Trijicon Reflex sight.

Although not known for great accuracy, the Ruger presents a compact and serviceable package. I went through three Mini-14s before finding one that shot with reasonable accuracy. The winner cut 5-shot groups that averaged around 2 inches at 100 yards; useful, if not stellar performance. Since then Ruger has made changes to improve results. You can buy them with synthetic stocks and stainless metal, which would be my preference. Although not suitable for major-power rounds, the system does offer utility. A Mini-30 would make a handy survival, boat, or truck gun, providing .30/30 power in a semi-automatic package. Its 7.62x39 ammunition is fairly common, and relatively inexpensive. A Ranch Rifle model would permit use of a low-powered scope, which would extend its useful range.

The Rugers use proprietary magazines, and come with 5-shot versions. Many states limit hunting to this capacity, but larger 20 and 30-round versions are also available. Disassembly and cleaning is simple so, overall, the design has merit. One big selling point is the Ruger's more politically correct appearance. A Mini-14 just looks more like a sporting-type rifle. Its configuration may also escape the onerous "assault rifle" restrictions imposed by several states. Cost is competitive as well.

Browning and FNH USA: Browning's well-established BAR line consists of some really nice rifles, although they are a bit time consuming to disassemble. They run off detachable magazines and are known as very good shooters. A .308 "ShorTrac Stalker" with a synthetic stock would be a good choice, and it's also available in .243, which generates less recoil. Those bent on hunting the largest

North American game can even buy versions in serious magnum chamberings. The .308 "Hog Stalker" offers features also great for defense.

FNH-USA is heavily connected to Browning. They offer a series of "FNAR" rifles similar to the Hog Stalker, with a few extra versions thrown in. Pistol grips and detachable magazines are a common theme. Picatinny rail sections permit use of lights, lasers, or infrared illuminators. A .308 "Competition" three-gun variant is set up more conventionally with a sporting-type, blue laminated stock and fluted barrel. To my eye it looks really sharp! The 10-round magazine would be illegal in many game fields, but it would be reassuring in tough times.

Benelli R-1: These rifles are more recent introductions, and perhaps not as widely available. They are also a bit pricey, but Benelli is well known for first-rate designs. The R-1's "Argo" gas-operated rifles employ a well-proven piston system similar to the one used in their M-4 Shotgun, which has been adopted by the USMC. As such, they are easy to disassemble. This feature justifies any added expense and assures reliability. I wish the R-1 was sold as a .308 synthetic model, but that chambering isn't even listed. However, like the BAR, it can be had as a .30/06, .300 Winchester Magnum, and even a .338 WM!

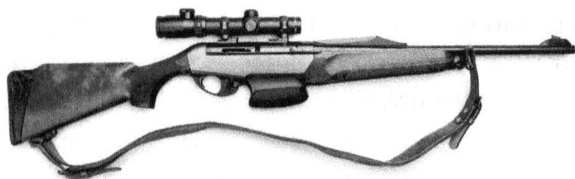

Benelli's R-1 is a reliable semi-auto with the added bonus of easy maintenance.

Remington autoloaders: When shopping for a running-deer rifle, I looked at all the options and then just settled for a plain old Remington Model 7400. I bought it used with a Bushnell 3x9 Trophy Scope, in excellent condition, for $450. It had a black, plastic stock, and 22-inch barrel. The trigger was better than expected and so was its accuracy. Being the consummate tinkerer, I made a few modifications. The first was a giant-head safety. Next, I added a Precision Reflex Picatinny scope rail. An XS Sights Backup Peep was clamped to the rear of the base. A different ramp and fiber optic Hi-Viz green front sight went up front. A compact Burris FastFire III dot sight was mounted to the rail, using a quarter as a screwdriver.

Here's the plan: The electronic dot is zeroed for 100 yards. During heavy snow (or if the battery dies), I can pop off the FastFire with a coin. The ghost ring peep is also sighted in at 100 yards. Combined with the big, green, fiber optic front bead, I have a backup, weather-proof aiming system. Either way, it's a fairly handy package. As purchased, with a full-sized scope, it wasn't. I've lost the long-range precision by removing it; but then again, the M-7400 is not my only rifle. I'd say this is also a good thing since durability is a concern. It's based on the older Model 742 series, which was designed around the .30/06. From what I've heard, it couldn't handle a whole lot of shooting. In fact, one of my cadre members shot his to destruction. The newest generation is the Model 750, available as a rifle or carbine. It's not too different from the Model 7400. One thing I find annoying is the lack of any bolt hold-open provision. The bolt WILL lock back upon the last shot as it engages the magazine's follower; but once the magazine is removed the means to trap the bolt is gone.

A business-like Remington M-7400 .308 equipped for fast action.

Another gripe involves disassembly. I can field strip it for cleaning – sort of. Taking it fully apart is another matter. Backing out one large screw in the face of the forend permits its removal. Afterward, the gas system is accessible for cleaning. I just brush everything out as much as possible. I've run into a bunch of these rifles that were almost impossible to take apart. The forend screws were nearly welded tight from accumulated carbon. Eventually, they quit running. Imagine that!

Despite its faults, my Remington does the job. It'll put three 150 grain, .308 Remington Core-Loct bullets into 1 ½ inches at 100 yards. Extra magazines are available, including a 10-shot version. I'll never shoot it enough to pound it to death, but if something does break, odds of finding parts are good. That said, I'm leery about pitching it as a sole rifle for use in extreme situations.

SEMI-AUTO THOUGHT

So, what's the final semi-auto recommendation, balancing features against cost? If it boils down to owning only one rifle, in keeping with our basic tenets, probably nothing.

CHAPTER 5

SLIDE-ACTION RIFLES

I've said it before and I'll say it again. If I had a brain in my head I'd only own three shoulder-fired guns: a Remington Model 870 12 gauge shotgun, a Remington Model 572 .22 pump, and a Remington Model 7600 slide-action in .308. Gee, that was simple! I just turned three chapters into one paragraph. The scariest part is that it makes complete sense. Are you black rifle junkies burning down now? Yeah, I am too. But, seriously, hear me out.

Ever hear of the Benoits? They're a serious deer-hunting tribe based out of Vermont. They are also a local legend in my parts, having killed 150 bucks exceeding a dressed weight of 200 pounds. Unlike most of the so-called "hunting" you see on TV, their deer are killed through old school techniques on public land. More impressively, the Benoits hunt New England's great North Woods, which are known for poor deer density. Their smart old bucks are literally tracked down on snow—a whole lot harder than it sounds. It's extremely tough hunting in the most adverse conditions, and their rifle of choice is a Remington pump gun! The more you think about it, the more it makes sense. Many of their deer are shot on the move in thick woods, where opportunities are fleeting. A second or third fast follow-up shot is essential, as is total reliability. When busting through snow-covered fir thickets, everything soon becomes coated with a mixture of water and ice. The pump guns run on demand, and that's why they use 'em. Calibers are .30/06 or .270, two classic American choices. I've seen video of these guys in action and it's really educational. Nowadays, you'll see pictures of rifles with scopes, but it wasn't all that long ago that the Benoits were using peep sights. Watching them blow up tossed cans of soup is pretty humbling. I'm sure they can use whatever they want, so their not-too high-tech choice speaks volumes.

Remington M-7600 series: Perusing a list of available pump riflepump rifles will bring you up short. It pretty much boils down to cowboy action shooting reproductions of the old Colt Lightning, or the Remington. My main instructor, Mike, had an M-7600 which he used to great effect. As a reigning New England sporting clays champ, he figured the rifle made sense. For him, it was just an extension of his Model 870 pump shotgun. After watching him shoot both, I had to agree. He's not planning on wining any benchrest matches with his .308, but he will fill his freezer. Ergonomics support fast shooting and his rifle carries well.

The M-7600 is another well-established system, originated as the Model 760 back in 1952. During 1981, Remington made some changes, adding the extra zero. The 7600 is presently listed with wood or synthetic stocks and 22" barrels. A more recent addition is the 7600-P, which stands for Patrol Rifle. With a ghost ring peep, synthetic stock and carbine-length 16" barrel, this .308 variation offers interesting survival features. It's cataloged in Remington's Law Enforcement website, but could probably be tracked down by a motivated dealer.

Another, slightly longer and conventional, 18" sporting carbine has been offered for forest use. It is chambered for the venerable .30/06 and would make a handy choice in the thicker places. The heaviest rifles are the longer 22" models, which still weigh in at only 7 ½ pounds. Receivers are drilled for scope bases and decent iron sights are standard. A one-piece Weaver base only costs a few dollars. QD rings that maintain scope zero are now fairly common.

Watching .223 AR-15 sales climb, Remington must have put on their thinking caps. Plenty of police departments still use M-870 pump shotguns, and not all are willing to make the non-PC jump to a black rifle. So, Remington performed some surgery on their Model 7600 slide-action design. The result was a rather odd Model 7615, which has a magazine well. It accepts M-16 magazines and is chambered for the .223 cartridge. Several versions are offered, including civilian models with conventional stocks, and LE/tactical carbines with pistol grips and collapsible, M-4 type stocks.

Out of everything available, two good choices would be that 7600-P .308 carbine, or a 22" synthetic 7600 in the same caliber. Whether you go with the 7615 or not, you still get a detachable magazine. The .308 remains a great, all-around caliber option.

Remington's M-7600 is a logical choice for any pump-shotgun owners.

The Remington pump rifle continues to survive, probably in large part because of semi-auto restrictions. Pennsylvania is a big-time deer hunting state and prime example. Regardless of the reasons, I'm glad it's available. We get a fast-handling and affordable, magazine-fed rifle, chambered for some serious calibers. The action uses a strong rotary bolt. It's not hard to scope and just may be the big sleeper among all rifle choices. An M-7600 is also legal just about everywhere.

Troy PAR: Slide-action AR variants have recently appeared as a means to circumvent so-called "assault rifle" restrictions. Troy Defense sells their "Pump Action Rifle" on AR-15 sized platforms in .223 and .300 Blackout. While they resemble AR-15s in appearance, they're actually quite different; the lower and upper receivers won't interchange.

Pricing begins at around $800. A somewhat more expensive folding stock model is also available, and should make for a very compact package. This feature is made possible by a lack of a buffer tube extension. There's no gas system either, so the receiver will see less fouling. The slide release is in the bottom of the trigger guard, but the safety and magazine release are in familiar AR locations. Running on standard M-16-type magazines, and sharing some common parts, these innovative rifles have potential for AR aficionados living in restrictive areas.

My initial take was dismissive but then I got to thinking (scary): The upper and lower receivers still separate, permitting compact storage and ease of maintenance. In .223 or .300 Blkt, weight isn't excessive. It should also digest a large assortment of ammunition with good reliability, and the small .300 seems like a great candidate for use with a suppressor. A larger .308 model is also offered on an AR-10 sized platform, but weight climbs to over 8 pounds.

Across the board, accuracy is reported to be quite good with the PAR line. Although they are new, proprietary designs, they do at least share some common AR parts. Actual use would no doubt require re-programming for self-loading AR fans, but practice makes perfect.

THE PUMP GUN PARADOX

It's somewhat ironic that a 12 gauge slide-action shotgun remains a go-to choice for millions of American shooters. A rifle that functions in the same manner would seem like a logical extension but, for whatever reason, that's not the case. It's too bad because, as far as I'm concerned, these rifles are real sleepers. They also handily squash just about all political correctness paranoia, while giving up little in performance.

CHAPTER 6

LEVER-ACTIONS

One might wonder why, in light of the more modern semi-auto or bolt-action systems available, we'd waste our time considering such an arcane design. The answer is a bit complicated. For starters, many households already have a perfectly serviceable lever gun floating around. It'll probably be chambered for .30/30, .32 Winchester Special, or .35 Remington; all of which have adequate power for many purposes. The lever-action is thoroughly ingrained into our culture, too. Many people just like them for their handy size and lively handling qualities.

I was recently viewing at TV program about the famous Winchester Model 94. Ed Head, who manages the well-respected Gunsight Academy, described an educational experience involving an older Montana sheriff. The guy showed up with an ancient, well-worn Model 94 and kicked everyone else's tail on a carbine course, thereby indicating that a lever-powered system is far from dead.

Comparing the Russian 7.62x39 to a .30/30, the edge goes to the older Winchester load. The capacity of most lever-actions is less, running somewhere around 7 rounds. But in most cases, the tubular magazine design does permit a shoot-and-replace strategy, similar to a shotgun. Now that Hornady has Flex-Tip bullets, the use of pointed projectiles is even possible. Prior to this design, less aerodynamic round nose bullets were required to prevent detonation of adjacent primers.

Browning's BLR solves nearly all problems associated with the lever-action. It's a completely different animal with a rack & pinion drive, detachable magazine, and a strong, rotary bolt. As such, it can handle modern cartridges, making it a viable contender. Its solid receiver permits easy mounting of optics, too. Superficially, we might consider the BLR an offshoot of the older Savage Model 99, which is no longer manufactured. Winchester's box magazine fed Model 95 was another design that mitigated pointed bullet issues. Unlike the Savage, it doesn't accommodate optics. Many of the other great old Winchesters are in the same boat. They can be fitted with aperture sights and many are. But, while a good peep sight is a major improvement over iron sights, the capability to employ an optical system will bring usefulness to a whole new level. Meanwhile, for those who own an older design, why not keep it? You'll still have a handy, grab & go rifle in a useful caliber.

RIFLES

If viewed in the context of one primary rifle, choices narrow. Three main types warrant a look. Some modern, competing brands are really just clones of what we'll cover.

Winchester Model 94: This great, John Browning-designed rifle has been around since 1894. It was the first design to use smokeless powder, and dates from an era preceding use of scopes. As such, it is built to eject spent cases straight upward. With more than 7 million Model 94s in circulation, it's certainly not uncommon. It has been offered in a number of chamberings, but by far, the most popular is the .30/30. Although production finally ceased in 2006, well-made Japanese clones are still produced by Miroku. Anyone referring to a "pre-64" is talking about rifles made prior to the big Winchester shake-up, which resulted in rifles of lesser quality. At least, that's the perception. Actually, all of them are serviceable. The later "angle eject" version is a re-design that throws empties to the side. A provision for scope bases was also incorporated. Although the Model 94 is a timeless choice, it wouldn't be my pick. The modified angle ejection disassembly is bothersome.

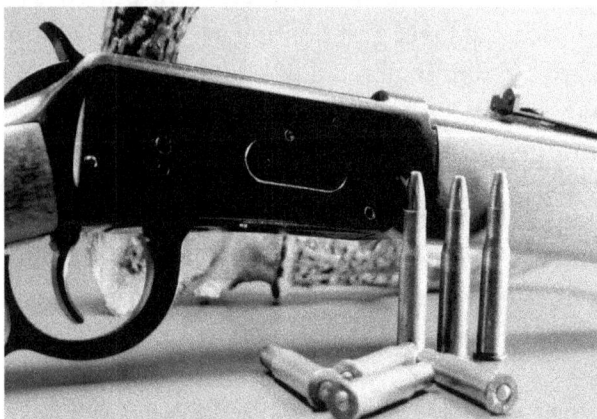

A classic combination is the Model 94 in .30/30. Older Winchesters are stamped .30 WCF.

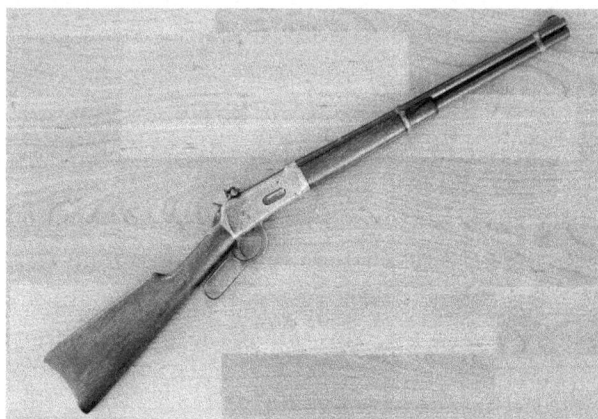

This old Winchester Model 94 is no doubt connected to many great stories. Note the side-mounted receiver sight. It's still an effective choice.

Marlins: The present Model 336 really goes back to 1893, but it has been produced in present form since 1948. Marlin has been the direct competitor of the Winchester Model 94. One big advantage of the M-336 is its solid receiver top with side ejection. Mounting optics on a Marlin is not a problem for this reason. More recently, quality has varied, in part because of aging production tooling, and possibly due to a learning curve associated with new management. Marlin's production has now shifted from the old North Haven, Ct. plant to modernized sites with a corresponding increase in precision. Much effort is going into re-tooling and quality control.

While a single-rifle owner would be well-served with a time-proven .30/30, the addition of a couple more Marlins would afford a versatile lever-action system for everything from small game to big bears. A Model 1895 will handle bigger calibers like .45/70 or .444 Marlin. The smaller Model 1894 is another neat design that fires handgun calibers. All three types, along with Marlin's companion 39-A .22, are very similar, and can be quickly disassembled for through-the-breech cleaning.

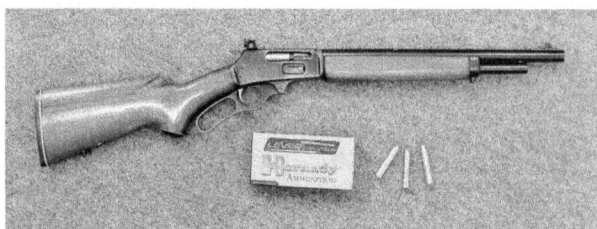

Behold "The Benedicta Bazooka," a battle-scarred, shortened M-1895 .45/70 made even more formidable thanks to Hornady's new flex-tip load. This carbine precedes Marlin's Guide Gun.

The .45/70 is a good old round that certainly has

plenty of power. The M-1895 I owned was fairly manageable and shot darned well. I screwed on a Williams peep sight and put a big, green fiber optic bead up front. Although it didn't seem precise, factory 300-grain bullets easily grouped inside 2 inches at 100 yards. A friend has a shorter Guide Gun that's similarly equipped, and is absolute hell on running big game.

CR-6 Rifle Marlin 45 70: Behold "The Benedicta Bazooka," a battle-scarred, shortened M-1895 .45/70 made even more formidable thanks to Hornady's new flex-tip load. This carbine precedes Marlin's Guide Gun.

I've owned several Model 1894s, all of which shot wonderfully. Two were .357 Magnums, also capable of firing .38 Specials. They were lots of fun, surprisingly accurate, and extremely quiet with the latter load. Such a rifle would make a nice companion to a .357 Magnum revolver. This of course, is an old idea that dates to the days of the Wild West. I still have an old, Lyman peep sight equipped M-39-A, which will digest any type of standard .22 ammo. It'll work on small game, and also makes a nice practice piece.

This brace of Marlins includes a M-39-A rimfire and a M-1894 centerfire. In a pinch, they'd cover just about all rifle chores.

Marlin's Model 336 has lots of nice features, including the ability to accommodate various aiming systems.

In my experience, all of these rifles are good shooters. I'd stick with the most common calibers. Marlin has a few proprietary chamberings like the .308 Marlin Express and .338 Marlin Express. Although they really boost performance, you wind up in the potential trap of hard-to-come-by ammunition.

Many of the Marlins are available in stainless steel, a design which may not be traditional, but certainly does make sense. The major parts are stainless but some minor ones are nickel-plated. The XLR-series are, to my taste, drop dead gorgeous with their laminated stocks. They balance well and are ready to hunt with right out of the box. The new and business-like 1895 GSBL .45/70 is a short, stainless carbine with a darkened finish.

One nice thing about the Marlin line is availability of accessories. The market isn't exactly swimming with extras, but some useful items can be found. XS Sights sells some interesting scope bases. Several other firms sell after-market sights, as well as stocks. Without much effort you could create a useful package without going broke.

Mossberg: This well-known firm sells a Model 94-type rifle, which is radical to say the least. It blends old west tradition with AR-type features, resulting in a wild-looking Model 464. You can have an M-4 type stock and a railed forend in a lever-action .30/30. At first glance I just shook my head but, thinking it over, the idea actually does have merit. Mossberg also offers more traditionally styled .22 rifles that would complement a bigger brother.

Henry Repeating Arms: Lever-action rifles are Henry's specialty, so they have a huge lever-action lineup. Most are rimfires, but their centerfire rifles are coming on strong. Like the Marlins, they have solid-frame receivers, drilled and tapped for scope bases. Their blued-steel .30/30 looks well-thought out. A very attractive .357 magnum version would make a great companion piece for anyone carrying a .357 revolver. New for 2016 are a brace of chrome-plated lever-actions with black, coated hardwood stocks. Each is designed for hard use in bad weather. The calibers are .30/30 and .45/70. Another new rifle is the "Long Ranger," which looks like a Browning BLR. The new Henry feeds from a detachable magazine that can handle pointed bullets. The lever-powered bolt locks into a barrel extension via six rotary lugs, in a manner similar to an M-16. This strong breeching system permits the use of a light aluminum receiver to minimize weight. The calibers are three great choices: .223 Rem, .243 Win, and .308. Despite its modern design, the Long Ranger manages to preserve traditional styling. The Henry line is worth exploring, for sure!

Rossi: This South American manufacturer sells the Rio, a .30/30 Marlin M-336 knockoff. They also have a line of Winchester '92 copies that are chambered for popular revolver cartridges. I have a real soft spot for Model 92 lever-actions and, supposedly, the Rossi clones are well-made. The top ejection negates a conventionally mounted scope, but one version sports a cheek piece riser and forward-mounted scope base. Some of the Rossi M-92s, including their .357 Magnums, are even available in stainless steel.

Browning's BLR: I owned an early model .358 Winchester, which shot extremely well. Upon close examination one can understand the reason. The lever drives a breech bolt using gears to impart a solid and smooth-feeling stroke. The rifle locks up much like a bolt-action, providing a strong connection. The trigger travels with the lever assembly and the power stroke is relatively short. Like most lever guns the BLR has a hammer, but it's of a slightly different design. You can fold a pivoting section forward for safe carry and unloading. Cock it and the unit orients for firing pin strikes. A detachable magazine feeds the rifle, which is chambered for a good assortment of high-intensity rounds. One rimless big-bore caliber is the .450 Marlin. The .358—based on a necked up .308—is there as well. In testimony to its strength, you can even buy a longer, magnum cartridge model. The BLR's biggest detraction is disassembly. The factory doesn't recommend it because function depends on proper indexing of gear teeth to the bolt. The guts are also captured by directional pins, which must be driven out and reinstalled correctly. I have successfully disassembled one, but Browning's advice is sound. It's a gunsmith operation, meaning the bolt is staying put. Cleaning must proceed with that in mind.

Despite this flaw, I really like the BLR. It's a modern design, but not without traditional styling. The rifle is well-proven, having been around since the late 1960s. It's another sleeper product, over-shadowed by the more traditional rifles. I had no trouble shooting 1.25 MOA groups with 200 grain .35 caliber spitzers through my .358. Thanks to a box-type magazine, pointed bullets are not a problem. A friend's .308 BLR shot closer to an inch. One thing not practical is breech-end cleaning, at least not with a conventional rod. But Otis sells a flexible cleaning arrangement which uses a coated cable. You drop it down the muzzle, attach a brush or patch, and pull it through the breech. It works and is a worthwhile accessory for anyone on the move.

Both of these rifles were older versions with steel receivers, sized for short action cartridges. Browning later came out with a long action BLR, plus alloy receivers designed to save weight. Strength is in no way compromised since the bolt's lugs engage the barrel. Lengthening the action permitted use of classic loads like the .30/06, but this change altered the rifle substantially. I personally prefer the short action models, which are lively and compact guns. The solid receivers are drilled and tapped for optics, but iron sights are provided. Besides the more classic-looking models, Browning offers a stainless/laminated rifle. Straight-hand stocks or pistol grips are there as well.

The coolest model has got to be the take-down version. A lever in the forend makes this process simple. A scout-type, barrel-mounted scope base can be used to help maintain zero, or a scope can be conventionally mounted to the receiver. With the barrel removed it can be easily cleaned through the breech end, and the bolt face becomes more accessible for cleaning. You could sign me up for a stainless Model 81 chambered in .308. Others might like their similar, Realtree camo, take-down, Hog Hunter model in the same caliber. Best of all may be the latest Black Label Takedown, which bridges lever-action operation with tactical features. Throw in a few extra magazines and add a short 1x4 scope. It might even work with a bipod, thanks to the very short lever throw. Nearly all bases will be covered, but…

For lever gun addicts, how about a .223? This BLR offering came and went, but has since reappeared. I think it's a great idea, providing a chance to own a duplicate varmint rifle on the same good action. Will it replace a bull-barreled bolt-action? No. You'll get a somewhat heavy hunting trigger and good, but possibly not phenomenal accuracy. But short of staking out a prairie dog town, the idea is pretty good.

One last BLR we'd want to add is Browning's .22 rimfire model. Voila, a three-gun set, capable of covering all bases!

CLOSING LEVER GUN THOUGHTS

Many of the classic tubular magazine types have a loading port in the right side of the receiver. This system affords an additional benefit that can be exploited with training. Namely, it's possible to shoot and reload when opportunity permits. Fire two shots and you can stuff two more rounds into the magazine while maintaining some semblance of a defensive posture. The proper location of spare ammo is a key part of this technique, which will also work for left-handed shooters.

In most cases, a bipod is probably not feasible due to mounting limitations and lever stroke (although that BLR might work). The more traditional Winchester types are also difficult to scope because of their vertical ejection. The solid-top receiver types solve this problem, but they often have stocks cut for iron sights. A simple solution is an add-on cheek piece, as discussed in the "Accessories" Chapter.

A .30/30 is more effective today than ever, thanks to recent ballistic enhancements. A .357 Magnum cartridge is no slouch either, offering companion revolver possibilities. If you happen to have a lever gun on hand, why not keep it?

Chapter 7

COMBINATION GUNS

A few different types of firearms fall into this category. The most common combination gun is one that can shoot rifle cartridges and shotgun shells through a pair of barrels using a selector. These guns are typically break-action designs with pivoting barrels, stacked in an over & under configuration. They're popular in Europe and sometimes seen as "drillings" with two shotgun barrels side-by-side and a third rifle barrel hung underneath. The significant engineering required to manufacture such a firearm is reflected by a substantial cost. Many are true works of art and some have trickled into the U.S. as imports or Word War II trophies.

An entirely different type of "combination gun" is one with interchangeable barrels. It is often an affordable single-shot of break-barrel design, sold as a two or three barrel set. A kit may include a .22 rimfire, shotgun, and centerfire barrel, all of which are fitted to a single receiver. We'll look at them in the next chapter.

LIMITING FACTORS

At first glance, one might think a true combination gun would be THE choice. After all, it's a shotgun and a rifle all rolled into one. I have an affinity for these firearms, having used them for years. Theoretically, all bases should thus be covered from birds to bears. However, when something seems too good to be true—it often is.

Combination guns really are useful tools under certain circumstances, but they do fall short in one key area—defense. You may have but a fraction of a second to sort out the appropriate barrel. With lots of practice, nearly instantaneous selection should be possible, but you'd better make it count. Defensively, missing has ominous implications. Since our theme involves choices capable of covering all bases, we're now weak in this crucial domain. Next, we'll need a way to aim or point, depending on our selected barrel. I've been trying to figure this part out for more than 35 years.

Any gun is better than no gun but, if we take the defensive aspect off the table, a combination gun begins to make some sense. I view it more as subsistence tool, best reserved for incidental encounters. For more serious hunting endeavors I'll bring the firearm best suited to a specific quarry. If I'm after ducks, one shotgun shell is limiting, and the rifle barrel will make a combo-gun illegal. For deer I'd really like good, low-light optics, decent range, and a quick, second shot. In other words, if a combination gun is your only firearm your horizons will be limited. On the other hand, if you add one to an established battery of working guns it can prove useful at times.

One thing to consider with stacked-barrel designs is sight height, relative to the rifle bore. Savage located their rifle barrels above the shotgun bore. With the supplied low-profile open sights, hitting close-range targets was fairly easy; however, most other manufacturers reverse the barrel positions, which greatly improves lock-up strength. If you add an optical sight to such designs, a large divergence occurs between the axis of optic and bore. It won't be such a problem on deer-sized game but on smaller targets it can cause some missing.

Herein lays a dilemma common to just about all combination guns: You don't aim a shotgun, you point it. Adding any sort of alternate sighting system defeats the whole shotgun concept. On the other hand, the supplied iron sights work poorly beyond close range—which defeats the rifle advantage. What to do? I've tried ghost ring peep sights, dot sights, and low-magnification scopes. The latter created a top-heavy package, which also worked poorly for flying targets. A small dot sight improved handling but lacked precision for rifle work, and still wasn't great with the shotgun tube. The same was true with a peep sight. Things get easier if wingshooting is off the table but, for me, that capability is desirable.

COMBINATION GUN CHOICES

Domestically, the most common type is probably the pedestrian Savage Model 24. Although out of production now, it has been around since 1939. Over the years several versions were offered in different calibers. The most common were .22 LR or .22 WMR over .410 or 20 gauge. Others were sold in .22 Hornet, .222, .223, .30/30, .308, and .357 Magnum atop 20 or 12 gauge barrels. The Model 24 is a break-action over & under with an external hammer. Barrel selection originally occurred with a frame-mounted button, but a simplified, hammer-mounted lever soon became the norm. I had a .22LR/20-Ga. DL model that carried fairly well. It was exceptionally accurate due to its rigid barrel attachment design. For knocking around the woods it was lots of fun. The hard part involved any sort of practical sighting system beyond the tiny, factory-issued open sights. The small-diameter rifle barrel was grooved for a scope, which was prone to slippage from shotgun recoil.

The Savage Model 24 was built in large quantities and calibers. It can still be found as a used but dependable combination gun.

I once owned a Valmet .308/12 gauge; and a Tikka .222/12 gauge. They were interesting guns, although the Valmet was fairly heavy. It also had a spare set of 28-inch O/U shotgun barrels which did handle quite well, providing real versatility. The combo-barrel configuration was laborious to tote, but its .308-accuracy was phenomenal, even using iron sights. A scope mounting system looked so ungainly that I skipped it. The gun had a single, selective trigger and was laid out like any conventional over & under shotgun. You can still buy these in various combinations from Double Gun Headquarters. Although not cheap, the Valmets cost less than other European guns that can run into the thousands of dollars.

Until recently, CZ sold a Brno, Czech-built combination gun. It was at one point chambered in .243, .308, and .30/06, under 12 gauge. I've yet to handle one, but you can see it online. Used guns occasionally surface on the gun sites.

This 12 Ga./.223 Tikka was re-chambered from .222 Rem. The barrel selector is visible on the receiver. The Burris FastFire was switched out for a lower Konus dot sight. A Bear Tooth stock riser helped. Note the extreme offset between the rifle barrel and sight.

I bought my Tikka-Ithaca Turkey Gun used in 1980. It has an external hammer, frame-mounted barrel selector, and accepts tip-off scope rings. A neat little folding rear sight pivots downward into a solid barrel rib. It's still going strong today although it has been a .223 for at least 25 years. I simply had it re-chambered, crossing my fingers that it would retain its stellar accuracy. Afterward, no real degradation was noted. It shoots sub-MOA, as long as time is allowed between shots for barrel cooling. It's now easy to feed thanks to common .223 and 12 Ga. ammo. We've shared many interesting miles while tramping through the North Woods. It lurks in the nether regions of the gun safe until my deer tag is filled.

At that point it appears for scouting missions, taking an incidental grouse, porcupine or coyote. I consider it an old friend, but I've yet to fully solve the sighting riddle. At the moment it's wearing a small Konus dot sight that has withstood 12 gauge recoil.

The same Tikka combination gun with a Konus Atomic dot sight. The switch was made for slightly lower sight height.

Springfield Armory sold a civilian version of the M-6 folding survival gun for a while. It was chambered for .22LR and .410, presenting a somewhat strange appearance. It was mostly metal, folded in half, and had a bar for a trigger. The one I owned was hard to shoot and I can't say I miss it.

Remington tried a run of Russian IZH combination guns, which were built like tanks. They had two triggers, permitting instant barrel selection. Various calibers were offered including 12/.223 and.308/.30/06. A smaller .22 LR or .22 WMR .410 was also offered. Prices were reasonable. Recently, EAA has resumed distribution of these guns, although prices are now higher.

Savage Model 42: The latest combination gun is another Savage. This one looks different from its predecessor, but shares many common features. One big difference is the copious use of plastic. You can buy it as a .22 LR or 22 WMR over 3-inch .410. Either choice offers possibilities. The .22 LR model would also handle CCI "Quiet" loads or CB Caps for stealthy subsistence. The .22 Magnum is

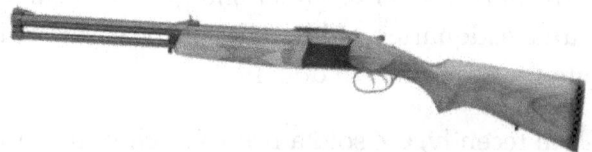

Russian built IZH Combination guns are on-again, off-again imports, which are built like tanks.

by no means a great deer cartridge, but it does at least afford additional power. Yes, you can shoot .410 slugs, but they're pretty anemic. I'd want to carefully shoot some groups in hopes of nailing an accurate load.

Three-inch .410 shells will harvest small game and birds out to at least 25 yards. I've successfully hunted pheasants with an over & under using a 3" #7 ½ shell in the more open choke, backed up by a three-inch #6. Normally, a .410 would be a poor ringneck choice, but I was shooting over a phenomenal pointer, owned by a guy who could really shoot. Ranges were close and, with two .410s in action, pheasants tumbled reliably without being shredded. Nowadays, there are some interesting .410 loads geared for defensive use in large revolvers. They'd also work in the Savage, although you'd only get one shot. I'd strongly recommend shooting some patterns on paper before relying on them.

We'll need time to see how the latest Savage does. So far so good since a take-down version has been announced for 2016. At least, with this model, if something breaks, service is available from a reputable company. If my Tikka breaks, owing to its age and obsolescence, I'm probably just plain screwed.

A WORD OF CAUTION

One important thing we all need to remember is that doggone barrel selector. More than once I've lined up for a tricky rifle shot and touched off a shotgun shell instead. In reverse it could be pretty dangerous. Firing a rifle skyward is never a good idea so, for that reason, I always park my selector on the shotgun barrel. Better to be safe than sorry.

CHAPTER 8

SINGLE-SHOT RIFLES

While black rifles and high-capacity magazines are all the rage, a quiet following of single-shot rifle buffs lurk on the sidelines. The finer European stalking rifles from firms like Blaser and Merkel handle wonderfully, and are true works of art. Domestically, a few great American examples like the Ruger Number One and Winchester 1885 are available for single-shot connoisseurs. But, for our purposes, utility is the driving force. I wouldn't want all my eggs in a single-shot basket so, without an effective self-defense capability, why tie up money on a high-end model?

Winchester's Model 1885 was made in two action sizes. The smaller "low wall" is an elegant rifle. Although this one is a .223, it only offers one shot for a significant cash outlay.

The single-shots we'll examine are more basic types. They employ hinged barrels and exposed hammers, which must be cocked prior to firing.

TRUE INTERCHANEGABLE BARREL SYSTEMS

Some of these guns are really affordable, while others may exceed $500. The more costly types often offer a menu of accessory barrels. Owners can purchase them as needed in different calibers or gauges to meet their personal needs. A high degree of precision manufacturing is required to maintain universal fit, so costs are higher than the factory-fitted, multi-barrel kits. Guns within the latter category are typically sold as cataloged packages, with barrels in .22 rimfire, 20 gauge shotgun, and .243 Winchester (or others). They're often advertised as "combination guns," which can cause some confusion. With either version, changing barrels is usually simple. In most designs the forend is removed by loosening a screw or two. At that point, a hinge pin can be driven out of the receiver to separate the barrel.

T/C: The most well-known interchangeable-barrel guns are sold by Thompson Center, which got the ball rolling decades ago with their break-barrel Contender pistol. Dual frame-mounted firing pins and a hammer-mounted selector permitted the use of centerfire or rimfire barrels. Unlike other systems from that era, they required no fitting, which opened up all sorts of possibilities. Before long, rifle barrels and stocks appeared, presenting the option of a universal system. Choices proliferated, but the Contender was never designed for popular high-pressure rifle cartridges like a .30/06 or .300 Winchester Magnum.

T/C sells an innovative break-barrel single-shot, which can be configured as a pistol or rifle. Interchangeable barrels provide great versatility.

A beefed up "Encore" eventually solved this problem, and it's still on the market. In fact, an updated Contender "G-2" version is as well. Removing the forend exposes a strong hinge pin that can be tapped out for barrel exchange. This simple and strong design affords many stock and caliber choices, along with shotgun and muzzle-loading options. The T/C systems are really firearm "transformers" in their own right. Users will need to be aware that installing a pistol-length barrel on shoulder-stocked frame is a federal violation without a BATF short-barrel permit. A rifle barrel shorter than 16-inches falls within that category.

For a while, I was working off two Contender frames with an assortment of pistol and rifle barrels, grips, and stocks. None were inaccurate and some were real tack drivers. My Encore experience is limited but those I've seen in action performed extremely well. Their ease of disassembly permits a shooter to field a compact kit.

CVA Apex: A more recent import is the "Apex," which works in a similar manner to the T/C. Both systems employ a spur on the trigger guard to unlock a tilting barrel. Unlike the T/C, which was an adaptation of a handgun, the Apex was built from the ground up as a true rifle. Its lines are therefore more traditional, although barrel choices are fewer. The trigger is adjustable. The Apex is both strong and accurate with barrels built by the Spanish Bergara factory on modern equipment. Each comes with barrel-mounted scope rings which, like the T/C design, ensure a constant zero. The stainless receiver and barrels provide good weather resistance and they attach through a process similar to the T/C.

I bought a muzzle-loading Apex several years ago. Besides the features noted, a main attraction was its weatherproof action. Like the T/C (and others), the powder charge is still loaded from the business end, but it's ignited by a breech-inserted, 209-type shotgun primer. Once the barrel is snapped shut, a fairly weatherproof system results. The breech plug is threaded for easy removal, providing direct bore access for cleaning. In this form the Apex is a real ringer.

This CVA Apex was originally purchased as a .50-caliber muzzle loader, but an extra .308 barrel extended its usefulness.

In fact, the whole system worked so well that I added a spare .308 barrel. A slightly different but inexpensive "standard" forend was required due to the thinner barrel and lack of a ramrod. The switch was easy and initial testing produced 5-shot groups of one MOA. A good trigger didn't hurt. Again, this capability also applies to a T/C Encore.

Somehow, I stumbled onto a third Apex barrel chambered for .300 Blackout. It worked with the standard forend and made a very interesting ad-

A brace of CVAs. The less expensive Scout lacks an interchangeable barrel feature.

dition. It's very short, measuring a shade over the legal 16-inch minimum. The muzzle is threaded 5/8 x 24, which is also common to .30-caliber AR-10s. A simple collar protects the threads, which will also accept muzzle devices like a suppressor (silencer). Once so equipped, the overall length of the rifle still isn't excessive. The small Blackout round is a dual-use cartridge designed to fire very heavy subsonic .30-caliber bullets. It can also shoot lighter and faster bullets that approximate 7.62 x 39 AK-47 ballistics. Without much effort, mine also achieved MOA accuracy. A suppressed, sealed-breech rifle can also attain maximum quietness. Overall length is still quite compact, so this Apex barrel is an intriguing addition. Disassembled, the receiver and a barrel will stow nicely in a soft takedown shotgun case or pack. Cost will run around $550 for an Apex with one barrel.

Rossi Wizard: This Brazilian manufacturer has been making affordable single-shot firearms for years. Their latest effort is the "Wizard," which offers true, switch-barrel capability. Whether rimfire, centerfire, shotgun, or muzzle loader, you can just keep adding barrels to the same receiver. No fitting is required and most popular calibers are available, along with common gauges. After removing the forend, the barrel will just tip off when the action is opened. Cost is much less, but obscurity is a hurdle. I logged onto the Rossi site and immediately found a link to spare barrels. The actual Wizard rifle didn't appear until I clicked on an archives link which indicates it's still in production.

When using subsonic .300 Blackout loads, a suppressed single-shot rifle can be very quiet.

SINGLE BARREL, FACTORY-FITTED TYPES

This category includes a few lower-tier-but-still-viable choices. Besides simplicity and low cost, many of them are darned good shooters.

Rossi: Besides the Wizard, a separate line of break-action firearms is offered. Some can be purchased as two or three-barrel sets in rimfire/centerfire or rimfire/centerfire/shotgun. There's even a two-barrel combo-pistol in .22 LR and .45 Long Colt /.410. The barrels are all pre-fitted by the factory so adding extras isn't possible.

I bought a Brazilian-made .357 Magnum rifle, which has a black, painted hardwood stock and nickel-plated metal. It's your typical break-action hammer gun, although it does have a pretty useless side-mounted safety lever. While not the finest example of gun making art, a bit of tweaking has turned it into my poor man's stalking rifle. The stock had dimensions suitable for Goliath. With only $130 in the rifle, I opted for do-it-yourself surgery, shortening it and re-carving the stock into something a bit more graceful. The butt and forend were then sprayed with black wrinkle-paint for texture. The supplied sling loops were easily modified to QD studs and a T/C Contender scope base was mounted on the factory-tapped barrel. I slapped an adhesive comb-riser pad on the stock and shopped for an inexpensive, low-powered scope with lots of eye relief. A Rossi hammer extension wouldn't clear its ocular bell, but I managed to modify another type. The finished product is very light and carries well. Have you ever seen revolver speed strips? You couldn't get a more handy spare ammo carrier and loading device for this rifle. Just slip a cartridge into the chamber and peel it off of the flexible carrier. For the consummate minimalist, the addition of a used .357 Magnum revolver would meet most needs. The wheel gun could cover defense and the rifle could pick off game at further ranges.

Peering through the not-too-wonderful 2X scope, the first volley from the Rossi produced encouraging results. I've been happy ever since, shooting my way through a collection of old Remington .38 +P, 125-grain Golden Saber Brass Jacketed Hollow Points. Off sandbags, this rifle will consistently put five inside 2-inches at 100 yards. I sight it in just a touch high at 50-yards and it prints a couple of inches below point of aim at 100. Figuring on seeing more bullet drop, I broke out the chronograph and recorded 1400 fps. Wow! Recoil is almost non-existent and the report is very mild. I've shot enough critters with this load to know it really works; however, for something really large I'd opt for a bit more horsepower. With a tougher .357 Magnum bullet, in a pinch, I'd even tackle a moose. For plinking or small game, a standard .38 Special round will do.

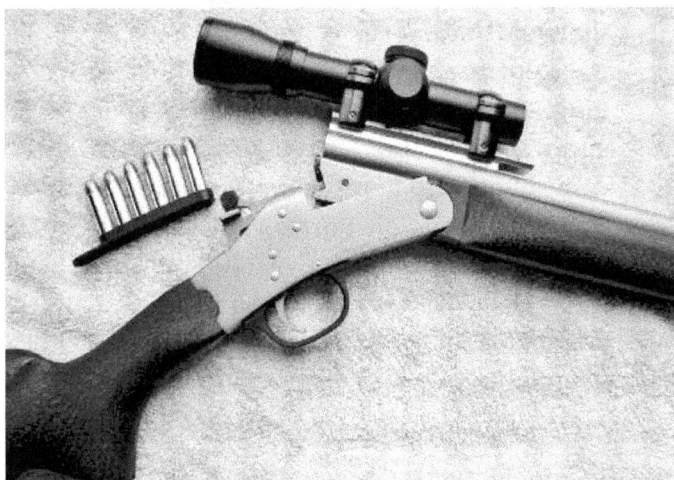

38 Special and .357 magnum velocities see dramatic gains in rifle barrels. A speed strip is a handy way to stoke this slightly tricked out Rossi.

Unscrewing the forward sling swivel permits removal of the forend. The barrel can then be opened and simply lifted off the frame. Reattaching the forend secures it from damage and both halves fit nicely in a soft take-down shotgun case. We liked the idea so much that I wound up modifying a second rifle for a friend. His works fine, but mine had occasional misfires. The problem appears to be fairly common with Rossi's transfer bar hammer arrangement. Careful removal of a few thousands of the hammer-face increased primer indents to improve ignition. For most, the procedure is best left to a gunsmith.

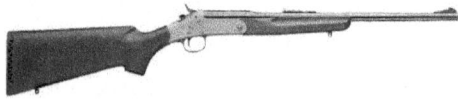

An H&R like this "Sportster" provides good bang for the buck.

H&R: Extending this concept a bit further, H&R offers their two-barrel "Handi-Rifle" combos. They catalog an interesting .357 Magnum and 20 gauge set, which most certainly would handle larger game. The rifle barrel comes without sights, but a scope base and hammer extension are included. Also available are .223 .30/30 and .308 break-action rifles. A "Survivor" version has a synthetic thumbhole stock with a built-in storage compartment. The "Tamer" is a nickel-plated 20 gauge version with shell holders in its stock. Youth models are available, and other "Topper" shotgun models are available in 12, 20, and .410. Like the Rossi, the H&Rs are reasonably priced, providing a utilitarian solution for those seeking a very basic firearm. They are domestically produced and have been around for years. You'll also see NEF (New England Firearms) guns, which look nearly identical. The explanation is simple: All of these guns come out of the same factory. Closely related is the AAC .300 Blackout version, sold by a subsidiary entity, Advanced Armaments Corporation. It has a short 16.1-inch barrel with a Picatinny optics rail and a threaded muzzle.

CVA Scout: Besides the Apex, CVA sells a similar-looking stainless "Scout.." It's more reasonably priced, but not available in all of the calibers referenced in this book. Among those offered, you can buy a .243 Winchester, a 45/70, and even a .300 Blackout. Shorter, youth-length versions are offered as well. It's actually a sharp-looking rifle, although interchangeable barrels are out. I see no mention

This CVA Scout may not be a big-ticket item but it obviously shoots. The photo precedes the addition of a YHM muzzle adapter, and shows a G.I. flash cage.

of Bergara barrels, which really might not matter. I lucked into a .300 Blackout Scout for a great price and deputized it as my truck gun. It fits in a very short, soft AR-15 assault rifle case with magazine pockets. They make a handy spot for spare ammo, as does an elastic stock-mounted sleeve that holds nine spare rounds. Like the Apex .300 Blackout barrel, this one is also only 16-inches long and threaded. I screwed on a spare YHM suppressor adapter, mostly because I could. It comes with a one-piece scope mount, so I next threw on an old 4X Burris Mini scope. Right out of the box it punched five 110-grain handloads into 7/8" at 100 yards. Recoil is nil, so with the shorter youth stock, it wouldn't be a bad choice for smaller shooters.

SINGLE-SHOT RATIONALE

Some folks will rank a single-shot firearm as an auxiliary tool, useful for specialized circumstances. The more basic domestic models are still very inexpensive, and could be stashed until needed at fall-back locations. If need be, one could even be ditched without losing a fortune; and for someone on a really tight budget, any gun is better than no gun. In fact, with careful shopping you can wring out two or more guns from one thanks to factory-fitted switch-barrel shotgun & rifle combos.

The repeated mention of the .300 Blackout chambering may seem contradictory to the principle of "widely available.." It's a fair argument but, as we'll see in the AR section, this load is really catching on. Part of its popularity is directly related to suppressor technologies, but this caliber can also be used for a quick AR-15 conversion from .223. People interested in either/or both fields might therefore want an extra single-shot .300 Blackout rifle. Installation of a suppressor can often cause a zero shift, so a dedicated, handy, sealed breech system does provide advantages. Given the expense of a suppressor and $200 tax, an affordable rifle can also keep a lid on costs. There are also quite a few handloaders who are now forming their own .300 Blackout brass from abundant 5.56 cases.

For everyone else, a lightweight single-shot can just be fun to shoot!

CHAPTER 9

AMMUNITION

A comprehensive listing of all centerfire rifle cartridges would make quite a list. Since we're dealing (in part) with the prospect of societal collapse, it would also be a waste of time. Even during good days many calibers can be difficult to locate. If things tip over, imagine trying to track down a box of .307 Winchester, which was introduced in 1982 for use in specially reinforced "angle eject" Model 1894s. The odds of tracking some down at the general store are far from good. The chance of locating some old-fashioned .30/30 rounds is *much* better.

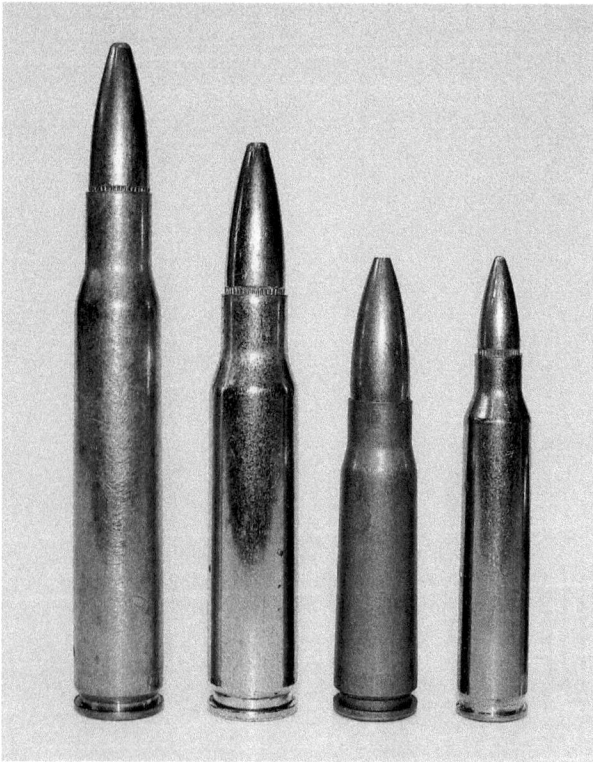

Choices based on mainstream military cartridges are safer bets for resupply. Shown L-R: .30/06, .308/7.62x51 NATO, 7.62x39 Russian (steel cased), and .223 Rem/5.56x45 NATO.

Availability: Sales of firearms and ammunition have recently exploded. Even .22 rimfire ammo is hard to find. Whether the situation will ease remains to be seen. This situation may be an indicator of just how bad things can get if our social order topples. Clearly, if things go completely to hell, ammunition will be a valuable commodity. It's entirely possible that certain calibers could assume the status of currency. In such a case, a large stash of .308 or .223 would have real value. A portion could be bartered for fuel and, if low on ammo, the odds of locating common calibers would be higher.

So, unlike the previous chapters, I won't beat the caliber choices to death. Instead, just a small list of practical choices will be covered. When it comes right down to it, there really isn't a huge amount of terminal difference between many of the popular choices anyway. For example, the .270, .280, and .30/06 are all based on the latter caliber. They have similar velocities and bullet diameter varies by only 0.031." Three one-hundred's of an inch is probably not worth sacrificing for availability.

The same can be said for a number of short action rounds based on the .308. Three fairly popular calibers include the .243, .260, and 7mm/08. Out of these, the .308 will be the easiest to find, and will also be available in a larger assortment of rifles. Believe it or not, velocity won't be all that much slower than a .30/06, either.

The .308 Winchester is essentially a civilian offshoot of the 1950s 7.62x51 NATO.

The .308 Winchester (center) soon gave birth to a number of offspring. Two examples are the .358 Win (L) and .243 Winchester (R). The fat .358 is a great cartridge but factory ammo remains scarce.

In fact, even some of the Magnum calibers aren't a vast improvement over the old-time '06, which has benefitted from modern propellants. For anyone who already owns a rifle chambered for a popular round like the 7mm Remington Magnum or .300 Winchester Magnum, great. Stock up on ammo when you can.

Projectile designs: Everyone seems to get hung up on caliber comparisons, but that's only part of the equation. Bullet construction is equally important and all bets are off without a suitably designed projectile. Some folks like heavier-for-caliber bullets on the theory that they hit harder. Others like lighter types in hopes of rapid energy transfer. While either camp can pose valid arguments, one key piece that can't be ignored is the actual construction of the projectile. We need to consider expansion balanced against penetration. Too little expansion may result in a deep but narrow wound channel. Too much could limit penetration, resulting in superficial wounding. Velocity plays a huge part in the upset of a bullet. The manufacturers expend much effort into covering as wide a spectrum as possible, but there limits on both sides of optimum performance. Excessive velocity could cause a bullet to disintegrate, whereas insufficient speed could create a full-metal jacket effect.

The size and tenacity of our quarry must also be considered. These are factors that will govern our choice of bullet, which now include many innovative designs. Some cost a small fortune and may consist of several materials all rolled into one projectile. Many are designed to control expansion for optimum penetration while still delivering necessary tissue damage.

Our military bullets conform to Hague Convention terms and are non-expanding, full-metal jacket types. They typically consist of a lead core surrounded by a copper jacket. The rifle bullets are sharply pointed and may contain a hard steel or tungsten insert, designed to increase hard-target penetration. They make a poor choice for hunting since tissue damage is lessened. Although it's true that some rounds like the 5.56mm can tumble in flesh, there's no guarantee. Particularly with smaller projectiles of this type, controlled expansion becomes more critical.

STOPPING POWER

Defensively, we may be addressing a determined 200-pound adversary. There really isn't any "magic bullet," and bigger isn't always better. For every action there is an equal and opposite reaction and, with more projectile mass at higher velocity, that reaction is recoil. Taking this Newtonian concept to the next level, guess what that level of force would do to a shooter if the projectile was capable of knocking an opponent off his feet? Much effort has gone into the science of defining so-called "knock-down power." A number of theories exist, but they all boil down to placing a bullet in the vitals, where wounding will produce the most rapid effects.

Big-bore loads: Elephant hunters may use large, .45-caliber "solids" that weigh more than 500 grains (there are 437.5 grains in an ounce). These big bullets penetrate deeply while substituting increased diameter for penetration-limiting expansion; however, precise placement is still necessary for decisive results—which come with serious recoil. Recovered bullets may look very much as they did before firing, except for rifling marks or a possible dent. Their aerodynamically poor round nose profile is perfectly adequate for close-range use.

Conventional loads: Our classic American big game bullets are designed to "mushroom" in their quarry. These projectiles are typically smaller pointed types, which are fired at high velocity for better long-range trajectory. Many are .24 to .35 calibers which, upon contact, expand to greater diameter. A larger wound channel results while their mass and velocity provide adequate penetration. Still, it's not uncommon for a well-hit deer to travel fifty to one hundred yards (or even further) before piling up. In my neck of the woods, their live weight probably averages around 160 pounds, factoring in mature does and smaller bucks. A broadside 40-yard hit from a .30/06 that clips the heart and traverses both lungs can produce no visible reaction other than a rapidly disappearing whitetail. We're talking about an *expanding* 150-grain bullet with a muzzle velocity (MV) of 3000 feet-per-second (fps). So much for knock-down power! Expect a long and possibly unsuccessful tracking effort from a military-type full-metal jacket. Even with the best expanding bullets, I'd wait at least 20 minutes before taking up the trail. Experienced hunters know it's best to give an animal time to lie down and expire.

These .223 bullets all weigh 55 grains, but their terminal performance will vary greatly. L-R: A fast-expanding Hornady TAP, deep-penetrating Barnes copper, and military FMJ.

Smaller-caliber choices: The so-called "assault rifle" calibers like the military 5.56/.223 fire light, small-caliber bullets at relatively high velocity. Their diminished mass decreases recoil and increases high-volume control. Lethality supposedly occurs through high velocity, along with some projectile tumbling. Still, I know of no deer hunters who would choose a .223 FMJ bullet. In many locales it would be illegal and, in some states, the caliber would be as well.

Some real world examples: Even with expanding .223 bullets, we had a devil of a time anchoring 40-50 pound coyotes. We were hunting them during winter months over bait with night vision-equipped AR-15s. These tough critters would run considerable distances after soaking up a bullet, which was a big problem after dark. They quickly disappeared within thick stands of softwood despite good upper body hits. In theory, they should have been easy to track on snow; however, a maze of coyote tracks leading to and from the bait, combined with an absence of blood, quickly dispelled that notion. We nearly gave up and switched to a bigger caliber like a .243 Winchester, but further research provided the cure.

A heated blind is essential during nocturnal coyote operations. Watching a bait site can still make for a long winter night.

A maze of fresh coyote tracks leads to this brush-covered bait pile. Each dimple in the snow is a footprint. Good luck tracking one down without a blood trail. Exit wounds help.

Recovery is tougher without snow. The hit, as indicated, resulted in a speedy departure of this smallish coyote. Recovery took lots of searching the next morning.

The 55-grain, .223 Hornady TAP round we started with was designed for rapid expansion. TAP stands for "Tactical Application Police," and the idea is to limit ricochets and over-penetration in urban areas. Here is where we need to delve further into the nebulous realm of so-called "stopping power." In this case, the fragile TAP bullets dumped all of their energy into our targets, which should have theoretically produced significant effects. Instead, we watched 13 consecutive coyotes run off with little to no reaction. We eventually found some, neatly punched through the vitals. In all cases, blood loss was minimal due to the small entrance hole, lack of exit, and thick absorbent winter coats of the coyotes. Bear in mind that these critters are part wolf and not like the smaller southwestern breed.

The fix was fairly simple: tougher bullets. In bigger calibers the Nosler Ballistic-Tip can sometimes be a quick expander, but as loaded by Federal, the 55-grain .223 version acts more like a miniature big game bullet. With complete penetration and controlled expansion, we anchored coyotes on the spot. Another winner was Federal's 60-grain Nosler Partition, which is a well-established design known for deep penetration and expansion. We could have shot full metal jackets but, without any real expansion, those coyotes would have just kept running. The key was a combination of both expansion *and* penetration, assuring maximum tissue damage. Interestingly, the Federal BT was endorsed by a trusted tactical law enforcement source, based on actual defensive shoots.

You can extrapolate these results to defensive scenarios or larger game. I once lost a dandy buck after shooting it head-on from only 40 yards with a .350 Remington Magnum. Believe me, he was hit hard. The next day a friend's dog found a pork chop-sized piece of meat with a rib attached. The 200-grain factory bullet hit bone and blew itself to bits. Since then I've shot a pile of deer with the same rifle, and none have required a second round. The cure was as simple as a switch to a somewhat tougher, but basic soft-point bullet; in this case Hornady's 200-grain Spire Point.

None of these larger northern deer were actually "knocked down." Being red color blind, I try to solve tracking issues by placing a large bullet on the shoulders and base of the neck. Still, you never know. I recently shot a buck broadside through the front end. He exhibited no reaction whatsoever, and bounced away as if un-hit, piling up on the other side of a ridge, some 75 yards away. Well, if a 200-grain, .35-caliber bullet with a muzzle-velocity of 2,680 fps won't blow a 200-pound animal off its feet, you can bet that a lighter bullet won't stop a determined adversary dead in his tracks either. Now think about handgun bullets, which travel only half as fast.

The deer described above was recovered in low light after soaking up a well-placed .350 Rem Mag bullet. He's no whopper, either. So much for "knock-down power."

Shot placement counts. Even a .22 LR bullet will be lethal if it damages the central nervous system. The trouble is, especially in defensive scenarios, adrenaline kicks in. Moving targets and low light just make things worse. Hit probability goes down and recoil can impede the placement of follow-up shots, so we need well-designed loads capable of bridging the gap between effective terminal performance and control.

BULLET CHOICES

Lately, an interesting assortment of premium bullets has appeared. Their use may or may not be warranted. Although often effective, they're not cheap, and in some cases an old school design may suffice.

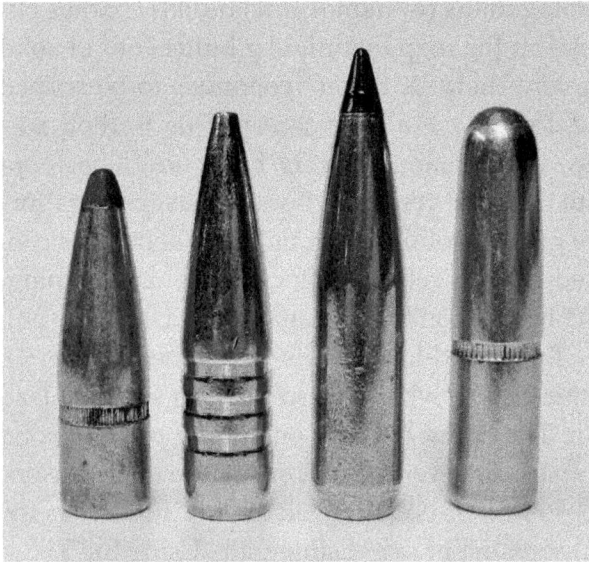

A collection of .30-caliber bullet types (L-R): 150 grain SP, 150 monolithic (copper) boat-tail, 180 polymer-tipped boat-tail, and 220 RN. The 150s illustrate how composition and profile can affect bullet length.

Basic cup & core designs: Bullets falling into "old school" category have a lead core encased in a copper-alloy jacket. The tip may have a "hollow-point" for rapid expansion or an exposed lead nose that will still expand, but at a somewhat slower rate. One good example is Hornady's recently introduced "American Whitetail" load. It's offered as a more affordable alternative to the premium loads and relies upon Hornady's simpler "Interlock" soft-point bullets. Among them are 150-grain Interlocks in .308 and .30/06. As it turns out, we've successfully used hand-loaded versions in both calibers to harvest dozens of deer. Many of our bullets were unrecovered. Those that were sometimes lost core material, but we've yet to lose a deer. Remington's .30/06 and .260 "Core-Lokt" loads have also worked reliably. We shoot the pointed (or "spitzer") types with a drag-resistant profile.

Up in the North Woods, some folks still shoot a round nose version, claiming it has better thump and brush-bucking ability. In truth, neither type will reliably travel true after even the slightest contact with a branch. A round nose will provide maximum weight in a bullet of a given length. This explains its popularity with dangerous game hunters who need deep penetration to reach the vitals of an elephant. Since most of us will be less challenged, a pointed type will minimize drop as ranges increase. Some will have a tapered "boat-tail base" for a slight reduction in turbulence. Others will be "flat-base" designs, but either should suffice for general purpose uses.

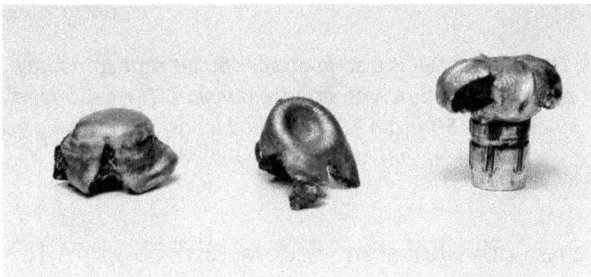

Bullets recovered from deer (L-R): A 150-Grain .30 Hornady Interlock, 90-grain .243 Nosler Partition, and 150-grain .30 Barnes TSX. The forward portion of the Partition peeled off in typical fashion. The solid-copper Barnes lost very little mass.

Evolutions: Nosler's "Partition Bullet" is a tried and true design consisting of two lead cores separated by jacket material. Picture a copper "H" filled on both ends by lead with the upper part formed into a tip. While the upper section can shed material, the lower portion generally survives for good penetration. The more rapidly expanding Nosler "Ballistic Tip" is a newer and different design with a streamlined plastic insert. You'll now see such types from several manufacturers. Some even offer "bonded" cores and jackets, combining sleek profiles and quick initial upset with good weight retention.

The Swift Scirocco is a bonded design with a reputation for toughness. Its core is soldered to the jacket for controlled expansion.

Homogenous (or monolithic) bullets: Barnes put these on the map by building bullets out of solid copper. Their "X Bullet" continues to be refined and some have a polymer tip. Due to their success, other manufacturers have now come out with similar versions. For serious penetration, I've gone to solid-copper bullets. Their use is confined to high velocity rifles like my .300 Remington Short action Ultra-Mag (.300 SAUM). The bullet I'm hand-loading is a Barnes 150-grain Triple-Shock, which doesn't have a speck of lead in it. The entire bullet is one pretty piece of solid copper and it expands nicely without risk of blowing apart. Believe it or not, one of the main reasons I use it is for insurance against over-expansion on close-range shots. Driven at very high velocity, some of the good, conventional cup & core bullets can separate or just disintegrate. Using the TSX, I won't hesitate to shoot a deer from any reasonable angle. The bullet will drive through the vitals producing text-book expansion and near-100% weight retention. The consensus is that solid-copper bullets behave as well as heavier, conventional types. I have a pair of 150 TSX bullets sitting here that traveled lengthwise through two bucks, coming to rest in their hind-quarters. One was found by our butcher's band saw after it blew the blade off the pulleys.

A tough bullet can prove valuable at close range where velocity is highest. Shown here is the author's .300 SAUM "Green Machine" and 40-yard Barnes TSX results.

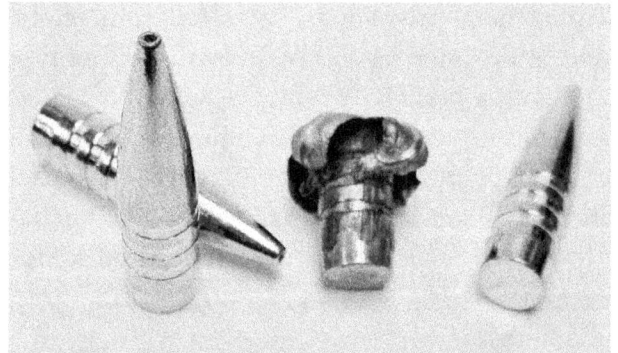

The Barnes TSX is a solid-copper bullet that combines deep penetration with good expansion. The expanded .30-caliber 150-grain TSX travelled lengthwise through a deer with almost zero weight loss.

We recently shot some Federal .223, 55-grain TSX through the FBI ballistic protocol involving glazing. It's probably as fair a test as any when properly executed. A special, temperature-controlled ballistic gelatin block is calibrated by measuring penetration of an airgun pellet at a specified velocity. Loads are then fired through specific protocols involving coverings of denim, dry-wall, and glass. The translucent gelatin blocks reveal 'wound" cavities as well as penetration. Out of over a dozen .223 loads tested, the TSX was undisputed champ

Classic bullet expansion in ballistic gelatin. This one is a handgun slug.

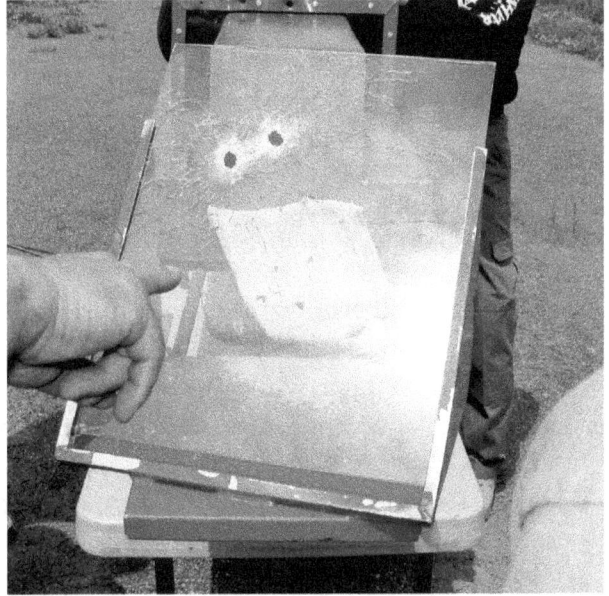
Bullet testing, per FBI protocols. The gel block is visible behind the glazing barrier.

for penetration and weight retention. It's the bullet I'd use on deer if limited to this caliber. A solid-copper bullet would also be a good choice in those locales mandating non-lead projectiles.

Flip-side choices: So, does that mean a solid-copper .223 bullet is the perfect all-around load? Heck no. For starters, although the TSX is generally known for great accuracy, I've seen mixed results in several .223 rifling twists. I also wouldn't care to use it for home defense. Instead, I'd look at something with less penetration—which might include that 55-grain TAP load. Like many of today's bullets, it has a polymer nose-cone, which improves aerodynamics and helps initiate expansion.

Varmint-type bullets are often designed as hollow-points for explosive expansion on thin-skinned varmints. In fact, many of the polymer-tipped lead-core projectiles behave in a similar manner. Others don't, so some homework is necessary before making a selection. The trick involves matching an appropriate design to your chosen caliber.

For those still shopping, here's a useful albeit fairly short list broken into three general categories.

ASSAULT & VARMINT RIFLE CALIBERS

These cartridges present in large quantities and can provide some useful services. They are often not the best for universal use including larger game, but they may get you by with careful shooting and proper bullets.

.223 Remington / 5.56mm: This choice goes hand-in-hand with an AR-15. Both designations refer to a very useful caliber and, in well-built bolt-actions or ARs, great accuracy is possible. Some people hunt deer-sized game with this round and I'd use it in a pinch, but it makes a better varmint load.

It's worth noting that the .223 Remington and 5.56mm NATO are really not interchangeable. For starters, the 5.56 round is loaded to pressures approximately 3000 PSI greater than a .223. To help handle this extra pressure, the NATO chamber has a bit of extra clearance ahead of it. This extra 0.125" space helps relieve pressure while serving as a small funnel to guide fired bullets into the rifled portion of the barrel. Lacking this extra clearance, the shorter leade of a civilian .223 chamber can easily develop extra pressure with mil-spec rounds. What does this mean? You CAN safely fire .223 loads in a 5.56mm chamber; however, you should NOT fire 5.56mm rounds in a civilian .223! Most barrels are marked according to their actual chambering for this reason. Clues that things are unsafe include cratered or loose primers with smudges and sticky extraction or bolt lift.

In a precision bolt-action rifle, I want a .223 chamber just to reap the accuracy benefits of its tighter dimensions. From a survivalist perspective that's probably not the best idea. The NATO chamber will handle everything, while producing useful accuracy. A good all-purpose rifling twist is 1x9. That means the bullet will rotate 360 degrees within nine inches of bore travel. Twists are available from a very fast 1x7 up to a slower 1x14 rate. Longer or heavier bullets require a faster twist. Short or lighter ones prefer slower rates, so a 1x9 is a good compromise.

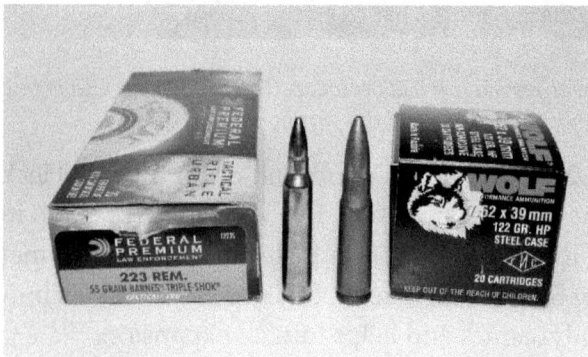

The global "assault" cartridges: Note the Barnes TSX .223 load, which can be fired in 5.56 NATO chambers.

7.62x39 Russian: This round has been manufactured in great quantities all over the globe. It has similar ballistics to a .30/30, but fires a lighter 123-grain bullet. Rifles chambered for the 7.62x39 are typically AK-47 variants or SKS designs, with a smattering of AR-types thrown in. The latter can be balky in this chambering, while the Soviet systems run and run. Tolerances are looser to improve reliability, but accuracy suffers. Now and then a bolt-action appears in this chambering, and with the CZ 527, I shot one MOA all day long. Owing to its mild recoil, with proper expanding bullets, it would make a great youth or ladies combination. As a weapon to be stashed, or for repelling boarders at close range, an AK or SKS will do the job. As a medium range hunting choice, it'll work on deer or hogs with good, expanding bullets. Ruger's Mini-14 is another option for those interested in this caliber.

UTILITY CARBINE CALIBERS

While they don't afford long-range performance or heavy-hitting clout, these cartridges do have some useful qualities. Of the three shown below, the second is included strictly as a companion handgun round. The third appears in deference to the many rifles already in circulation. Note the absence of another popular joint handgun and carbine round, the .44 Magnum. In our experience, even full-strength .357 loads are intimidating to many shooters. The product of recoil and muzzle blast is poor shooting caused by flinching. It's an all-too common occurrence, greatly exacerbated by the potent magnums. The few folks who can actually handle a .44 Magnum handgun could certainly handle a carbine. Like the .357 Magnum, it will greatly boost velocity. Milder and somewhat less expensive .44 Special loads could also be shot for small game or practice. Meanwhile, practicality and the K.I.S.S.

principle justify these picks:

.30 Carbine: The little M-1 was quickly approaching collector status, except for a smattering of post-WWII copies; however, production of well-executed, new M-1 Carbines has commenced. One reason for this is that they're still a handy little package with adequate power for close-range defensive use. Ammunition is also still plentiful and reasonably affordable. Practice 110-grain FMJ might set you back $25 for a box of 50 rounds. For defensive use, Hornady's 2000 fps "Critical Defense" 110-grain Flex-Tip load seems just about perfect. Cost is double, but the cheaper stuff will suffice for practice and even some small game. Half way around

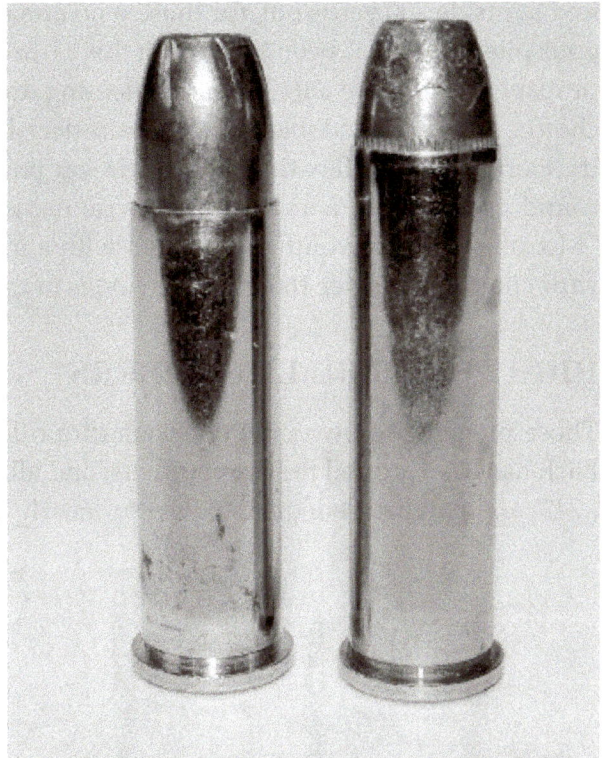

The .38 Special (L) and .357 Magnum loads can be fired interchangeably in the Magnum's chamber. If .38 Specials won't reliably feed they can probably be single-loaded.

Three useful utility carbine choices. Many .357 carbines will also feed and fire lower-powered .38 Special loads for small game and practice.

the globe, I once shot a deer with a military 110 FMJ. It worked, but I was lucky. The M-1 Carbine doesn't jump off the page as a whitetail pick, although I'd use a Hornady in a pinch, carefully placing my shot behind a shoulder. Be sure to perform a live fire function test prior to any serious use.

.357 Magnum: For anyone toting a revolver, this caliber may make sense. It wasn't long after the Civil War before people connected the dots. Colt single-action revolvers and lever-action rifles often traveled in tandem, chambered for handgun rounds like the .38/40 or .44/40. While I wouldn't choose a .357 to tackle elk, it will work on deer at fairly close range. In a revolver, the same round is known as a top defensive choice. When fired from a rifle, the .357 Magnum really gathers up a head of steam. Much recent effort has gone into bullet designs and some, like the solid-copper Barnes, will remain intact at higher rifle velocities. Lower-powered .38 Special rounds can be fired in .357 chambers as well. I've chronographed .38 +P loads in a rifle that actually exceeded .357 Magnum handgun velocities. If they feed in your rifle, standard .38s can stand in for less expensive practice.

.30/30: This caliber is synonymous with lever-actions, which exist in huge numbers. Even though they're great to carry, the stocks are often built for iron sights. Even with a scope, range will be limited to inside 200 yards but, for those who already have one, a .30/30 will do. As proof, one humongous pile of deer has been taken with this cartridge. Also, just about any place that stocks ammo will probably have some .30/30 rounds floating around. Lastly, it won't make a bad personal defense choice. Pick a dependable 150-170 grain deer load and you're off to the races. To spice things up, try Hornady's new flex-tip loads. Their soft pointed noses offer an aerodynamic improvement over round nose bullets, which are otherwise necessary in tubular magazines. The Hornady 140-grain "Monoflex LEVERevolution" is listed with a muzzle velocity of 2465 fps, making it an honest 200-yard choice. A heavier 160-grain version is in the same boat, with a slight increase in recoil.

HIGH POWER RIFLE CALIBERS

Those planning to own only one centerfire rifle could do worse than one of the following choices. Each has been around for over 50 years, and all will provide decent range. One will offer mild recoil (.243) and two have adequate power for nearly any use.

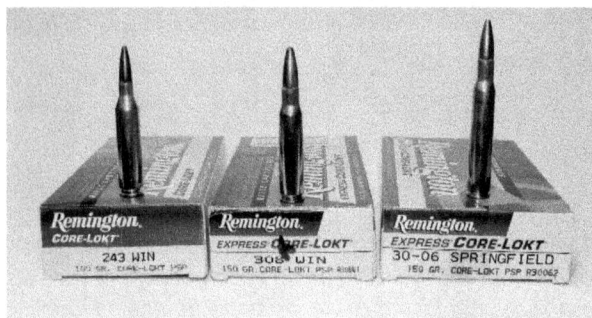

This basic trio of Core-Lokts is widely available for around a buck a shot.

.243 Winchester: Although not as widely distributed as the others, this 60-year-old cartridge is still a popular choice. The .243 is really a necked-down .308, which was envisioned as a dual-use varmint and deer load. Big game bullets run around 100 grains, which helps cut recoil. Light varmint bullets are also available that can achieve high velocity. I've owned several .243 rifles, using them for both roles. As a varminter it's loud, but that isn't always an issue. Plenty of deer have fallen to the .243, and I've taken several with hand-loads. It did the job, although I didn't find any exit holes. Since then, bullet design has greatly improved. Nowadays I'd look for a premium bullet, mainly for extra penetration insurance. One that comes to mind is the Barnes 85-grain TSX, which is loaded by Federal. Normally, that weight might be a bit on the light side but, thanks to its solid design, an 85-grain TSX should behave as well as any 100-grain bullet. Another well-proven design is Nosler Partition, which I have used in this caliber. The .243 is listed here to cover those who don't want the recoil of the next two choices.

.308 Winchester: You can't go wrong with this caliber, another military design. The cartridge case evolved from a shortened .30/06, but velocity remains close thanks to modern-day propellants. Ammunition is widely available, and you can find a .308 in any of the popular action-types. Many bullet choices exist, although the more common weigh between 150–180 grains. With premium bullets, just about all North American big game could be taken. The plain cup & core designs are adequate for deer. The .30/06 we'll examine next has a bigger boiler, which helps it handle heavier bullets; however, monolithic copper slugs provide the same attributes in a lighter weight. A 165-grain TSX may achieve penetration similar to a 180-grain conventional design with somewhat flatter trajectory. A light, 110-grain version is also available. It wouldn't be my first choice for big game, but it would provide a defensive option for recoil-sensitive folks. In any semi-auto system, I'd give them a thorough function test. Most such rifles are designed to operate within certain pressure parameters obtained with popular weights. "Managed Recoil" loads are sold to soften its kick, but most people should be able to handle a standard .308. Recoil is present, but not to the extent of magnum calibers. In a short action rifle, size will be a bit less, which helps provide a handy package. The .308, although designed for the U.S. M-14 Rifle, just seems right.

.30/06 Springfield: Most of the comments made about the .308 apply to the "ought-six" as well. I've listed the .30/06 due to its long-standing popularity, meaning rifles and ammo are widely distributed. For many experienced shooters, the '06 has long been the benchmark when comparing other calibers. Count me among them. The US Model 1903 Springfield bolt-action rifle was adopted in that year and was fully refined by 1906 to fire this cartridge. Since then, just about everything that could be done to this cartridge has been. The result is a wide spectrum of very useful loads. Like a .308, light 110 grain bullets can be found. On the heavier end, very long 220-grain loads are available for use on the biggest game. Trajectory won't be flat but penetration will be impressive. Unlike the .308, the .30/06 needs a long action receiver. The result will be a somewhat larger rifle with a correspondingly longer bolt stroke. For many, this will be a non-issue. My oldest son hunts with a stainless Remington Model 700. I seriously doubt this minor concern has ever crossed his mind. Having fought in three major wars, the .30/06 is a well-established performer. The huge assortment of bullets will cover nearly all bases. Premium bullets and modern propellants continue to nudge it closer to magnum levels. Anyone with access to a .30/06 is in darned good shape. Just stock up on ammo and call it good.

COMMON LOADS AND ZEROS

Again, there are a pile of similar-performing calibers like the .270 Winchester, etc. They'll do equally well, so if a large stash of ammo is on hand, your crisis is over. However, to avoid several pages of caliber listings, here's a synopsis of what we've just covered:

Common rifle calibers, ballistics and recommended zeros:

Many of these calibers have matured to the point where it's hard to identify a "standard" bullet weight. Additionally, Hornady's line of "Lever Evolution" and "Superformance" cartridges jump velocity by a measureable notch. Again, the .357 Magnum is listed in deference to those considering one dual-purpose handgun and rifle round.

Practical range: You'll sometimes see an "effective range" assigned to a firearm or cartridge. To my mind (much like the data shown above), such a figure can be arbitrary. Many factors come into play, including the shooter's abilities. Bottom line: A "practical range" is likely closer than any listing.

Experienced "tactical rifle" shooters know full well that a .308 is effective way beyond 300 yards. For others, please weigh reality against Chris Kyle expectations. Sure, you could run out and buy an accurate, heavy-barreled .308 bolt-action rifle. For nearly the price of the rifle again, you could add a sophisticated scope. Next, you'll need a rangefinder, anemometer, bipod, scope-level, other doo-dads, plus lots of top-shelf ammo. When the dust settles, hopefully you'll have found a practical load capable of *consistent* sub-MOA accuracy. At that point, having expended several thousand dollars, you'll be ready to learn the fine art of long-range shooting! You will also be the owner of a very heavy rifle, best fired from prone in a wide open space to allow such long distance shots.

Common rifle calibers, ballistics and recommended zeros:						
Caliber	Weights	Standard	Velocity	100 Yds	200Yds	300 Yds
.223 Rem	35-77 grs	55 grains	3250 fps	+ 2.0"	zero	- 9.0"
7.62x39	123-125	123 grains	2300 fps	+ 2.5"	- 2.0"	n/a
.30 Carbine	110 grs	110 grains	2000 fps	zero	-12"	n/a
.357 Mag	110-180	158 grains	1800 fps	zero	n/a	n/a
.30/30	125-170	150 grains	2400 fps	zero	- 8.0"	n/a
.30/30 Rev*	----------	160 grains	2400 fps	+ 3.0"	zero	- 12"
.243 Win	55-105	100 grains	2950 fps	+2.5"	+2.0"	- 6.5
.308 Win	110-190	150 grains	2800 fps	+2.5"	zero	- 8.5"
.30/06	110-220	165 grains	2800 fps	+2.5"	zero	- 9.0"
* .30/30 Hornady 160 Grain Lever Evolution with pointed, flex-tip bullet.						

For a mere (sarcasm) $7,000, hits beyond 800 yards are entirely possible. Most of us could get by with less sophisticated (and lighter) equipment.

Assuming your equipment will provide the necessary elevation corrections at distances out to 800 yards or beyond, what about wind? Don't assume the readings from your hand-held meter will correlate with down-range conditions. Wind drift data is typically listed using a 90-degree, 10 MPH figure. Inconsistencies, angles, and speeds will require adjustments. Speaking of degrees, we can't forget temperature's effect on ignition and velocity. Temperature and elevation also change air-density, which affects a bullet's aerodynamic drag. In other words, there's a whole lot more to this than meets the eye! Technologies can closely connect trajectories to targets but correct wind allowance is both art and science. In other words, experience counts!

Real world shooting: For most of us, the data listed in the chart above is more relevant. There's a reason military snipers prefer engagements on the far side of 400 yards—it's beyond the capabilities of most enemy troops. Adding some adrenaline, an elevated heart rate, and real world field positions will illustrate the limitations. Most prepper-bent folks will need to prioritize their expenditures. Learning how to make reliable hits from relevant field positions is a more practical beginning. Consistent off-hand results on a paper plate at 100 yards will make a darned good starting point. Even some so-called tactical shooters might have trouble there.

OTHER FACTORS

Accuracy is dependent on many factors, including good rifles and consistent ammunition; however, some well-recognized loads and rifles just don't get along. Experienced shooters will try several choices in hopes of achieving optimum accuracy. Only then will they buy in volume, seeking common production lot numbers to ensure consistency. We'll explore this process further in the training chapter.

The tarnished .243 cartridges on the left were hand-loaded during 1984. Resurrected from a G.I. ammo can in 2016, they held their own against factory-fresh cartridges during chronograph and accuracy testing.

Reliability: Function is another key consideration which, like accuracy, shouldn't be based on just a few rounds. In fact, some systems like the M-14 are designed to function within somewhat narrow pressure windows. Gas operation requires properly metered pressures, so use of incompatible ammunition can cause stoppages or increase wear. For all firearms, avoid someone else's handloads. Decent ammo helps and proper storage is essential. Two big enemies are moisture and heat. G.I. ammo cans are a great way to store ammunition. They have handles and can be stacked. Once empty, they'll serve nicely for other purposes, too.

Interchangeable zeros: Each brand will probably shoot to a slightly different spot, requiring a new zero. Premium hunting and defensive loads tend to be fairly expensive due to their more elaborate bullet designs. In the most popular military and law enforcement calibers, less expensive FMJ training loads are available. With luck and planning, you may be able to use the same zero with each. To exploit this principle, it's often wise to search for common weights prior to picking a final load. For example, we shoot lots of 55-grain .223 FMJ for training and qualification. A couple of our expanding service loads share the same velocity and weight. The choices we made can be used interchangeably with one zero. The Q-loads aren't match grade, but they still shoot less than 2 MOA while providing significant savings. For a run-and-gun combat course they work just fine.

The A-2 type G.I. flash hider is a common commodity. It helps, but there are better muzzle devices.

Flash: Another consideration is muzzle flash, a very big deal in low light. I mentioned shooting coyotes with night vision scopes. Two key pieces of this technology are the right load and an effective flash-reducing muzzle device. We've gone to great lengths to track down winning combinations. Night vision devices (NVDs) are often gated, meaning they'll shut off when exposed to bright light. Hit assessments and follow-up shots are then impossible, so terminal effects are not the sole criteria. We've found several winning combinations that will be discussed in the AR section.

These .30/06 cartridges are loaded into 8-shot M-1 Garand clips. The year of manufacture is indicated on military head stamps. A '42 will indicate WWII vintage, which may be corrosive.

Military loads: Since many of the calibers covered here began as military cartridges, it's possible to run into surplus rounds. Some are imports while others are of U.S. origin. A domestic 7.62x51NATO (.308 Win) or .30/06 will be loaded to pressures compatible with M-14 or M-1 Rifles. Some civilian loads don't take this into account and could actually damage operating rods over time. A further concern is the possibility of encountering corrosive priming. This *could* happen with very old .30/06 ammunition, but it is more likely with the various imports. Armor piercing (AP) and tracer rounds can also be encountered. The APs have a black tip and are designed to drill through steel. They'll also ricochet due to a very hard core. U.S. tracers have red tips and will be revealed as a brilliant red projectile. They're tempting to shoot, but fire danger is a major concern. They also can't be good for a premium barrel. When all is said and done, a good domestic commercial load seems like a better bet. We shoot a bunch of .223 and .308 Federal American Eagle.

RESEARCH

To evaluate accuracy and reliability, live fire testing will be necessary. You might also want to fire a few defense loads in darkness. Many military and LE service loads are formulated with propellants suitable for equivalent systems. They also may use flash-retardant powders, which are less of a concern with sporting ammunition. Shooting a .44 Magnum revolver in the dark will perfectly illustrate the problem. It's probably going to be a very dazzling one-shot deal. Even though the 5.56 / .223 is a military/LE choice, a barrel with a bare muzzle may cause similar issues.

I once shot a bobcat in low light with a 20-inch Remington M-7 chambered in .223. The range was around 110 yards, but I had a good rest and the shot felt great. Upon squeezing the trigger, a blinding flash obscured the energetic reaction of the cat, which was no longer in sight when my vision returned. I found him the next day in brush about 40 yards away, hit squarely through the shoulders. A duplicate event occurred a year later with another bobcat. The same load fired from an 18-inch AR-15 with a Smith Enterprises flash hider produced no visible flash. The difference is amazing, and could justify the choice of a threaded muzzle.

Other firearms are now sold with this option, permitting the use of muzzle devices. One reason for their appearance is a surge in suppressor interest. Two common thread patterns are 1/2x28 and 5/8x24. The smaller-diameter matches 5.56mm AR /M-16 barrels. The larger-diameter is common with many 7.62mm AR-10s. Most threaded sporting-type rifles are sold with a protective collar. It can be swapped out for a flash hider or QD suppressor coupling. In some cases, both features are built into the same device. A muzzle brake is a similar device that redirects propellant gas to counter recoil. Since some of these attachments can kick up dirt and debris from prone, they may not always be advised. A brake will also be really loud!

Think about your own likely scenarios before jumping in with both feet. Firearms and equipment play key roles, but so does ammunition. Their effective use is contingent on some planning, which may determine your optimal system choice.

CHAPTER 10

SIGHTING SYSTEM BASICS

For a general tutorial, the *Rimfire Rifles* edition makes a good reference. As far as actual centerfire sighting systems, open and aperture (or peep) sights *may* work, but an optical system will be more versatile. Why? Because many centerfire calibers permit accurate shooting out to a quarter mile or more. Nevertheless, with only one rifle I'd feel more at ease if it had a backup set of iron sights (BUIS) for emergency use.

IRON SIGHTS

A good example of an iron-sighted rifle is a Winchester Model 1894 lever-action. Its front sight bead is aligned with the notch in an adjustable rear blade. Such arrangements are also referred to as "open sights." Windage (left or right) corrections are made by tapping the rear sight assembly, which moves within the barrel's dovetail cut. Vertical corrections are accomplished through a sliding, stepped elevator. The rule of thumb is to move the rear sight in the same direction you want the bullets to go. It's a simple trial and error process, but it's not uncommon for different shooters to require personalized zeros. An aperture system tends to be more precise, explaining its use on target rifles.

Open sights: They have served for centuries and still work, although there are limiting factors. The shooter will need to consciously locate a fine front sight blade (or bead) in a small rear notch and then align this "sight picture" with the target. Since the eye can't simultaneously focus on all three things, the front sight is the right choice. Although it needs to be clearly seen, vision and light are issues. As we age, a clear front sight becomes a difficult prospect, even in broad daylight. For all shooters, the dawn and dusk lighting most common when game moves can make aiming tough. The latest fiber optic front sight beads help greatly, and even radioactive Tritium self-glowing sights are available.

Typical open rear sight with a stepped elevation adjustment.

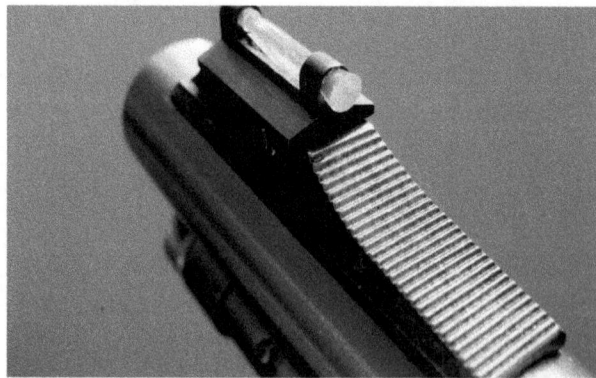

This Hi-Viz fiber optic front sight is a real eye-grabber, especially in low light.

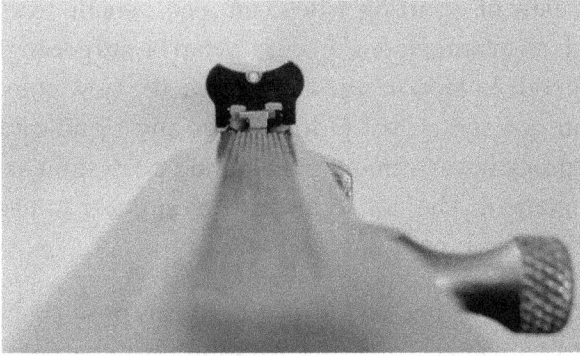

The proper alignment of the front and rear sights results in a "sight picture." Focus on the front sight!

Regardless of their designs, iron sights lack the precision for small or long-range targets. That's why they've been largely supplanted by telescopic sights, most commonly referred to as scopes. Still, I like the idea of a backup set of iron sights. More than one scope has been damaged afield and, with the right mounts, you can quickly remove it to remain operational.

Aperture (peep) sights: With this design, the open rear blade is replaced by a more rearward-mounted small metal loop (or aperture). As it turns out, our eye will naturally center an object in a hole, so viewing the front sight through a rear "peep sight" can produce surprisingly accurate results. There's no obsessing over the exact placement of the front sight in an open rear notch. It's both intuitive and fast with the right combination.

Military forces were quick to recognize the advantages of such a system during the advent of long-range smokeless cartridges. This reasonably durable but compact sighting system improved accuracy, and many designs permitted precise user adjustments. Like many other Cold War soldiers, I used an M-14 with good effect against 600-meter targets. During the same period, the M-16 appeared with its familiar built-in carry handle. The upper rear portion also contained an aperture sight, which soldiered through tough conditions. Nowadays, the A-1 carry handle system has morphed into a flat topped M-4, equipped with optical sights; however, a good rugged peep sight does have virtues. If you stumble onto an M-1 Carbine or M-14 Rifle (or other military-type rifles), an aperture sight will be standard.

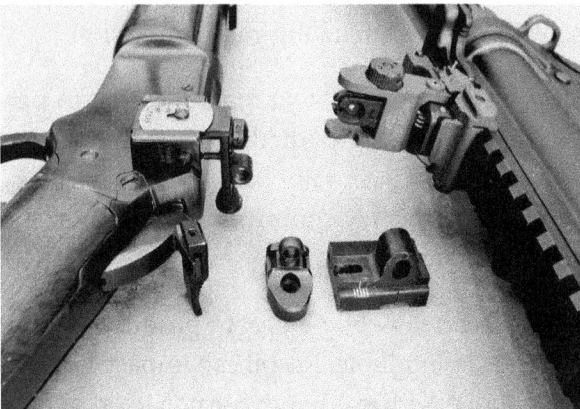

A small collection of aperture (or peep) sights in civilian and military form. The adjustments on the Lyman (L) are fairly precise.

Peep sight alignment is intuitive. In this case, the Lyman's finer aperture disk has been removed. The resulting "ghost ring" image is deadly in the woods. It's also weatherproof!

A WWII .30/06 M-1 Garand, shown in action against 400-yard silhouettes. The aperture sighting system is fully up to the job. Note the expended 8-shot clips.

Civilian or sporting rifles can also benefit from such an arrangement. Accuracy can be surprisingly good. In fact, in our experience, the now common dot sights really don't offer any significant accuracy improvement over a good peep sight arrangement. The dot sights are just quicker to use and better in poor light.

Like open sights, vision and light can pose problems with aperture sights. Although better accuracy is possible, the precision necessary for engagement of small targets at further ranges remains challenging.

SCOPES

More correctly, we should refer to such a system as a telescopic sight. That's a mouthful, so "scope" serves to describe a tube with magnifying lenses and some means to aim it. Initially, most were of fixed magnifications like 4-power (4X) using fine wire crosshairs. External mounting adjustments moved the tube until the crosshairs and target coincided. The concept dates back to the 1800s and was slow to catch on, so for decades rifles were stocked for lower head placement with iron sights. By the 1960s, things had changed with rapid advancements in scope designs. Variable magnification became common with 3-9 X being the most popular choice. Plain crosshairs gave way to a whole series of aiming reticles, which could be internally moved by precise turret adjustments. Rifle makers followed suit with higher stocks and receivers came pre-drilled for scope mounts. The age of the optical sight is now fully upon us, both in civilian and military worlds. Some are highly precise instruments with illuminated range-finding reticles, high magnifications, and large dimensions needed to accommodate such features. When paired with the right rifle, these optical marvels can produce reliable hits in excess of 1,000 yards. Other technologies like rangefinders, wind meters, and ballistic apps play key roles. Comprehensive training is an essential piece of such long-range precision.

Although less sexy, many of us will be well-served with a basic scope of lower magnification. A personal pet peeve involves decent rifles outfitted with lesser-quality, big-bodied, high-magnification scopes. For starters, some of the internal lenses in cheap scopes may actually be plastic. Regardless, anti-reflective coatings may not be present and their cheesy innards may compromise repeatable adjustments. As we'll soon see, there is more to a good scope than its external appearance.

Fortunately, scope manufacturing has come a long way. You can now buy a decent product without breaking the bank. That said, "decent" doesn't necessarily mean infallible. Recoil can impart cumulative effects leading to problems. The average hunter might not ever fire enough rounds to cross a reliability threshold which nevertheless exists. Heavier recoiling rifles like a .300 Winchester Magnum can quickly unravel a marginal scope, but a bit more shooting with lesser calibers can produce similar effects. Even a light .308 Win-class rifle can exert plenty of inertial force on a mid-to-large size scope.

Additional shock and vibration can be transmitted to an optic by energetic semi-automatic actions. Sometimes problems creep in through wandering zeros or group shifts. Other, more obvious clues may involve tilted or absent reticles, rattling lenses, loss of turret adjustments, and fogging. I've experienced them all, along with a few that were more dramatic. The first instinct is to blame zero shifts on the rifle. Since discovery of the actual culprit can involve a fairly large expenditure of ammunition, associated costs are better directed toward a scope. Your sanity is worth something, too. Nothing will get your blood boiling like a 6 MOA group shift after a ½ MOA adjustment.

So what constitutes a "good" scope? Shooters obsess over optical clarity free from edge-to-edge distortion and maximum light transmission. Such features are great, but what about the mechanical aspects? Reliable adjustments, weather-proof seals, and rugged construction are equally important features—if not more so. Nail them all and you'll have that good scope. It won't have a rock-bottom price, either. The top-shelf tactical products are built to survive battlefield conditions with reinforced lens supports and extra-thick bodies. Additional technical features can drive their costs toward $2,000 or beyond. Can we really expect similar performance from an outwardly similar $200 product? Nope.

Fortunately, there are ways to keep a lid on costs. To ensure reliability, it's worth forgoing ginger bread items for rugged construction. A more basic design suited for general field use will still cover plenty of bases. Believe it or not, a small but sturdy fixed-power 4X scope will do the job. The extra cams, internal tubes, and slots required for a variable-power type can be omitted. Attendant costs and potential problems will thus be minimized. Granted, a variable scope is nice, but one thing you can probably skip is an adjustable parallax feature (which will be discussed shortly). I'll take it on a dedicated tactical or varmint rifle, where precise long-range shots are common. For other general shooting chores within 300 yards though, you can live without it. A few things you will want are a decent field of view, a fairly generous eye relief, and good low-light performance.

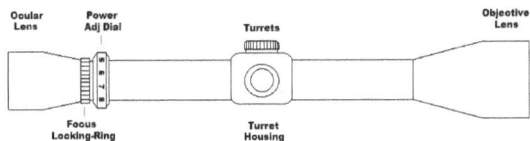

Generic scope nomenclature.

Low-light performance: A cut-away view of a scope's interior will show a series of lenses. The surface of each will cause some light reflection, as will the tube's interior. Fortunately, designers have discovered effective coatings and other tricks, which greatly improve light transmission. But, good lenses with quality coatings still cost money. No matter how big a scope's front end is, it won't transmit more light without decent glass.

Another key factor is the exit pupil. The light that strikes your eyeball is really just a narrow beam. That shaft of light, if properly focused, will flood your pupil with a useable image. The relationship between the diameter of the light beam (exit pupil) and your eyeball's pupil is important. The diameter of a human pupil runs around 5mm in normal light. In low light it dilates to around 7mm. If the scope's exit pupil (the beam of light) exceeds the diameter of the user's pupil, the excess light is wasted. Fortunately, an easy formula can be used to help calculate this process.

We only need two measurements to calculate exit pupil: the diameter of the objective lens and the scope's magnification. The objective lens is the up-front surface, excluding its mounting hardware.

A 4x scope with a 32mm objective will produce an 8mm exit pupil, about the maximum the eye can use. We determine this number by simply dividing the objective diameter (32mm) by the magnification (4X). You can easily see the 8mm shaft of light by pointing the scope's front end at a bright light source. Hold a dark flat surface (like a piece of cardboard) perpendicular with the other end (the ocular lens). At its rated eye relief distance, a small bright spot of light should appear, and that's what enters your eye.

All bets are off without decent lenses, but there are other fish to fry. I once shot a good eight-point buck during terrible weather within the last few minutes of legal light. During a final mad dash, he almost ran me over, piling up 30 yards to my rear. Although I could barely make him out, I soon realized he needed a finishing shot. The trouble was I couldn't make out my duplex crosshairs in the gloomy conditions. I finally aimed at a patch of dim sky, found the crosshairs, and maintained solid stock contact while centering the vague shape in the scope. It worked perfectly, but illustrated the importance of a good low-light reticle.

Objective (front-end) bells: A variable-power scope may have a larger objective lens to provide a brighter image on higher magnification. Although many 3x9 models employ a 40mm objective, some now use big, 50mm lenses. Doing the math, we can see that the 40mm will flood the eye with light on its lowest setting. At 9X, the beam will shrink to only 4.5mm; however, if we crank its power down to 5X, the resulting 8mm exit pupil will be more than adequate. By increasing the front bell to 50mm, our exit pupil will increase to 5.5mm on 9X, which is a marked improvement. We could theoretically achieve full light transfer at around 7-power, but other factors cannot be ignored. These include the previously mentioned optical qualities.

Really big objective bells can also cause mounting headaches. The scope will likely need higher rings for proper barrel clearance. It may also require offset rings to gain the necessary eye relief. I've had several instances where a satisfactory arrangement wasn't even possible. When all is said and done, you want a good, positive cheek weld. I'll gladly trade some magnification for that, every time. I still don't mind a *good* 3-9x32 scope for lower mounting, but nowadays they're much harder to find (a trimmer 2x7 often helps as long as we don't forget bolt handle clearance).

The very best low-light performers are built by firms like Schmidt & Bender, Night Force, etc. No corners are cut but, with prices starting at around $2,000, you'd better have deep pockets. For us working stiffs, a compromise of less magnification, moderate size, and good, if not stellar optics may be necessary.

Field of view (FOV): Tying in with less magnification, the size of the area you see through your scope is a very big deal. Bottom line: Greater power translates to a smaller visible area, known as the field of view. I don't know how many times I've heard someone condemn a scope just because they couldn't locate their quarry in time to make a shot. Check further and you'll probably discover it was a 3x9 set on maximum power. In America, more is better, right?

Well, in my corner of the country, the deer hunting is lousy. Plenty of people go an entire 4-week season without seeing one at all so, if a chance arises, everything needs to be just right. I've had a couple of very close calls involving spitting-distance deer and scopes set on higher powers. In both cases, "higher" was only 7X, which at 20 yards became a problem. It's pretty disconcerting to get on target only to see an all-brown image. These days, my big game scopes stay on around 2X. I can crank them up if time permits but, if not, I'll still prevail. Bear in mind, our hunting usually takes place in wooded country. Even in open terrain, a 4 or 6X scope provides adequate magnification for many circumstances.

If it's hard to locate a stationary target, try centering a moving one within a small field of view. Things get harder as the magnification increases. My often-used Leupold 2X7s have a fairly generous 45-foot FOV at 2X. On maximum power though, that number shrinks to only 18 feet. These are 100-yard measurements, meaning things get worse at closer distances.

The latest rage involves hog hunting with purpose-built optics. Many shots occur in low light on moving targets. A popular choice is a low-magnification 1X4 scope with a very generous field of view. On its lowest setting, Leupold's Hog scope boasts 75 feet at 100 yards. Many patrol-type AR-15 scopes are similarly configured for the same reason. A good, sturdy 1x4, 1.75x5, or 2x7 scope is not a bad choice. Nor is a solid 4-power unit, which will often have adequate tube space for mounting purposes.

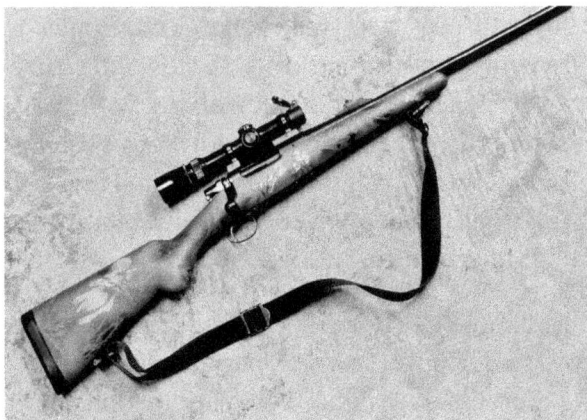

A business-like package is this .350 Remington Custom Shop Model Seven with a Leupold 1.75-5x20 VX-3 Scope in Leupold QRS Rings. It weighs almost nothing thanks to the Kevlar stock—and is darned handy in tough terrain.

Ocular (rear) bell: A clear image and sharply focused reticle are essential, so a provision for personalized focus is necessary. Two methods are commonly employed, the first and oldest relying on a threaded ocular housing which can be spun on fine threads until the sharpest image is acquired. A knurled locking ring can then be cinched up against the housing to lock it in place. The finer threads are more tedious to adjust but the process is normally a one-time deal. Read the directions first since some brands have cautions about excessive rotations. Most scopes are purged and filled with inert, non-fogging gasses like nitrogen. Their integrity requires unbroken seals. Some, *but not all* manufacturers add a built-in stop. Once locked into place, a friction-fit protective lens cap can be pressed onto the ocular housing where it'll remain correctly oriented.

Lately, fast-focus eyepieces have become popular. Individual adjustments can be quickly made by twisting a coarser-threaded ring on the rear of the scope. Although more convenient, they can be inadvertently moved. Still, for shared users, a fast-focus design makes the most sense. A lens caps is worthwhile and a tight-fitting one will also help hold a fast-focus ring in place. A piece of electrical tape also works.

One of my favorite scopes has a heavy German reticle. It's perfect for fast action in dark spruce, but the magnification adjustments are integral with the ocular bell (which also has a fast-focus eyepiece). The rotation necessary to go from the lowest to highest settings is about 120 degrees, which interferes with a hinged scope cap. Since I normally park this scope on 2X, it isn't a huge problem, but this is something else to think about before buying.

Power ring: Most variable scopes have an annular ring just ahead of the ocular housing. This ring is rotated to change magnification. Sounds simple enough, right? Well, we can sometimes get tossed a curveball or two.

The power ring will normally be inscribed with a series of numbers indicating the magnification settings. Most are visible in bright light, but small numbers can be tough to see in twilight or bad weather. The last thing I want is a scope inadvertently cranked to its highest setting. An occasional check can be reassuring and, if the need for more power does arise, a fast and effortless shift is helpful. I love the tactile detents on my 1.75-5 Leupold VX-3. Although it also stays on 2X, I can quickly change its setting in any light, without contortions. Such a feature is also handy in prone. Some power rings have a small raised spot or other index point that can be used as a tactile reference. At 12:00, it should equal a specific magnification from which adjustments can be made. You'll need to learn which direction increases magnification.

Some scopes may also include power ring symbols. Leupold uses two small reference triangles to match the relationship of their ballistic reticle models with certain trajectories. Each mark corresponds with a group of cartridges within a listed velocity class. Their VX-3 models also have yardage scales for range estimation. The space between the crosshair junction and tip of the lower duplex post equals a constant 16 inches, which is the approximate back-to-brisket depth many whitetail bucks. If the power ring is rotated until a deer's body fills this gap, the approximate yardage will be indicated. Such features are all well and good assuming time and lighting suffice.

Eye relief: Especially with high powered rifles, we need some clearance between our eye and the scope. Otherwise, at best, recoil-induced "scope eyebrow" will result. At worst, permanent eye injury is possible. The optical engineers are adept at striking a necessary balance between magnification, field-of-view, and eye relief. Most rifle scopes will have somewhere between 3-4 inches of clearance. A few may be a bit more generous, extending to 5 inches.

Handgun scopes have arm-length eye relief since that's the way they're shot. FOV is typically much smaller, but the shooter's greater peripheral view can overcome this problem. The "Scout Scope" is a niche design with intermediate eye relief and low magnification. It was popularized by Col. Cooper of Gunsite Academy fame for use on compact bolt-action rifles. The concept involved mounting a small 2X scope forward of the receiver, resulting in a handy, fast-handling "Scout Rifle." Ruger's recent M-77 "Gunsite Scout" embodies this design, although it does offer barrel or receiver-mounted scope options. Scout scopes are still available and some shooters barrel-mount them ahead of top-ejecting actions like a Winchester M-94 lever gun.

I trend toward conventional scopes with generous eye relief because of my build and shooting style. I'm stumpy and shoot heads-up, so my scopes are further rearward. With 3 ½ inch types, a front bell or turret housing will often contact a mounting ring before I can acquire a full image. Tall, lanky stock-crawling folks will probably have the opposite problem.

A properly mounted scope should present a full image without any contortions. Two things affecting this are clothing and position. It's best to mount your scopes while dressed for anticipated conditions. Allowance should also be made for various shooting positions. I mount most scopes for off-hand shots, but I'll also check some from prone. Usually, your eye will then be closer to the scope, and your head will probably be higher as well. The best time to sort this all out is before final tightening of the scope rings.

Tube length: Big scopes seem right on heavy-barreled long-range rifles, but they can make a typical sporter feel top-heavy. The larger objective bells of high-magnification scopes can also shorten overall tube length resulting in less mounting latitude. The lower-magnification scopes are more forgiving, which is one of the reasons I like a 2x7. A straight-tube 1.75x5 is even better for mounting purposes. Ideally, the rings should provide maximum support through locations nearest the ocular and objective housings. More than once I've been stymied by a totally incompatible scope and rifle combination. You may pay more at your local gun shop, but it's better to discover such a problem before forking over hard-earned cash.

Tube diameter: The trend is toward large, tactical-type scopes with high magnification, target turrets, and fat main tubes. Again, on big rifles they match. On smaller sporters, some can be clumsy. The standard U.S. scope-tube diameter is one inch. Some people seek the bigger-diameter 30mm tubes expecting a brighter image, but the main advantage is increased elevation adjustment related to long-range shooting. A larger-diameter main tube has more room for reticle housing movement, so additional vertical adjustment can be applied. Even larger 34mm types are now showing up since, way out at 1,500 yards, every extra bit of internal elevation helps. Scopes with illuminated reticles also benefit from greater diameter to accommodate their circuitry.

Nowadays, you can buy fairly compact, lower-power 30 mm scopes with lots of neat features. Some are oriented toward the "modern sporting rifle" (MSR), which is a politically correct description of an AR-15. For many of us, a somewhat simpler and more affordable one-inch body should be adequate. Whichever type you choose, make sure your mounting system matches. In fact, some bases are designed to provide extra elevation. A "20 MOA" base has that amount of inclination built in (and roughly equivalent to the internal elevation gained with a 30mm scope); however, a do-all, field-expedient package needn't be adorned with too many bells or whistles. The KISS principle is worth remembering.

Magnification: By now you may appreciate the value of lower-powered scopes. For purposes of this book, a 2½ x 10 should be more than enough glass and a 3x9 should be plenty. A 2x7 will work fine, as will a 1.75x5. Many will still seek the big-bell 50mm designs in quest of better low-light performance. The non-belled objective end of my 1.75x5 VXIII Leupold has a 20mm lens, which might not seem like much; however, on 3X it still provides an exit pupil of nearly 7mm. Its straight tube makes it easy to mount, and its mass isn't excessive. This helps it stay put under recoil, which can be significant on a lightweight rifle. I have a fly-weight custom magnum that moved a not-too-large 3x9 during recoil. For any Marlin lever gun shooters, a fixed-power 4X, or even a 2.5X version makes sense. Their smaller sizes permit easy mounting with low rings. Since some lever-actions have more stock drop, less scope height is helpful.

The highest magnification scopes I use are 4.5x14s, reserved for heavy-barreled varmint rifles. The rifles themselves are already large, so *truly* giant scopes just add unwelcome weight; however, 14-power (or maybe 12X) is around the *minimum* magnification I'd want for a western prairie dog shoot. Back east, I often crank varmint scopes down to 8X, since most shots are inside 200 yards on woodchucks or crows. Bear in mind we're not talking about the latest, greatest long-range tactical craze with heavy rifles in big calibers and high-end, super-sized scopes. They require plenty of technical savvy and practice, along with a large supply of greenbacks. The ensuing package will resemble the varmint combinations that remain in my safe during serious freezer-filling expeditions.

This decked out tactical rifle sports a Vortex Gen II Razor HD 3-18x50mm with a 34mm tube and side-mounted P/A feature. The ballistic turrets are very precise. The whole package is far from featherweight!

Anyone considering a large scope with extra bells and whistles would probably be better served with two rifles, one of which should be more portable. Skeptics should try slinging a 12–14 pound rifle while stumbling through the boonies.

Parallax Adjustment: As mentioned before, a general purpose rifle/scope combination really doesn't need a P/A feature. A scope's focal plane and reticle only coincide at one distance. When parallax is evident, shifting your eye position toward the outer circumference of the scope's image will reveal a bit of reticle movement relative to the target. This inconsistency will be evident on a target. Most manufacturers set their lenses to match at 100-150 yards. At extreme distances (whether close or far), there will be some divergence, but within average field distances on big game, it won't be enough to matter.

Purpose-built airgun and rimfire scopes often have a feature permitting adjustments as close as 10 yards. Most centerfire P/A scopes are graduated for long range and stop at 50 yards. In either case, the user can adjust to a target's range, eliminating reticle divergence. The most common designs have a rotating objective ring, which is aligned with a yardage marking. Another increasingly popular type employs a graduated knob in the turret housing. The latter system is big with tactical shooters who often fire from prone. In theory, P/A scales will match actual yardages, but there's no guarantee. As is the case in general, price is commensurate with precision—and actual testing is prudent.

This adjustable-objective (A/O) airgun scope has close-range parallax graduations.

I want a P/A system on an airgun scope, and prefer one on a rimfire model. As for centerfire rifles, I've noticed that even with this feature, I'll often leave a higher-magnification varmint scope set on 200 yards. This is especially true during high-volume prairie dog action. I will make a parallax adjustment during deliberate, long-range shooting, but thick eastern woods call for something simpler and more compact. Not too coincidentally, this terrain mirrors many average conditions in which a basic scope is suitable. A proper mounting system helps since, if the shooter's eye remains consistently centered behind the scope, the effects of parallax are minimal or non-existent.

Turrets: Extended "target turrets" are part of the tactical craze. Some have protective caps while others are exposed, leading to concerns about accidental adjustments. Most run-of-the-mill sporting scopes are sold with lower-profile dials protected by waterproof caps. In either case, two dials located on a saddle (or turret housing) permit vertical and horizontal reticle adjustments. Each may display a graduated reference scale shown as "MOA" or "1/4-inch at 100 yards." While inch values might seem simpler, they'll only match at one distance. Since a minute-of-angle is an angular value, we can apply it to any range. Clicks are common, permitting consistent movements in fractions of these values. If our rifle was shooting two inches low at 100 yards, coming "up" eight ¼ MOA clicks should put us on the money (remember, one MOA equals approximately an inch); however, a 2-inch low error at 200 yards would require only one MOA of correction, or 4 upward clicks. The same would be needed with a ¼" 100-yard scale, since out at 200 yards each click would equal ½-inch.

Target turrets offer precise, repeatable adjustments – assuming the scope is properly built.

Small arrows on the coin or finger-operated dials will indicate "up" or "right." A few moderate taps on a turret can help settle it down after an adjustment is made. Some dials work on friction instead of clicks, providing infinite settings. Many of either type have a surrounding reference ring. Once zeroed, it can be carefully rotated until a mark lines up with the "0" on the turret. It's worth using since you can find your way home after a future adjustment. Some folks also "shoot a square" to test repeatability. Once a zero is established, a series of groups are shot in a box-type pattern using the windage and elevation dials. With a properly mounted, quality scope possessing an identical series of clicks, the final group should coincide with the previous zero. If so, the adjustments are consistent for practical field use.

For a general purpose rifle, capped field-type turrets are hard to beat. They'll offer few surprises during rough handling. Note the superfluous A/O feature up front.

For basic use in tough conditions, I'll take lower-profile turrets with caps. A straight-forward system can direct costs to lenses and overall quality. Once a zero is established I can still dial in a different setting if need be.

Reticles and trajectory-compensating systems: The advent of rangefinders has spawned major interest in systems permitting spot-on aiming at longer distances. Adjustable target turrets can be calibrated to specific loads and then dialed to match pre-ranged distances. Another popular compensating system involves holdover marks on the lower, vertical crosshair. In principle, they'll mesh with the trajectory of popular loads, providing consistent reference points for holdover aiming. The latest technology employs a built-in lasing rangefinder with an internal, automatic compensation.

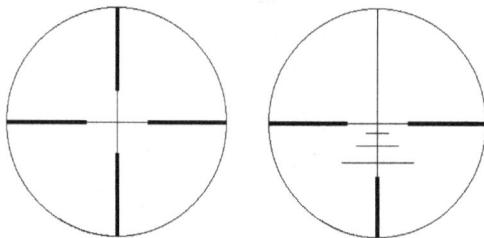

Generic renditions of a duplex reticle (L) and ballistic type.

Ballistic reticles: Of the three designs, for intermediate-range field use, I prefer basic holdover marks. Burris popularized this design with their "Ballistic-Plex" and others have since followed suit. Once properly sighted in, horizontal hash marks coincide with a bullet's path at longer distances. At least, that's the theory. Confirmation will require live fire testing since a number of variables can introduce errors, including elevation, temperature, and ammunition choices. Still, when combined with a hand-held laser rangefinder, calibration is often close enough for practical use. I like this concept because it's simple and fairly intuitive. On larger targets, it'll work for many mid-range field situations.

Target-type turrets: Serious long-range shooters will use "come-ups," dialing their turrets for precise shot placement. After establishing a baseline zero, the scope's turrets can be set to "0" using graduated scales. From there, the requisite elevation clicks can be applied to achieve long-range hits. The turret may be graduated in inches, MOAs, or Mil-Dots. A few newer types use yardages instead, designed to be used with specific loads. Once the fine points are ironed out, a precise and repeatable system will be at hand. The technology costs money and is a bit slower to use. It's also easy to forget a setting and can be harder to use in low light. Still, I prefer come-ups for deliberate shooting at distant or carefully pre-ranged targets. On the other hand, I prefer hold-offs for wind. It plays a huge part in long range success, but its precise judgment is a challenging mix of art and science. A laser rangefinder can provide a close elevation solution that can be mechanically applied. Wind is an ever-changing variable that may need reactive adaptations, so sometimes a combination of target-turret come-ups

AND ballistic aiming features may prove handy. Lots of elevation will be necessary for a shot at extreme range. Although turret designs vary by manufacturers, it's possible that several revolutions may be necessary. Afterward, a return to zero will be necessary. Some scopes have "zero stops" to prevent going too far; others don't. Depending on the design, the fix may be as simple as an O-ring spacer located to limit excess revolutions. Particularly on tactical-type scopes, turrets are uncovered. Others are furnished with jumbo caps to prevent inadvertent adjustments. Some in-between designs use lower-profiled turrets and caps. Adjustments can be effected using fingers, but clearly marked graduations further simplify the process.

Tactical systems: These are often hybrid designs involving ballistic reticles *and* turrets. Using the ballistic reticle, one can place the appropriate elevation mark on the target and squeeze off a shot. Some also have wind hold-off marks for the reason noted above. The sniper-type Mil-Dot reticles employ a series of spaced dots or ovals on all four wires, which mathematically correlate to known-sized targets for long-range engagements. Just about every serious long-range shooter (or sniper) is using a Mil-Dot system. It can be used to range targets or to establish their lead and wind hold-offs. When time permits, elevation will typically be applied via turret adjustments. All such shooters have dusted off their math skills, which are essential when correlating a constant angular measurement with the trajectory of a bullet. At ranges well beyond 500 yards, any seemingly small variable will introduce major errors. Shots at 700–1,000 yards (or more) are possible with the right skills, ammunition, and equipment. The shooters know that just because a scope is advertised with specific elevation values, doesn't necessarily make it so. The proof is in live fire testing, which may reveal different results.

The KISS principle: The civilian sporting systems are simpler for average shooters. We've used Leupold's Varmint Hunter reticles with great success during high-volume prairie dog shoots. They present a fairly "busy" image, but hits out to 500 yards are possible with .223 AR-15s. One thing we do first is make sure the reticles actually jive with our ammunition. As it turns out, the VH system can come darned close to the advertised data when using 24-inch barrels. Another version more appropriate for general field use is Leupold's "Boone & Crocket" system, which is geared toward big game hunting. It has heavier graduations which are more visible in low light. You still get windage points, too. I have a 2.5x8 so equipped, which permits well-centered hits on steel IPSC silhouettes out to 500 yards. Leupold's third sporting-type range-compensating system is their LRD, which stands for "Long Range Duplex." It's similar to the Burris system and you're just "holding high" with reticle reference marks. Nikon uses a series of descending circles that work the same way. One downside I've noticed with these arrangements involves rifle canting (tilting the rifle left or right), which can introduce windage errors. We also see this during long-range stages using dot sights. Without any horizontal reference lines it's easy to cant a rifle. The extra height of AR sights exacerbates this problem. Also, many ballistic aiming systems are "Second Focal Plane" designs, which require maximum magnification for correct calibration.

Illuminated reticles: These have gained popularity as the technology improves. Especially for low-light uses, the idea has merit. Most are battery-powered, which leads to the foibles of electronics. The overall package will also trend larger, with a 30mm tube being likely. Some, like our tactical Leupolds, have a motion sensor that will shut off the electronics after a period of inactivity. They preserve battery life and will reactivate when the rifle is moved. They also switch off between numbered rheostat settings. Many are just "off" or "on" with adjustable intensity. Illumination may display complete crosshairs or just a small central point of light. Trijicon is a well-known supplier of military optical sights that employ Tritium lamp technology. They also sell a nice line of sporting scopes that work the same way. These radioactive systems work without any batteries!

The main illuminated-reticle markets are probably defense, hog, and varmint hunting (with big game thrown in). More than once, I've considered a 50mm illuminated scope for nocturnal coyote operations. My thought was to power up the crosshairs as darkness fell and later switch it off while attaching a rear-mounted night vision device. Any standard illuminated designs will kill a rear-mounted NV unit due to image "blooming;" however, scopes with NV settings are now more common. You'd never know they were "on" with your naked eye, but they emit just enough light to accent an aiming point (check them after use to make sure they're actually switched off). The new front-mounted NV units solve these problems by coupling with the objective lens. Either method works without zero change (for significant additional expense).

You can probably survive without an illuminated system, but if you must indulge yourself, look for a model with visible crosshairs, whether or not the diode works.

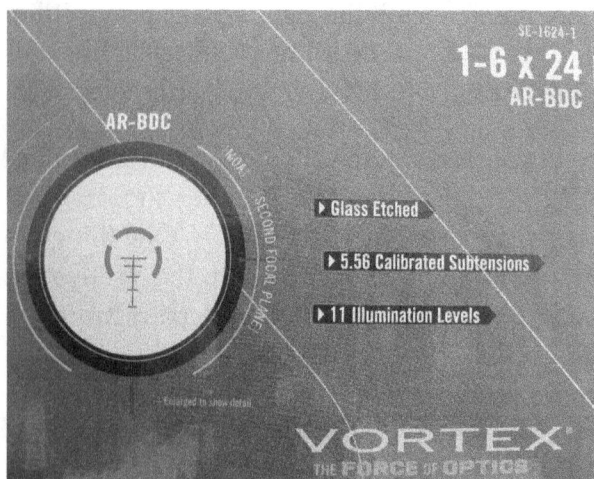

The image on the box is a good representation of this Vortex illuminated reticle. The 1-6 Strike Eagle's reticle still works with a dead battery. It's a second focal plane type.

Other reticle choices: Note the many references to Leupold, which also offers a series of interesting tactical reticles housed within more expensive scopes. Many other excellent brands compete within this market, and some cost thousands of dollars. In fact, this whole field has exploded in the last few years as technology improves. A properly equipped long-range artist can now measure necessary atmospherics like temperature, elevation, and pressure, inputting this data with range and trajectory numbers for an interfaced smart phone app solution! Trouble is, without a thorough understanding of all technical aspects, blindly purchasing equipment would be a monumental waste of money. For many Prepper types, funds could be better spent on basic gear, which constitutes only part of an overall plan.

Focal plane designs: You'll see scopes advertised with first or second focal plane construction. Until recently, most U.S. scopes were of the latter type. Regardless of their magnification, the crosshairs present a consistent thickness. The first European focal plane types caused the crosshair size to increase as the magnification is turned up, which can be disconcerting; however, FFP scopes are now increasingly popular with snipers and designated marksmen who may need to shoot on the fly. Because the crosshairs expand or contract relative to magnification, they offer a constant scale for ballistic reticle systems. Second focal plane values will change with power settings, so their ballistic reticles only coincide at one magnification—typically the highest. Experimental shooting can sometimes reveal other useful settings though. My shorter-barreled M-700 Compact Tactical develops less velocity than its scope is graduated for, but a reduction of 2X changes the reticle and target relationship. At that point things match up again.

What about "regular" crosshairs? Good news: Basic crosshairs still work! They not only support level holds, but also present an uncluttered image. Designs like Leupold's often-copied "Duplex" reticle are common, intuitive, and fast. The tip of the lower thick-thin vertical crosshair juncture will also coincide with a bullet's impact at *some* longer range. The gap between Leupold's crosshairs and lower duplex tip equals eight inches. Many popular rifle calibers print about that amount low at 300 yards when zeroed at 200 yards. Real shooting will reveal the actual distance.

You can also compare the relative scale of reticle points by aiming at a 100-yard target with one-inch grids. The squares will translate to MOA increments, which are useful for longer range calculations. If the space between your crosshair juncture and lower duplex tip equals four squares at 100 yards, it can provide a 16-inch holdover point at 400 yards, the equivalent of 4 MOA.

Taking the process a step further, you can also use the gap for ranging purposes. Charts are available that list the average depth of game animals. In this hypothetical example, if a mature antelope fits within the two points, there's a good chance it's around 400 yards away. Of course, excitement can get us in trouble. Since most standard scopes are 2nd plane types, the values change with magnification shifts. Suddenly, a fixed 4X scope isn't such a bad idea!

A few variations use thinner crosshairs, which don't work well in low light. A fix is a simple system with thicker posts like a "German" or "Heavy Duplex" reticle. The only use I have for fine crosshairs involves varmint hunting' and I'd Just as soon skip them for ballistic crosshairs.

Other details: Hard-kicking cartridges can unravel many optical sights, and the full-power magnum loads are prime offenders. A steady diet of .308 can also take its toll, so a well-built product is advised. A not-overly-large scope can minimize inertial effects, and each extra feature redirects cash that could be better spent on construction.

DOT SIGHTS

During the past two decades, non-magnifying, battery-powered dot sights have become popular. The Swedish Aimpoint firm did much to get the ball rolling and is still a key player. Instead of crosshairs, a highly visible dot is displayed. It's normally illuminated by a battery, although Trijicon uses a radioactive element instead (or in some cases, both). Unlike a laser sight, these units don't project a beam. Instead, the "dot" is a reflected image, emitted by a diode located within the sight. Intensity can often be regulated, using a dial or toggle-switch.

The rheostat switch on this small Konus unit also provides two color choices.

A collection of dot sights. The small Burris is representative of the latest tubeless genre.

A bright, central dot is an intuitive design that works well in dynamic events. Just place the dot on the target and squeeze the trigger! Dot size is usually described in a minute-of-angle values, with many running 2–4 MOA. At 100 yards, a 4 MOA dot will subtend about four inches. At 300 yards, the same dot will cover one foot, so precise aiming can be challenging on smaller targets. Lately, dot size seems to be shrinking with 1 or 2 MOA versions becoming common. While I like a smaller dot, it's not *always* the best choice. We had good luck with AR-15 mounted Trijicon Reflex 6.5 MOA sights during close-quarter shooting. Although large, we found the reticle effective on combat silhouette targets out to 300 yards. Furthermore, they don't use batteries, relying instead on a combination of fiber optic and Tritium-powered illumination. Since few things are truly perfect, their downside is a washout effect during some light conditions. This was most prevalent when aiming from with-

Tactical-grade dot sights like this 2 MOA Aimpoint can be bought for a lot more money. Note the mounting height, which is right on an AR-15, but too high for most other rifles.

in a darker area toward a bright target. We also dealt with reticle flare when shooting into sunlight. We've since switched to battery-powered "Aimpoint Pro Patrol" units with 2 MOA dots. We change their batteries annually, but thanks to their rated 30,000-hour life, they'll run for three years!

We'll cover the dot sights more thoroughly in the AR-15 chapter. At the moment, for general purpose use, I'd recommend just staying with a scope. Not that the dots don't have merit—they do. I remain a fan and use a fair assortment of different brands. But for those looking at a smaller firearms collection, a scope will greatly stretch your range. The dot sights generally lack the precision afforded by a magnified image and well-defined crosshairs. Also, most rely on batteries, some of which are less common. Those without crosshairs may also cause canting, which can create windage errors at further range.

CLOSING THOUGHT

By now, one thing should be fairly obvious — the KISS principle. You could do a whole lot worse than a solid Leupold 2.5x8 Vari-X-3 with a Boone& Crocket reticle. Simple, not overly-large scopes are easier to mount and more likely to stay put during recoil. They'll also save weight, and most importantly, they will cover just about all practical contingencies.

CHAPTER 11

CHOOSING YOUR RIFLE

As part of a greater collection of firearms, a reliable, general purpose centerfire rifle should do the job. We'll want one with adequate range and power, but without excessive recoil. Although weight can lessen that effect, portability is also important. A popular model will more readily accommodate optics and accessories, which expands versatility. A good rifle choice will likely be a compromise that runs off common ammunition and parts. Simple operation and familiar function shouldn't be ignored. These considerations will contribute to the true bottom line: increased odds of effective hits.

BOLT-ACTIONS

Despite the proliferation of semiautomatic designs, the bolt-action rifle is in no immediate danger of obsolescence. In fact, besides the numerous factory offerings, a new wave of semi-custom actions and rifles has appeared. Not too coincidentally, many are advertised with a "Model 700 footprint," meaning they accommodate Remington-designed scope bases and stocks. There are plenty of other great choices but this trend is a good indicator of a solid foundation.

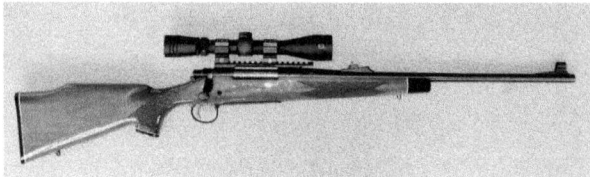

Remington's timeless BDL. This one is wearing a newer Redfield scope on a one-piece Picatinny-type base.

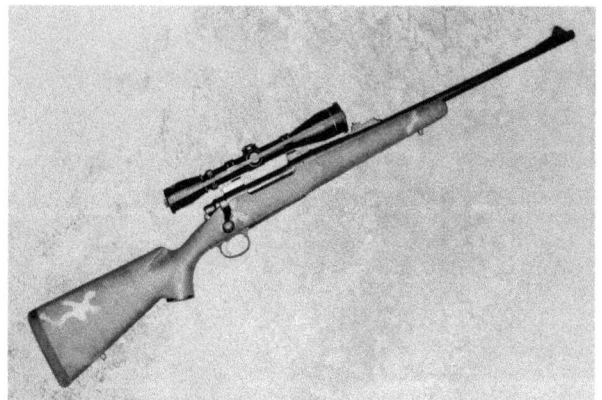

This discontinued, mid-80s BDL factory variant is a synthetic stock, matte-finished, long action .30/06 with a Leupold scope in Talley rings. It has seen plenty of use in terrible weather, but keeps on chugging.

Top Pick—Remington's Model 700 in .308 Win: With several million in circulation, availability of parts is assured. The same can be said for accessories. If extras are desired later on, the odds are good of finding them. That's because of all the bolt-actions out there, the Model 700 has the biggest list of add-ons. In fact, it's now possible to turn a plain-Jane Remington into a futuristic AR-looking platform. I wouldn't go too hog-wild, though. It's just not necessary for most of us. If you shop carefully for off-the-shelf features you should be good-to-go. In fact, even some non-cataloged Remingtons are available through larger retailers.

The Remington M-700 Compact Tactical is a short action factory offering, available in .223 and .308. The 20-inch barreled action is stainless steel with a non-reflective coating, and the fluting saves weight.

This buck was taken at 150 yards with a .260 Remington M-700 Mountain Rifle and one well-placed 140-grain Core-Lokt. He piled up on the spot, in the middle of a swamp.

An older .243 Remington Model Seven with a 3-hole receiver and one-piece Leupold base. The 2-7 scope and rings are also from Leupold.

With two dozen cataloged versions, the hardest part is figuring out which one to buy. Some are heavy-barreled varmint or long-range renditions, while others have pretty wood stocks. Somewhere in between lays an all-around, weather resistant choice that won't break the bank. The stainless version of the SPS is an example. It's a 24" all-stainless rifle with a synthetic stock and QD sling studs. I owned a detachable magazine version, which I shortened to 21-inches. You can expect good handling qualities, simple operation and excellent accuracy for a reasonable price. For another $300, Remington offers an M-700 Mountain SS with a 22-inch barrel. It has a much nicer synthetic stock and weighs only 6 ½ pounds, thus shaving 16 ounces off the SPS. Both versions are available as short action .308s.

Another neat idea is a Remington Model Seven. This rifle is similar to a short-action M-700, but uses an even shorter rear receiver bridge. The earlier M-7s had a three-hole scope mounting pattern, with only one in the rear bridge. The latest variant employs four holes. They're all handy, and beyond this compact rifle line, an interesting version is sold through Advanced Armaments Corp. It has a very short 16" barrel threaded for a sound suppressor. When so equipped, using the .300 Blackout and ultra-heavy bullets, velocity remains subsonic, which greatly quiets the report. More pedestrian Model Sevens are cataloged by Remington in several calibers and variants. Among them are blued, carbon steel, synthetic, and laminated stock models. During 2016, stainless 20" versions reappeared. We shoot several Model Sevens in various calibers and configurations. I owned an earlier stainless/synthetic .308, which was handy in the woods, but somewhat difficult to shoot offhand. My identical .243 seems to handle better, probably due to greater barrel mass. The same is true of my son's stainless.260 Remington. Its factory synthetic stock has been replaced by a Bell &

Carlson. The latest run is also available again in .223 Remington, another practical choice.

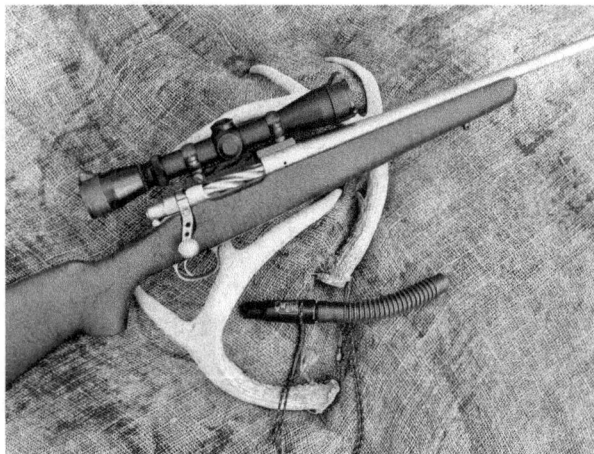

The same M-7 .243 after a few custom touches, including a Bell & Carlson Medalist stock. The skeletonized and fluted bolt work was done by Red Hawk Rifles.

This fully customized John Gallagher .300 SAUM Model Seven has a lightweight Bansner stock and lightened action. The action is a newer 4-hole type with Talley one-piece rings.

Another full-blown Gallagher custom M-7. This one is a .223 with a Kreiger barrel and Bansner winter-camo stock. Yes, it really shoots, but the plainer factory configuration will work just fine.

Among the tactical crowd, shorter barrels are becoming popular. Many are bull-barrel types, which may be fluted to save weight and promote cooling. A Model 700 with a 20-inch barrel isn't a great Magnum choice, but that length will make a handy .308 companion.

Most no longer come with iron sights, one exception being the timeless M-700 BDL; however, you can have them installed by a competent gunsmith. In fact, some innovative backup peep sights are also available. I have a very compact XS backup unit which clamps directly to a Weaver-type scope base. It'll attach with a coin and seems to hold its zero, but of course, you'd need to have it with you. A great alternative is the XS peep with an integral Weaver-type base. The aperture dovetails into a small cut and it's located far enough rearward to clear many clamp-on scope rings. A scope in a QD ring set would permit convenient use of either system. As for more common arrangements, everyone makes scope mounts. Other options include after-market detachable magazine and trigger guard assemblies, stocks, custom bolt knobs, and triggers.

Honorable Mention—Ruger's Model 77 Gunsite Scout Model: Believe me, this one was a tough call. I almost listed it as the top pick. The proprietary detachable magazine is one reason I didn't, but this could be overcome with a stash of spares. You can buy the Ruger as a right-hand or left-handed rifle, in blued or stainless steel. I'd get the stainless version just for increased weather resistance. The barrel is only 18-inches, designed for portability. It's chambered for the .308 Winchester and has a flash hider attached to the muzzle. The short barrel will give up some velocity (maybe 100 fps), and would produce a dazzling flash without it. The laminated stock looks sharp and has a series of stock spacers. Length of pull can be adjusted through a generous 2-inch range. The odds of achieving a proper fit are very good. QD sling swivel studs are included.

A great utility rifle: Ruger's Model 77 Gunsite Scout.

The Scout model comes with a forward, barrel-mounted scope base, plus the normal receiver mounting points. You get a set of rugged Ruger rings that will clamp to either spot. A very useful set of iron sights also come standard on this rifle. The rear is a Ruger peep that clamps to the receiver's scope base. To fully exploit the design, you'd want a purpose-built, forward-mounted "Scout Scope" with longer eye relief. The concept is similar to a pistol scope with low magnification but intermediate eye-clearance. In principle, it's used with both eyes open, sighting both through and around the scope for rapid target pick-up. By mounting the scope to the barrel base, the peep could remain attached (although the peep might interfere with the scope's field of view). The scope rings detach without trouble, and are also fairly repeatable. My personal inclination would be to add a conventional, low-powered scope like a 1.75x5 and keep the peep sight handy in a kit.

Ease of maintenance is part of our criteria and an M-77 rifle qualifies nicely. The bolt can be disassembled without undue effort and the trigger mechanism is easy to deal with. Many rifles use "cassette" type triggers with enclosed parts. The Ruger trigger is simple and can easily be accessed for removal of debris.

Ruger's Model 77 rimfire makes a perfect addition to the centerfire.

A Gunsite Scout is one hell of a useful rifle which could also compliment a rimfire 77/22. You could certainly improve upon your shooting skills by using the .22 model. Whether chasing small game or bigger quarry, all bases would be well-covered.

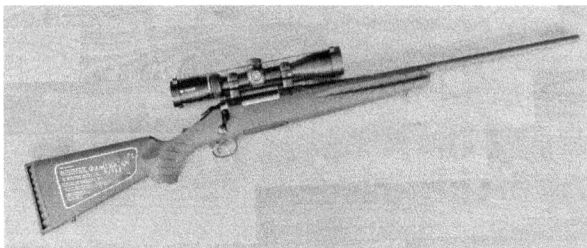

The Ruger American offers great value. This one was pulled off a dealer's shelf as a factory package gun with a Vortex Crossfire 3x9 scope. Note the Weaver base mounting system.

Another new Ruger, the "American": If the Gunsite model was a tough call, the latest Ruger is even harder. By itself, the centerfire "American" is but one of several new affordable offerings presented by the major manufacturers. But, besides a $450 retail price, it now has a new rimfire companion, ideal for small game and practice. As such, each really elevates the other to a new level of practicality. You could buy both "American" rifles for the cost of one traditionally-made Model 77. An "American" .308 in either full-size or carbine-length would nicely match a .22 LR and/or .22 WMR understudy piece. The adjustable trigger is nice and

Weaver-type bases present many scope mounting options. The synthetic, detachable 4-shot magazines are reasonably priced. Unlike the .22, you don't get iron sights. You do gain a tang-mounted safety, similar to the earliest Ruger M-77 centerfires. The latest design doesn't lock the bolt shut on "safe," so some attention will be required during carry to ensure it remains fully closed. The three-lug design offers shorter lift and a smooth action, plus a cocking indicator. The shroud can also be removed without tools for ready servicing. Thinking about commonality of function and the safety location, anyone considering a Mossberg shotgun may want to keep this in mind. The liability for either rifle will be limited availability of parts (although the rimfires use common 10/22 magazines).

AUTOLOADERS

The same rationale you'll see with the pump gun choice can be applied to a self-loading rifle. Essentially, it boils down to a finalist that shares common function with a shotgun and rimfire.

Top Pick—Remington autos: By tracking down a Remington Model 750 or M-7400 you'll have it. The trade-off will be ease of total disassembly, a shorter round-count life, and lack of a Ninja-like appearance. It'll also be somewhat heavy, but a shorter-barreled carbine version can help shed some weight. Many of these rifles are sold in .30/06, which was part of the original design. I'd go for a .308 and stock up on a few spare magazines. A synthetic stock model with a matte-steel finish will provide some extra weather protection. It's possible to trick one up through Accuracy Systems, which offers some unique modifications. The similar shotgun and rimfire models are Remington's 1100/1187 seriesand their .22 LR M-552 Speedmaster. The centerfires M-7400s are often seen as used rifles for $500 or less. While 10-round magazines can be found, reviews are mixed. I'd start with just one before stocking up. Meanwhile, a couple of 4-shot Remingtons will get you going.

Honorable Mention—Ruger Mini-14s: These rifles may work for some survival oriented shooters. A 7.62x39 would probably be the best compromise

Remington's .308 M-7400 in factory-issue form, with a Weaver base and spare magazine.

The same M-7400, set up for tough conditions with a Burris FastFire dot sight and XS backup ghost ring.

of power and ammunition availability. Higher-capacity magazines and accessories are available, and the Ranch models can be easily scoped. Unlike a .308 or '06, 300-yard range will be doubtful. The full-strength cartridges are also more forgiving when it comes to larger game. I'd be a lot fussier about a 7.62x39 hunting bullet choice. With the bigger .30s, a basic and affordable Remington Core-Lokt would do the job. They can be found about anywhere.

Browning and FNH sell several BAR versions. They're known as accurate rifles and handle well.

Also worth noting—Browning BARs/ FNH: Try to get your hands on one before committing to the others. That includes disassembly.

PUMPS

It's not the pinnacle of rifle evolution, but a pump-action rifle will nicely compliment a Model 870 Shotgun. Add a .22 Remington M-572 Fieldmaster and you'll have a not-too-glamorous but very useful three-gun set. These guns are also legal just about everywhere. Their manual operation is more tolerant of ammo variations and weather extremes. For shared use, a pump will be easier to operate by any lefties, too. A slide-action rifle is not a bad do-all choice!

Top Pick—Remington Model 7600 pump series: Unlike a Model 870 Shotgun, the Model 7600 barrel is, for all practical purposes, permanently attached. You'll either need to clean it through the muzzle or use a pull-through system. Without a gas system the process is fairly simple. The bolt won't come out for field stripping, but the trigger assembly will. Like the 870, just drift out two pins. This is handy after a trip in the rain, and it also exposes the bolt for cleaning.

Remington's tried and true Model 7600 in basic wood-stocked form.

While a pump may not be quite as fast as a semi-auto, it's still pretty darned quick. Capacity is 4 +1, and the detachable magazines permit use of modern, pointed bullets in full-size cartridges. The rotary bolt is plenty strong and fairly foolproof. A receiver-mounted Weaver or Picatinny scope rail will permit use of QD scope rings so that iron sights, which come standard, will then be available. A low-powered scope will help minimize weight resulting in a fairly trim package. For those who can handle the moderate recoil, a .308 is the obvious choice. If not, there's always the .243. Snag a few extra magazines when opportunity permits and you'll be good-to-go.

LEVER GUNS

Two strong choices top the list. One is a bit unconventional while the other will appeal to traditionalists (who may already have one on hand). Either will work handily for both right and left-handed shooters. Both have external hammers with built-in safety features.

Although not mentioned below, the latest Henry lever-actions also look like great rifles. They have classic lines and are available in .30/30 and revolver chamberings. Their tubular magazines load through the forward sections in a manner similar to rimfires. New "All-Weather" models are chrome-plated with coated hardwood stocks. Their "Long Ranger" also holds promise.

Top Pick — Browning's BLR: With its strong, rotary bolt and detachable magazine, the BLR can handle modern cartridges. Scoping is a breeze and backup iron sights are there if needed. A stainless, take-down .308 would be hard to beat. A BL-22 would be a handy companion, and a .223 BLR would make a handy walking varmint rig. I haven't tried a take-down version, but it should solve one complaint against the BLR design: You can't clean the standard type through the breech. As is the case with the Remington pump, an Otis flexible pull-through system will handle that chore. There are two other issues worth considering though. First, you can't field strip the bolt. Second, the trigger will be fairly heavy. You'll need to weigh these negatives against the many positives. One extremely attractive version is the recently announced BLR Black Label Takedown. It's got to be nigh on to the perfect survival lever gun. Picatinny rail sections are mounted to the receiver and barrel for a full gamut of aiming options. Additional sections are attached to the forend for use of lasers or lights. The take-down BLRs supposedly maintain their zero, making them a great pack rifle. One thing I'd add is some sort of cheek piece riser to inexpensively improve scope use.

Browning's BLR Black Label is a clever marriage of old and new features.

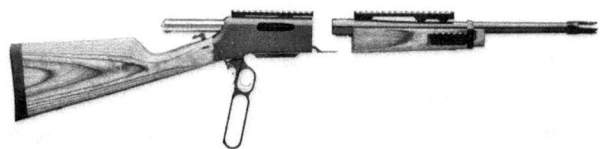

The Black Label's clever take-down design is the icing on the cake.

Honorable Mention — Marlin Model 336: Traditionalists could consider a Marlin .30/30. You'll lose the punch of a .308, but you'll gain an okay trigger, and a removable bolt. Accuracy will be useable, too. The stainless/laminated XLR version is a handsome and weather-proof rifle, but if its robust size and 24-inch barrel are an issue, a four-inch shorter carbine is available. The Marlin's solid-top receiver is easy to scope, and iron sights come standard. Add a .22 Model 39 and you'll have a useful, two-gun set. Since these rifles have been in continuous production for more than a century, they qualify as "well established." In fact, I wouldn't rule out a decent used Marlin, which will be quite affordable. Even during recent ammunition shortages, .30/30 cartridges have remained available. For general-utility chores, we could do worse. A similar M-1894 Marlin chambered for a .357 or .44 Magnum handgun round wouldn't be terrible either. Both rounds really pick up steam in a rifle bar-

Marlin sells their well-proven M-336 as a stainless model.

The trim lines of a handgun-caliber M-1894 can be maintained with a compact scope like this low-mounted 2.5X Leupold.

The Marlin M-336 is easy to scope, which can stretch out its range. This hog tipped over after one well-placed shot from 100 yards.

rel, and a .357 would make a nice companion for a revolver. Either will also fire .38 Special rounds for practice or small game. Does a Marlin have defensive capability? Watch the Cowboy Action shooters and you'll see that it's possible to squirt a whole bunch of lead downrange in a short amount of time. Here's another positive that's often overlooked: You can shoot and reload a centerfire Marlin (or Winchester), as opportunity presents, through the receiver's magazine port. With training this can happen quickly while maintaining a defensive posture.

COMBINATION GUNS

The higher-end guns are nice but, if we look at their overall usefulness, something more utilitarian makes sense.

The latest M-42 Savage combination gun employs a rimfire barrel atop its .410 shotgun tube. Those seeking a centerfire option can shop for a used M-24.

Top Pick — Savage: For most folks, a gun like the Savage is probably the ticket. It won't replace a full battery of firearms, but it will be at home in a pickup, boat, airplane, or cabin. You could look for a used Model 24 or spring for the new M-42. The former is well-known and ruggedly built, although parts could be a problem. Several centerfire rifle calibers were offered in the M-24 along with rimfire choices. The latter M-42 is strictly a rimfire, and is just so new that it doesn't have any history. A .22 LR or .22 WMR/.410 won't handle everything but should put some meat on a campfire. Some of the new .410 defensive revolver loads will up the ante, and hits on smaller targets will be a whole lot easier with the rifle barrel on top. I'd just stick with iron sights and call it good. A take-down version has appeared, which further increases the M-42's utility.

SINGLE SHOT RIFLES

Given the firepower limitations of this system, cost may be a factor. In that case, a strong and simple design will help.

Top Pick — Harrington & Richardson: They're ruggedly built, reasonably priced, ambidextrous, and surprisingly accurate. If something breaks you can get it fixed, and although the H&R may be an old design, it's far from dead. The latest AAC/H&R venture combines this basic gun with the latest technologies. Advanced Armament Corporation lists a tricked out rifle chambered in .300 Blackout. The barely-legal 16.25-inch barrel is threaded to accept an AAC sound suppressor. The heaviest loads are subsonic and designed specifically for suppressed use. With lighter 125-grain bullets, ballistics are similar to the 7.62x39mm Russian and close to a .30/30. The .300BLKT is relatively new, but catching on quickly. Still, it's far from "widely distributed." It is mentioned here to illustrate how an old design can adapt to new technology. Most folks would be better off with a plainer H&R chambered for a common caliber. They'll all disassemble without much effort for storage in small spaces.

A utilitarian H&R will normally shoot extremely well. This laminated version is chambered for .308 Winchester. Note the hammer extension and simple scope base.

CHAPTER 12

CHOOSING YOUR SIGHTING SYSTEM

A tour of shooting catalogs will reveal a mind-numbing assortment of aiming choices. This is especially true with optics, which are by far the dominant choice of rifle shooters. Nevertheless, a legitimate place remains for other systems.

IRON SIGHTS

These age-old designs encompass non-optical aiming systems. Their virtues are simplicity and durability. Drawbacks include less precision and limitations imposed by poor lighting. Some absolutely gorgeous 18th century flintlock rifles still exist. They typically have long barrels and fine open sights, made for precise shooting by riflemen whose eyes weren't fried by lights, TVs, and monitor screens. While some younger modern-day shooters may have excellent vision, it probably won't last. The trick then is to field a set of iron sights large enough to be seen in various conditions. At that point, the front bead will likely be large enough to obscure small or distant targets. A further drawback is that different zeros are often required for those sharing iron sights. The reason is that we're attempting to align three objects at three different distances: a rear sight, front sight, and target. The main focus should be directed to the front sight, but individual vision can cause discrepancies. A peep sight helps somewhat, so this phenomenon is more pronounced with open sights.

Old and newer technologies coincide on this flintlock rifle, equipped with a Lyman 66 Receiver sight. The rear sight slot has a filler blank.

Open sights: Although I seldom use them as a primary aiming system, open sights can provide a reassuring alternative to a damaged scope. You may already own a rifle so equipped. If so, a practical means to detach the optic will be needed. While QD zero-repeating rings are nice, many other Weaver-type sets use slotted nuts that can be removed with a car key or coin (I use a quarter to tighten them so I know they'll come off). The height of the scope bases will need to be lower than the iron sights, and you'll also need to factor in objective bell clearance. Some combinations just won't work, but a folding rear sight leaf may save the day. A front sight blade may be visible through a scope on its lowest magnifications. I just tune it out, but it bothers some shooters.

The "buckhorn" rear sight design was designed for fast shooting from horseback. It's recognizable by a pair of large ears and is still standard on many lever guns. I prefer a rear sight blade with a flat top and U-notch that matches a bright green fiber optic front sight bead. There are lots of alternatives to suit other tastes, but whatever is considered, think about visibility in dim lighting and bad weather. Some rear sights have a small moveable insert plate that contains the actual notch. Elevation changes are made by loosening small set screws. Other rear sights employ a stepped elevator ramp that slips beneath a spring-steel extension. Windage adjustments are commonly made by drifting the rear sight body in the barrel's dovetail (or sight body). Sighting in is a trial and error process with a small brass hammer or punch, so most open sights are a "set it and forget it" system.

Two extremes in open sight design. The F/O Williams unit (L) has small windage and elevation set screws.

Several manufacturers offer nice open sights. Williams sells "Fire Sights" with fiber optic elements. Marbles also produces a nice assortment of fiber optic front sights. Hi-Viz and Truglo are solidly into fiber optics. Lyman has been building iron sights forever; and there are others.

Receiver sights: Some rifles just seem "right" with a peep sight arrangement. Among them are the traditional lever-action Winchesters and Marlins. They are stocked for low-mounted irons, and their trim lines are better preserved without top-heavy optics.

A tiny but rugged XS ghost ring peep unit is perched atop one of my Marlin lever-actions. Another Marlin has a nice Lyman aperture sight. Its threaded aperture has been removed, and the larger-diameter housing serves as the actual "peep." Although a ghost ring may not seem very precise, field accuracy remains more than adequate. Any small loss is more than offset by the speed of this system, especially when used in conjunction with a large "Hi-Viz" fiber optic front sight. The eye will naturally center an object in a hole and the bright

The ramp-mounted F/O is a Hi-Viz with interchangeable elements. The barrel-mounted blade is a finer Marbles sight. It's higher than the original to accommodate a somewhat taller receiver sight.

The XS Sights Backup unit will clamp to a Weaver or Picatinny base. This one is mounted behind a dot sight for extra insurance.

The XS Sights ghost ring peep is a rugged little unit. Opposing set screws provide windage. They also lock the threaded aperture stem used for elevation.

Skinner sells another nice, compact aperture sight with adjustments similar to the XS unit. This one is mounted in a rear-sight barrel slot ahead of a top-ejecting receiver.

F/O bead will remain visible in low light. When a bit more precision is called for, I like a finer Marbles green bead. Why so much emphasis on this color? Because I have trouble seeing red!

Other rifles can benefit from a compact receiver sight as well. The small XS "Backup Sight" clamps to a Weaver or Picatinny scope base. I have one mounted to a Remington M-7400 semi-auto, right behind a small dot sight. It's reassuring, and it can also be used as a stand-alone aiming system when every tree or branch is coated with heavy wet snow. Backup iron sights (BUIS) are often seen on AR-15s. Many are spring-loaded pop-up types that will fit underneath a scope's ocular bell. We use A.R.M.S. 40-Ls on our M-4 type AR patrol carbines, to back up our electronic dot sights. I use a 40-L with a folding Diamondhead front sight on a personal AR-15. There are lots of similar products for the black rifle crowd.

Those with more conventional rifles can check out Williams, Lyman, XS Sights, Skinner Sights, and a few other firearm-specific brands sold for T/C Contenders and Encores. Many can be mounted using existing screw holes. The XS unit on my Marlin 1894 mounts to its rear pair of receiver holes. When adding a receiver sight, a taller front sight may also be necessary. The reason is that many are taller than a barrel-mounted open rear sight. Once finalized, I often drift out the rear iron sight and replace it with a dovetail filler blank.

Williams sells a nice line of aperture sights. Many are designed to mount on existing action holes.

Note: Brownells and Midway USA are two excellent sources for iron sights.

SCOPE CHOICES

Among the mind-numbing offerings, some well-known brands include Bushnell, Burris, Nikon, Weaver, Vortex, Leupold, and Redfield—just to name a few. In the interest of brevity, and at the risk of offending those other loyal users, I'll stick with a short list. Not shown will be some wonderful optics from firms like Schmidt & Bender, Zeiss, Nightforce, etc. The rifles we've examined are basic, so we'll scope them accordingly.

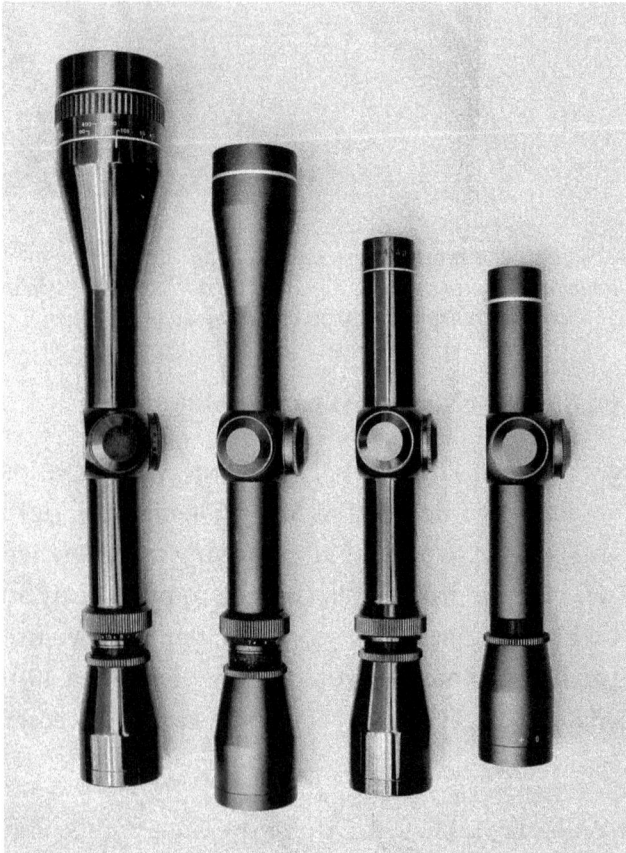

A collection of Leupold scopes in gloss and matte finishes (L-R): 4-12x40 AO VX-2, 2-7x33 VX-2, 1-4x20 VX-2, and 2.5x20 FX II Ultra-Light. Note the extra spacing afforded by the straight-tubed scopes for mounting.

Reliable turret adjustments with positive click stops are nice. Those with ¼ MOA clicks will work well, but even ½ MOA graduations can get you by. Friction dials work too, but should be left alone once zeroed. The big thing is repeatable adjustments. Low-end scopes probably won't have them for long, and they may also shift zero as magnification changes. Erratic adjustments are most likely products of mediocre tolerances or click stop wear, assuming the scope is near its optical center. Non-level crosshairs can also cause errors. Unless you're comfortable mounting a scope, it's worth spending a bit extra for a professional installation.

Leupold scopes: The market is getting crowded, but Leupold is still a benchmark brand. The few problems I've had were promptly fixed for free, which came as no

surprise. The scopes shown below are fairly basic models, but they'll do the job for most. Check the Leupold site for all of the features. Some are available with caliber-specific dials, ballistic-aiming, or illuminated reticles. All have plenty of eye relief and generous FOV. Comparing their weights against other brands, you'll see the Leupolds are often quite a bit

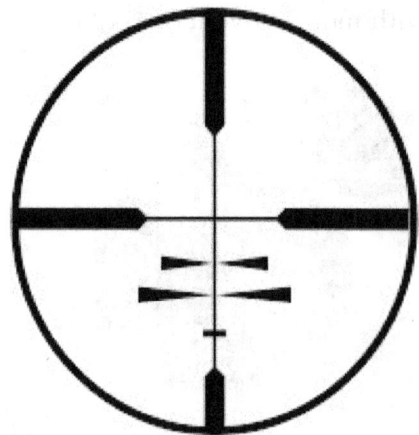

Leupold's "Boone & Crockett" system combines useful holdover aiming lines with a visible reticle.

lighter. They're hard to beat for the money.

A LEUPOLD SCOPE SAMPLER

Power	Obj Dia	Model	Comments
2 x 7	33 mm	Rifleman	Good basic scope; friction-dial adjustments
3 x 9	40 mm	Rifleman	Per above
3 x 9	40 mm	VX-1	Solid choice; friction-dial turrets
3 x 9	40 mm	VX-2	Better glass; click stop dials
1 x 4	20 mm	VX-2	Small straight-tube scope with big FOV and click stop dials
2 x 7	33 mm	VX-2	Great all-around choice with click stop turrets
1.75 x 5	20 mm	VX-3	Top-shelf straight-tubed scope with big FOV & click stop dials
2.5 x 8	36 mm	VX-3	Another great scope, available with Boone & Crockett reticle
2.5	28 mm	FX-2 Scout	Intermediate eye relief model (good for Ruger's M-77 Gunsight)
2.5	20 mm	FX-II Ultra-light	Nice little fixed-power scope for Marlin lever-actions
4	33mm	FX-II	Good, dependable fixed-power choice

Redfield: The name is well-known, but the original company is long gone. Good news: The brand has been resurrected by Leupold as a way to compete with lower-priced products. Costs are very reasonable and the scopes are all well-built. This should come as no surprise since Leupold is their source. For anyone on a budget, the Redfields are worth a serious look. The product line is fairly small, but it manages to cover most bases. Selections will fall in line with the Leupold scopes charted above.

Nikon: This firm has always been known for good optics. When it comes to scopes, there's something for everyone, beginning with the economy-priced "Pro-Staff" line and topping out with some very high-end models. Nikon is really into the ballistic reticle concept, which they've taken to the next

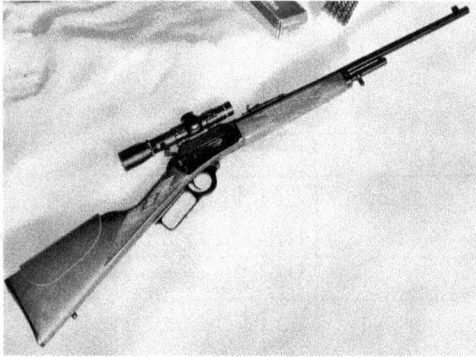

The scope on this Marlin 1894 Classic is a 2.5X Leupold FX-II, set up for optimum lever gun mounting. The rings are Weaver's lowest set on thin Warne bases. The cheek pad promotes a good cheek weld. Note the hammer extension.

Decent performance for reasonable cost is a hallmark of the Nikon line. This Omega BDC in Warne QD rings boasts 5" of eye relief. The Remington M-700 action may look a bit strange because it's a muzzle loader!

level with their "Spot-On" software. It will let you match their BDC reticles to the load of your choice. You'll even find a magnification slider that changes reticle values. For example, I have an Omega 3x9 with a BDC reticle. It's really built for modern muzzleloaders or slug guns, but I was interested in mounting it to a .17 HMR rifle. At 9X, the circles would've worked, but the yardages would have been oddball. By fooling with magnifications, Nikon's program revealed an 8X solution, matching 50-yard increments.

Burris: We can thank this company for getting ballistic reticles off the ground. Their "Ballistic-Plex" system is fairly simple, but it works quite well. Other innovations include the "Posi-Lock" turret, which locks windage and elevation adjustments. Burris also offers a diverse product line including many scopes with illuminated reticles. Their "Full-Field II" line represents real value. The latest "E-1" type includes windage hold-off lines. A new online ballistic program permits close match-ups of loads and reticles at various ranges. I have a number of Burris scopes which are all going strong. A few have been around for many years and my oldest 4x Mini has been to hell and back. I had a very old and obsolete 4x12 AO that seemed right for a .223 Winchester Model 1885 single-shot.

It had a duplex type reticle but Burris said they could upgrade it to a Ballistic-Plex style. I dutifully mailed it in with a $60 payment. Instead, Burris called to let me know they were replacing it with a brand new Timberline 4.5x14 AO model. As it turned out, the tube on my jalopy was slightly bent. I was happy enough with the new Timberline to buy a second one, both of which have Ballistic-Plex reticles. Burris must not be kidding about their "no fault warranty."

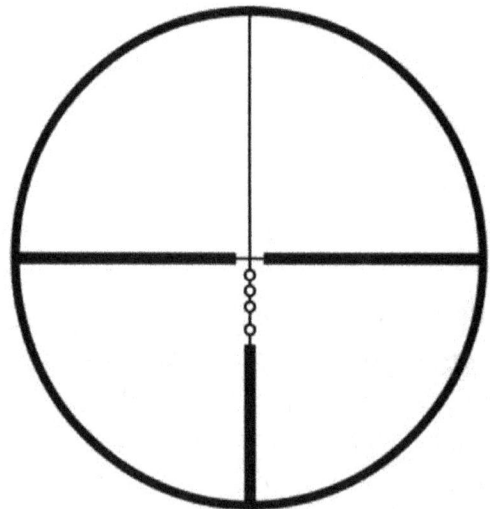

Several versions of Nikon's BDC reticle are offered to match various trajectories. Their Spot-On software is invaluable.

This Timberline is but one of many interesting scopes sold by Burris. The box indicates a Ballistic Plex reticle.

BURRIS Riflescope with Ballistic Plex™ **7mm Rem Mag** **.7mm WSM & SAUM** 175gr @ 2860 fps		BURRIS Riflescope with Ballistic Plex™ **.308 Win** 150gr @ 2820 fps	
Bullet Impact at Noted Yardage "-" = Low "+" = High	BURRIS	Bullet Impact at Noted Yardage "-" = Low "+" = High	BURRIS
0	100	0	100
0	200	-1	200
+1	300	-2	300
+1	400	-4	400
+2	500	-9	500

Burris includes caliber-specific labels with their ballistic reticle scopes. Similar velocities can produce different results, based on drag and weight.

Besides sending me a new scope, they even returned my check!

Bushnell: One thing I'll say about these scopes: Their glass is really clear. Again, you'll see a large product line. Even the lower-priced models seem to work. I have a beater Trophy 3x9 that came with a used rifle. It has since been shunted from gun to gun, but shows no sign of wear. I wouldn't take it to Africa (well, maybe I would as a spare), but it seems to survive all local adventures. Based on its performance, the higher-end models should work just fine.

Vortex: This brand seems to have come out of the blue but has quickly managed to establish a good reputation. The product line is innovative and diverse with broad pricing. A 30mm Strike Eagle 1x6 is now perched atop one of my AR-15s. Its illuminated ballistic reticle seems fast and intuitive. Later, we'll examine a few technical aspects of long-range shooting. The Viper PST 2.5-10x32 FFP might be just the ticket for that, on a compact bolt-action. Its first-focal-plane design will maintain ballistic reticle values throughout all magnifications. Ballistic turrets with zero stops are also offered in addition to a side-mounted A/O . Several illuminated reticles choices include an MOA-graduated type. The 32mm objective results in a more manageable package, despite 30mm construction. Cost is around $800, a fair deal considering its features.

We could keep going, but it's time to move on. Here's hoping you've noticed a trend: I've skipped the really cheap stuff. Don't go overboard, but spend a few bucks. Nothing will drive you as crazy as a wandering scope. Ammo isn't cheap… assuming you can find it!

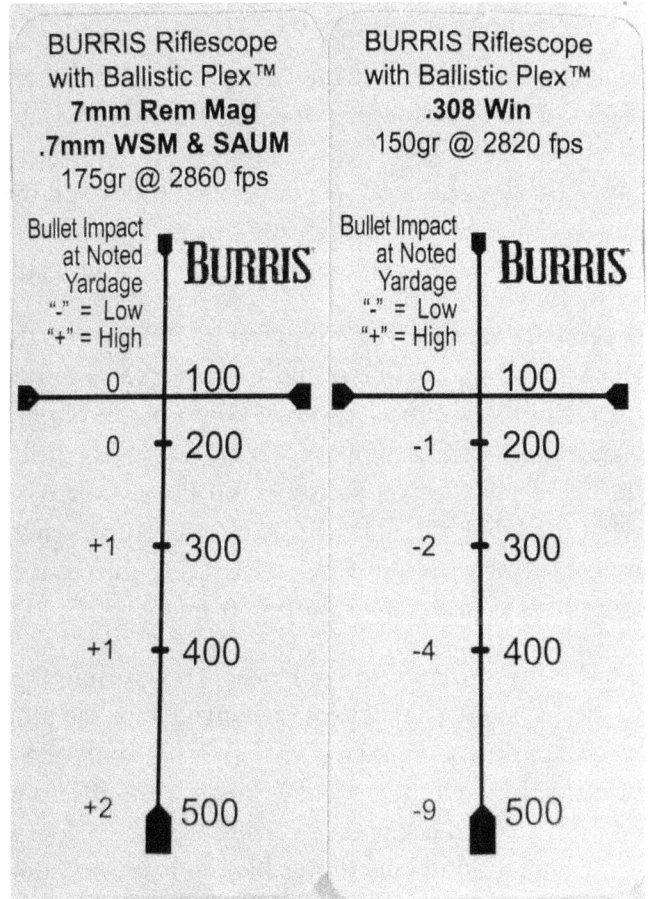

SCOPE BASES AND RINGS

Picking a viable mount can be more daunting than choosing a scope. The most popular rifles afford many options although some, like Ruger's Model 77s, require proprietary rings. On a positive note, the receiver's integral bases simplify the mounting process. For nearly everyone else, simple solutions are close at hand. If you review the scope listing above, you'll see none are behemoth models capable of exerting extra inertia during recoil. As a result, simpler base and ring sets will work. Listing every combination would be difficult so I'll stick with a few good choices.

A typical example: A Remington M-700 typifies the scope mounting process. Like many other rifles, its receiver top is drilled and tapped to accommodate popular systems. While its 6/48 thread pattern is fairly common, receiver contours and hole spacing require a specific match, explaining why Remington's more compact M-7 cousin needs different mounts. Both models bear two standard holes in their front receiver sections, but the rear bridges are different. In other words, we need to know what fits what. Thankfully, the manufacturers provide the necessary listings. Occasionally, the same mounting system will work with a few different brands, but we need to be sure. We've seen a few horrific zero problems resulting from use of an incorrect base section that looked "close enough."

Back to the Remington: We'll need a few different parts. First, we'll need bases, which will be screwed to the receiver. They'll provide a means for the attachment of scope rings, so these components must be compatible. Like many other models, both one-piece and two-piece base options exist. In the case of our M-700, we may need to know if the rifle is a long action or short action version. A .30/06 will be built around a longer receiver. Since a .308 cartridge is shorter, it'll fit into a short action receiver. If we're using something like a Picatinny one-piece base, we'll need the right length. Since the hole-spacing is the same on both long and short action Remington receivers, two-piece bases won't raise this concern; however, we'll still need compatible base and ring combinations. We might as well start with the parts that bolt onto the rifle.

Bases: Some scope rings are sold as integral designs, but most attach to separate bases. Complicating matters, there are several completely different systems. The trick is to make a good choice and match the parts.

<u>Weaver:</u> An inexpensive and lightweight-but-reliable design is their aluminum "Top Mount" system. These bases are also available in steel, and similar types are sold by other firms. Weaver has a huge selection chart that covers just about every type of rifle. We've used these bases extensively on many different rifles. They're plates with 0.180" wide cross slots that engage corresponding through-bolts on compatible scope rings. You'll either need a one-piece or two-piece arrangement depending on your rifle. When scoping Remington model 700s, I always go with a two-piece base set. The front base is reversible (thanks to an offset slot), which provides extra latitude for optimum scope positioning. The receiver's screw holes are degreased, and the base screws then get a drop of Loctite glue prior to tightening. The trick is to cinch them up sufficiently without snapping off a screw head. After that it's just a matter of choosing rings. One thing to be aware of is that some rings designed for a Picatinny base may cause minor fitting problems. I've had to occasionally widen the cross bolt slots on Weaver bases with a jeweler's file for proper engagement. You won't have this problem with sporting rings

like Weaver or Burris Zee types. They'll just clamp on. As a fan of low-mounted scopes, I'll often use Weaver bases with Burris "low" Zee Rings. Some optical sights employ integral dual cross bolts spaced for Picatinny rails. They probably won't index properly on Weaver bases, which typically employ just one or two slots.

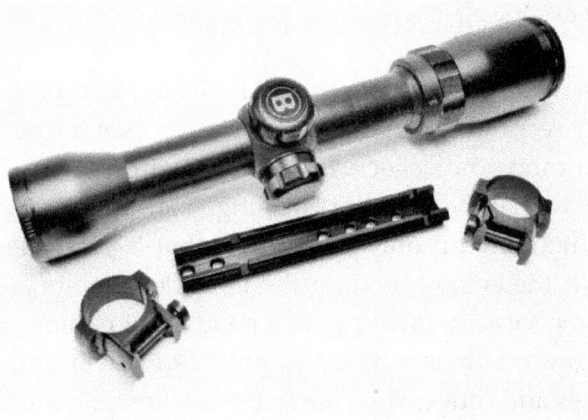

This older Bushnell Banner has seen good service. The base is a one-piece Weaver. The rings are Burris Zees. Note how their cross bolts engage corresponding slots.

Picatinny Rails: These military-designed bases are increasingly popular. They are similar to the Weaver rails, but have tighter tolerances and slightly wider (0.206") cross slots cut in regular 0.394" intervals. This design provides much fore and aft latitude, and is the base of choice for tactical rifles. Some have built-in inclines, typically expressed in MOA values, to gain increased scope elevation at extreme range. Picatinny bases are strong but do tend to be thicker, resulting in a higher overall scope system. To some extent, this issue can be overcome with careful ring shopping. Just about everyone with a big tactical-type scope will use a Picatinny base. In order to resist the inertial mass of such systems, larger 8/40 receiver screws are sometimes employed through gunsmith modifications.

A Picatinny base can accept numerous rings. The turn-in system (below) is a Redfield. Windage is attainable through opposing rear screws.

Turn-in systems: The old-but-proven Redfield design employs turn-in rings and is often seen with a one-piece base. The front ring is inserted into a dovetailed hole and rotated 90 degrees for very tight engagement. The rear ring will usually be captured by opposing screws that permit windage adjustments. An advantage is the ability to acquire optical centering of a scope's reticle. A variant is a dual dovetail design, which lacks this capability. Either system is strong, but somewhat heavy. Both types are best used as one-time couplings. Examples are now marketed by firms like Leupold and Burris. I like them for permanent installations on hard-kicking rifles. The rings are available in several heights. You can also buy extension rings for extra mounting latitude. The trick is to turn the rings until they're a true 90 degrees. That way the scope tube won't be dinged or damaged during mounting. As we'll see in the ring section, lapping helps avoid this. Most of the major mount manufacturers market this design.

QD variations: Leupold sells a somewhat similar "QR" base & ring design that use small thumb levers to engage ring studs. This design is also plenty strong. I've used QRs on my lightweight, Kev-

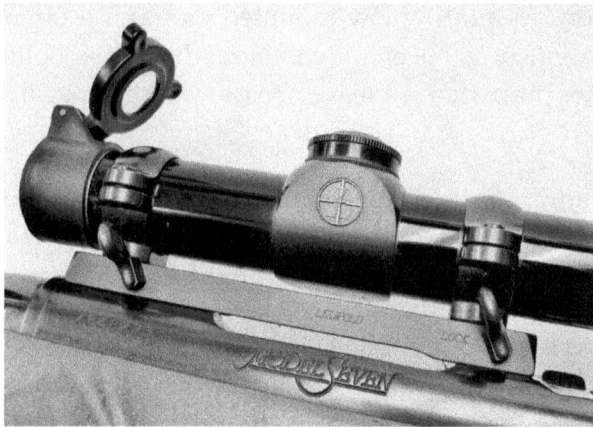

Leupold's QR bases and ring system is solid as a rock, but permits repeat mountings without zero loss.

lar-stocked .350 Remington Magnum for many seasons. The rifle kicks like a mule but its 1.75x5 Leupold VX-3 scope stays put. It can be instantly removed for use of iron sights; and repeat-zero is maintained. Leupold claims it'll be within ½ MOA, which matches my results.

Whatever type is chosen, the bases must be properly secured. A small dab of Threadlocker is good insurance, but check fit first. Sometimes a base screw may be too short or long. You might even tighten one up only to discover that it protrudes with the action, binding the bolt. Proper bits are also necessary (along with a good bit of patience). A gun cradle is advised to prevent inadvertently flipping a rifle on a kitchen table. Beyond less scratches and dings, your language may remain more civil.

Not every rifle needs separate bases. Some, like that Ruger M-77, already have them machined into the receiver. A flat top AR-15 normally has an integral Picatinny rail. You still need to understand what you have in order to buy the right rings.

Rings: You can buy a set of generic Weaver-type scope rings for $10 or less. They'll be made from some type of pot-metal with questionable quality. Their cap head screws may be metric and subject to buggering from use of standard Allen wrenches. Since the scope and rifle interface on its rings, why not spend a bit more? Many serviceable ring sets can be bought for less than fifty bucks. More often than not, they'll be types that mount to Weaver bases. High-end, long-range, tactical rifles typically employ large scopes that mount to Picatinny bases. Rugged ring construction and careful machining are cornerstones of such systems, which may cost several hundred dollars. Out at 800–1,000 yards, every little glitch is magnified. Fortunately, most needs are less demanding.

A small sampling of scope ring choices.

Weaver: Their "Top Mount" rings have been around for eons and are fairly inexpensive. They also tend to repeat zero fairly well. Those shopping for the lowest possible ring height should consider them on Weaver or Warne bases. Their downside can be difficulty maintaining level crosshairs during tightening (don't go overboard on this or you may cause tube indentations). They'll clamp firmly to Weaver or similar bases. A more streamlined and attractive-but-still-affordable "Grand Slam" set is also available in several heights. A variation is their windage-adjustable

A close-up view of Leupold's 2.5X Ultra-Light Scope in low Weaver rings, which are simple and strong.

version, which will help maintain optical centering of a scope. I haven't used their QD "Lever Lock" adaptation, but it certainly appears to be a viable choice.

<u>Burris:</u> Another good Weaver-base option is Burris's Zee Rings, which are machined from solid steel. They look good and come in various heights. They also sell a "Posi-Align" version that use polymer, eccentric inserts. Optical centering of a scope is possible with this feature, and rings with QD levers are also offered. I usually stick with basic Zee Rings, which are available in several heights and finishes. They've proven reliable during decades of hard use. Cost is also reasonable, so I always keep at least one extra set on hand for unplanned acquisitions. Their main drawback is that you can't tip them on from the side of a base. Each ring has notched legs that surround the base, so they must be slipped on from the front or rear. A cross bolt is then inserted to engage a base slot and cinch the ring. A relief cut in the ring provides adequate compression for tight purchase. Sometimes, after repeat usage, a Zee-Ring may not slide freely onto a base. If that happens, you can carefully pry the cut a bit for extra clearance. In most cases, these concerns are probably a non-issue. On Remington M-700s, the "low" set works well in standard Weaver bases with reasonably-sized scopes. A Leupold VX-II 2x7 is a good example of such a lightweight, compact package. The bolt handle may just kiss the side of the ocular housing when opened. A simple fix is a small square of black electrical tape, which will protect the scope's finish. Any base or barrel contact is bad, requiring higher rings.

Burris Zee Rings are another good mounting option for weaver-type bases.

<u>Ironsighter:</u> Among their other products, this company offers a neat set of Weaver-type extension rings. One ring is standard while the other has an offset base. Since it's a two-piece design, plenty of mounting options are possible. The extension will work up front or at the rear. By flipping both 180 degrees, extra fore or aft reach is possible. Since some Weaver bases are also reversible, all sorts of possibilities exist.

<u>Millett:</u> A large assortment of ring and base systems are offered as turn-in or clamp-on types. Their "Angle-Lock" windage-adjustable rings use opposing clamps to firmly engage Weaver-type bases. New scopes normally come "optically centered," near the middle of their adjustment range. Using Millett's "Angle Lock" system, the reticle can be closely aligned with a target for full windage capability. Only a few scope clicks should be needed for horizontal zeroing. These rings come in various heights, including some that are quite tall. They also offer extension rings in various heights and combinations. They look sharp, too!

<u>Warne:</u> They specialize in mounting systems, including quick-disconnect and permanent-type rings.

The QD types are surprisingly repeatable and strong. We've used them for many years with good results. Each ring has a lever that cinches rugged clamps to Weaver or Picatinny bases. Several heights and finishes are offered. I've been running an ongoing test for several years. Each spring I dismount the night scope on my AR-15 coyote rifle. In its place goes a 3x9 Leupold Compact, mounted in Ultra-High Warne QD rings. By saving one target I'm able to compare each group location, all of which have been remarkably consistent. The rife is a real tack driver, so any deviations will be readily apparent. So far, the turrets remain untouched. A lower set on a Remington inline M-700 muzzleloader permits dismounting during cleaning. They're handy and reliable, although a bit "fiddly" to set up. That's a small price to pay in more than one way, since their cost is reasonable. Similar, non-QD sets are also available for permanent mounting.

Warne's QD ring system is repeatable. The target shows an accumulation of several zero-check groups fired over several seasons after re-mounting this Leupold 3-9 Compact Scope.

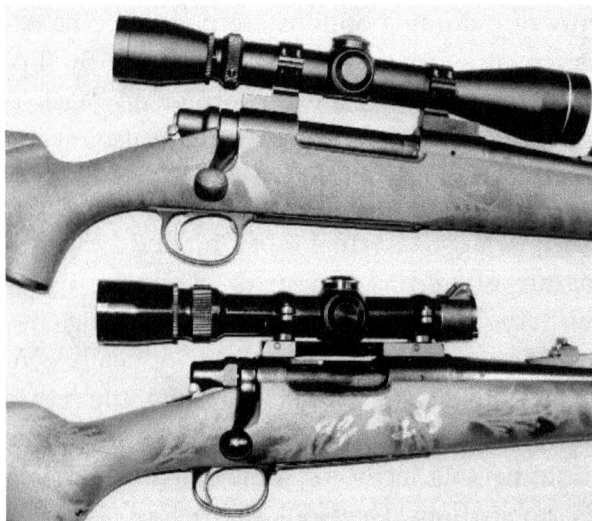

The long action M-700 has lightweight Talley one-piece rings. The short action M-7 is set up with Leupold's QR base and ring system.

Leupold: The huge product line includes a good looking, rugged "QRW" ring. I've been using these QD rings as part of a two-sight system involving a dot and scope. The upper ring sections extend a bit below the center of a scope, so they need to be snapped over the tube. At that point, tightening the screws will firmly draw everything together. Like the Warne's, repeatability has been great on Weaver and Picatinny bases. A simpler "PRW" version is designed for permanent mounting. Leupold also sells a number of rings for rifles with proprietary bases including Sakos, CZs, and Rugers. The previously mentioned "QR" types plug into corresponding base holes. All of the Leupold systems are well-built and handsome designs.

Ruger: Integral bases have long been machined into various Ruger firearms like their M-77 bolt-actions and single-shot Number Ones. The proprietary rings will supposedly maintain fairly consistent zero during multiple attachments. My experience tends to bear this out. Although proprietary systems can sometimes limit mounting choices, Ruger also sells extension rings. They're all built like bank vaults. Other manufacturers sell rings to fit Ruger receivers, too.

Talley: Lately, when scoping Remington bolt guns, we've used Talley dual rings. The bases are integral with the rings and their aluminum construction saves weight. They can certainly handle recoil, too. The Talley rings look sharp and are fairly affordable. Their main disadvantage is the lack of any QD capability, but on a rifle without backup iron sights, they have much merit. Anyone trying to field a lightweight rifle should give them a look.

Others: Several clamp-on designs are sold as extension rings, which offer more latitude in scope positioning. They can save the day during some otherwise incompatible rifle and scope combinations. B-Square specializes in conquering unorthodox mounting challenges with no-gunsmith systems. Besides offering a rakish set of strong sporting ring sets, S&K Scope Mounts sells non-gunsmithing military mounts. Many military-type optical sights are shipped with their own mounting systems, designed for a Picatinny rail. The extra height necessary for AR rifles is usually factored in, making them too high for other types.

SCOPING A RIFLE

Considering all possible base and ring combinations, a full-line gun shop begins to make sense. They'll probably have a good assortment of practical alternatives from which to choose. Remember that not every scope and mounting system is compatible. Since you may not be able to acquire the right eye relief or scope height, a trusted shop becomes a good place to figure these things out. They may also have a collimator, which permits bore-sighting at the counter. Considering the cost of ammunition, professional help may actually be cost effective. There's nothing as unsettling as firing a carefully aimed shot at a large target which remains unscathed.

If you do decide to go it alone, line up the right tools first. Then think about safety. Please make darn sure the rifle is unloaded, and remove any ammo from your workspace. If possible, remove the bolt. In fact, it's easy to go a step further with an AR. Pulling two receiver detents will allow the whole upper receiver to detach. Some other types (like single-shots) have removable barrels.

Bases and rings: Threadlocker agents are good base insurance, but you should skip them on rings. Instead, just degrease everything. Make sure the bases match the receiver's hole patterns. The latter may have small filler screws installed, which will need to be carefully removed. A jeweler's screwdriver will often work well on those with small slotted heads. When installing the base screws, check for varying lengths. In some cases they'll be different. Locate the bases, paying attention for interference with action function. The screws can be lightly installed until each one is aligned. At that point you can remove each separately and apply a dab of Threadlocker. Tighten them up evenly using the correct bit. Work the action to make sure a screw isn't protruding within the receiver.

Rings are sometimes machined and bored from one piece of metal. The relationship of their upper and lower halves should therefore be maintained (you can mark them prior to disassembly). Prior to tightening the halves, check for proper scope positioning. I like to stop at the point where the scope can still be moved for leveling and eye relief. During final tightening, strive for equal gaps, working on the screws in a consistent and alternating pattern. After each one seems snug, you can give the screwdriver an extra rap. Odds are you'll see a bit more play.

Location and fit: With hunting rifles, I'll establish eye relief while wearing a hunting coat. The scope will be set on its maximum magnification since relief is usually shorter. The scope should be located just far enough rearward to acquire full FOV, a step that should prevent "scope eyebrow." If prone is on your menu, perform the final setup there. Your head will probably be closer to the scope. Final tube positioning can also detect any hang ups that could damage the tube. Some people lap machined rings for this reason. A special, close fitting rod is coated with lapping compound and run back and forth through the mounted rings, knocking off burrs or high spots. Although the furthest ring spacing will provide the strongest support, avoid hard contact with bells, turret housings, or power rings.

Reticles: Leveling can be a smooth process or a maddening event. When possible, I'll use a level, working off corresponding flats on the rifle and top turret (commercial kits are available). At other times it may be possible to slip a feeler gauge between a base and the flat underside of a scope's turret housing. Trial and error is another resort, best performed on low magnification. I'll sometimes rest the muzzle on a padded floor and lean over the rifle and scope, comparing the crosshairs to the action. Some people use the vertical edge of a building as a reference. It's worth bringing the ring bit to the range in case things don't look right. More than once I've wondered what in God's name I was thinking after setting up on sandbags. I'm not averse to getting a second opinion, either. Level crosshairs are especially important with ballistic aiming reticles, to prevent windage errors. Another foible involves ballistic-compensating turrets near the limits of their adjustments. Unless the scope's interior reticle housing is close to center after zeroing, its radius can cause unusual tracking shifts when elevation is applied. New scopes often ship "optically centered" in the midpoint of their adjustments. Ideally, only modest turret adjustments will put them on target. The beauty of adjustable mounts is that they can often make this happen. Dot sights tend to be simpler. Most recent tactical units just clamp onto a Picatinny rail. It's still worth striving for plumb turrets, so their adjustments track properly.

Final steps: As for the tightening process, how much is enough? Too much may snap a screw, cause a dent, or even bend a scope. Its internals could also be damaged. Insufficient torque will result in the scope creeping forward during recoil. It doesn't take much movement to change zero, either. Some screws are slotted, others use Allen heads, and Torx-types are now common. The right-sized bit is crucial, and so is the amount of force. If in doubt, go with the manufacturer's recommended inch-pounds, using a torque wrench. I just proceed carefully and, so far, so good. After the screws are snug you can give each one that rap, and then tighten them a bit more. As mentioned above, reserve the Threadlocker for bases. Now and then a scope will creep. It's more common with hard-kicking rifles and large scopes, but ring tolerances can be a factor. Some people apply a bit of rosin to the rings. I've used a thickness of masking tape and one persistent creeper was cured with double-face tape. Sometimes it's hard to tell if movement is the culprit. For suspects, I'll apply a small strip of electrical tape to the top of the scope adjacent to a ring. It'll indicate movement and may actually curl at its abutting edge.

Once everything is secured, perform a final check. You should have a good cheek weld, unimpeded action function, and level crosshairs. The objective bell shouldn't contact the barrel, receiver, or any extension ring surfaces. The thickness of a business card is about the minimum bell and barrel clearance, but more will be necessary with lens caps. Higher rings will solve many such issues–to a point.

That cheek weld is important for proper shooting. Some folks use see-through rings, which also permit use of iron sights. Count me out.

Bore-sighting: We can establish a rough zero without firing a shot by bore-sighting. Special laser inserts are sold that project a fine beam for adjustment of the crosshairs. A Collimator is another option, employing a tight-fitting bore spud. It supports an optical device that extends above the muzzle. The device displays a reference grid that can be seen through a scope. The turrets are then dialed until everything lines up, providing an approximate zero. Most full-line gun shops will have such technology on hand.

Redneck technique: I usually just figure out a way to stabilize the rifle while looking through the bore and scope. After both coincide on a distant object it should be roughly zeroed. With the luxury of a home-based range, I'll just set the rifle up on a benchrest near the workbench. A 100-yard, round 8" white plate serves as a reference point. The bolt is removed and the crosshairs are aligned to see where the bore is pointing. It's rarely on the money, but the known distance and size of the plate permit predictable scope adjustments. If the plate isn't initially visible, things could be out of whack. In that case, searching through the bore will eventually locate the target. Without disturbing the rifle, a peek through the scope should show the relationship of the crosshairs. Adjustments can then be made, although turret revolutions will be reversed. The process seems more logical when the crosshairs serve as a constant reference. In that case, an off-target bore will have the same effect as a projectile. Once the plate is visually centered in the bore, I know the first fired shot will probably strike within a few inches of a 100-yard bullseye. I've used a notched cardboard box as a makeshift rifle holder in a pinch, lining everything up on a neighbor's stove pipe. While other distances will work, 25-yards is a good alternative. It'll translate well with many turret scales at 25% of their value.

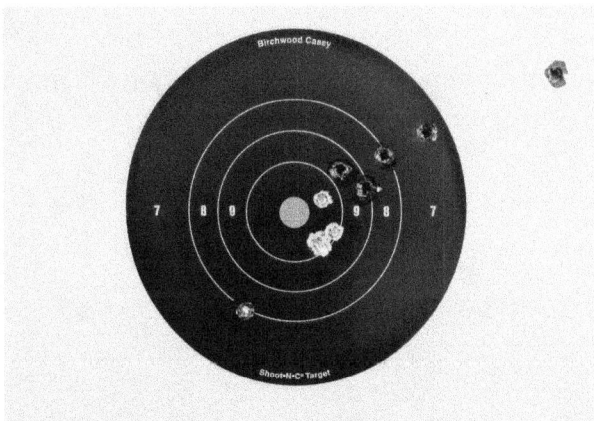

100-yard redneck bore-sighting results. The furthest 2:00 shot was the first. A few more adjustments resulted in the unmarked group.

What if you can't remove the bolt? I've resorted to a dental mirror more than once. Last year, I had a devil of a time indexing a dot sight on an S&W .44 Magnum revolver. The sight had been used on another firearm and was grossly out of zero. The first shot at 25 yards wasn't even on the paper! Because ammo isn't cheap, it was time for Plan B. I was able to secure the S&W in a small, portable vise, set on my home benchrest table. After many contortions, the dental mirror's image of the 25-yard bullseye was visible through the bore. A glance through the sight revealed a very high dot. In other words, placing the dot on the target would result in a very low hit. Fortunately, adequate elevation existed to quickly adjust the sight. The process was time consuming, but a whole lot cheaper than randomly blasting away.

An alternate method involves firing an actual shot while aiming at a large target from very close range. In the case of the revolver, it could've been 10 yards. Measuring the bullet's deviation would indicate the necessary adjustments at $1/10^{th}$ their values. The same technique will work with rifles at 25 yards. If it's something like a Winchester M-94 lever-action with iron sights, the rear sight will need to be moved toward your desired impact point. We'd move the rear sight up if rounds were striking low. A stepped elevator will often provide incremental movements. Windage is typically changed by tapping the whole rear sight in its barrel dovetail. Proceed cautiously, using a brass tool face. Although formulas are available, most of us will use trial and error.

One more zero trick: After firing a careful shot, note the bullet hole. The rifle's position is maintained with crosshairs on the bull. Turret adjustments are then applied until the reticle and bullet hole coincide. The trick requires a complete lack of gun movement throughout the process—easier said than done!

Cheating: We sometimes need to zero a large batch of AR-15s. We'll just head for the range and set up a 50-yard "assembly line." Actually, it's a disassembly line, since each upper receiver will be pulled off its lower. The bolt is then removed. From a 50-yard bench it's easy to stabilize the upper for bore-sighting. The first shot won't be far off the mark, and final adjustments can be called by a spotter. The ARs have Aimpoint dot sights with ½ MOA turrets. The target has 1" grid lines to indicate the necessary clicks (¼-inch at 50 yards). A rifle is usually zeroed within two or three shots, and not too coincidentally, a 50-yard AR-15 zero is also on the money at 200 yards.

I'd rather perform bore-sighting near a workbench in case gross misalignment is evident. Lacking adjustable mounts, remedies may include thin base shims—or an entirely different system. Once in a blue moon I've been able achieve zero by reversing a base or ring. Sometimes the fault can lie with a rifle that has misaligned screw holes or an off-center bore. Fortunately, these issues are now less common thanks to precision manufacturing.

Assuming everything progresses smoothly, it's important to remember that bore-sighting is not a replacement for the live fire sighting in!

CHAPTER 13

ACCESSORIES

A rifle, scope, and ammunition constitute a good chunk of money, but not the final amount. Here's a list of extras broken down by essentials, handy accessories, and other useful stuff. Of course, we'll also want to look at cool things like night scopes and suppressors. They're not for everyone, but window shopping is fun.

ESSENTIALS

This list is short and bearable. In fact, many items (slings, gun cases, and cleaning gear) can be used with other firearms that may be on hand now or in the future.

Sling: If your firearms have QD studs, it's easy to transfer a sling. I prefer the nylon types, light and quiet. They dry quickly and can be rolled up in a pocket. The simplest designs are the most compact, although those with a thin rubber section tend to remain situated on a shoulder better. The most common are one inch wide and easiest to stuff in a pocket. I'll sometimes do so when hunting a tight spot where the slightest extra noise can ruin an opportunity. A sling swivel moving against a synthetic stock can be the kiss of death. During long treks with heavier firearms, I like a wider 1 ¼-inch version. Quick-detachable swivels are sold to fit either width.

Another type of swivel system employs a push-button, which causes a series of ball detents to retract from a plugin stem. A corresponding receptacle sits flush with the stock. It's fast, but won't accept the more common external stud-type swivels. I have a shotgun so equipped and always wind up fishing around for its dedicated sling. The clip-on hook arrangements seen on AR-15s will be covered in that section.

Basic but useful items include a soft case and QD sling.

A hard-shell case is a better bet for traveling, and a locked one is required in some locales. Two rolled up shooting mats are visible here.

Gun case: A soft, zippered version will do, and some are waterproof. With careful shopping you can find a size that fits more than one rifle. Besides protecting your finish, a good case will cushion your scope to help maintain its zero. One thing you shouldn't do is store a rifle in a soft case for a long period of time. Sooner or later the liner will absorb moisture, ruining its contents.

For more demanding conditions, a hard-shell case is better. When traveling you'll need locking models in some areas just to stay legal. You'll get what you pay for. I'll sometimes tuck a one-piece cleaning rod between the foam liner and interior shell of a rifle-length case. Be sure to include your address and phone number, just in case it disappears.

Extra magazines: This is obviously a non-issue for those with integral systems. For others, think "Murphy's Law." Besides loss, malfunctions can often be tracked down to a bad magazine. Having at least one spare can help identify the cause, and numbering each one helps. Defensively, the ability to execute fast reloads is paramount, meaning several will be necessary. Extra magazines can also provide a means to quickly switch loads. For a pure sporting rifle, one spare may suffice, but defensively, it's better to have too many than not enough.

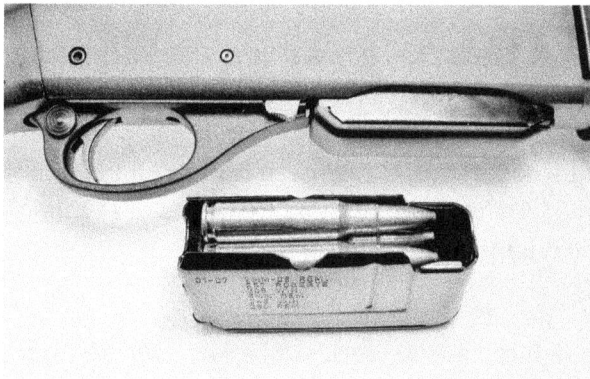

Extra magazines are essential and this Rem M-7400 type accommodates a number of short action calibers. The rifle is also fitted with a giant head safety button.

Ammo carrier or magazine pouch? The type of rifle will dictate your choice, but some type of system is advised. Single-shots, lever guns, and bolt-actions are typically reloaded with individual cartridges. Some folks prefer elastic stock-mounted carriers which offer a self-contained and convenient package. Since freezing rain and snow are common, we prefer a simple weather resistant alternative. During deer season the same 9-round elastic carriers can be worn on a belt, shielded by a coat.

Defensively, ammo management is a very big deal. Although they're accessible, stock-mounted carriers can interfere with ambidextrous cheek welds. Loose rounds in pockets are problematic since reloads should be possible from any position. The same applies to spare magazines. A well-built pouch can be a valuable commodity when properly positioned for either-hand access.

Cleaning kit with bore guide: The one you bought for your rimfire should also work with your centerfire rifle. You can just add the proper brushes and patches. One-piece rods are best, but they aren't very portable. A pull-through kit can cover mobile missions, tucking nicely in a pack.

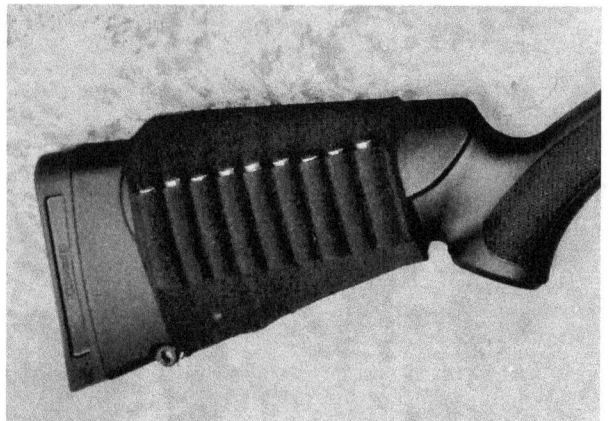

Stock-mounted ammo carriers can also be worn on a belt.

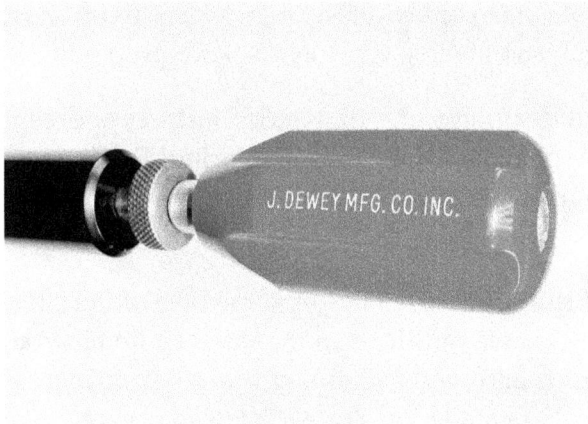

The brass collar on this Dewey rod is a bore guide, which can help protect a rifle's muzzle.

Bore snakes will work on the fly as well. Jointed rods will work in a pinch, but they can be hard on rifling. One thing a flexible system won't do is clear a barrel obstruction.

When rifles must be cleaned from the muzzle, a guide is advised. It may be as simple as a small tapered collar that slips over a cleaning rod. Thread a patch on a patch-loop and the collar won't slide off in storage. A bolt-action rifle can be cleaned through its breech after removing the bolt. For this chore, a longer bolt-like guide can be inserted into the rear of the receiver. It'll keep your rod centered and help channel solvent away from the action and stock. I could probably get fancier, but a pair of plastic MTM guides in short and long action lengths seem to work just fine. They're inexpensive, too. AR-15s can be cleaned in a similar manner, using purpose-built guides.

Rifle-specific tool kit: This is just a small and portable collection of bits or drivers that will support on-the-move maintenance. Sit down and take a look at the various screws or scope ring fasteners to figure out what you'll need. In some cases it might just be a multi-tool.

I'm never to eager to remove a stock (or most rings) since zero can shift during reassembly. On those rare occasions when I do, the chore is performed at my workbench. One tool that will minimize this problem is a torque wrench. Although not essential, it's worth owning a small unit. Every serious shooter should invest in a gunsmith screwdriver set. The assortment of bits will prevent damaged screws and make life a whole lot simpler. Besides slotted heads, today's fastening systems often include Allen and Torque-bit screws. Forget about carpenter-type, angled-blade screwdrivers, which will quickly bugger machine screw slots.

A good set of lens caps should be part of any scope purchase. The rear cap has a fast pop-open lever.

HANDY ACCESSORIES

Most of these items are relatively inexpensive and some like lens caps and cleaners will extend the life of costly optics.

Lens caps: Several designs are out there. Many have hinged covers. You work their flexible sleeves over each end of a scope and pop the covers free when needed. I like the see-through types, which have saved the day on several occasions. On some designs, the cover can make a noise as it fully opens. Offenders can be silenced by pressing a small piece of adhesive weather stripping against the contact point. Besides protection from snow and rain, lens caps will keep your scopes free of dust during storage. Your best bet is to buy them from a gun shop where you can check for proper fit.

Lens pen: These little jewels have a built-in brush and cleaning pad. The exterior surfaces of decent optics have anti-reflective coatings that may become damaged from minor abrasion. Don't grind your glove into an objective lens; use the lens pen. Your scope caps are part of the equation, too. Less debris equals better protection.

Bolt disassembly tool: As previously covered, the firing pin assemblies of some bolt-action rifles need a mechanical assist for disassembly. It could be a simple punch, or in the case of a Remington, a specialty tool. Failure to perform the requisite maintenance will eventually lead to misfires, so a Kleinendorst or Sinclair tool should be part of an M-700 cleaning kit. You won't need it very often, but you *will* need it! A little-known alternative involves hooking the bolt's disassembly notch on something like a boot lace, but life will be a whole lot simpler with the right tool.

Gun cradle: Trying to run a long cleaning rod through a rifle barrel will illustrate the value of this device. Besides freeing up both hands, your rifle will be less likely to sustain damage. One slip is all it takes to sustain a screwdriver –induced scratch. You'll appreciate a cradle when fussing over cleaning details and mounting scopes.

G.I. ammo can: They're handy for lots of different uses, including long-term ammunition storage. You can even turn one into a mobile cleaning kit with solvents, patches, and oil. A separate can with padding can transport binoculars and rangefinders.

Cheek piece riser: You may or may not need one, depending on your rifle. My pet peeve is a scope mounted too high for solid cheek contact. This becomes most evident when shooting off a bipod from prone. Low rings help, but they won't always solve the problem. For this reason I have a few guns with accessory cheek pads. I've had good luck with Acu-Riser, Beartooth, Cheek-eez, and the Beretta

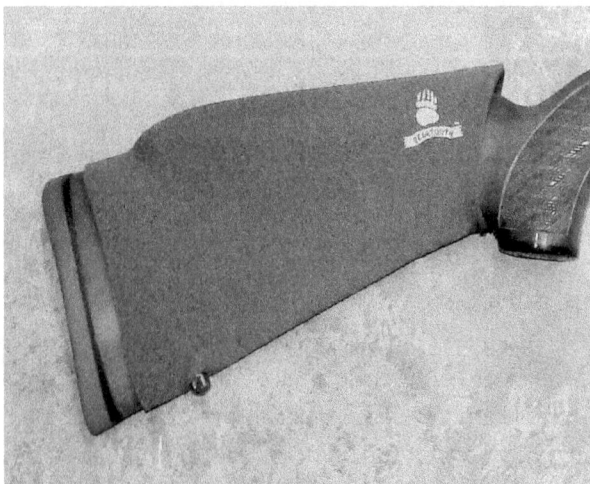

An old but tricked out Remington M-510 .22 rimfire with an Acu-Riser cheek piece. Installation here is via two screws, but straps are supplied.

This elastic Bear Tooth riser comes with foam spacers of various heights.

Gel-Pad. The latter two are adhesive and, although I have successfully removed them without incurring any damage to finishes, they're probably best considered a semi-permanent fix. The Beartooth uses a slip-on neoprene sleeve that captures foam spacers (elastic slip on ammo carriers will sometimes work).The Acu-Riser affords strap-on or screw-on options. I chose the latter, firmly anchoring one to the walnut stock of a .22 rifle. It's actually my favorite cheek piece. There are plenty of other products available, including those with Velcro straps. Some have side-mounted pouches and cartridge loops, the theory being that everything is self-contained. While such designs do offer sporting advantages, they could present defensive concerns when switching hands and eyes. Whatever type you choose, make sure it won't interfere with operation of the rifle's bolt, hammer, or charge handle.

After-market stock and/or detachable magazine system? This one is a "maybe," geared toward bolt-action rifles with floor plates. I'm thinking of a Remington Model 700 BDL and that affordable Magpul system. The Howa magazine conversion is also inexpensive. In either case, the idea is to increase reloading speed along with possible capacity. Be sure to consider the extra length of a higher capacity magazine.

USEFUL SHOOTING AIDS

Collectively, these items could put a major dent in your wallet. Still, I'd hate to be without them. A possible exception is a set of shooting sticks which, ironically, is the least expensive of them all.

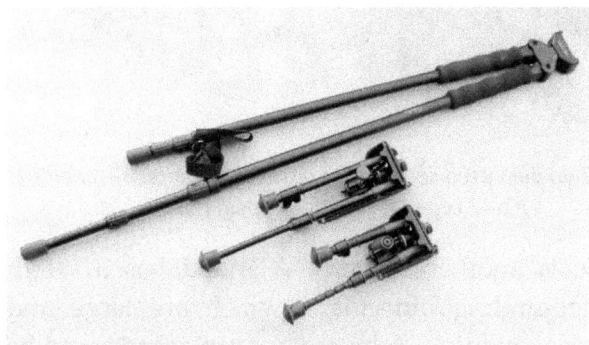

Shooting sticks and bipods: The Harris units are 6-9 and 9-13 inch bipods with friction and notched-leg features.

Bipod: Like a sling, one bipod can cover several different rifles. I own two in different heights and both are Harris products. One is the shortest 6-9" and the other is 9-13." The short one doesn't see much use, being more of a benchrest model. The next size is a well-used veteran that has served for over 30 years. These units have spring-loaded, folding, telescoping legs, and clamp to a forward sling swivel stud. Installation is quick and an alternate attachment-point permits re-attachment of the sling. Several taller models are offered at the expense of increased mass. My preference is for those with click stop legs and a tilt feature. Several competitive brands, with which I have no experience, are available for less money. Off a bench I'd much prefer a good sandbag arrangement. From prone, a bipod will provide less accuracy than a benchrest, but it's possible to come fairly close. This is well and good in an open field, but won't help much in the bush.

Shooting sticks: Acting somewhat like extra tall bipods, sticks now appear with frequency. You'll see them in use during outdoor TV shows, often in Africa. They serve as a makeshift support during hunting situations. They also aren't a new idea, having been used by American buffalo hunters on the Great Plains. Nowadays, commercial models are sold in several heights, with telescoping legs. Designs include one, two, or three-legged models. Out of these, I prefer the dual-leg designs. They're not as steady as a tripod, but offer simplicity with less weight.

Rangefinder: There are plenty of laser-ranging instruments to choose from these days. By sticking with those from well-known scope makers, odds are good of buying a serviceable unit. Like everything else in gun land, prices vary in accordance with features. The advent of this technology has spawned the long-range shooting craze and today's ballistic scope systems. A few new high-end rangefinders are more like ballistic data systems, offering accurate firing solutions for precise trajectories. Others, like my older Bushnell ARC 1500, are perfectly adequate for general field use. It has seen plenty of action while running reliably off a long-lasting 9-volt battery. The "ARC" stands for "angle-range compensating" whereby inclination is calculated with yardage. Steep-angled shots, whether uphill or downhill, actually require less elevation correction across a given distance. The Bushnell's built-in inclinometer displays the target's vertical angle and its corrected yardage. This feature is probably more useful in mountainous terrain but, since it's fairly affordable, why not have it?

Two well-used sets of roof prism binoculars: Bushnell's 10x42 Legends (L) and Leupold mini 7x20s.

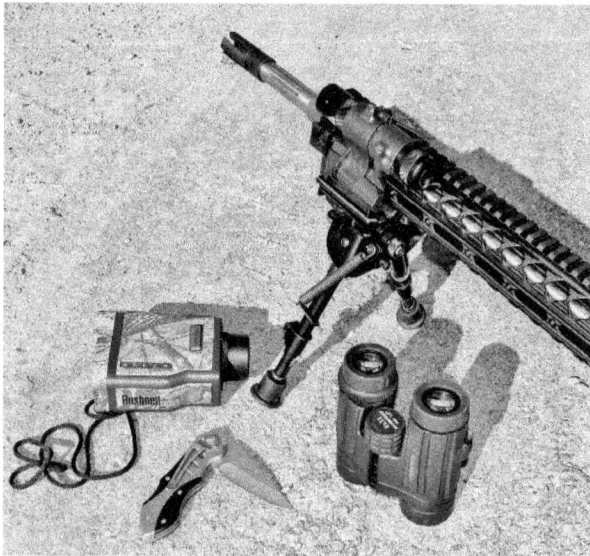

The Bushnell Elite 1500 ARC Rangefinder has seen lots of use. The Redfield 8x32 Binos live in a truck. The rifle-mounted Safariland RLS light sees regular duty on a number of firearms.

Size is another concern. A friend has a set of range-finding binoculars, which are large and more expensive. A basic laser rangefinder can be had for $250 or less and will carry without difficulty. The basic operating concept involves bouncing a laser beam off the object to be ranged. A rangefinder advertised with 1,000-yard capability will likely be less effective during field conditions. Some of the variables include lighting, reflectivity of an object, intersecting brush, and weather. Since the latter can also affect durability, a waterproof rating helps. Besides providing an accurate distance reading, a rangefinder presents a way to sharpen up "guestimation." This skill can be improved by throwing in an estimate just prior to pushing the button. Now and then you'll get quite a surprise!

Binoculars: Another key piece of gear is a set of serviceable binoculars. Some hunters will skip them in favor of a scope. Overall, this is a very bad plan. I've been "glassed" by more than one scoped hunter, which didn't make my day. Binoculars are much safer and will offer better performance. The two main types are Porro and roof prism designs. The Porro prism versions have ocular lenses which are offset outboard from their centers. Roof prism binos employ two straight tubes for a narrower package. Although a good set of Porros can provide a somewhat enhanced 3-D image, many outdoor types go with more compact roof designs. In addition to lenses, both versions employ a series of prisms, all of which must work in concert. Based on results of equipping a fairly large armed force, we've found the roof prism types to be more durable. If good optics help with scopes, they're essential with binoculars, which are much like two rifle scopes placed side-by-side. Any collimation (alignment) errors will manifest themselves through eyestrain and headaches.

When perusing the sporting catalogs, you'll see a huge range in prices, generally reflecting quality. Those who spend long hours glassing open terrain for bighorn sheep or other western game will buy the best optics possible out of sheer necessity. Since ignorance is bliss, nimrods and casual users will often go the opposite route. For many of us, a useful compromise exists somewhere in-between. At least, that's the route I've chosen, using three sets. A newer Redfield 8x30 Rebel lives in my truck year-round. Since it could "disappear" at any moment, economy is a factor. This set is still going strong despite severe temperature extremes. Its optical quality is also surprisingly good considering my $110 investment. Normally, I'd never look twice at something in this price range but after a chance opportunity to try a set, I snapped them up for occasional use.

My oldest bino is a tiny European-made Leupold 7x20, which has seen tough use for more than two decades. Many successful hunting stories are directly attributable to this glass despite limitations imposed by small lenses and marginal low-light capabilities; however, I can just throw the miniature set around my neck and forget it's there until needed. We all have treasured equipment and these old Leupolds make my list. Nevertheless, I wouldn't recommend something this small as a stand-alone choice. Those going with minis should spend more and not less, since their limited optical constraints require every advantage.

My third selection is a general utility set of Bushnell 10x42 Legends, purchased after reading good reviews. One evening I had an opportunity to pass them around a group of a dozen shooters who were participating in a low-light firearms training program. We also had a set of $900 European binos on hand for comparison. Everyone got multiple tries on various objects as the light faded away. The consensus was that the European glass was better, but not by very much. My Legends cost a bit under $250 around ten years ago. Since then they've seen lots of use; much of it after dark while scanning coyote baits. The eye strain and headaches associated with inferior optics are thankfully absent with mine. Performance is good enough that we normally only use our night vision scopes to execute a shot. Our initial target detection occurs with the binos, preserving our vision. We equipped a surveillance team with an 8X version for better low-light performance. They do have a slight edge, but my all-purpose 10X set also works, providing a useful 315-foot, 100-yard field of view. The Legends are still available for under $300. There are a number of other brands in this price category, which is probably the lower cut-off point. Spending more is certainly not a bad thing.

The larger sporting emporiums often stock a wide array of binoculars, permitting opportunities for hands-on comparisons. The cheapest sets may seem okay in a well-lit retail store but don't forget, the acid test involves prolonged use during real world conditions. Look for binos rated as waterproof (instead of "water resistant"). A rubber-armored exterior will greatly increases their odds of surviving inevitable bouts with gravity. Read the online reviews and don't be afraid to ask questions.

RANGE EQUIPMENT

Clubs and commercial ranges are often equipped with things like shooting benches or rests. Nevertheless, a good many shooters will be using an improvised site. Regardless of the location, the first items are essential!

Eye and ear protection: You'll need these items, not only for you, but for others in close proximity. You can always tell when you're in the presence of older shooters (plan on repeating every sentence at least two times). Ear plugs aren't as effective as muffs, but are worth having when afield. Particularly with muzzle brakes, sound blasts can be severe. Prolonged wingshooting won't help your hearing either. Anyone into firearms will probably acquire several types of hearing protection, ranging from plugs, through basic muffs, and upward to electronic models. I'd start with a basic set of muffs. Shooting-specific eye protection is also highly recommended. Lenses will probably be made from tough polycarbonates, which can take a surprising beating. Shoot long enough and you'll be thankful you were wearing them. Keep them on when doing maintenance, too. Many parts are under spring pressure and can launch with great force.

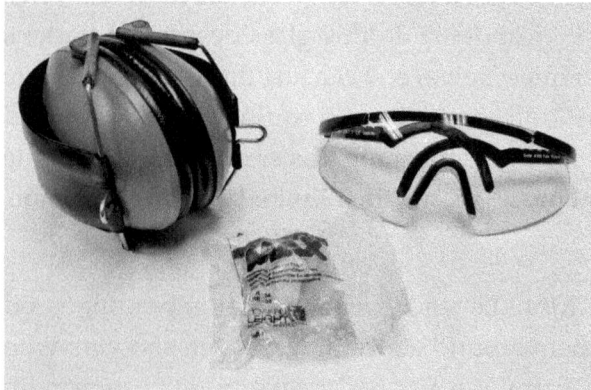

Two essential safety items are a set of shatter-resistant glasses and hearing protection.

Testing in progress over a sturdy wooden bench and Wichita tripod.

Range bag: Some sort of rugged, compartmentalized bag is convenient for lugging assorted range supplies. A stapler, targets, hearing and eye protection, spare magazines, and ammo are just some of the items we'll typically lug to a range.

Shooting mat: Mine sees infrequent use, but it's still appreciated. Like many other types, it's a large roll-up mat, intended for shooting from prone. I'll rarely have it afield, but it sure comes in handy for bipod practice. The alternative is plopping down on dirt or wet grass. Some of the fancier tactical types serve double-duty as "drag bag" rifle cases. You can buy a basic but useful mat for around $50, depending on what you want.

Benchrest systems: Serious accuracy testing requires a means to eliminate human error. Such a system typically consists of five key pieces: a sturdy shooting bench, chair, adjustable rest/sandbag, and extra rear bag. Stability, proper orientation, and comfort are crucial. This excerpt from *Rimfire Rifles* might help:

You can spend several hundred dollars on a top-end, fully adjustable, heavy cast tripod with fitted bags. We maintain a Wichita unit on our range, along with several sandbags. It's made from a heavy casting and has *pointed, screw adjustable feet at the end of each low tripod leg. A central threaded stem adjusts to various heights using a large thumb-wheel. A metal cradle on top holds an eared leather sandbag for proper forend support. A separate, larger eared bag is positioned at the rear of the shooting bench to cradle the rifle's stock. Once properly set up, rock-steady support can be maintained. That takes most of the human equation out of serious accuracy testing. Caldwell sells a similar, but more reasonably-priced unit for less than $130. It's called "The Rock Shooting Rest & Rear Bag Combo," which comes range-ready with both bags.*

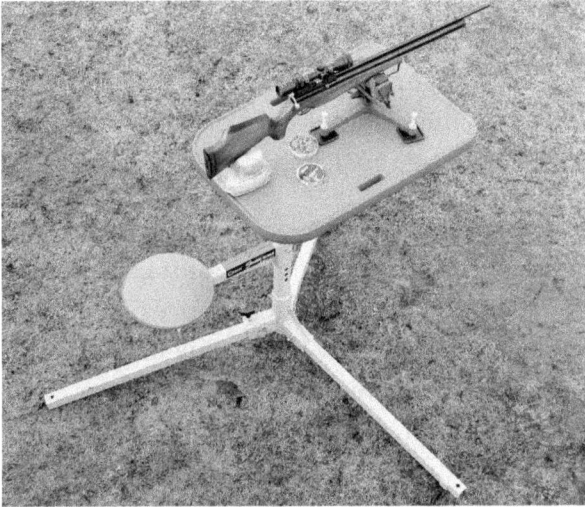

This British air rifle is set up for accuracy testing atop Caldwell's "The Rock" system. The bench is their "Stable Table."

Cabela's sells a Herters bench that easily unfolds.

Some sort of wiggle-proof bench is necessary. A heavy, fixed shooting bench of the type commonly seen on established ranges is best, but portable types are available. Two I have experience with are Caldwell's Stable Table and Cabela's "Herters" unit. The former disassembles for transportation and the latter folds up. The Caldwell unit is built like a tank but it should fit into most vehicle trunks. The folding Herters bench seems a bit less accommodating but easily folds flat. It's probably too large for most car interiors, but it'll slide into the bed of a pickup truck.

Since recoil is amplified when shooting off a bench, Caldwell's Lead Sled has become popular. It's an alternative to a tripod, built as a long, one-piece tubular unit. Fore and aft supports are integral and a cradle is provided to hold 25-pound bags of shot. A butt stop, combined with extra mass, soaks up recoil. They start around $80.

PAST shoulder pad: This item is another recoil-reducing accessory for those seeking relief from hard-kicking rifles. Two models are offered, serving as strap-on shoulder pads. The "Super Mag Plus" costs $30. I haven't tried one but I know a few folks that swear by them.

Spotting scope: Those who hunt in vast, open spaces will pack one to help locate game. This spot-and-stalk technique saves miles of aimless walking and is a great way to judge trophies. For our purposes, bullet holes are the main intent. A spotting scope can still save a whole lot of time and walking—especially at longer ranges. You may want one—or not. It is an extra piece of gear, so more often than not, ours stay back at headquarters. A good 3x9 rifle scope will resolve .22 holes at 100 yards (or more against the right background). A 12-14X will reveal them from 200 yards. Remember the mass-production AR/dot sight bore-sight and zero process previously described? We use a spotting scope for this job even though it's only 50 yards. The extra magnification will establish the necessary turret clicks. For simple projects, we'll often just use a scoped rifle and in many cases, it'll involve the one we're shooting. A Leupold 2x7 will easily spot .30-caliber holes at 100 yards. This is sport-related shooting. Long-range marksmen absolutely *need* a spotting scope, but only if it's a good

A Leupold spotting scope in action on a long-range course of fire. It saves a lot of walking when distances exceed a quarter-mile!

one. Like other optics, quality comes with a price. You'll see a huge spread, and at least a middle-of-the-road product is advised. You might consider one as a long-term goal, depending on your needs.

Chronograph: This item isn't essential (or even necessary) for many shooters, but it can provide valuable information. Given the price of ammunition, a chronograph may be worthwhile since, like many other electronic devices, costs have come down. Getting an accurate read on the velocity of a bullet will permit calculation of its trajectory. This information is essential for long-range shooters and can prove useful for those with ballistic aiming reticles. Programs from Strelok, JBM Ballistics, Burris, and Nikon can provide an accurate plotting of trajectory, once a velocity is determined. We've spent lots of time working up consistent subsonic loads for suppressor use.

The two sensors are visible on the top surface of the chronograph. The display indicates a projectile's velocity in feet-per-second.

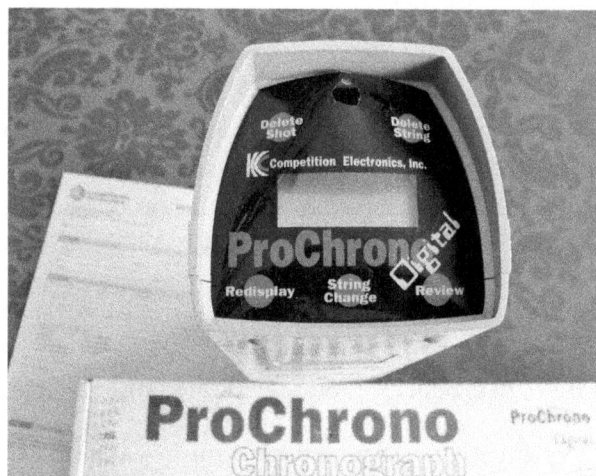

Ideally, a projectile will pass over the sensors, but it was lights out with this low airgun shot. Surprisingly, the data remained intact after a factory repair.

We use a self-contained Competition Electronics unit, which easily mounts to a camera tripod. The chronograph is a long plastic housing full of electronics. On each end, skyward-looking sensors "see" the projectile and calculate its time of passage. Results are displayed in feet-per-second on the face of the instrument, which is typically positioned around 15 feet downrange, beyond peak muzzle blast. Bullets are then carefully fired just above its long axis and sensor windows. The operative word is "carefully." Let the owner do the shooting to avoid any unclean thoughts resulting from shots "not quite high enough." Nothing will ruin your day like the big "oops." It took a while, but I finally drilled ours right through the display with an airgun pellet (Competition Electronics made it whole in short order). It's easy to use and displays the velocity of each shot, average velocity, extreme spread, and standard deviation. The latter two figures can indicate the consistency of a load.

In many cases, velocity will be lower than advertised—sometimes by a considerable amount. Plugging the wrong data into a ballistic solution will obviously cause problems, which will be manifested at longer ranges by mystifying misses and elevated blood pressure. You might say that a chronograph has medicinal purposes!

OTHER NEAT STUFF

These items are fairly pricey, so most might be longer-term possibilities for those of us bitten by the gun bug. An exception might be a muzzle brake, which is fairly affordable by itself; however, since it requires a threaded barrel for mounting, extra gunsmith costs can be involved. Fortunately, a by-product of recent silencer interest is factory-threaded barrels. Through careful shopping, one might conceivably purchase a rifle, muzzle brake, and suppressor that all share a common thread-pattern.

Muzzle brakes: Unlike a flash hider, these devices are designed to cut down recoil. There are a number of after-market designs, and a few rifle manufacturers now catalog them as factory options. I own an after-market Gentry "Quiet Brake." It probably emits less extra noise than other types, but hearing protection is essential. Mine was installed on a hard-kicking, custom lightweight .300 Short-Mag that ate good scopes. The barrel needed gunsmith threading, which added to the cost of the brake. It was money well spent, since recoil went down to below .260 Rem level—maybe to around a .243! Shortly afterward, I shot a deer with it and my ears were ringing for hours. A buddy in a tree stand 1/3 mile north said he almost wet himself. For this reason, Ruger includes a dummy device with their heavy-hitting M-77 Guide Gun. Its factory-fitted brake can be exchanged for an equally-weighted blank device that won't affect zero. The brake provides relief at the bench, and the weight is intended for the woods. It's a good idea since some professional guides won't allow a muzzle brake in their camps! Back to that Gentry brake: The already-lightweight Model Seven underwent a number of custom modifications that made it even lighter. I'm by no stretch recoil shy, but this thing was vicious. The installation of the brake made a *huge* difference; much better than expected. It was money well spent.

With careful shopping, you may be able to buy a dual-use brake (like an AAC) that will also accept a suppressor. Barrel diameter plays a key role related to the common thread patterns. A bare muzzle will require machining for threads, so thickness must be considered. Brakes are sold in a number

The Gentry "Quiet Brake" resulted in a huge recoil reduction. The same cannot be said about noise. Hearing protection is critical!

Another effective brake installed on a 7mm Remington Magnum. The M-700 is a DMB version on a Wichita benchrest.

of thread patterns beyond the common military 5/8x24 (.308) and 1/2x28 (5.56) types.

Suppressors (silencers): Threaded barrels segue nicely into these devices, which are shrouded in mystique. For many non-shooters, Hollywood images provide the main point of reference. As often as not, the actual silencer will be a small attachment emitting minimal noise, employed by a sinister character. The reality is completely different and it's now safe to say that silencers are going mainstream. This accounts for the proliferation of new firearms sold with threaded muzzles. Nevertheless, you can't just buy one off the shelf. Since the 1930s, suppressors have been heavily regulated by The National Firearms Act (NFA). Beyond the legal aspects, unique mechanical and ballistic factors must be considered.

This Thunder Beast suppressor is mounted to the business end of a tactical .308 bolt-gun. It's a direct-thread attachment, meant for semi-permanent installation and maximum accuracy.

<u>The process:</u> You will need some money and a fair degree of patience to own one of these federally-regulated devices. Ownership isn't legal in all states and others restrict hunting use, so your first step should be to check. The next hurdle involves BATF paperwork, endorsement from a local law enforcement head, two passport photos, and a one-time payment of $200 for the special registration. For a bit less money, ($150) a "trust" can be established, which lists multiple users. The trust is simpler in a sense since LE approval is skipped. It also solves potential estate headaches, but the process may require a lawyer. These steps are on top of the cost for the actual device, which may run $450 to $1,000. Due to the red tape, patience will be needed during a waiting period that can encompass several months. During the interim,

your bought-and-paid-for suppressor must languish in the custody of an NFA dealer. At some point paperwork will arrive, bearing a $200 Stamp, and the serial number of the suppressor. A copy should be readily available for inspection by law enforcement. Loaning the device is prohibited, although others could use it in your presence. The trust process allows the listed users to share the same suppressor. Either way, it can't be possessed until all legal hurdles are cleared. Some NFA dealers, like The Silencer Shop, can guide you through the process. Their trust-specific application packages can be purchased in lieu of an attorney.

Factors: With subsonic ammunition, a suppressor can be *very* quiet. In rimfire calibers, the sound of the action working may be nearly as loud as the report. Centerfire rifles will be louder, but much less noisy. The key to success is use of projectiles that don't produce a telltale supersonic crack. A normal supersonic .223 round will still be fairly loud, sounding similar to a rimfire .22 Magnum; not ear-shattering, but definitely detectable. The right ammunition is essential, but it can pose function issues in semiautomatic firearms. On top of that, there are different types of suppressors for pistols and rifles. In other words, there's more to consider than meets the eye.

Attachment: The device will need a way to attach; typically accomplished with a threaded muzzle. There are several thread patterns in use, depending on the caliber. Most rimfire and .223 barrels are machined 1/2x28, which matches the threads of AR-15 flash hiders. The 5/8x24-pattern is often seen with .30-caliber AR-10 barrels. Some manufacturers (like Yankee Hill Machine) have developed QD muzzle devices. The "can" is screwed on to the device (which also serves as a flash hider) by hand. It cinches up using spring-loaded detents, much like a shotgun's magazine cap. The correct device is necessary to avoid inadvertent firing of a .30 bullet through a .22 suppressor.

I'm perfectly happy with the YHM coupling system since mounting is a breeze. A few quick twists are all that's needed to mount or remove the "can." I could've purchased a model that screws directly onto a barrel but the QD system is more versatile. Its click stop detents also assure repeatable mounting for consistent zeros. Right now I'm using one "can" on five different rifles in two calibers. Two are single-shots and three are AR-15s.

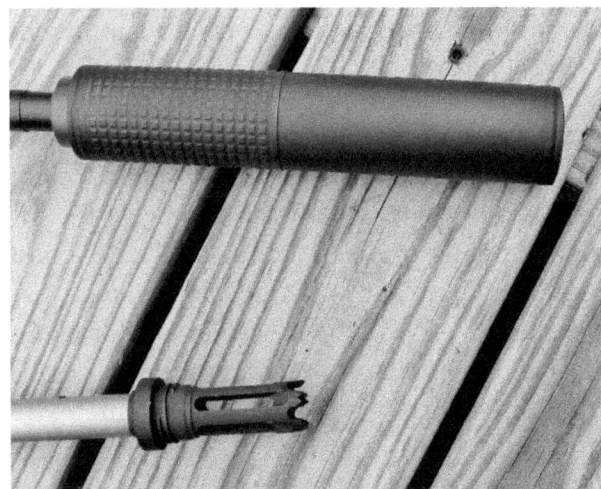

The YHM system employs a combination flash hider/QD muzzle device. Their Phantom suppressor quickly spins on until captured by a click stop.

Depending on the rifle, zero may shift. One of my .300 Blackout AR-15s has a thin M-4 profile barrel that shoots 4 MOA lower when the can is attached. A heavier-barreled twin shifts right by 1.5 MOA. When the same suppressor is attached to a fairly stiff AR-15 .223 barrel, zero is, for all practical purposes, unchanged. You won't know until you shoot some groups. Decent scopes permit easy corrections through turret adjustments.

Plusses and minuses: Once these details are sorted out, new possibilities exist. I can use the same YHM Phantom on any of four .300 Blackout bar-

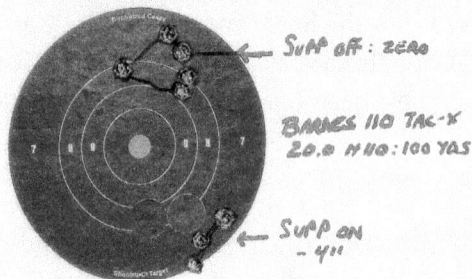

Handwritten on target:
300 BLKT AR-15/BURRIS 1¾-5X/25F-CAM
YH SUPPRESSOR TEST
SUPP OFF: ZERO
BARNES 110 TAC-X
20.0 H110: 100 YDS
SUPP ON
- 4"

Attachment of a suppressor caused a 4 MOA shift down-ward with this .300 Blackout AR combination. Accuracy remained quite useful with Barnes 110 TAC-X bullets.

rels, as well as a .223 AR-15. Yes, the muzzle end of the suppressor's hole is greater, but it still works. As mentioned above, the .223's report won't be all that quiet, but it'll still be much less, and muzzle flash will be non-existent. Supersonic .300 Black-out loads sound more like CCI .22 LR Stingers. Using subsonic loads, the report will be *much* less! I backed off around ten yards while my son popped off a shot, which sounded more like an airgun report. A single-shot or bolt-action is even quieter, largely due to the lack of action noise.

At 100 yards, there is a noticeable delay until my heavy 220-grain .30-caliber round nose bullets smack a target backer. Depending on the load, they strike 12 to 14 inches below the crosshairs (with a 110-grain zero). The heavy subsonics do better at 50 yards, landing 5 inches below the crosshairs. Obviously, trajectory is a major issue. Fortunately, several scopes are now available with dual-velocity reticles to help overcome this problem. I can adjust a Burris 1.75x5 to around 2.2-power. At 100 yards the loopy subsonic 220 RN bullets will then coincide with the tip of the lower thick-thin duplex reticle. Although not a perfect solution, it's better than guessing. My Vortex Strike Eagle 1x6 has a ballistic reticle, offering all sorts of new possibilities.

Of course, the steep trajectory issues are mitigated with conventional loads. Last week I shot a coyote after dark using a suppressor. The rifle was a .223 AR-15, which shoots plenty flat. The price was some extra noise, but the report was still much more tolerable. It was also less likely to alert new

The same .30-caliber suppressor works on this .223 night vision equipped AR-15 with the correct muzzle device. Probably due to a stiffer barrel, zero remains usefully constant.

customers. The load was our preferred 55-grain Ballistic Tip. Zero and function were unchanged. Accuracy appears to be better with the suppressor attached.

To achieve semi-auto function, extremely heavy subsonic bullets are necessary. Their extra weight develops sufficient gas pressure to cycle the action with lighter propellant charges. The heaviest subsonic 5.56 bullets won't develop enough gas to operate an AR-15. Much heavier .300 Blackout bullets allow pressure to build, but the process is a ballistic balancing act which can require extra tinkering. The slow and heavy .30-caliber bullets will obviously have a loopy trajectory, and they may also be unstable without fast rifling twists. The wrong combination (or off-center mounting) could further result in a baffle strike that would demolish the can—a very costly mistake!

Regular suppressor maintenance is also necessary. I could attach my relatively inexpensive YHM Phantom to a .22 rimfire rifle, but since it won't disassemble, lead fouling would quickly accumulate. Its diameter may also obstruct iron sights.

Worth it? The NFA paperwork is essential. Fortunately, in my state, ownership and hunting is legal with the proper credentials; however, for many shooters, considering the expense, red tape, and local restrictions, a companion rimfire capable of firing .22 CB Caps or Shorts might be an attractive alternative!

Night Vision Devices (NVDs): These instruments fall under three general categories: light amplification, thermal detection, and digital image enhancement. The latter two categories are more recent developments.

Ambient light amplification: The first instrument I used was a 1960s-era "Starlight Scope." It was crude by today's standards and as large as a section of toilet plumbing. It displayed a greenish image, accompanied by a subtle high-pitched whine. Nowadays, thanks to military developments, night vision devices (NVDs) are much improved and more compact. Some prior-military users will relate to a PVS-14 monocular, which stands for "passive viewing system." Our agency's Gen-III, ITT #6015s are similar civilian models. They don't project a beam, accounting for their "passive viewing" designation. Instead, a special tube converts any existing light photons into electrical energy (electrons).

Night vision performance is thus dependent on the degree of available light, with some amount being necessary. In absolute darkness, an NVD won't work at all. Furthermore, exposure to supplemental lighting will damage the instrument and defeat its purpose. Fortunately, an infrared illuminator can fill in the darkness by projecting light invisible to a naked eye. An IR beam is, however, detectable by opposing night vision users. Also, the rear lens of an NV device will emit a small amount of light that can be reflected off a user's face. Rubber boots are often included to contain the image and minimize this problem. Military users may also use monocular-type instruments with their off-side eyes to help maintain defensive night vision.

Typical NV designs consist of monocular, binocular, or weapon mounted systems. Their capabilities are often listed by three generations, the oldest or least expensive being Gen I. The Gen III units cost *much* more money, accounting for popularity of Gen II (or II-Plus) among many civilian users. Some manufacturers muddy the waters through other performance ratings like CTG or HPT. Gen IV is the latest option. The heart of an instrument is its image intensifier tube, which has a finite life. Pricing is commensurate with the ratings and longevity of these instruments.

No pun intended, but there is more than meets the eye with night vision use. One consideration is its intended use. Our Agency's Gen III monoculars serve for hand-held surveillance and weapon-mounted use. A pair of AA batteries will power one for hours on end if its integral IR assist is limited. They cost in excess of $3,000 apiece back in 2002, but they're still going strong. Similar versions now start around $3,500, a huge chunk of change. Quick-disconnect GG&G mounts permit their use on AR-15 flat top receivers behind compatible dot sights. The tactical-grade sights have special night vision settings which barely illuminate their reticles. This essential feature prevents "blooming," phenomena that will overpower an NV image and damage the unit.

Lately, a number of NV-capable optical sights have appeared, and when coupled with a good instrument, can be highly effective. Thanks to some Rube Goldberg engineering, I was even able to adapt an NV monocular to a conventional scope. I scrounged a short length of PVC plumbing and modified it to serve as a coupler. The PVC adapter was slipped over the ocular lens of a 3x9 Leupold scope and the NV monocular was plugged into its rear. The whole affair was held in place with a jumbo elastic band. It looked ridiculous but worked surprisingly well during many nocturnal coyote hunts. On most nights, the Leupold scope worked best at 3-5 power. A full moon and snow easily permitted 9X. In dimmer conditions, infrared augmentation was necessary. Mounting an ITT #6015 behind an optical sight obstructs its built-in IR port, but an auxiliary illuminator solves the problem. The big drawback to my jury-rigged PVC arrangement was the extreme rearward location of the monocular. On a soft-kicking AR-15 it wasn't a problem. A .308 would be another story. A major plus was that I

A Rube Goldberg aiming adaptation of a 3rd Gen ITT #6015 Monocular.

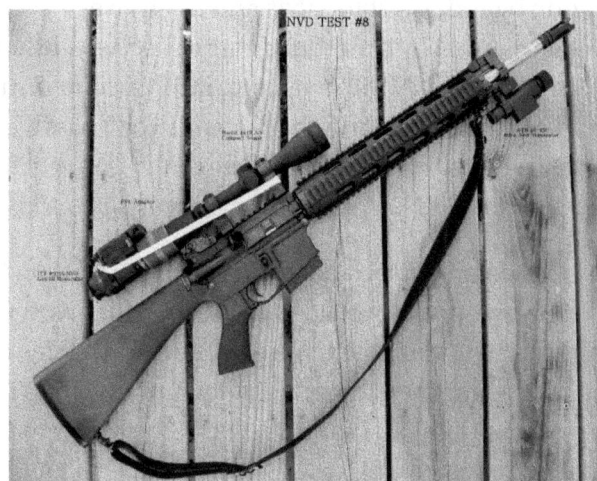

The evolution continued with the addition of an IR illuminator. It looks dumb but works—on a soft-kicking rifle.

had a 24-hour system. The scope served for daylight use and the NV setup could be easily attached as darkness fell. No re-zeroing was necessary after adding the device.

A dedicated night scope makes life a whole lot simpler for aiming purposes. We have extensive experience with several ATN Tridents. Mine is a 4X "CTG-Tube" scope, which is no longer cataloged. ATN's Night Arrow 2 appears to be a replacement with a somewhat lower price ($1400). CTG stands for "Custom Tube Grade," with performance similar to Gen II+. The Tridents run on a single #123 battery, good for at least 40 hours. They also come with an accessory ATN M-450 infrared illuminator that uses the same battery. These relatively small IR units have an integral clamp, which can mount to a short Picatinny rail section on top of the scope (mine is mounted further out on the forend). The actual Tridents weigh over two pounds and are configured for AR flat top height. The ensuing package will be somewhat large, and it will also be a dedicated night-only system. A more recent introduction is the PS-28 clip-on model that mounts in front of a conventional scope. An AR with a Picatinny forend seems ideal for this device. The QD PS-28 permits simple mounting when darkness falls with no need to re-zero. Cost depends on its performance rating, starting below $2,000. For those who can bear such cost, this system seems perfect.

Think "vampire" with your night vision device, meaning bright light is harmful to the instrument. A thick rubber cover shields the objective lens of our Tridents. It has a small aperture that accepts just enough light for daytime zeroing. I've gone this route but I much prefer to shoot in true darkness. It's not only fun but easier on the instrument, with an added bonus of some actual hands-on low-light practice. The Trident's QD mount has so far maintained zero after remounting. On my accurate AR coyote upper, tight sub-MOA clusters seem like magic after dark.

Night vision does have limitations. Again, since some ambient light must be available, extreme darkness will affect performance. Our pricey agency ITT units have small built-in IR illuminators, best used indoors where distances are shorter. The ATN auxiliary IR units turn night into day well beyond 150 yards on the darkest nights (when conditions are right). Add some fog or mist and you'll see nothing more than a white out. Cold weather dictates use of Lithium batteries, but our IR units still suck through juice in short order. Although we have picked out glowing coyote eyeballs more than once, most IR use is limited to an actual shot. Speaking of that, since many NV units are "gated," they can briefly shut down during muzzle flash. You'll only get one shot without a good flash hider.

ATN's Trident is a dedicated night scope. The addition of a suppressor results in a heavy package best reserved for stationary use.

Thermal: This technology works off heat emissions, a good example being military FLIR gun camera footage. Civilian instruments have grown in popularity but equivalent performance cost *much* more than conventional NV units. Pricing will be measured in thousands of dollars. As a whole, the thermal units tend to be more compact, and size really does matter when traveling on foot.

The latest craze of civilian thermal aiming is centered on Texas hog hunting. These critters are highly destructive to agricultural enterprises, behaving like four-legged rototillers. Ranchers want them gone but feral pigs are smart and quickly learn to feed after dark. Their Achilles heel is a pronounced heat signature. Of course, they also eat like pigs (imagine that,) so the use of thermal scopes over game feeders has come to the front.

ATN's M-450 IR illuminator is included with their night scopes, but it can also be purchased as an accessory. It will QD-mount to Picatinny rail sections.

My experience with this technology is zero, and owing to its cost, will probably not increase anytime soon. Since the lower-priced thermal units just aren't in the same league, Gen II+ night vision instruments continue as a viable alternative.

Digital: This new and entirely different design is quickly gaining ground. The technology is similar to a digital camera where the image is pixilated rather than optical. As such, an NV-capable digital scope can be used during daylight or darkness. During low-light conditions, IR augmentation is employed. The digital NV scopes offer some interesting features (among them being cost). Magnification can be digitally zoomed, and several reticle options are often programmed in. Some of these units will even interface with a smart phone for shared imagery. Personal reservations involve wet conditions and cold weather.

The glowing eyeballs of this coyote are the result of infrared illumination. Note how the branches reflect an IR source. So do snowflakes and water droplets.

It's the nature of today's technologies that my few-year-old NV system is now eclipsed. That said, it still does the job. In fact, we've used ours for some unusual tasks. All of the major outdoor emporiums now sell trail cameras. Prices have decreased to the point where many hunters now own several. These autonomous digital cameras are motion-activated with a built-in IR flash. They are typically strapped to a tree or fencepost and left to monitor game movement. Others use them for security purposes. Although invisible to a naked eye, a burst of movement-triggered IR light is brilliant through a night scope. The combination of both technologies results in a clandestine trip flare, visible at considerable distance.

One last thing: NV instruments are complex and should be handled with care. Dropping one will likely cause serious damage to the unit and your wallet!

CHAPTER 14

RANGE WORK AND TRAINING

It's about time to hit the range. But first, what about safety? Even a "lowly .22" can launch a bullet in excess of a mile. Distances easily double with most centerfire rifles, and regardless of the type, we'll need to observe an established set of safety protocols for the welfare of everyone. This topic is covered more thoroughly in *"Survival Guns: A Beginner's Guide."*

THE UNIVERSAL SAFETY RULES

Don't attempt to fire a shot until these five "Universal Firearms Safety Rules" can be recited by heart.

#1: Treat all firearms as if loaded! We don't care if the safety is on or not, whether the gun is unloaded or not. It doesn't matter if the action is open or closed. It's *ALWAYS* loaded, and should never sweep any part of you or anyone else!

#2: Don't allow the muzzle to sweep something you're unwilling to destroy! This rule *always* applies, whether in handling or in storage. On a range, vertical racks are useful. Stow your gun with its action open, and watch your head when you retrieve it. Further caution will be necessary when using a sling. If carried muzzle-up, it's easy to sweep others while bending forward, and a careless rearward dismount can produce the same effect. Horizontal vehicle racks will as well. Be aware of your muzzle at all times!

#3: Keep your finger off the trigger until ready to fire! Find an index point on the gun. Typically, the trigger finger will be extended forward, parallel with rifle. You can disengage a safety while committing to fire, but the trigger is off-limits until the gun is fully mounted. You can also bet that most "accidental" shootings are the result of a failure to follow this rule (as well as the others). The safety is never a substitute for sloppy muzzle discipline. YOU are the safety!

#4: Be sure of your target, and what is beyond it! If you shoot it, you own it, so an adequate backstop is essential. The entire down-range area should also be considered since an uncontained projectile can be lethal in excess of two miles. Bullets can also ricochet off water. We need to exercise situational awareness at all times.

#5: Check any type of gun upon handling it. Bolt-action guns are easy to inspect since their chambers are exposed when the action is opened. Auto-loaders, lever-actions, and pumps are often a different matter, so check them and then do it again. Proper gun etiquette dictates that a firearm should be passed to someone else unloaded and on "safe" with its action open. The recipient should immediately check it as well. One more thing: If you don't know how a gun works, leave it alone!

OTHER SAFETY CONCERNS

An extractor can sometimes slip off the rim of a loaded cartridge, leaving it lodged in the barrel. The floating firing pin on some semi-autos (like an AR-15) can cause a light primer indent. If the same live round is re-chambered a few times, it just might go off! Point the muzzle toward the backstop when going hot.

Squibs and bore obstructions: If you detect a mild report, stop shooting, unload, leave the action open, and check for an obstruction. You might have just experienced an under-powered "squib-load." It's also not a bad idea to check a barrel if a gun has been in storage for a while. If you take a fall, check for mud or dirt. The wrong carry in snow can cause the same problem. So can small branches.

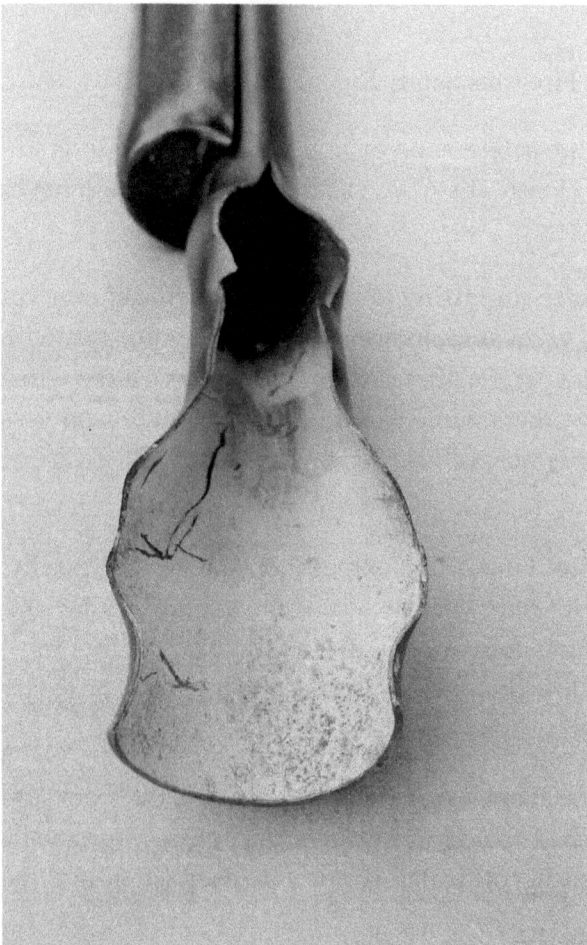

Results of a bore obstruction test. You're actually looking at two tests involving mud near the muzzle. It's ugly enough with relatively low-pressure shotgun shells!

Target hazards: Careless people shoot themselves from ricocheting projectiles every year. They bounce off tires, old TV screens, trees, or other make-shift targets. Commercial steel reactive targets are safe, but only if the manufacturer's cautions are followed. The hotter types, and magnum loads, may dent them. At that point such targets are unsafe with *any* projectile.

Common sense: It goes without saying that alcohol and drugs don't mix with firearms. Neither do unsupervised children or careless types. Unattended firearms are a huge problem that require responsible storage. Firearms safety and storage is covered in depth within the *"Survival Guns"* edition. Read it if you haven't.

Lead: The discharge of conventional ammunition involves some exposure to lead. It's not only the primary material used for projectiles, but is also used in many priming mixtures. We can minimize concerns by shooting in well-ventilated areas and washing up afterward. Perform any cleaning chores with similar precautions—away from your kitchen table!

Safety gear: Before firing a shot, track down a good set of shooting glasses and some hearing protection. Wear them anytime firearms are discharged in your proximity and make sure everyone else is properly equipped. Most centerfire rifles are loud enough to quickly cause permanent hearing damage without adequate protection. A ruptured case will expel hot particles, and ejected brass can injure an eye. We're dealing with hot brass, too. A piece inside a shirt can cause rapid reactions, so appropriate attire is essential. A hat with a visor will help prevent one from lodging behind your shooting glasses.

GETTING STARTED

I've tried to stick with a short list of useful basic shooting drills throughout this series of books. The centerfire rifle itinerary can pose challenges because of ammunition cost. This is one of the key reasons I'm always pushing an understudy .22. Using one with similar function, you can program yourself for proper big-bore techniques.

Hopefully, through the previous editions, you've already learned the fundamentals of marksmanship. You might even be programmed to run a gun while it remains mounted to your shoulder. You may also have learned how to shoot from various positions: field positions, improvised rests, sticks, and bipods. If not, we'll touch on these skills again. But first, we'll need to get comfortable with our rifle.

Some folks will be experienced shooters while others may be starting from scratch. Yet another class will fall somewhere in-between. Those versed in one firearm type (like shotguns) may lack knowledge about another. When setting up a scoped rifle where do we begin? Everything must be properly aligned and the rifle must be sighted in before any serious shooting can take place. Depending on the type of rifle, barrel cleaning could come into play. A new rifle with serious accuracy potential deserves some tender care right from the beginning. Many accuracy devotees ascribe to pet "break-in" techniques involving minimal initial shooting. More information is provided in the next *Accuracy and Distance* chapter. It's worth a look before live fire commences. In most cases, that will involve initial "sighting-in." A recent experience with an old friend and co-worker may help illustrate the process.

The sighting-in process — a two-step example: Don decided to get back into deer hunting after many years of absence. He bought a .30/06 Remington Model 700 ADL "package gun" that came with a 3x9 scope. This was a whole new frontier for a guy who grew up hunting in a red flannel coat with an iron-sighted .30/30. The pre-scoped Remington offered some promise of simplicity, which was only true to a point. An out-of-the-box setup is really a generic compromise that won't work for everyone. Those unaware of details like eye relief and focus will suffer as a result.

Don asked for some help in getting started, so we settled on a two-step process. Step #1 was a preliminary off-range session that involved personalized adjustments and bore-sighting. Although his scope was pre-mounted by the factory, the process is essentially the same for do-it-yourselfers. Step #2 involved actual sighting-in on a range.

The first step occurred at my house. It involved repositioning the scope in its rings for proper eye relief, individualized focus, and careful bore sighting. These chores are often easier at a workbench. We loosened the rings enough to permit scope movement, and then established Don's eye relief. He brought his hunting coat to ensure optimal field of view. With the crosshairs level and the scope rings retightened, we next worked on focus. It's a trial and error process that results in a sharply focused reticle and clear target. Instead of continuously staring through the scope, we used incremental trials to gain clarity. This helped prevent Don's eyes from acclimating to a marginal arrangement. Next we turned to bore-sighting. The rifle was located on a rest with its bolt removed. It was then aimed through a window at a white 8-inch steel plate hanging 100 yards away. By looking through the scope and bore, we determined it was fairly well bore-sighted by the factory. With the crosshairs centered on our target, the bore was pointing a half-plate right. Unscrewing the windage cap revealed ¼ MOA graduations. After moving it clockwise 16 clicks, the scope and bore were closely aligned on the target. We also carefully checked the rifle for any loose screws or obvious problems. None were noted, so we hoped for a smooth range experience.

As for the second step, that's how things worked out. Some initial loading and unloading practice preceded live fire, along with gun mounts and dry fire. Before long we could see the nuances of a scoped rifle come together. It took Don a while to find a comfortable position when firing from a bench. One concern was a bit of excess stock-crawling, with the potential for a "scope eyebrow." It's often better to proceed slowly and carefully than to jump in with both feet. The first shot was loaded singly and fired off a sandbag rest.

Live fire began at 25 yards. I felt certain we'd be able to record a bullet hole at this close distance. I'd also seen Donny in action during our agency's firearms training sessions, so I knew he was a competent shot. A 150-grain Remington Core-Lokt was discharged smoothly and touched the six-inch bullseye. We measured its proximity to the center, did some math, and applied the requisite clicks. The second shot moved accordingly, hitting just below the center. We picked up the rest and moved back to a 100-yard bench, shooting with a full magazine. A bit more fumbling was encountered during loading, but before long, Donny was more comfortable with his rifle. He was also soon properly zeroed, for a total expenditure of just eight rounds. By using a ruler, application of the necessary scope clicks made adjustments simple. Three things I learned were that Don could shoot, his rifle was a tack driver, and his scopes ¼ MOA clicks were actually around 1/5 MOA. A lesson Don learned was to think about eye relief. He has a new scab on his nose to serve as a reminder. It's a lot easier to crawl up a stock from a bench (or from prone).

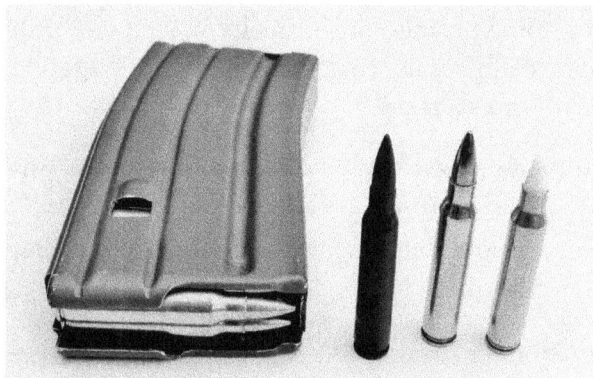

Dummy cartridges can be useful for a number of uses beyond function checks. Mixed in with live ammo, they afford good malfunction clearance practice. A solid aluminum A-Zoom is shown on the left.

Here are a few more takeaways: Loading and unloading were a bit foreign to Don. He needed lots of practice to perform these tasks competently—especially in low light. The M-700 ADL has a blind magazine, meaning it lacks a hinged floor plate. Unlatching the bottom to dump out live rounds is out, so they must be cycled through the action. Some people run them fully in the chamber and then extract them with the bolt, but there is a safer way to clear the rifle. After extracting the chambered round, the bolt can be nudged forward just far enough to free the next round from the magazine. Once it pops loose, it can be rolled out of the action. A bit of minor bolt manipulation will permit the process to be repeated until the rifle is unloaded. With newer Remingtons (and many other brands), the safety can remain engaged.

Like me, Don lives in a rural area. He can practice loading and unloading with live ammo right in his backyard. A safer option is the use of Snap Caps like well-built aluminum "A-Zooms." A few minutes of daily practice with an empty rifle will also result in a spot-on gun mount. Meanwhile, Don now understands the sighting-in process. He'll also be able to check his zero.

I would have thrown my .22 Remington Model 504 in the truck for an in-depth practice session, but there was no way my eye relief would've worked for Don. Food for thought: A .22 rimfire is a great training aid for all of us! Fortunately, in Don's case, things came together nicely. Based on experience with Remington Model 700s and Cor-Lokts, I wasn't too surprised. He'll be well-served by this rifle when chasing whitetail deer. There's no sense making things unnecessarily complicated when you don't need to!

PRACTICAL SHOOTING DRILLS

A rifle that will put three shots inside two inches will serve well enough for field practice. We're talking about basic use at reasonably close distances inside 200 yards. You can use the previous example to achieve a workable zero. When you're on the money at 100 yards, the rifle will be sighted in well enough for the upcoming "field position" section.

We'll stretch out the range later, but the basics come first. They involve a few unsupported positions like standing (off-hand); kneeling; sitting; and prone. Too many people rely on a shooting bench, and are ill-equipped for real world encounters. The result will be a wobbly rifle and an uncertain outcome. As hunters, we have a moral obligation to do better. As defenders of our loved ones, well-grounded skills are essential. Let's get comfortable with our rifle.

Pre-fire regimen: A few minutes of daily dry fire practice can really smooth things out. Just make sure you start with an empty rifle and a safe background. The "target" could be just about anything. Assuming you have a scope, it'll probably need to be far enough away for clear focus. Proportionally, it may resemble an 8-12" target at 100 yards.

Ready positions: Instead of mounting the rifle haphazardly, we should think about a starting point. Defensive is part of this equation, which involves both readiness and muzzle control. Two common ready positions are "high" and "low-ready." With either, the trigger finger must be outside the trigger guard until the stock makes shoulder contact. A safety should be "on" or a hammer should remain un-cocked. We can activate either during the actual mounting process.

High ready: The stock hovers around the bottom of the ribcage while the muzzle indexes on the target. A taught string extending from the shooter's strong-side eye to the target would contact the muzzle (or front sight). The business end of the gun isn't too high, nor is it too low. If done properly, the muzzle is a hinge, remaining on the same plane as the stock is moved smoothly to the shoulder and face.

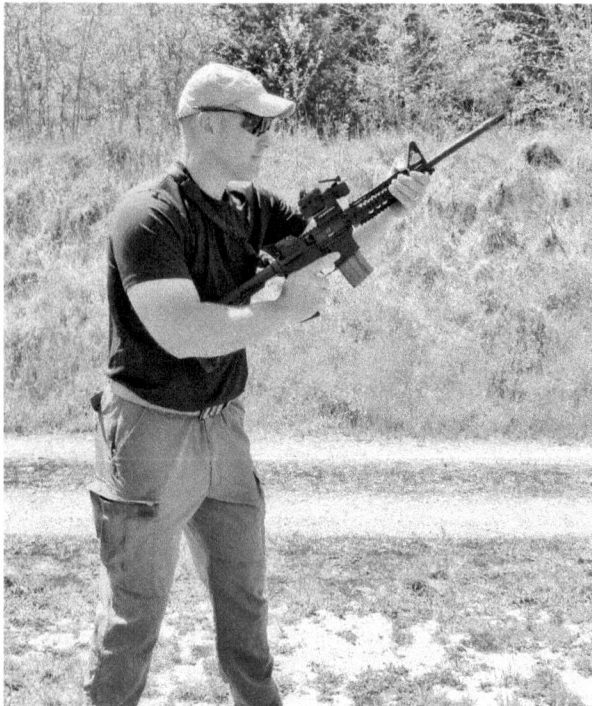

An effective universal "high ready." Note the location of the buttstock and muzzle.

A few negatives: The high ready is a poor choice for entering doorways, and it can be also tiring, but an unintentional discharge will send a shot above a target, instead of into it. The trigger finger can be lightly positioned against a safety button (or hammer) in preparation for a gun mount.

Low ready: This position is primarily defensive. The stock is on your shoulder and the muzzle is depressed. The degree of depression will depend upon the situation and proximity of threats. You don't want your muzzle to sweep your feet! The toe of the stock acts like a hinge against the shoulder, so this position needs to be maintained for effective engagement. Again, the trigger finger is

outside the trigger guard. It's a better position for addressing entrances, so the low ready is better in serious social situations.

Either position has advantages, depending on the situation. Don't discount the advantages of an effective ready position. Also, don't forget trigger finger discipline! If all practice commences from the ready, this vital step will be reinforced.

<u>Marksmanship:</u> Your mission is to work on the fundamentals: stance, grip, breath, sight (or crosshair) alignment, and trigger control. Develop the gun mount from a ready position. As long as the sights or crosshairs are wandering within the borders of your target, keep applying trigger pressure. Sooner or later the rifle will fire. Pay attention and you'll be able to note exactly where the crosshairs were at that moment. This is known as "calling your shot" and dry fire is a great way to learn it! Some rifles, such as Marlin

The "low ready" is another universal shoulder-fired position, geared for defense. The toe of the stock acts like a hinge on the shooter's shoulder. The muzzle can be lower in tighter quarters.

lever-actions, can be damaged by prolonged dry-firing, but Snap Caps will solve that problem. Off-hand is a good position for this practice regimen. Since higher scope magnifications really amplify the wiggles, go with a lower setting. At first, the tremors will seem imposing, but your confidence should grow. The gun handling aspect is also valuable, which leads us to…

Operation: Run the rifle on your shoulder! As dry fire confidence grows, don't dismount between shots. With a bolt-action, lever gun, or pump, immediately cycle the action and remain on target for 2-3 seconds. This will program you for fast follow-up shots. Skip it and you'll ingrain a bad habit that just wastes precious time. We can scan for other targets or threats after returning to a ready position.

As for simulated follow-through, semi-autos can be trickier. The action won't cycle, but you should still be able to manually cock it with the rifle on your shoulder. While you're at it, hold the trigger rearward after the shot breaks. When the action goes back into battery, ease the trigger forward until you feel the sear reset. Pause at that point and don't let go. You're ready to squeeze off another shot. In systems like an AR, the reset is quite pronounced. This skill will greatly improve overall control during fast-paced shooting. The dry fire semi-auto regimen won't work with a magazine seated. Why? Well, with most types, the bolt will lock back on an empty follower. Make a real effort to practice the reset during the live fire drills.

This balanced offhand position is well-suited for a fast response. It will support quick follow-up shots while controlling recoil.

Field position live fire drills: A logical progression of techniques is helpful. Besides marksmanship, we should think about the actual operation of the action, and access to spare ammunition or magazines. Problems can arise which won't be evident if you only shoot from off-hand. A pump-action rifle can provide lightning-fast shots. Sure, an auto-loading rifle easily solves this problem, but you may need a quick reload. If you're lying on top of those spare magazine, well, good luck.

The following itinerary could be called practice, but it should really be viewed as a training regimen. By incorporating the pre-fire operational skills, you can kill multiple birds with one stone. Let's add another to the mix: reloading. Think about where you'll be carrying spare ammo or magazines. The latter can be fed from a pouch. Others may be reloading individual rounds. Remember this: You'll need to get at it from any position.

Offhand: As always, begin from a ready position. A few initial dry fire shots are recommended. The dry fire and first live fire stage can commence from 25 yards. Instead of a bullseye you might want to staple a paper plate to a brown cardboard backer for contrast (IPSC targets work well). Experienced shooters may sneer at such "close range," but it's a good confidence builder. In fact, there's nothing wrong with starting even closer. For safety's sake, it's not a bad idea to start with just one round. As familiarity improves, progress to full capacity, but don't neglect the unloading aspect. *Cease fire with at least two remaining rounds, and then focus on safe unloading procedures.* Whenever possible, apply the safety first! Detachable magazines should be removed prior to clearing the chamber. Check your rifle carefully afterward, and then do it again! The action should remain open while advancing to subsequent stages. Unsupported shooting is hard, so don't bite off more than you can chew. You can back out further as your confidence grows. The next stop can be 50 yards. Sooner or later, head back to the 100-yard line.

Sitting: Although prone offers excellent stability,

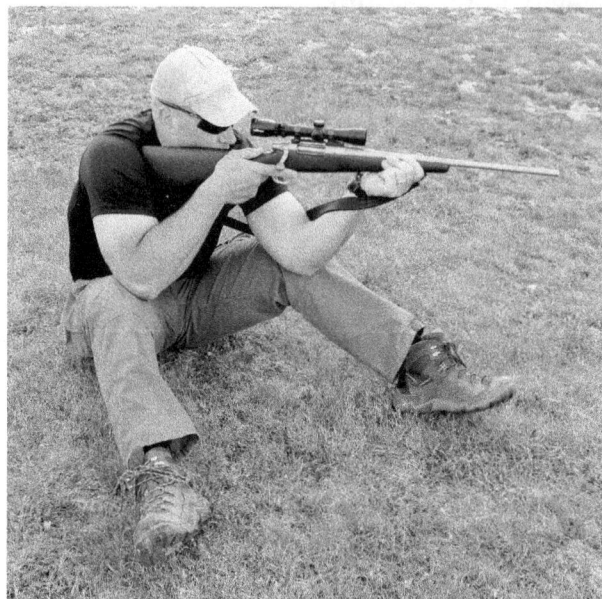

A classic sitting position. Note the elbow locations.

One of several kneeling techniques, dictated by individual flexibility and preference.

it won't always work due to brush or terrain. A crossed-leg sitting position can provide stabilizing elbow contact points, just ahead of the knees. Avoid joint-to-joint contact to minimize wobbles and get as comfortable as you can. A few dry fire shots should iron out problems while checking for safe eye relief. Again, a simple paper plate makes a nice 50-yard starting point. Maintain a conscious effort to run the rifle from your shoulder, and note any action-induced issues. This is often where an "uh oh" moment happens while reloading, too. Surprise! Those side trouser pockets are now inaccessible.

Kneeling: There are a few variations of this position. A couple speed versions involve dropping to one or both knees, as dictated by urgency and cover limitations. Either is fairly fast, and you will gain more height than sitting. Competition shooters will place their strong-side knee on the ground, and then sit back on their trailing leg. The support-side leg will be up for use as an elbow brace. Dry fire is strongly advised while practicing these positions. It'll let you know what works for you, as well

A solid prone position, enhanced by the use of a sling.

as what doesn't. The latter version is particularly stable but less mobile. During live fire, continue to operate the rifle on your shoulder. The same 50-yard target is a good beginning. You can load and unload from kneeling as long as your balance isn't jeopardized.

Prone: Although this position is extremely stabile, it can pose new loading and operational revelations. The 50-yard line makes a good starting point, but don't load until you're in prone. It is also a good time to check for potential scope-eyebrow problems. After consistent 5-shot groups occur, you can back out further, but unload first. It'll be a lot safer if you return to standing with an empty rifle. You can then hike back another 50 yards and repeat this stage. The same paper plate is fine at 100 yards for the time being. A commercial steel plate or gong is better, as long as the recommended minimum distance is maintained (often 100 yards). You can paint it and touch up your splats with spray paint. Hits will be announced by audible impacts and, with the right terrain behind it, any misses can be seen as puffs of dirt. You'll no doubt have some, but they'll help you learn where to hold.

Don't forget to run the action on your shoulder. It'll be much trickier from prone, especially with pumps and lever-actions. Also, think about spare ammo access. If it can't be reached, you'll need a better system. You might even discover that it's missing. Prone is the spot where we often see shooters futilely searching for gear. Pouches and holsters with retention capabilities are strongly recommended. Laying out gear and spare ammo is defensively bad since any unanticipated movement can cause its loss.

Points to ponder: Note the absence of a round count. More experienced shooters may wish to try only a few shots from *some* of the above positions. Nearly everyone could benefit from more, but too much centerfire shooting in a single session can be counterproductive. Recoil and muzzle blast contribute to flinching. Fouling and heat aren't good either—especially with a new barrel. You can break your range time into daily blocks, cleaning between sessions. Throughout this process you'll begin to get a handle on your ability and limits. Experience and proficiency won't happen overnight, so don't beat yourself up over misses. You can always shorten the distance and, by all means, go back to a rimfire or airgun! Either provides a great way to improve your shooting without much cost. In fact, those with a decent air rifle could refine their skills inside a basement or garage. Just scale down the targets accordingly. A ten yard 0.8" target is the equivalent of a 100-yard eight-inch plate. The downside is that most airguns are single-shots. They need to be dismounted for reloading, which can quickly become a habit. The cure is to consciously work on operating your centerfire with it mounted to your shoulder. It's one reason why that similar rimfire makes so much sense!

A goal: Strive for reliable hits on that 8-inch target from 100 yards. Not everyone will be able to use all four positions, but those who can should. Off-hand is the benchmark. At that point you'll be ahead of many self-professed outdoorsmen. You'll also be ready for more...

More skills: By now your confidence is probably increasing. The actual operation of your rifle is likely second nature—during controlled conditions. All bets are off under stressful circumstances and, as we turn up the heat, unexpected problems may arise. "Buck Fever" is a classic example, manifested through marginal skills.

Multiple targets: These can be combined with *quick* repeat shots. Distances can be relatively short, and targets can be generous. Beginning from "the ready," two fast 20-yard shots on a pair of 8-inch plates make a good starting point. Thanks to disciplined practice, you should be programmed for shouldered operation, so don't dismount! As everything comes together, you can increase the range. A friendly competition won't hurt either. This drill can be applied to various positions. Semi-auto shooters should also work on sear reset, which will greatly improve accuracy. As the tempo increases, you can add more targets. Better yet, use a shot timer that will record initial and follow-up shots in hundredths of a second. Expect some function glitches as the pressure increases. That's exactly the point; our manual dexterity degrades under stress, so practice is essential.

A shot timer is a great training aid. After emitting a start tone, this one recorded a 2.14 second interval to the first shot. Any subsequent shots can also be reviewed.

Flinch check: Throwing speed into the mix can add adrenaline. While this is actually a good thing, an unwanted by-product is flinching; an involuntary reaction to noise and recoil, exacerbated by stress. The effect is muzzle dip and resulting low hits. A flinch is easy to develop and hard to cure. Trigger control should be the same whether the rifle is empty or loaded, but recoil will obscure a flinch, making it hard to detect. On the other hand, an anticipated live shot that results in a click will be painfully obvious. An assistant can provide some humility by use of dummy rounds. Have him or her load the rifle while mixing a few into the magazine. The shooter's objective is to pretend the rifle is unloaded during trigger squeeze, whether it is or isn't. This is easier said than done. In fact, the majority of shooters from all walks of life seem to have an ingrained flinch. It's often not obvious either. The "ball & dummy drill" is a great cure for flinching. It can be supported by more dry-firing and, again, a nearly recoilless rimfire really helps. To exact revenge and cure inevitable laughter, switch roles! There's a good chance your "experienced" partner's muzzle will dip.

Reloading skills: it's always a good idea to maintain a state of readiness. That's hard to do with an empty rifle! There are occasions when the loudest sound in the world is a "click" - especially during a fight. The exact reloading process will be dictated by the firearm type, but the idea is to get it done quickly. Some systems like lever guns are conducive to sustained loading techniques. The concept involves inserting new rounds prior to running out. While the first priority is to maintain defensiveness, there may be breaks where top-offs are possible. Detachable magazine systems like an AR-15 will require rapid exchanges, best accomplished with the support hand. In all cases, spare ammo should be accessible from consistent locations. Reloading skills can often be practiced by shooting two pairs of shots, with a reload in between each. This drill saves ammo while refining technique. You'll probably try it from off-hand, but think about other positions. We call the whole concept "ammo management" for good reasons. It gets even more interesting after dark. In fact, so does unloading. That's why it was part of the previous practice.

Ambidextrous operation: A skilled tactical shooter should be able to engage threats in any light, from any position, using either hand (or shoulder). Beyond a wounded extremity, a shoulder-fired weapon poses other challenges. An injury to the dominant eye could result from bullet or hard-cover fragments (which might even be from your shots). The need for single-handed operation could arise when fending off a threat or dragging a wounded ally. True ambidextrous proficiency also extends to clearing malfunctions and reloading skills. These advanced skills require professional training, but we can keep things simple by skipping the tactical aspects. I've shot a few deer off my left shoulder in close situations where I just couldn't get turned around. You can try this on a range, proceeding with caution. Control will be diminished and recoil will seem greater, so dry fire practice is essential before going hot. Live fire should commence with only one round. You might as well try loading it from the reversed position, which will be educational. A singly loaded shot is a whole lot safer with any firearm, and more so with a self-loading rifle. Once again, a rimfire is a great tool for the initial attempts. Besides attention to control, take sure to switch eyes as well as shoulders. We've seen some overly-excited ninjas who could have sustained recoil induced eye injuries from head contortions. Beyond accuracy, the actual operation will pose challenges. Bolt-action shooters will get a quick reality check, but hot brass can cause excitement with many systems. Lever gun shooters will probably maintain a smug demeanor—until they try it from prone. Again, professional training is strongly advised, especially for advanced drills.

Supported shooting: Stability is essential for consistent accuracy, but curved ground, brush, or deep snow can put the kibosh on prone. It's worth thinking about a full list of practical options from which to choose. Here's the menu:

- Unsupported: Fast and often necessary, especially from off-hand; at the expense of best accuracy.

- Sling: Provides a noticeable improvement, especially from prone or solid sitting and kneeling positions. The operative word here is "solid" (if I get in a solid kneeling position call 911).

- Improvised rest: Think about a tree, fencepost, or other solid object. When used properly, a rifle can become *much* steadier.

- Shooting sticks: A portable alternative to a tree, permitting sufficient height for clearance of brush and terrain.

- Bipod from prone: A huge improvement, approaching but not quite equaling benchrest results.

- Benchrest: Wrings out the maximum accuracy potential of a rifle.

Think about what you want to lug around. Since unsupported shooting (particularly offhand) is challenging, we can improve the odds.

Sling use: There are several types designed to draw a rifle more securely into the shooter. Isometric tension and proper sling adjustments do the job. The simplest are carry straps, adjusted so the shooter's support arm can be slipped through. A half-wrap then follows. It's about as far as I normally take the whole sling concept, although I could certainly do better. Still, a sling is an indispensable carry mode which can serve double-duty. It's worth practicing with one, especially from different positions. You should see more stability, and you may also be able to resolve any unexpected issues related to an action type (a pump gun can get interesting after the first shot, even from off-hand). When playing with a sling, don't ignore a carry dismount. Muzzle management plays a key part, since it's all too easy to sweep others.

Improvised rests: Since we won't be toting a tree, we'll need to look for one; or some similar object that can help brace our body. Here in New England, nature makes 'em every day, so more often than not, a tree is close enough to use on the fly. Contact with the support hand greatly reduces the wobble quotient, although the strong elbow will still be afloat. A sling helps, but some other object like a big rock is even better. If it's large enough to crawl onto, a prone-like position may be possible. I'll do whatever it takes to brace my support hand and shooting elbow. Further body contact is icing on the cake. Just be aware that contortions can result in a serious case of scope eyebrow. A hat between the support hand and object can provide cushioning, and will protect a stock during recoil. A fencepost will work, but don't rest a rifle directly on any hard surface. A pack is great. On a range there will often be structures to practice from. A pole will work as well as a tree. Out on the Great Plains, it may make more sense to grab a set of shooting sticks…

Shooting sticks provide a portable all-terrain solution.

A tripod is better, but mobility can be a factor. You wouldn't want to lug this gear too far.

An improvised rest. Note the forward hand position. The shooter's hand is between the forend and hard surface.

Shooting sticks: With proper technique, they'll greatly improve field accuracy. One problem with sticks is lugging them around. I'll always keep a set, but they don't see much regular use. Now and then though, they're the perfect solution. Mine has two telescoping legs with ample adjustments for sitting or standing shots. More often than not, they see use in pre-scouted locations. I usually preset them for off-hand height and just spread the legs against a limiting-strap. The gun rest portion is then positioned near the forend tip so my support hand can encircle both. At that point I can draw everything rearward until stability is achieved. Like a tree, the shooting elbow remains afloat, so tucking it downward helps. One surprise you may encounter involves quick follow-up shots. Operating the action may cause your setup to unravel, providing another great excuse to head for the range. I sometimes practice from sticks with an accurate air rifle, shooting at small metal spinners. It's a great confidence builder and lots of fun!

Bipods: These rifle-mounted, two-legged folding rests will take your shooting to a whole new level.

A bipod affords great stability in terrain that will permit its use. Note the stabilizing effects provided by wide-spread feet and a low center-of-gravity.

The rifle on the left may not look like an airgun, but it is. At 40-50 yards, paintballs set on golf tees provide challenging backyard practice.

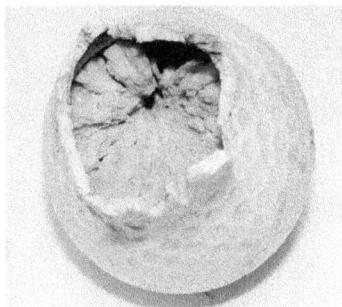
Extreme golf, .308-style from 100 yards. Don't try this with airgun projectiles, which can bounce back!

Still, it's best to master the basics prior to falling in love. Lugging a bipod-equipped rifle can also turn into misery. Besides extra weight, the rifle's center of gravity will change. During sling carry the brackets will dig into a shoulder blade, so my bipod often stays behind. There are other times when you just can't beat having one. Some people tuck a bipod in a pack for a QD hook-up. While this sounds good in principle, it takes practice. For starters, the bipod mounts to the same stud that secures the sling. Switching things around requires plenty of fiddling at best. Some forends are equipped with an extra stud, which certainly helps, but the hookup still takes time. After jumping through these hoops, you may be stymied by terrain. A small intervening rise is all it takes to kill the bipod option. Many of these problems can be sorted out on a range. The 100-yard line is a good place to start. Done right, a bipod from prone is amazingly steady. The butt may float around a bit, but it can often be stabilized using the support hand. Loading a bit of forward pressure into the legs also helps. Your eye relief will probably change, but practice can sort through that. Shoot carefully to note if any zero shift occurs from the bipod. Hard or soft surfaces can play a role, and we've seen slight shifts, even with one folded up. It takes a while to learn the ins and outs of bipod shooting. As experience grows, you may find it easier to match both leg extensions when standing. Don't forget, you might be able to hook one on a rimfire rifle. My British pre-charged air rifle has sling swivel studs just for this reason. Paintballs on golf tees make nifty 40-50 yard targets. They translate well to real golf balls out beyond 100 yards.

Adapt and overcome: While much bipod use is geared toward bolt-action and AR designs, a stabile platform can be acquired with other firearms. You'll just need to adapt and overcome. With the possible exception of Browning's BLR, two systems that are difficult to shoot from prone include pump guns and lever-actions. Neither is really compatible with bipods, and some gyrations are still necessary for reliable operation. It's no big deal as long as you're willing to adjust to their limitations. You can substitute a pack for a bipod or use your shooting sticks from sitting. With a pump .308, shots out to 300 yards should be doable. That's still a pretty good poke east of the Mississippi.

If you've suffered through all or even part of these live fire drills, your comfort level should be sound. You may be ready to seek new long-range shooting horizons. If so, great, but your accuracy requirements may need attention first.

CHAPTER 15

ACCURACY AND DISTANCE

So far our focus has been relatively close-range shooting, geared toward deer-sized targets. Back to Don and his stalwart Model 700's out-of-the-box accuracy, other people may not be so fortunate. They may also use several loads, depending on their requirements. If Don lucks out and draws a moose tag, he might want a tougher bullet. Different loads will often shoot to different spots, even if they show great accuracy. The way to figure this out involves some serious testing. You might want to read the *Rimfire* book since it pertains to this phase.

REFINING ACCURACY

We'll need to discover at least one good load, but how do we know when accuracy is "good?" The following table is just a rough guideline based on personal experience. Believe me, there are some rifles that can do much better. Unfortunately, the reverse is also true. Some loads may be incompatible with certain rifling twists. Slower rates work best with lighter bullets, and fast twists help stabilize heavy (or longer) ones. Wild groups or keyhole impacts indicate something has gone awry and the fix may be as simple as a bullet change. As an example, a 1x14 .223 barrel would work best with bullets of 55 grains or less. It will probably perform poorly with 70 grain projectiles, which need a faster twist like a 1x7. This assumes the scope and stock are properly secured to the action. If so, here are some expectations:

Accuracy expectations with centerfire rifles				Average groups	
Rifle	range	Rds per group	Groups per load	Good	Great
AK & SKS	100 yards	3 rounds	5 each (15 rds)	3.50"	2.50"
AR-15 standard 5.56	100 yards	5 rounds	5 each (25 rds)	1.50"	1.00"
AR-15 Varmint .223	100 yards	5 rounds	5 each (25 rds)	1.00"	0.60"
Lever-action .30/30	100 yards	3 rounds	5 each (15 rds)	3.00"	2.00"
Bolt-action sporter	100 yards	3 rounds	5 each (15 rds)	1.50"	1.00"
Bolt-action heavy bbl	100 yards	5 rounds	5 each (25 rds)	1.00"	0.50"
Groups from sandbag rests, fired carefully in calm conditions.					

Eliminating the human quotient: Since we all have built-in tremors, assessment of true accuracy is dependent on minimizing this effect. Leaning over a vehicle's hood just won't cut it for more than a casual zero check. Some experienced shooters can come close to benchrest-grade accuracy from prone off a bipod using a rear sandbag for additional support. This skill takes time to acquire, so a stable and purpose-built shooting bench is a much better arrangement. It can be used to support a forward rest of some sort, as well as a rear bag. The two contact points are typically a set of contoured sandbags that impart form-fitting stability. The front bag is often mounted to a low tripod, permitting adjustments for optimum positioning. It will cradle the forend with the rear bag located to support the toe of the stock. Once properly set up, the shooter can climb into a seat at the bench and impart minimal influence. A rock-solid, permanent bench is best, but lacking access to one, the portable units listed in the Accessories Chapter will work.

A solid benchrest, combined with the right technique, is essential for accuracy assessment. This heavy, portable arrangement is 60 miles from the nearest pavement.

Targets: The design is best matched up to what we're shooting. For an iron-sighted rifle, believe it or not, there are times when I may just use a large white cardboard IPSC target which, excluding the head, measures 24x18 inches. At 50-yards, I may apply a heavy black "X" with a marking pen and hold below its juncture. Back at 100 yards, which is a good sight-in distance for plain irons or peeps, it can be easier to skip any sort of precise aiming mark. We need to focus on a clear front sight and that can fade out while trying to resolve small marks. The result can be second-guessing during alignment; so it's often simpler—especially with older eyes—to aim for the plain white chest area. This technique may not seem very precise, but I've fired a bunch of sub 2-inch, 5-shot groups this way at 100 yards. I often use this trick with a large fiber optic front sight, which can cover considerable aiming area.

Low-powered scopes like 2.5X types work well with paper plates. It's easy to bisect the white circle, which can be stapled to a brown background. Since two-tone cardboard IPSC targets have white and brown surfaces, they're handy for many uses. In this case, the brown side becomes a target backer with contrast, which can capture errant shots. Peep sight systems with smaller beads will also work this way. The aperture helps increase depth-of-field, increasing resolution.

There's no denying the effectiveness of this 100-yard 12 Ga. rifled slug group.

General purpose 2x7 or 3x9 hunting scopes work with bullseyes, my favorite being the adhesive Birchwood Casey "Shoot-N-C" types, around 6-inches in diameter. Once again, an IPSC target has value, this time serving as a white-sided backer. It'll accommodate several bullseyes, which will display highly visible yellow borders

The white surface of this IPSC Target displays 75-yard groups shot while sighting in a muzzle-loading rifle.

A white paper plate on a darker-colored background can provide good contrast with coarser crosshairs or iron sights. This 100-yard group was fired with a heavy-duplex 2.5 X Scope.

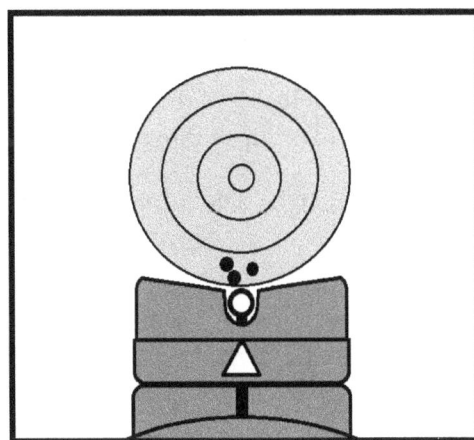

When using bullseyes with iron sights, a 6:00 hold lends more precision. Adjust the rear sight in the same direction you want bullet strikes to move.

Thanks to a "Shoot-N-C" target, tiny .17 HMR holes were clearly visible through a Burris 3x9 Timberline scope from 110 yards.

WIN 1885 .223 AFTER RE·BED 40 TAP

Squares can work well for precision shooting with higher-magnification scopes. The "F-1" hole is the first fouling shot from the 100-yard series.

when shot. If zeroed around two inches high at one hundred yards, many loads will be on the money out at twice that range. Using a six-inch bull, you can adjust a scope until groups develop around 2/3 of the way above its center. A black marking pen can be used to cover up yellow edges of the holes, permitting the use of the same target for up to three groups.

With higher-magnification scopes, I like bold black 1 ½" squares, drawn on a white backer. Again, the trusty IPSC target works well. I use a cardboard template and draw them with a marking pen. It's easy to space out nine squares in three vertical rows. Even .17-caliber holes should be visible through a decent scope of 9X or greater. With many fast loads, a group that forms just above the square should result in a 200-yard zero.

Zero: The ballistic-reticle scopes are often designed for a 100 or 200-yard zero. Target-turret scopes are frequently sighted in at 100 yards, using come-ups for further distances. In that case, center your groups at 100 yards using the techniques described above. For those using scopes with conventional reticles in cartridges like a .308 or .30/06, a 200-yard zero is a serviceable compromise. Your best bet is to confirm this by actually

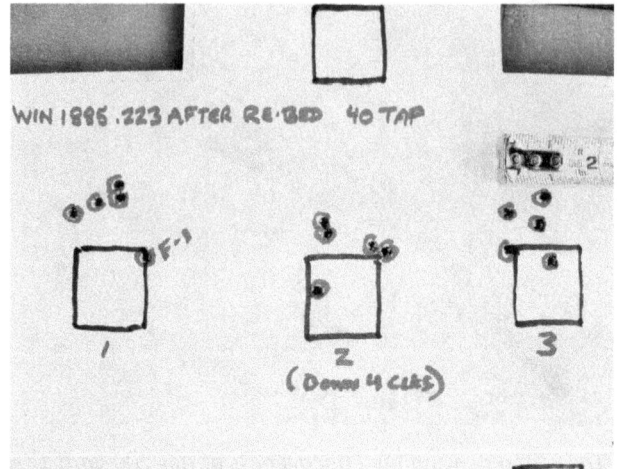

Power-Point
Assures quick and massive knock-down

Strategic Notching
Provides consistent and reliable expansion

Contoured Jacket
Maximum expansion performance

Alloyed Lead Core
Increases retained weight for deeper penetration

BALLISTICS TABLE						
	Muzzle	100 YDS	200 YDS	300 YDS	400 YDS	500 YDS
Velocity	2960	2697	2449	2215	1993	1786
Trajectory	–	1.9	0	-7.8	-22.6	-46.3
Energy	1945	1615	1332	1089	882	708

The chart on this box of 100-grain Winchester .243 ammo illustrates the value of a 200-yard zero. Since barrel length will affect velocity, confirm this on a range.

firing at that distance in calm conditions. Establish final zero in temperature and altitude representative of field conditions.

With many high powered rifle loads, a 200-yard zero should be somewhere around 7-9 inches low at 300 yards. Those in wide-open spaces sometimes opt for a "Western Zero," which involves sighting in for 250-300 yards. Although this approach helps minimize holdover concerns, 100-yard shots will strike around 3-inches high. In the woods, this increased deviation can cause a deflection from a branch. In that case, all bets are off, including strikes from purported "brush-busting" loads with big round nosed bullets. In my experience, the KISS principle is advisable when things get exciting. It's all too easy to forget about extra allowance.

Heat: Barrel heating can be a major impediment to accuracy testing. It can cause barrels to wander. Thinner barrels are more susceptible, which is why most sporter groups are only three rounds. Direct sunlight also plays a role. My ideal test conditions will involve temperatures in the low 50s with a light overcast and no wind. Plenty of time is allowed for cooling between each series. High-volume shooting is also hard on barrel steel.

Barrel break-in and fouling: Some folks are fanatical about barrel break-in procedures. When starting with a new rifle they may fire only one shot and then clean their bore. At some point after 5-20 singles, they may increase to pairs of shots. Several pet techniques exist, and some premium barrel-makers will recommend a version of this process. Others may tell you to skip it. I've always wondered how many bores or crowns were damaged during the break-in process by zealous devotes. A protocol that makes sense to me comes from a premium barrel maker with which we have experience. Bartlein Barrels recommends a process that is simpler than some. They just fire a couple shots, cleaning after each, to look for copper fouling. If little or none is evident, a five round group comes next, followed by another cleaning. If accuracy is good and cleaning is easy, the process is complete. If not, a gradual progression is employed, cleaning between groups of 3-5 shots while looking for telltale fouling. The barrel governs the break-in procedures since, even with good accuracy, some can clean harder than others. Fouling typically extends from the throat area so attention should be paid to that area. Using copper solvents, it will be evident on patches as greenish deposits. Sometimes it takes a while for a bore to smooth out, but in general, a properly cared for barrel will become easier to clean over time.

I trend toward a fairly simple routine, depending on the firearm. When baptizing a potentially accurate rifle like a heavy-barreled bolt-gun, I'll give the bore a thorough cleaning and check it for loose screws. The first range session probably won't exceed eight shots, and could be as few as five. Depending on copper residue, the second session probably won't exceed ten rounds, but could be less. I'll avoid exceeding 18-20 rounds between future cleaning sessions. I also prefer to test only one load between each cleaning. It sometimes takes a few fouling shots before a new one settles down. This can also happen from a spotless barrel during the first (or sometimes few) "cold-bore" fouling shots.

With more utilitarian rifles, the standards will be lessened. We won't be busting aspirin tablets with a pump or lever gun. Instead of sub-MOA accuracy, we should be happy with 1 ½ - 2-inch 100-yard groups. Still, it's worth thinking about the variables. As a general rule of thumb, the appearance of copper fouling can dictate cleaning frequency.

Testing protocols: As for serious accuracy testing, I'll commence at 100 yards, zeroed and set up as described above.

Precision rifles: When shooting tack driver class rifles like .223 heavy-barreled varminters, each group will consist of 5 shots. With a series of aiming points laid out, I start on the upper left, numbering each square. The first round or two may (or may not) print a bit out of the main group. I like to write an "F-1" or "F-2" by those to indicate fouling shots. You'll sometimes see this phenomena disappear as shooting progresses. With such a rifle, I'll assess results from five groups totaling 25 shots. The targets can be saved or digitally photographed for future reference. This amount of shooting exceeds my normal 18-round limit, but it also may not happen in just one session. Depending on how easily a bore cleans up, I may quit after 3-4 groups, or I may push things a bit further. There's also a very good chance the whole series will be repeated on another day. It's a time consuming process, but one that will yield useful data. Ideally, you'll see consistent groups that don't shift from one range session to the next, during similar conditions. Results will be far more reliable than firing a couple 3-shot groups, which I call "feel good" testing. Keep going and reality will probably reveal its ugly head through fliers. It's a real mind-bender to fire the fifth shot in group with four close holes — especially during the fifth series! Relax, re-breath, squeeze, and think happy thoughts…

Sporters: Three-shot groups are a common standard for many hunting rifles. The overall protocol remains the same, with a couple possible changes. With light rifles I may place a folded towel on the front bag. This acts as a recoil cushion similar to the support hand when afield. It'll also protect the forend of a rifle that jumps during recoil. Some light sporters may shoot more accurately if the forend is controlled by the support hand.

200-yard groups? Well, it depends on what you have. I'd skip it with an iron-sighted .30/30 lever-action (a 100-yard zero makes more sense). On the other hand, a scoped Marlin with Hornady's new Flex-Tip load is at least worth a try. A bolt-action chambered for a .243, .270, .30/06, .308, etc. will shine with a 200-yard zero. Although a 100-yard group around 1 ½ -2-inch high (approximately) should provide that, you may note a discrepancy. The error could be due to elevation, windage, scope height, or other factors. Moving back to 200 yards is the best way to find out. Just remember that your scope's click values will be double their 100-yard movements. Wind can also be a factor, so wait for calm conditions.

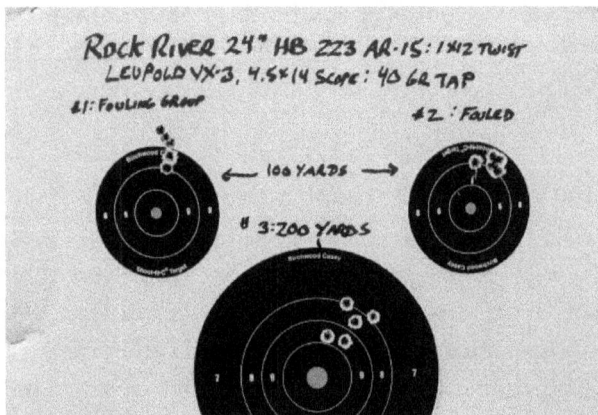

Bolt-gun class accuracy from an AR-15 is evident with these consistent groups. The first one shows possible effects of fouling. The 200-yard series reveals the need for a zero tweak.

Consistency: Group sizes are measured center-to-center from the furthest shots. Ample time is allowed between each series for barrel cooling. I'll often reach forward to feel the barrel just ahead of its chamber. Although far from exact, it does provide some indication of what's happening. During sunlit conditions, I'll look for a shady spot in which to place the rifle between groups. Ideally, testing will occur in overcast skies, during still air. This often translates to an evening period with adequate light. Since ambient temperature can affect load pressure, disparities between test and field use conditions can cause problems. These may be as simple as group shifts; or more serious issues revealed through sticky bolt lift—a sign of excessive pressure. The culprit might just be hot weather.

A really good rifle is often evident right from the get-go, offering few surprises. Sure, you may hit upon an incompatible load, but a winner should be quickly evident. Such jewels are possibly more common nowadays thanks to manufacturing precision, but most rifles fall somewhere in between. Once in a while you can encounter one that's downright irritating. It will typically throw fliers from an otherwise encouraging group. It's true that overall accuracy can improve within the first hundred or so shots, but erratic performers won't normally shoot their way out of miscreant behavior. The temptation of some will be to disregard errant shots. Everyone can blow a shot, but a competent shooter should be able to "call" a poor one. This becomes possible through a proper testing arrangement; in conjunction with full awareness of the crosshairs, before and *during* the shot. Proper breathing and trigger control are essential, as is follow-through.

Persistent fliers: If the trend of fliers continues, something is probably amiss. The cure might be as simple as switching to a different load. Some barrels are especially susceptible to barrel heating effects, so cooling time may help. If these options are exhausted, I'd cease fire, pack up, and give the problem child a thorough examination under lower blood pressure. Things worth checking are scope bell and barrel contact, loose mounts, stock screws, or uneven barrel channel clearance. A clean barrel free of copper fouling is important, and so is a non-damaged muzzle (crown). I'll often give a rifle a moderate "karate chop" with the heel of a hand, in hopes of detecting some rattle or looseness. A decent scope is reassuring, whereas a cheapo-type just throws another wild card in the mix (although anything is possible). I once did battle with an ultra-lightweight rifle in a hard-kicking caliber. As it turned out, the rifle was fine and so was the scope, which gradually crept forward in recoil. The movement, although nearly undetectable, was sufficient to cause small zero changes. A poor action and stock fit is another culprit. A popular solution involves glass bedding (also known as rifle bedding), whereby a thin epoxy layer is applied between the stock and action. When done properly, the result will be a form-fitting connection that eliminates accuracy-robbing shifts. Most shooters would be better off paying a qualified gunsmith to perform this process, which beats the alternative of a permanently bonded stock and action!

Playing the odds: Although no rifle is exempt from problems, a well-respected brand can tip the odds toward success. Remember the sighting-in example with my friend, Don? His stainless/synthetic Remington Model 700 ADL "package gun" cost around $500, excluding two boxes of .30/06 Remington 150-grain Cor-Lokt ammo. As it turned out, this combination drilled 3-shot groups of around 3/4 MOA right from the start. That's not too shabby by any standard! I was expecting results more on the order of 1.25 MOA, but then again, M-700s are known as accurate rifles.

Moving on: Assuming your sanity remained intact during the testing process, a usefully accurate

Shooters in action on a steel silhouette course with targets placed from 100-400 yards. Their Aimpoint dot sights are up to the task.

rifle should be on hand. In that case, why not explore its capabilities? Shooting beyond 200 yards is fun, but two huge factors will be trajectory and wind. We can overcome the former with reasonably flat-shooting cartridges, ballistic aiming systems and rangefinders. On the other hand, learning how to effectively dope wind is a fine art. You won't learn it if you don't stretch out the range.

INTERMEDIATE-RANGE SHOOTING

What exactly is that? Well, it depends on what you're shooting. For our purposes, let's define intermediate range as a distance beyond normal sight-in, but less than "long range." Using a .30/30, it might be 150 yards. We want some assurance of a hit, so even with a hotter caliber like a .30/06, three-hundred yards is a fair poke for average hunters; however, many western hunters shoot antelope out to a quarter-mile, or beyond. Their choice of rifles, calibers, and optics makes this possible. In fact, due to recent technological advances in rifles, optics, and ammunition, this distance is less of a challenge. Assuming we're shooting a more common scoped hunting-type rifle in a caliber like .308, let's define "intermediate range" as inside 450 yards. Particularly as we stretch out the distance, stability becomes essential. A well-developed prone position will serve as a great foundation—especially with a bipod. Sometimes other solid objects can be employed like rocks, roof peaks, etc. Once in a while a shot may need to happen in hurry without any extra aids.

Practical ranges, KISS style: Here's what we do for our dot sight-equipped .223 patrol rifle shooters. A series of steel IPSC silhouettes are set out in multi-target arrays at ranges of from 150– 400 yards. We've deliberately chosen an open area with plenty of full-value crosswind. Owing to the basic Aimpoint Patrol optics, all shooting employs "Kentucky Windage" or guestimated aiming. Everyone gets a very basic holdover & hold-off class prior to any live fire. Participants then split into two-man shooter/spotter teams, firing from unsupported prone (which is probably a real world *best-case* scenario). It's an educational experience which has noticeably improved wind and elevation calls. Target ranges change from year to year, just to keep everyone on their toes. We always precede each event with a range estimation exercise which, in itself can be pretty entertaining! During one event we had a couple of well-known state firearm instructors show up from another agency. They seemed reluctant to try their luck, and we soon knew why. Without any pre-fire point of reference, both guys, who have plenty of other experience, were pretty well lost. Across the board, they were darned good shooters, too.

Applying science: We'll need an appropriate rifle and a place to shoot. A spot capable of squeaking out 500 yards would be nice, but you could live with less. We'll also need a target capable of capturing our results. A cardboard IPSC target with a white background works well. You can stick a "Shoot n' See" adhesive bullseye to it. Hits on or off the black will them be visible with scopes on their highest settings. Attach the IPSC target to an even bigger backer so you can record wide shots. Two other essentials are a rangefinder and notepad. For purposes of this exercise, let's assume our rifle is a bolt-action .308, with a 3x9 scope (or 2x7). The scope can be one with a duplex or range-compensating reticle. Crank it up to maximum power.

Conventional duplex crosshairs: If your scope is so equipped, a 200-yard zero is darned useful for general field purposes. With this zero, a .308 or .30/06 will hit less than two inches high at 100 yards, and less than nine inches low at 300 yards. As noted in the last section, the best way to get a true 200-yard zero is to actually fire at that distance.

If you haven't done so, start out with the same benchrest techniques used to establish accurate loads at 100 yards. Assuming things are still working, you should be able to place 3 centered shots inside three inches at 200 yards with an off-the-shelf bolt-action rifle. Once that zero is established, read the instructions for your scope's turrets and align the witness scales to "0." From there, you can make any future adjustments without getting lost. Click stops are preferable for this purpose. One last test is worth the trouble—magnification shifts. Shoot a group on three different settings, just make sure everything jives. At 200 yards you'll quickly see any discrepancies.

Next, it's time to hook on your bipod and assume a good, prone position (of course, you've already learned how to do so by firing your .22 rifle). Carefully re-shoot a 200-yard series. Your group may or may not form in the same spot. Regardless, it will probably be a bit larger, maybe measuring around 4-5 inches. If it shifts you'll either need to re-zero or compensate by hold-off. Assuming both groups correspond, it's time to back up another 100 yards. Leave your turrets alone.

At 300 yards, a 6-inch bull can become challenging. A new IPSC target without one may work better. If you have the luxury of a similarly sized, rifle-rated steel silhouette, by all means use it. Hits should be clearly visible if its surface is painted white. If not, plan on some extra walking with a black marker. Your 300-yard groups will probably strike around 8-9 inches low. In calm air you might see a windage shift, which could be caused by either canting or non-level crosshairs. Correct scope mounting solves the latter problem and the former can be rectified through careful aiming. Note the relationship of your group to the cross-

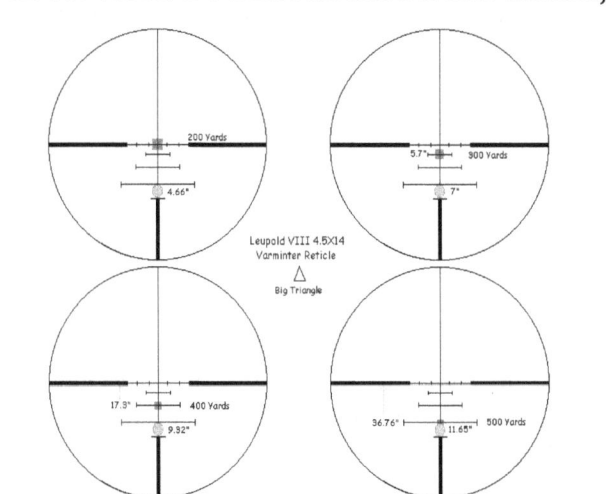

Leupold's Varmint Hunter reticle: 200 yards is the baseline zero here. Note how the value of the lowest prairie dog estimator changes with distance. Holdovers coincide with 40-grain .223 bullets and a MV of 3,800 fps.

Remington M-700 CT, 20" Bbl: .223 Federal 55-grain Balistic Tip				
Yardage (65F)	100	200	300	400
Leupold 4.5x14 VX-3 VH hold lines	+ 1.5"	0	1st	2nd
Magnification	N/A	N/A	11X	9X

Set power ring on small arrow

Shooting on steel while changing magnification settings resulted in this chart. The corrections now account for shorter barrel velocity.

hairs and lower duplex juncture. Rounds may strike somewhere near the lower duplex post. Instead of adding come-ups, leave your scope on "0" and gain more distance.

At some further distance like 400 yards, your groups will probably strike well below the duplex tip. If so, you may be able to merge them again with a magnification decrease. It's not a perfect system, but it can work. Once you have things figured out you can record the data on a small, stock-mounted label.

Ballistic reticles: If you have a scope with a ballistic aiming reticle, you'll want to sight it in per the manufacturer's directions. The zero distance will depend upon the caliber and bullet weight. Once established, you can perform the test described above. The difference is that you'll be using the appropriate holdover marks for the various ranges. Assuming the scope is a common 2nd focal plane type, begin on its maximum magnification setting (some have two settings for different loads).

Hits may or may not coincide with holdover lines. Discrepancies may become more evident as distances increase. In that case you have a few options. You can compensate by noting your hold-offs, or by re-locating the target. A steel plate affords another possibility thanks to visible impacts. You may be able to decrease magnification a bit, until the reticle and impact realign. In the end you can get a useful if not perfect solution. It's a lot better than a "guestimation" using plain reticles; however, there are a few wrinkles. Among the most common concerns, temperature extremes can affect velocity and trajectory. Altitude and atmospheric pressure variations will also cause problems. I try to solve temperature issues by shooting in the same type of weather I'll encounter afield.

I live in near the coast at a 200-foot elevation. When traveling to western destinations, the increased elevation results in holdover problems. During prairie dog shoots I'll range a dirt mound and adjust the elevation turret until dirt flies behind the appropriate reticle line. A big game hunter wouldn't have this luxury, which is where the latest ballistic smart phone apps can help. Check out "I-Strelok," which offers accurate ballistic corrections for a number of reticles and loads. After entering localized atmospheric data, corrected reticle values will be shown. Technology is a wonderful thing!

One thing I don't advocate is applying turret adjustments for wind. Too many variables exist and it's easy to forget you cranked the dial. Some of the ballistic systems have windage marks, which can be very useful.

Ballistic turrets: The basics are similar, but shooting will involve dead-on aiming through the use of "come-ups." The scope's manual should provide a necessary understanding of its turret values. After a baseline zero is established, it can serve as the starting point for adjustments at greater range. The question is how much? We can figure that out with load-specific data. The safest bet is to use a chronograph when inputting muzzle velocity. Lacking one, published velocity will have to do. Handloaders will use data from a loading manual, while others will consult a manufacturer's chart. Either way, actual velocity will likely be different due to barrel length, temperature, and numerous other factors. Still, it'll be better than nothing, and should serve as a rough starting point. From there, an online Strelok or JBM Ballistic Calculator program can be sourced to figure trajectory at various ranges. Using a rangefinder, turret adjustments can then be applied to compensate for drop. Your

Serious long-range work combines precisely calibrated scope turrets with the elimination of variables.

shot probably won't be spot-on, but a large target may at least record the hit. Two more carefully fired rounds should form a group from which to work off of. Be sure to return to "0" when done.

Some turrets, like Leupold's "CDS," are graduated in yardages. After sending data to Leupold, a custom dial is machined that can be user installed. Once zeroed, the dial can be turned to match a target's range, permitting a dead-on hold. Obviously, accurate data is necessary, which is why a chronograph helps.

Recording data: These exercises all involve a fair amount of time and ammunition. If results are not recorded, they'll soon be forgotten. A notepad will solve that problem, and so will a small label, affixed to the rifle. Once you have your elevations figured out you'll need more experience shooting in wind. At 400 yards, things will get interesting in a 10 MPH crosswind.

LONG-RANGE WORK

At ranges beyond 500 yards, precise target turrets are the answer. A heavy-barreled, accurate rifle is another key ingredient. Suitable scopes typically have 30mm or larger main tubes to provide additional reticle adjustments, necessary for the arcing trajectory of long-range projectiles.

Turret values: Assuming you've spent a good chunk of cash for a decent scope, the use of "come-ups" can provide precise bullet placement at predetermined distances. Trajectory compensations will be accomplished by using a series of clicks, referenced off a graduated scale on the elevation turret. It's a mathematical process, assuming everything jives, which may or may not be the case. Users of such scopes should take the time to find out under controlled conditions. One way to do this involves calm air and an exactly placed 100-yard target with plenty of vertical surface. Draw a line running from the bottom of the target to its top edge. This mark must be plumb, so don't align it with a target frame. Instead, use a level or plumb-line.

Now, near the bottom of your line, place a small aiming point. Assuming you're already sighted in for 100 yards, carefully fire a 3-shot group. You may want to shoot off your bipod to simulate field results. After a group develops on the lower aiming point, set your turret scale to "zero." Next, apply a bunch of elevation come-ups. Assuming you're firing a .308 with a good long-range load (like Federal 168 Gold Medal Match), you'll need to gain about 28 MOA for 800-yard hits (excluding wind). With a 1/4 MOA turret, that means somewhere around 112 clicks will be needed. Many of the larger tube tactical scopes possess this capability, but with one-inch tube sporting-type scopes, you could run out of vertical adjustment. If so, go with what you have (or shop for a 25 MOA base). Alternately, try coming up 20 MOA (80 clicks). Fire a group at this setting and measure its proximity to the lower group. At 100 yards, the second group should be about 21 inches higher (MOA = 1.047"). If not, your scope's click values are probably not as advertised. More calculations can provide a solution to seemingly unexplainable misses at long range.

Other factors: We're not out of the woods yet. What about windage? Hopefully, the higher group has formed on the vertical line. If not, your scope's tracking might be off kilter, which could drive you nuts when doping wind. In the .308 example, a 10 mph crosswind will induce 32 inches of drift at 800 yards, so the last thing we need is another variable. A non-level scope can cause this problem, as can a canted rifle. The line on the target must be plumb as well.

Optical centering is another less-known culprit that can introduce tracking problems. Ideally, your scope should be mounted so its reticle will remain near the mid-point of its adjustment range after bore-sighted. It will then be "optically centered," requiring only minor turret adjustments for final zero. This step will prevent running out of adjustments during the initial zero process, or at longer ranges. Since most new scopes are shipped with centered reticles, optimum alignment can be checked during bore-sighting. Used scopes can be corrected by first adjusting their turrets through their full limits, and then dividing them by half. If gross reticle adjustments are necessary for initial zero, tracking problems can result. The turret knobs transmit pressure to the scope's internal reticle housing. When their contacts don't engage the fullest diameter of the housing, its radius can introduce tracking shifts. Fixes include shimming of rings or bases and windage-adjustable mounting systems.

Take great care to establish your setup. Long range shooters should also shop for a rifle-mounted level. Once a final zero is established, the turret scales can be set to "0." This will help find your way home after applying come-ups. Some higher-end scopes have zero stops to prevent dialing a revolution too far down. Lacking this feature all is not lost. Something like that O-ring spacer can limit excessive revolutions in some turret designs.

Stretching the range: Having ironed out the specifics of the scope, it's time to deal with atmospherics. These include details such as altitude, barometric pressure, temperature, and that doggone wind. All of this is pointless without an extremely consistent load fired from an accurate rifle by a shooter with the requisite marksmanship skills. A good rangefinder is essential, and a wind meter can be valuable. Thanks to recent technologies, some of these devices (like the Bluetooth-capable Kestrels) will interface with

A rifle-rated steel target can save lots of walking. This one can handle .300 Win. Mag. hits at 100 yards or farther.

ballistic apps in smart phones! Again, the Strelok programs are worth a look.

With access to a good location, try to round up an experienced spotter and at least one reactive steel target. A few strips of orange surveyor's tape can serve as makeshift wind flags. Before getting too fancy, start at 300 yards and apply the necessary come-ups. It's also a good distance to note the effects of wind and capture initial hits. From there you can stretch out the range in hundred-yard increments. Advance research will inspire confidence as extra elevation adjustments are applied. Wind will be an ever increasing factor, and so will other atmospheric influences like temperature, altitude, and barometric pressure. Out at 800 yards or beyond, every subtle influence will be greatly magnified. We can all have a good day, but consistent success will be data-driven. A log book is as important as your rangefinder. It will help identify elusive effects, which will also include your first or "cold-bore" shot shots.

Having a blast: Ever heard of Tannerite? It's a two-part mix that explodes with gusto when struck by a bullet. The directions need to be followed carefully, which includes shooting from a safe distance. As of this writing, a video is going around of a guy who stuffed a couple pounds in his dead lawn-mower. After the *KA-BOOM*, he almost was as well (although he did blow off a leg). The "Binary Target" components are sold in separate containers, and mixed immediately prior to use. It takes a hard blow (high powered rifle bullet) to set the stuff off and you'll know when it happens. We were very glad the 1-pound unit we shot was a mile from the nearest residents! Besides the noise of a Civil War cannon, there is plenty of smoke. The stuff provides an awesome grand finale on a long-range course.

CLOSING THOUGHTS

Although this chapter provides direction, it's really just an overview of the basics. For many average shooters (including me), a ballistic reticle may be the simplest bet for ranges inside 400 yards. Yes, you could stretch the distance by another hundred yards, but conditions are always a concern.

The further ranges are a specialist's domain. A suitable rifle will be large and heavy, excluding it from general bush-beating uses. It will also be expensive, so buy some books, surf the net, and do your research first. You'll see a plethora of excellent optics and supporting technologies. None of it will be cheap and even unlimited funds won't guarantee success. You'll need to brush up on math skills, locate a suitable site, and invest much effort in practice. Even at that, professional training will be needed to truly master this art.

Sticker shock will probably keep most of us in KISS mode, and truthfully, it'll do. In wooded terrain, that .30/30 lever gun is far from ineffective. Intermediate and long-range distances will shrink, but try even *seeing* 200 yards in the woods. Those darned trees always seem to be in the way.

CHAPTER 16

CLEANING, MAINTENANCE AND STORAGE

Shotguns: A Comprehensive Guide and *Rimfire Rifles: A Buyer's and Shooter's Guide* have fairly detailed cleaning chapters, and much of the same equipment will work for a centerfire rifle. As noted in the *Rimfire* edition, "periodic cleaning will not only ensure reliability but will also extend the life of your rifle. Regardless of the technique, this process is best done somewhere other than in the kitchen!" Since we'll be dealing with lead and caustic solvents, any sort of food preparation or dining surface makes a poor workbench. But, first things first…

SAFETY

Inspect your rifle carefully to ensure it is unloaded! Then, do it again. *Move any live ammunition to some out-of-reach location*, and put on a set of safety or shooting glasses. Solvent splatter and flying springs are real concerns, so better to be safe than sorry. Beyond direct ingestion, residual lead can be inadvertently deposited on doorknobs, clothing, or vehicles. When the job is finished, wash up thoroughly.

CLEANING KITS

At a minimum, you'll need a cleaning rod (or pull-through system), bore brush, patches, solvent, lubricant, and a few other minor items like a toothbrush and rag. Pre-packaged kits make a good starting point, but most will be equipped with jointed aluminum cleaning rods. Although simple, their seams can pick up crud that can damage a bore. Take-down rods are handy at times, but a one-piece rod is also advised.

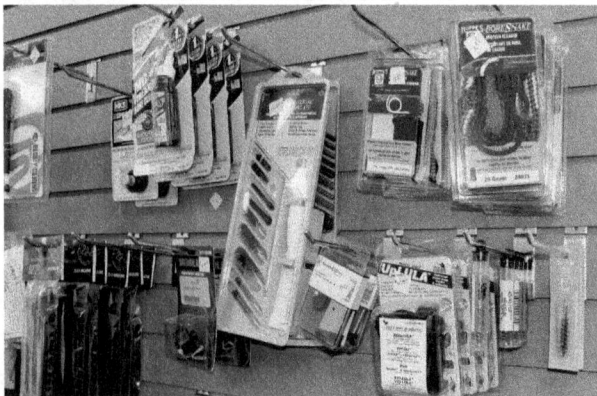

This display contains a whole bunch of useful cleaning items from three well-known sources. Among them are Hoppe's Bore Snake, Ventco's Shooter's Choice solvent, and Outers Universal Cleaning Kit.

We should clean the barrel through the breech when possible to avoid muzzle damage. Since this isn't always feasible, check out the Otis pull-through systems. A rod is replaced with a nylon-coated length of braided stainless wire that has threaded fittings on both ends. It's a compact alternative that can be uncoiled and pulled through a barrel. Mine comes as a kit in a small pouch that doesn't occupy much space. The similar "Bore Snake" has a weighted end that can be inserted through an open breech and down a barrel. It can then be pulled through from the muzzle end while bristle and swab sections clean the bore. Flexible systems are great on the move, but they can't dislodge an obstruction.

Instead of using a commercial cleaning kit, I just employ an accumulation of gear. My one-piece rifle rods see regular use, but they are too long for emergency travel. Although the jointed rods see very little use, a section is sometimes used for action cleaning. The Otis pull-through kit sees service when breech-to-muzzle cleaning won't work.

Back at the ranch, a gun cradle can make things a whole lot more manageable. It'll stabilize the rifle while freeing up both hands. Mine also works well during scope mounting projects.

Solvents & lubricants: Although we buy some of these products by the gallon, you could easily survive with small quantities of the first two items. Be sure to read their labels prior to application. Some readers will disagree with our choices; they work well for us.

Shooter's Choice: This is our go-to solvent. It doesn't have the aroma of Hoppes, but it sure is hell on fouling of all kinds. It's worth applying a small test drop to an inconspicuous area to ensure nothing dissolves. Many firearms now have plastic parts and synthetic stocks, some of which are film-dipped.

Breakfree CLP: We use it for general lubrication of metal-on-metal contact points. It also works well for final wiping of metal surfaces, and it effectively inhibits corrosion. The military uses it for the same reason. CLP stands for "cleaner, lubricant, and preservative." Actually, in a pinch, it could stand in for everything else!

Rem Oil: This general purpose gun oil can be used to lubricate action parts, or to wipe down exterior metal surfaces. A small bottle will last a long time.

Gun Grease: A little goes a long way. We use it sparingly to maintain lubricity on bolt lug contact spots, cocking cam surfaces, hinge pins, and other hard-contact surfaces.

These solvents represent a useful collection of essentials.

Gun Scrubber: This evaporative, aerosol solvent effectively cuts fouling in hard-to-reach areas; however, it will leave them bone-dry. Be careful not to get any in your eyes, or on night-sight elements.

Rust Prevent: As a final step, we often spray on an aerosol-borne film. It quickly dries, leaving a protective coating that won't attract debris. It smells good, too!

Copper solvent: A neglected barrel will often show streaks of copper, left by bullet jackets. Other well-cared for barrels are susceptible to copper fouling, due to rougher interiors. At some point an accumulation will degrade accuracy, and the cure is a dose of this medicine, *applied strictly in accordance with directions*.

JB Bore Paste: This is one of those seldom-used items that can prove invaluable for stubborn barrel fouling. It's a very mild abrasive paste, which we reserve as a last resort. Clean normally and then run a JB-impregnated patch through the bore. You'll probably be surprised by the amount of crud that comes out. We only use it on very dirty barrels, taking care to flush them out afterward with a solvent-soaked patch. *Be sure to read the directions!*

Rods, patches, and brushes: The list may look long, but many of the items can be used with other firearms. Note the emphasis on one-piece cleaning rods. You may want to add a separate pull-through system as well. It won't occupy much space and can be augmented with a few jury-rigged extras. The following items will provide a useful home-based inventory of gear.

Rods: You may wind up buying a self-contained cleaning kit, *and* a separate one-piece rod. Some folks swear by carbon-fiber types, while others prefer nylon-coated versions. I like a one-piece stainless rod because its surface can't trap imbedded particles. As previously mentioned, a pull-through kit will prove useful at times.

Bore brushes: We use Brownell's "Brass Core Special Line Brushes" in various calibers. We flush them with Gun Scrubber after each use to wash off copper-eating chemicals.

Patch holders: Slotted tips are standard in most kits. The brass versions are less likely to cause bore-damage, but a jag is also useful. It's a caliber-specific brass drum with an O-ring guide and a pointed tip to help center a patch. Using the correct patch, it will squeeze through the bore with uniform contact for more thorough cleaning.

Patches: You'll need the right caliber sizes. We seem to get by well with just three types. We use lots of 5.56mm GI M-16 patches, which are 1 ¼-inch squares. They are a bit thick for use with a jag, but can be sized down by pulling off a few loose strands from the edges. The .30-caliber size fits a number of similar calibers. Our square 3-inch shotgun patches cover larger bores. They are also handy when cleaning disassembled parts and actions. When placed on a short handgun rod with a slotted tip, they'll swab out receivers and AR-15 bolt carriers.

M-16 toothbrush: Picture a toothbrush with an extra set of small bristles on its handle. It's good for brushing out small parts and actions. You can also use a regular toothbrush.

Stainless steel toothbrush: These are heavy-duty toothbrushes with thick black plastic handles and stiff metal bristles. They'll really cut through heavy fouling when used with Shooter's Choice, but they need to be used with caution. A disassembled bolt *may* get some careful brushing with one on its heavily fouled face, while avoiding the extractor. Any muzzle scrubbing is out!

Cotton swabs: The wood-shaft medical-types permit access to tight spots like extractor cuts and AR bolts. Q-tips will do the same job but the longer, medical types are a bit handier.

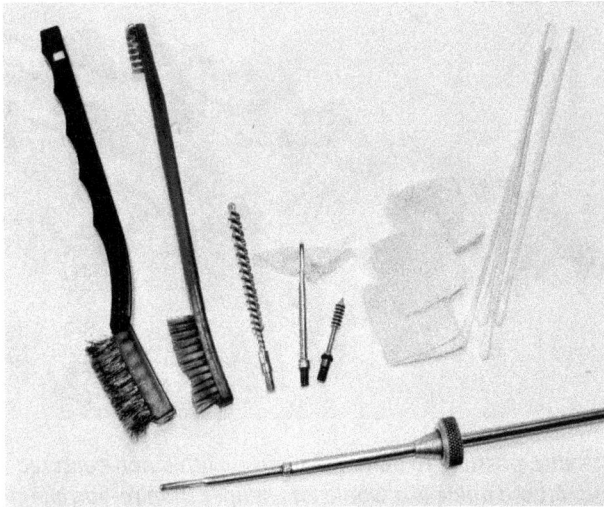

Handy cleaning gear from brushes to patch holders.

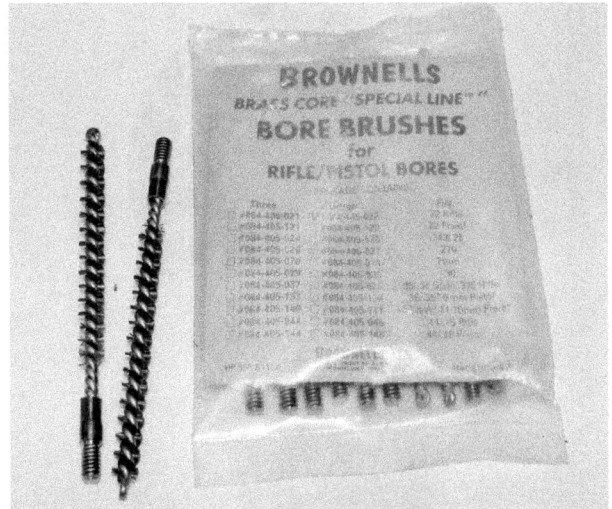

The Brownell's Special Line bore brushes have a brass core. They're easier on rifling than steel types.

CLEANING

I'll seldom fire more than 20 rounds through a prized centerfire rifle without cleaning its barrel. It only takes a few seconds to disassemble a bolt-action for easy maintenance. An AR-15 has extra nooks and crannies to deal with, but bolt removal is nearly as simple. Both types tend to be the choice of accuracy buffs and either can be cleaned through the breech. Pumps, lever-actions, and semi-autos often pose greater challenges. Some are cleaned rarely, as evidenced by streaks of copper fouling in their bores. The action is also subject to wear. It's a machine with metal parts that need to run freely on lubricated surfaces! The most ignored rifles are semi-automatics. More than one has quit running due to something as simple as a dirty chamber, and fouled gas systems usually accompany this problem. At some point, a seized firing pin or heavily fouled breech face *could* result in a dangerous out-of-battery discharge.

There is often a way to remove a bolt for proper cleaning. Most bolt-action rifles will have some sort of easy release catch. Other designs may first require a bit of disassembly. A few like Browning's lever-action BLR and Remington's auto-loaders are better cleaned without bolt removal. It's still possible to clean them, but the process requires extra effort. Although it's less sporting, an owner's manual can make things a whole lot less aggravating, and nowadays, it's often easy to locate an owner's manual online. "Steve's Firearms Page" has dozens of scanned, PDF owner's manuals listed by manufacturer.

A magnetic parts tray is handy for small parts. Once in awhile, one may decide to launch toward places unknown, so an uncluttered area helps. Safety glasses are strongly recommended. If you have a gun cradle, this is the time to drag it out.

Barrel: You can degrade accuracy not only through neglect, but also by careless techniques. Again, cleaning from the breech end is generally the best approach. Fouling won't be as likely to enter the

It's also possible to damage a barrel with a non-centered rod. A bore guide is a whole lot cheaper than re-barreling!

Clean through the breech when possible to avoid damaging a barrel's delicate crown. It only takes one small nick to degrade accuracy. Note the protective recess.

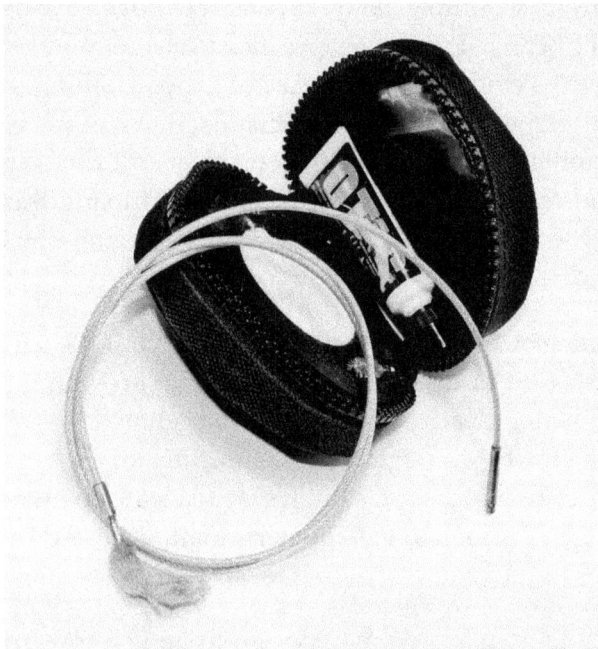

The flexible Otis pull-through kit has another bonus: It'll fit in a small, mobile space.

action, and damage to the barrel's crown will be prevented.

To reiterate, the pull-through systems are the best solution for guns that won't accommodate a rod. That said, I may clean a non-match grade barrel through its muzzle with a rod. A Remington Model 7400 auto-loader is a good example. Mine will provide useful field grade accuracy, but is unlikely to appear in any Olympic events. Mainly to save time, I'll just break out a one-piece rod and proceed with care. A small, brass cone-shaped rod guide will keep the rod centered in its muzzle.

As for Marlins, removal of one screw will separate the lever. The bolt can then be removed for direct breech-to-muzzle cleaning. Bolt-actions warrant tender loving care, due to their simplicity and accuracy. With some types, like Remington M-700s, the bolt can removed and replaced with an insert guide that keeps the rod centered. A similar device is sold for AR-15s.

Regardless of the action, bore cleaning procedures remain similar.

Step #1: I'll usually start with a patch on a slotted tip that's been sprayed with a shot of Gun Scrubber. The patch is discarded after it exits the barrel (don't pull it back through the barrel). It'll pick up any grease coatings or debris to help make the next steps easier.

Step #2: A solvent-soaked bronze brush is passed through the barrel while taking care to maintain a centered rod (we use Shooter's Choice). The brush should fit snuggly, but should not require excessive force. Accuracy of the best-shooting rifles can be maintained by unscrewing the brush every time it emerges from the muzzle. At that point, the rod can be withdrawn and wiped off. It's much easier on a good barrel than running the brush back and forth while fouling accumulates. In all cases, make sure the brush exits the barrel before reversing direction! Depending on how many rounds have been fired, you may need as few as three or four passes, or possibly a dozen or more. A good rule of thumb is one pass per shot fired. Take care to prevent solvent from running throughout the action and stock.

Step #3: Swap the brush for a well-fit patch attached to a loop or jag. The first patch should turn into a mess! The second should look a bit better. Keep going until the patches begin to come out clean. They probably won't be spotless, but at some point they should show only minimal discoloration.

Step #4: Depending on duration of storage, an oiled patch can be passed through the bore to prevent corrosion. Be sure to run a clean patch through the barrel before it is fired (it's a good idea to check for a clear bore, too). So far, thanks to a stable storage environment, I haven't found this last step necessary.

Note: If the barrel seems excessively fouled, it might be time to break out the copper solvent, or JB Paste. Read the directions and repeat Step #3, afterward. The copper agents sometimes contain ammonia. Prolonged barrel exposure can cause damage.

Once the barrel is cleaned, don't forget to flush solvent off the bronze bore brush using a shot of Gun Scrubber.

Action: An M-16 toothbrush with a bit of solvent will clean fouling from the receiver, bolt face, and breech. Most centerfire semi-autos employ gas-operated systems that will quickly foul. In the case of the aforementioned Remington M-7400 (and similar Remington models), removal of the forend is necessary for cleaning. One large, slotted screw holds it in place. Access is fairly simple — IF regular maintenance occurs. The trouble is some shooters just don't bother. At some point, the gas system will seize, rendering the rifle inoperative. There's a good chance the forend screw will also be bound up. An overnight soaking of penetrating oil may help. Assuming you can get it apart, a solvent-soaked stainless toothbrush may come in handy. We see this situation on similar semi-autos, like Ruger Mini-14s, M-1 Carbines, Winchester M-100s, etc.; all of which use simple gas systems within the forend. Excessive lubrication in these areas is bad, but lube the forend screw on that Remington prior to reassembly.

Many bolt-action owners never think about the innards of a bolt. Its massive spring-loaded firing pin assembly will, at best, accumulate carbon fouling. Exposure to rain will cause corrosion and the first indication of a problem will probably be a misfire. Even with Joe Saturday use, it's worth disassembling the bolt on an annual basis. As noted in the Accessories Chapter, Remington owners will appreciate a disassembly tool. A dab of gun grease will minimize wear on bolt lugs and cocking cams, but use oil on the striker assembly. Grease can stiffen up in cold weather, impeding reliability. This explains why arctic hunters often completely degrease an action.

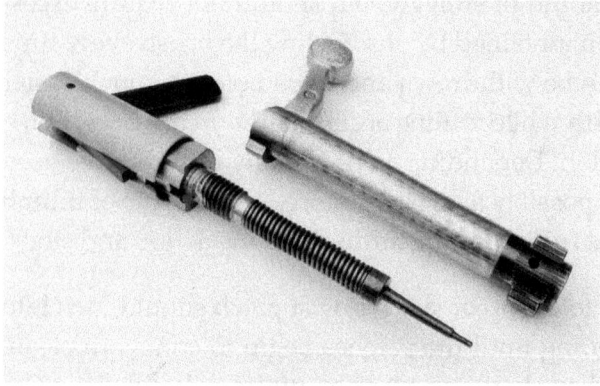

The innards of a Remington bolt are easily exposed for servicing with the right tool.

With all types of rifles, make sure the extractor moves freely and is cleared of any fouling. Trigger groups should receive periodic attention. Gun Scrubber is sometimes a good way to flush out powder residue. The stock will probably need to be removed, which isn't a bad thing. We usually find stray needles in ours, due to jack-fir hellholes (they penetrate everywhere in wet weather). Apply a couple drops of Breakfree or Rem Oil to the firearm's moving parts afterward. Then cycle the action a few times. Too much lube can attract grit and damage wood stocks, so in most cases, sparing applications are best.

Magazines: Springs and followers should be periodically cleaned. The tubular types can sometimes be cleaned like a barrel using a patch on a rod. The muzzle-end often has a steel plug secured by a screw. Be careful during removal since the spring is under pressure! Before disassembling any detachable magazines, it's worth keeping a spare on hand to serve as a reference during reassembly. Mostly, I just flush them out with Gun Scrubber. Oily magazines will attract dirt, resulting in stoppages. Some lubes, like WD-40, will also kill primers. Depending on the environment, they may be better off without any lubrication. I'll sometimes mist internal parts with a light shot of Rust Prevent, which will leave a dry-feeling protective coating less likely to capture debris.

Exterior: The last step involves applying a protective coating to metal surfaces. You can wipe on a thin film of Breakfree or Rem Oil; or spray on a light layer of Rust Prevent. Watch out for your optics though! Scope rings and metal magazines can be lightly wiped afterward with the same cloth. We don't want a rifle dripping with oil—just a light sheen should do. Many owners store their guns vertically in a gun safe or cabinet where excessive applications can migrate into stocks. Old guns often show an area of dark discoloring right behind a receiver. It's oil-soaked wood, which can weaken a stock in that critical area.

Scope: Lens caps are a wise investment. They'll not only ward off water or dust, but also solvents and oils during gun cleaning. The best way to clean the lenses is to blow them off. Since that won't always work, a "Lens Pen" is a wise investment. One end has a small brush and the other has a special tip designed for removal of stubborn spots. You *can* clean a lens with caution, by misting its surface with a breath, followed by gentle attention and a very soft cleaning patch or eyeglass cloth. Just remember that the special anti-reflective coatings are very thin. Don't mess with any screws in the scope. It's a sealed unit and disassembly will ruin it.

An inexpensive tackle can serve as a handy organizer for cleaning accessories.

ENVIRONMENTAL FACTORS

Conditions can vary greatly, from hot weather with blowing sand to arctic cold and ice. Maintenance will need to be tailored for reliable function, and there isn't any "one size fits all" strategy. I've operated in military environments where fine grit was driven into every nook and cranny by rotor wash. In these hot and sandy conditions, anything beyond minimal lubrication quickly disabled most weapons. Within the same theatre, operations often shifted to tropical rain forests that required frequent lubrication. In all conditions, maintenance was performed with religious zeal. We'll hopefully be operating under tamer conditions, but weather is always a factor.

Wet weather: Since stainless actions and synthetic stocks afford additional weather resistance, they are the go-to choice of my hunting tribe. After a raw day in wet woods, you can bet each rifle will get TLC; but at least we can jump into dry clothes first. During the interim, we can position a rifle to help drain out water. It'll probably be a bolt-gun, permitting easy removal of its bolt. Thanks to QD swivels, the sling can also be pulled off and set aside to dry. There are times when the stock may need to come off, but more often than not, judicious use of a hairdryer will do the trick. It eliminates worries about zero shifts caused by varying stock bolt torque. The same cannot be said of wood stocks, which can warp. If one receives a good soaking it most definitely should be removed. Wipe out any water and let it dry without undue heat. Well-sealed internal wood surfaces are the best insurance from unexpected zero shifts, and although laminated stocks are better, they can also soak up water. The synthetics are noisier and less attractive, but they do have their place. With any type, don't forget the bore and other metal surfaces. Even stainless will rust, so we provide these rifles with the same level of care given to a blued firearm. The stainless construction just provides another level of insurance. My son's battle-scarred .30/06 Remington M-700 has seen decades of action in truly horrible weather, but thanks to regular maintenance, its matte-blued finish is still in good shape.

Don't forget a wet sling, which will hold water and rust any adjacent steel. The push-button QD swivel disengages from a socket within the stock.

Snow: The same wet weather regimen generally

applies, with a couple of twists. It's all too easy to plug a barrel with snow, so a makeshift cap is good insurance. Electrical tape works great and it'll safely be blown clear of the muzzle by air pressure. Snow-covered branches will quickly coat everything, so lens caps are essential (QD scope mounts and iron sights can come in handy, too). You should think about ice as well. We've seen a few semi-autos that were frozen shut, whereas a bolt-action normally can exert enough leverage to free its action. In the end, it really boils down to keeping a rifle as snow-free as possible. Some diehards apply a light coating of wax, which can help shed water.

Cold: Moisture will quickly condense on a cold firearm when brought into a heated area. The entire gun will be immediately covered with fine water droplets. Those spending time in remote winter locations often leave their working gun outdoor for this reason. A gradual warm-up with constant attention is otherwise necessary. Extreme cold also calls for different lubrication practices. Sometimes it's safest to completely strip off all lubricants, using white gas or a degreasing agent. Graphite is sometimes used on parts requiring lubricity. I don't live in the arctic, but our area can get pretty darned cold. Grease will really stiffen up during cold weather. For this reason, we limit application to small quantities, in spots that won't impede firing pins or other action parts. A new lubricant reported to work well in deep cold is "Liberty Lube CLP." With a freeze point of -85F, it ought to get most of us by!

One leap and this whitetail will be gone. Take up its trail and you'll be covered with snow. At that point, weatherproofing details will become immediate priorities.

Blood and other corrosive effects: Since blood will quickly damage most metal finishes, it should be quickly removed. Its effects are similar to salt water, which can quickly raise havoc. I once was accidentally submerged in seawater with a nice Beretta O/U shotgun. After crawling ashore, I dried the gun as much as possible and made a beeline toward the house. The entire shotgun went in a bathtub full of fresh water for a thorough flushing out. I spent lots more time blotting up every water droplet, and then generously applied oil to all of the metal surfaces. This treatment was a success—or so it seemed. A few weeks later I encountered occasional misfires. Experimentation showed they only happened when the muzzles were elevated. It turned out a bit of salt had eaten through the return spring on the cocking bar. When pointed skyward, the bar

slipped back against the hammers and retarded their full impact force. The fix was relatively simple but devilish to figure out. One thing I did remember was its gun case. Since the gun had gone back in it during the trip home, the safest long-term bet was just to trash it. Believe it or not, we have sea duck hunters in our area who consider their shotguns as disposable items. Most of these guys are commercial fishermen who treat them as any other piece of boat gear. By the end of the season, salt water has taken its toll, rendering even a well-made shotgun inoperative. To me, it's like using the Mona Lisa as a floor mat, but then again, this practice does emphasize the price of neglect.

STORAGE

The following from *Shotguns: A comprehensive Guide* applies equally well to other firearms, as well as airguns.

Periodic inspections and basic cleanings go a long way toward peace of mind and will also help maintain your investment. The means of storage is equally important. External corrosion can appear in a surprisingly short amount of time, and if undiscovered, it can cause pitting and permanent damage. Long-term gun case storage may result in transfer of moisture from padded surfaces, which can accumulate through humidity. Believe it or not, sometimes the moisture can appear in minutes. We've seen firearms literally covered in water droplets after their soft-cases were exposed to intense sunlight. These guns were properly stored, and only cased for a trip to the range. The soft interiors had probably absorbed moisture over time, and upon arrival, the cases were placed in the sun. Soon afterward, their interiors turned into saunas, causing "sweating" that condensed on the guns. The same situation can occur in reverse upon entering a warm area from low temperatures.

A good gun safe provides stable and secure non-portable security. It also makes a great organizer.

Besides gun cases, wrapping a gun in cloth can wreak havoc, even if stored indoors. Any damp place like a basement or shed is just as bad, but long-term vehicle storage can cause similar problems. Ammunition is also best stored in a cool, dry location. It will last for decades with care, whereas heat will cause rapid deterioration. Moisture is as bad for ammo as it is for guns!

That's why a good gun safe located in a dry and stabile environment is worthwhile. Desiccant packs and dehumidifier rods should provide adequate protection from rust if some thought goes into the final location. I haven't had any issues using a safe alone, which is located in a primary living space. The extra peace of mind afforded by a good safe is another major dividend. The *Survival Guns* edition covers safes and other storage options in detail. We all have an obligation to ensure that our firearms and ammunition don't fall into the wrong hands. A locked case or trigger-lock may deter kids or honest folks but they are really just interim steps for a thief.

Springs & storage: During long-term storage, we prefer to relax the tension on a few key springs.

Opening the action will typically cock a hammer or striker, which is normally powered by a strong-coil spring. A semi-auto also has a recoil spring that undergoes compression while its bolt is locked rearward. On a range, a shoulder-fired gun should be racked that way for safety's sake. It'll be fine during short periods, but not for long-term storage. A compressed recoil spring will gradually weaken over time. It could eventually degrade function and cause damage to the gun from excessive bolt velocity.

Bolt-actions can often be un-cocked by first lifting the handle, and then squeezing the trigger, as the bolt is slowly eased downward. The same basic idea will, of course, apply to any hammer guns. Semi-autos will need to be dry fired prior to long-term storage. An occasional dry-firing won't hurt most types, but for reassurance, you can insert a Snap Cap, a dummy cartridge designed to cushion the blow of a firing pin.

Note: Whatever technique is employed, please make darned sure the gun is unloaded! Then, store it responsibly.

Sources: Brownell's and Midway USA catalog a large selection of gun cleaning gear and solvents. The major outdoor retailers like Cabela's, Bass Pro Shops, Gander Mountain, and others have walk-in locations for hands-on shopping. Your local gun shop is worth a visit as well. Since some also provide gunsmith services, a good customer relationship can prove valuable. Sooner or later, there's a good chance you'll need their help!

CHAPTER 17

GENERAL PURPOSE RIFLE SUMMARY

So far, the main focus has been on a portable, general purpose rifle capable of firing a high-powered cartridge. Such a firearm in a caliber like .308 Winchester should cover contingencies out to 400 yards, or even a bit further. The good news is its overall cost, which will remain fairly affordable with careful shopping. The well-established models will readily accommodate a wide array of mounts and optics to maximize their potential.

As a bolt-action guy, I'll take three in .223 Remington, .22 LR, and .308 Winchester. This battery will handle everything from squirrels to moose. A .223 works great for varmints, and thanks to affordable ammo, it can also double as a centerfire practice tool. The .22 LR is a perfect trainer and plinker that won't tear up camp meat. When combined with specialty loads like .22 Shorts, its already mild report becomes nearly inaudible. A bolt-action downside for some will be lack of ambidextrous operation, but as we've seen, there are lots other good choices that won't break the bank.

The three-gun idea is feasible with a Browning or Henry lever-action, and if the .223 drops off the list, a less expensive pair of .30/30 and .22 LR Marlins will work. A .30/30 won't get you a quarter-mile of range, but thanks to advances in ammunition, it'll cover at least 200 yards. Throw in the smaller list of essential accessories and system will be affordable. In fact, some readers probably have a serviceable rifle on hand.

A minimalist might opt for just one centerfire rifle, in which case a pump-action .308 Remington M-760 could work. The future addition of a 12 gauge Model 870 twin would cover everything from birds through burglars, and of course, Remington rimfire pump remains another possibility. Since all of these firearms are manually operated, they're not picky on ammo. The latest "managed recoil" loads will soften a centerfire bite without concerns about function. The scary black rifle aspects are also missing, so few restrictions exist.

When it comes to semi-auto types, a basic choice may lack the exotic luster of fully decked out "modern sporting rifles," but it'll still perform similarly. Much of the same rationale applied to Remington's pump gun line extends to their semi-autos. Reduced loads are off the table but equivalent shotgun and rimfire models are sold. As we've seen by now, similar function remains a constant theme throughout this series of books.

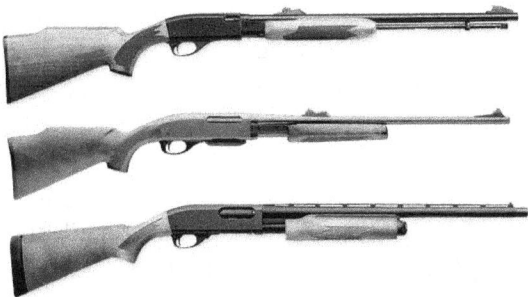

A systems approach makes sense. All bases are covered with this line of Remington pump guns in 22 Rimfire, .308 Centerfire, and a 12 Ga. shotgun. They're not fussy about ammo, and legal just about anywhere within the U.S.

However, some people will find the allure of a military-type rifle irresistible. If so, factors like controllability and flash signature will come into play. So will ammunition, parts, and extra expenses. Hence, the next section…

SECTION II: THE AR-15

CHAPTER 18

AN OVERVIEW

It was tempting to title this as an "assault rifle" section, but for starters, such a weapon is actually select-fire, meaning it can be discharged with either semi-auto or machinegun-type bursts. Although civilian rifles look very similar, they lack full-auto capability. In other words, they're not really assault rifles at all!

Many of these rifles are judged largely by their appearance and poorly understood. The addition of a pistol grip or black stock won't alter the semi-auto principles common to a host of well-established deer rifles like a Browning BAR, Remington Woodsmaster, or Winchester Model 100—all of which exist in 7.62x51 NATO/.308 persuasion. They also share gas-operated mechanisms, detachable magazines, and one shot per trigger-pull function. Even the "scary" civilian AKs work the same way, despite their lower-powered 7.62 chambering.

Among the numerous military types, the two big players are the AK-47 variants of Soviet origin and the American M-16/AR-15 models. Other larger-caliber military-type firearms include the M-14, AR-10, FAL, G-3, etc., all of which are full-size battle rifles. Legalities aside, most of us will manage just fine sans a select-fire option, if for no other reason than the logistics involved with feeding such a weapon. Recoil and size are further concerns.

Although the utilitarian AK works, it's no accuracy champ. The most affordable 7.62x39mm Russian rounds are typically foreign-produced and Berdan-primed, often using steel cartridge cases, or even steel-bullet jackets. Quality will vary, but thanks to its generous tolerances, a Kalashnikov will digest just about anything. Ammo is now fairly common, and the 7.62x39 develops ballistics similar to the venerable .30/30 (but with lighter 123-grain bullets). Another modernized variant, the AK-74, fires smaller-caliber 5.45x39mm ammunition similar to American 5.56mm NATO. Regardless, most AK-type rifles are closely configured. The original military designs are really laid out for massed-fire at close-to-intermediate distances using iron sights. Equipped with a 30-round magazine, a semi-auto AK could be handy for use against armed intruders. Based on previous experience, dodging Chinese-produced rounds, I certainly respect the design (which is not without its faults). Although globally distributed on a vast scale, here in the U.S., popularity is subservient to the Stoner-designed AR system.

The 7.62x51 NATO/.308 Winchester (L) is much larger than the 7.62x39 Russian (steel-cased) and 5.56x45 NATO/.223 Remington (R).

Lately, the term "modern sporting rifle" has come into vogue. At first it seemed like a bit of a stretch, but it now fits some systems very well. This is particularly true of the AR-15 platform which, unlike the AK design, is available in a stunning array of configurations, along with an interesting assortment of calibers beyond the standard 5.56mm/.223. Considering the widespread availability of parts, magazines and ammunition—combined with the versatility of the system—our focus will be directed toward the AR-15. Costs went through the roof a few years back, but lately they've really come down. It's now possible to own a $700 AR from a mainstream manufacturer. That puts this system well in line with other potential choices, with the added benefit of huge customization potential.

THE AR CONCEPT

As originally developed by Eugene Stoner, this 1950s design was a radical departure. Like the full-size M-1 Garand and M-14 battle-rifles, it harnessed propellant pressure to function. Everything else was brand new. Steel forgings and walnut were gone. So were full-power .30-caliber cartridges.

Instead, the new AR used weight-saving aluminum and plastic construction. The smaller 5.56mm cartridge evolved from a modified .222 Remington Magnum, and fired a light .224 diameter projectile. The "AR" moniker referred to ArmaLite. The cartridge and rifle actually came second. The AR-15 was an evolution their initial AR-10 design, which fired standard .308, M-14 ammunition.

Advantages: Reducing the cartridge size cut back on recoil and decreased system weight. The unique straight-line action further improved muzzle climb during full-auto fire. Initially fed from a 20-round, detachable box magazine, this controllable firepower was an answer to the Soviet AK-47. The United States finally had a true "assault rifle" known as the M-16.

During the 1960s, aluminum and plastic were hard to accept, despite their clear advantages. I remember much grumbling about our "plastic rifles," which had some early teething pains. A series of catastrophic battlefield stoppages were eventually tracked down to poorly understood maintenance procedures, incompatible propellants, and the wrong lubricants. Chrome-plated chambers and bores helped resist the effects of tropical weather. A "forward assist" was added to help seat the bolt. Shortly thereafter, I carried a now-vintage, triangle-forend M-16 through two combat tours without stoppage.

Colt began selling semi-automatic AR-15 rifles, which were very similar to the military M-16. The civilian .223 Remington version of the 5.56 NATO arrived in 1964. The military continued to tweak the design while civilian interest grew. The entire system steadily evolved and the dreaded "black gun" eventually made strong sporting inroads. It's doubtful that even Mr. Stoner could have fully envisioned the present incarnations of his system.

DESIGN AND FUNCTION

An AR-15 consists of two main components: the lower and upper receivers. The lower receiver contains the fire-control system, pistol grip, magazine well, buffer tube, and stock. The upper receiver contains the bolt carrier assembly, barrel, gas system, forend, and sights. Both receiver halves are connected by two easily retractable pins for quick separation. Maintenance is not only simplified, but different uppers can be readily installed. An AR owner can thus reconfigure the rifle to any number of options and calibers, within the dimensional limitations of the platform.

The lower receiver is the serial numbered half. Manual retraction of its two pins permits easy disassembly or mounting of different upper receivers.

Direct impingement: The AR-15 operates as an inline design, whereby the bolt recoils within the stock. Upon discharge, some of the propellant gas is diverted through a port within the barrel, near the front of the forend. From there, gas is diverted rearward through a tube, impinging upon a bolt carrier housed within the receiver. Pressure

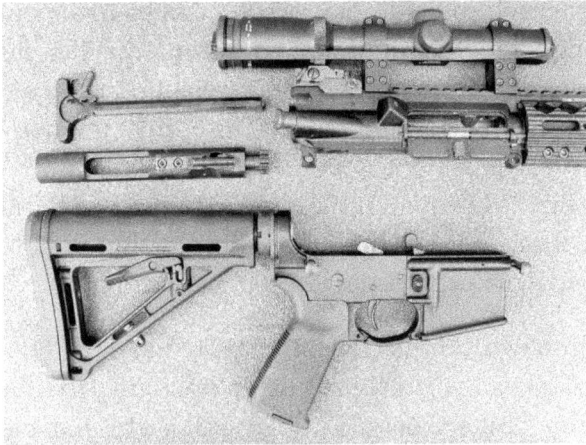

The lower and upper receivers are separated. The charge handle and bolt carrier assembly are withdrawn from the upper. The magazine release button is ahead of the trigger.

drives the bolt carrier rearward, camming a separate rotating bolt head out of engagement with the barrel. Once unlocked, the lugged bolt head and carrier assembly continue their rearward movement. The fired case is ripped from the chamber by a bolt-mounted extractor claw. A spring-loaded plunger within the bolt face then ejects it through a port on the right side of the action. Meanwhile, the bolt carrier assembly continues its rearward travel, compressing a spring-loaded buffer housed within the stock. Upon full compression, the spring-powered buffer drives the bolt carrier forward again, stripping a new cartridge from the feed lips of the magazine. As the bolt goes home, it chambers the cartridge and the locking lugs re-engage. A magazine-activated bolt stop locks the bolt to the rear upon the last shot.

Depression of a button will allow the magazine to drop free for rapid reloads. The separate bolt stop can then be manually tripped to release the bolt, allowing it to run home. An independent "charging handle" is provided for manual retraction of the bolt carrier assembly; however, since it isn't solidly connected to this assembly, it can't be used to seat the bolt. On earlier versions, if the bolt didn't fully engage, there was no ready recourse. A forward assist was added to solve this problem. It's a large button behind the ejection port, which can be used to exert pressure on the bolt carrier to fully seat it. Some economy-grade civilian ARs don't have this feature, but it is reassuring. As part of an ingrained military habit, I routinely use mine when chambering the first round.

The AR's small cartridges and shorter action travel result in fast cycling. The straight-line function serves to minimize vertical recoil effects. The benefits include less muzzle climb during full-auto fire, and overall control. The bolt's steel locking lugs engage corresponding steel recesses at the rear of

The standard DI system employs a gas key (the upper tube), which surrounds a gas tube in the receiver. The rotating bolt is surrounded by a massive bolt carrier.

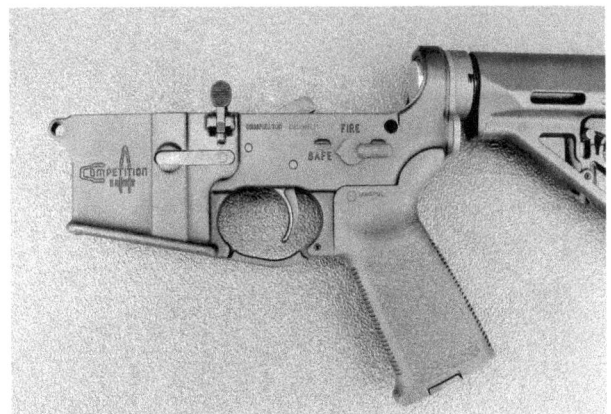

The hammer is cocked and the safety is "on." The bolt stop is the small paddle above the receiver. Below it is part of the magazine release mechanism.

The "forward assist" button was an early addition that could fully seat a recalcitrant bolt.

Similar views of two different AR types. The DI AR-15 (top) is a .300 Blackout. The much larger .308 calls for an AR-10 sized platform like the piston-driven Patriot Ordnance Factory.

the barrel, so the upper receiver can be made out of lightweight aluminum. Unlike many other gas operated designs, the Stoner system lacks connecting linkages and pistons. Its "direct impingement" gas system is often referred to as a "DI" design. While it's simple, carbon fouling and heat are transferred to the action. Routine but not obsessive maintenance will keep one running.

Piston evolutions: The latest genre includes "piston" rifles, which substitute an operating rod for the gas tube. The gas port is still there, but the corresponding block is modified. Pressure is used to shove a piston against the rod, driving the bolt carrier rearward. Such designs run cleaner since no propellant residue enters the action; however, several proprietary designs exist, leading to worries about spare parts. While the general piston design does have merit, a few problems have been encountered. DI bolt unlocking is a carefully orchestrated process that controls related stresses. A piston-driven unlocks from one violent shove. The bolt lugs disengage quickly when the rod strikes a lug on the carrier (which replaces the gas key). Lacking lateral gas tube guidance, this blow can tilt the bolt carrier downward, causing wear on rear contact surfaces. Manufacturers have developed various methods to deal with this problem, at the expense of proprietary designs.

On a positive note, the integral lug on the bolt carrier won't be loosening up. The same cannot be said of a standard DI gas key, which is a separate piece. It bolts on with two heavy cap screws, which are then staked. A solid connection to the bolt carrier is needed to prevent gas leakage, and loose or broken screws are a common source of malfunctions. Most armorers will have a torque wrench and staking jig just for this reason.

Thinking back a few decades, I can't remember a single time when anyone in my Recon squad lamented the lack of a piston. If maintained, a

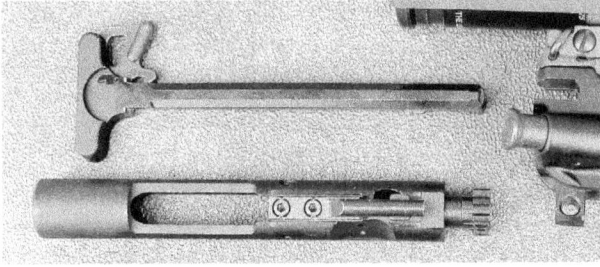

The DI gas key is a separate part. Its two cap screws need to be securely staked in order to maintain a tight pressure seal.

This piston-driven bolt assembly has a roller cam unlocking system. A recess on its integral "gas key" interfaces with a gas-powered operating rod.

An adjustable gas-metering valve is visible just above the barrel on this piston-drive rifle. Pressure shoves the long operating rod rearward within the forend.

well-built DI rifle will run, and after 50 years of continuous production, parts are not a problem. We've taken an agency plunge into the piston world, with a small and auxiliary battery of Patriot Ordnance Factory .308 AR-10-type rifles. Having tested a few, we found them well-made with a number of innovative features. Among them is an adjustable gas metering system, which permits fine tuning (not all ammunition is compatible with gas operated systems, and use of a suppressor can further affect function). Sig Arms is producing some highly intriguing AR-hybrid rifles which lack Stoner-type buffer tubes. As a result, they can employ folding stocks.

Meanwhile, we recently procured 70 more Windham Weaponry AR-15s. They reliably support all standard operations via the original Stoner design. We've seen WW's gas key staking process, and it will probably nail down a tank. Our large accumulation of existing AR parts will keep these carbines running, and our prior-military staff can operate them in their sleep.

Configurations and calibers: The modularity of the AR design also hasn't hurt efforts to reconfigure the initial solid-stocked, 20-inch barreled platform. Before long a 16-inch carbine appeared with a telescoping stock. As the nuances of pressure and inertia were better understood, more versions sprung forth, driven by specialized tactical requirements. Chopped down sub-gun sized ARs showed up with barrels that were *much* shorter. In some cases, buttstocks were entirely removed, resulting in pistol-type variants. The caliber list expanded accordingly, with 9mm versions showing up. Moving in the opposite direction, 24-inch (or longer) heavy-barreled AR-15s chipped at the domain of bolt-action tack drivers.

Variations of the larger AR-10 reappeared, to whet the appetites of those seeking .308 performance. Like the original version, size and weight increased proportionally. So did recoil. Although manageable, the extra mass of the bolt carrier assembly was hard on triggers and bolt stops. Evolution continues and popularity is increasing. This large AR platform has been tweaked, or even super-sized for other centerfire chamberings. Charitably, many will not be handy in the bush.

Meanwhile, just about any cartridge that could be adapted to the smaller AR-15 has been, so today you really can "have it your way."

Chapter 19

THE CIVILIAN AR-15

Political heartburn to the contrary, a properly set up AR-15 can be a very useful multi-tool. As an example, during a recent prairie dog shoot, we dragged out our Remington heavy-barreled M-700 bolt-action .223s. Hits instantly diminished, so this lasted *maybe* 15 minutes. We very quickly returned to our black rifles. During three days of steady shooting the ARs, ran reliably, scoring consistent hits thanks to good scopes, fine accuracy, and fast follow-up shots. Our hamster-sized targets were no closer than 200 yards, with many far beyond that range. Once home, I just disengaged two pins and swapped out the heavy-barreled, 24-inch upper receiver for a shorter "tactical" unit. The second flat top upper had an 18-inch barrel and was pre-zeroed with its own optical sight. The whole process took less than a minute. My modern sporting rifle was now a defensive carbine, thereby fulfilling two roles off one serial-numbered lower receiver. Additional uppers, which are not serial-numbered, can be ordered by mail.

These cute little critters are just part of a huge prairie dog town devastating South Dakota grazing lands.

Impending pink mist from a 1x9 twist, 24" Bushmaster Varminter. The bench swivels for good coverage of the prairie.

Prairie dog control AR style, with a 24" Rock River. Note the receiver-mounted spirit level.

CONSTRAINTS

A case might be made to just dispense with any other centerfire rifle system in favor of the AR platform; however, there are a few flaws with this argument. If widespread ammo availability is important, AR choices will likely boil down to just two: either the 5.56 NATO/.223 or the 7.62x51 NATO/.308.

AR functionality is maintained with a .308 at the expense of size. The AR-10 moniker is a generic description of several large variants. Armalite actually claims the title.

5.56x45mm NATO/.223 Remington: The 5.56 NATO is by far the most common AR chambering due to the M-16/AR-15. The similar (but slightly different) .223 Remington is a civilian version of the military round. An AR-15 can be had in a compact and lightweight carbine, but there's always a catch. Unfortunately, these cartridges lack the terminal punch necessary to humanely harvest big game. We're talking about elk, moose, bear, and larger deer. No doubt all of these species have been taken, but there are much better choices.

7.62x51 NATO/.308 Winchester: These cartridges offer plenty of wallop, but a much larger AR-10 rifle is necessary. The ensuing platform will resemble a jumbo AR-15. Besides durability, proprietary replacement parts are a concern, and for many of us, an AR-10 will handle awkwardly. Nevertheless, .308 AR-10 type rifles are increasingly popular. Today, they are cataloged by many AR manufacturers. I'm betting many spend most of their time on a range or in a truck.

Other issues: Back to an AR-15, there are other interesting caliber choices, but most are less common. The 7.62x39 Russian is fairly abundant, but it poses functional challenges in an AR-15. Another problem for some prospective AR buyers is restrictive legislation. It's hard to have that perfect cake and eat it too, so for general high power rifle chores, I still prefer bolt guns. They're simple and adaptable to a wide assortment of calibers.

CIVILAN ADVANTAGES

Caliber limitations aside, the AR-15 has merit. Some of its best attributes are not readily apparent, extending to defensive *and* sporting applications. A more unusual sporting example related to both uses involves nocturnal coyote hunting. The parallel may seem a bit strange so here goes...

Unlike the typical daytime open-country calling you see on TV, our operations involve thicker cover, with bait and heated blinds. Because the action happens after dark, some specialized accessories are necessary. These include weapon-mounted lights, night vision scopes, and infrared illuminators. In our experience, an AR-15 is superior to a bolt-action for this type of work. Not too coincidentally, some of its key attributes also extend to the tactical theatre. Note the similarities below.

Accessories: Although some bolt-gun manufacturers have begun attaching rail sections, the military Picatinny system really is the domain of the black rifle. Besides conventional optics, our night vision scopes, lights, and infrared illuminators also need attachment points. I mount my IR unit and a tactical light on forend rail sections. They can all easily quick-disconnect when not in use. A dedicated night scope mounts to the receiver rail in lieu of a standard scope, and it also employs a QD mount. The NV scope can be quickly exchanged for a conventional scope without any loss of zero. In fact, some of newer NV units mount forward of a conventional scope, on a forend top-rail. I have cobbled together some bolt-action arrangements, but they were really just temporary solutions.

Picatinny Rails permit attachment of all sorts of accessories from bipods through lights and night vision scopes. The muzzle-device is a Smith Vortex.

Beyond night-related accessories, bipods and forward-mounted pistol grips come to mind. There are lots of other gadgets, too. Caution: One big trap to be avoided is over-accessorization. We've seen shooters arrive for rifle training with every device known to mankind. Before long, most of the extras were coming off. KISS is a good principle to bear in mind!

Muzzle-flash reduction: A bare muzzle can be as bad as an old-time flashbulb at night. The military A-2 flash cage offers some improvement but a few of the latest devices do a superior job. Loads with flash-retardant propellants can result in a BIG difference when combined with a good muzzle device! From experience, we can tell you that a Yankee Hill Phantom and Federal 55 grain Ballistic Tip produce almost zero flash. The same is true with a Smith Enterprises Vortex. I was watching them both, side-by-side, during a recent night fire event. The Smith appeared to hold a slight advantage, and is now standard on our patrol carbines. We fire an A-2 and Vortex for low-light comparison during basic rifle training, and their difference is amazing. The Surefire unit also works very well, and there are no doubt many others.

Adding a night scope to the mix, a good flash hider will greatly improve its effectiveness. You'll get exactly one shot with an NV scope and a bare muzzle. The flash will instantly shut down most units, which are gated to prevent over-exposure. The same visual effect can occur with conventional aiming systems in low light. So, with or without an NVD, a good flash hider can prove useful. Picture touching off a short-barreled AR-15 in a darkened hallway! Choosing an AR with a standard (1/2x28) threaded muzzle will solve the problem, while also protecting the barrel's crown. A suppressor will further mitigate concussive effects, although maneuvering can be impaired.

Fast follow-up shots: You don't always need one, but extra shots are reassuring. Oftentimes during nocturnal coyote operations, we're just shooting at dim silhouettes. Lots of action may be forthcoming when the rifle goes bang. Things can then get pretty entertaining! Our state law allows 5-shot magazines, so that's what we use for hunting. I've never emptied one, but we have all fired multiple rounds on numerous occasions. For more serious social occasions involving semi-auto fire, a 20-rounder should suffice. For best reliability, we load them with only 18 rounds, which is still a bunch of ammo. Many folks will opt for fully loaded 30-rounders. In that case, fill 'em up! If you do need a reload, it can happen quickly with an AR.

Fumble-free loading & unloading: Ever load little cartridges into a top-fed bolt-action magazine? It's a bit "fiddly" during daylight and a real pain in low light. We're prior military and well-drilled on the black rifle. Under stress or in the dark, loading is much simpler with the AR-15 system. Pre-loaded magazines are easy to insert and at least one spare is always close at hand. I'm not a fan of connected (or coupled) mags. They're susceptible to dirt and weather, adding extra weight as well. A readily accessible magazine pouch is preferable during harsh environments.

Carry-case convenience: This is a bigger deal than one might expect. Many of the better AR-15 specific "assault rifle cases" have side pockets for extra magazines, ammo, and gear. They also have padded slings. You can throw the whole enchilada over your shoulder, leaving both hands free for other gear. This "grab & go" package can be very handy both in and out of a vehicle. Mine always contains three extra loaded magazines plus two boxes of ammo. When traveling out-of-state through non-gun-friendly territory, I just drift out both receiver pins to separate the upper and lower units. Both halves will then fit inside a lockable hard-shell take-down shotgun case that stows nicely in a vehicle.

Battery storage: Electronic sights are all the rage and some of the latest units are really good. With the right AR-15 stock and pistol grip choices, you can find handy places for spare batteries. Not having spares guarantees a failure, which will probably occur sometime around midnight, almost certainly during the worst possible circumstances.

Compact size: A shorter-barreled AR-15 with a good, collapsible stock can be handy in tight spaces; like a vehicle, hallway, or small blind. The stock will also accommodate varying layers of winter clothing or different physiques. It's no coincidence that this configuration originated with the military. One additional and happy consequence is that matching the rifles minimum length to the right tactical case will provide an extremely convenient package. In fact, a disassembled AR will go down another complete notch in size. Once separated, my 16-inch ARs will fit within a spotting scope case.

Pull two captive pins and collapse the stock. Presto, you have a very compact package!

Conversion: The capability to separate upper and lower receivers facilitates an easy change to other configurations; or completely different calibers. This capability is possibly one of the best and least recognized AR features.

THE ULTIMATE TRANSFORMER?

My previously described 18 and 24-inch .223 uppers are a good example of an AR's versatility. Until I procured an extra lower, I also ran a 16-inch .300 Blackout upper, feeding all three from the same set of magazines. Manual depression of two disassembly pins makes each conversion a snap. Since each sighting system is mounted to its own upper receiver, zero is maintained. It almost sounds too good to be true, but switch-top uppers are completely practical.

Possibilities: I use a separate rimfire AR, but a .22 LR upper will mount as easily as anything (with a rimfire magazine). Many other calibers are now available, within the dimensional limits imposed by an AR's action size. You can't fit a .308-zized cartridge in an AR-15, which is why the super-sized AR-10 exists.

However, Colt introduced a novel hybrid AR-10 system that uses interchangeable magazine wells.

An AR-15 is the ultimate transformer. The Aim-point-equipped .300 Blackout carbine can morph into a precision heavy-barreled .223 without losing zero. The same magazine will feed either upper.

Their AR-10 type .308 upper can be attached to a special lower receiver with a large QD mag well. A smaller QD well can be exchanged, that accepts standard AR-15 magazines. At that point use a 5.56 upper is possible.

Windham Weaponry upped the ante with an AR-15 sized "RMCS" that will eat 5.56mm, .300 Blackout, 7.62x39 Russian, and 9mm. It's based on a Maine-made "Hydra" design, employing modular magazine wells and interchangeable barrels. A pair of strong pivoting forend arms will unlock a barrel for an easy exchange. The absence of a .308 is due to the smaller AR-15 platform.

Ruger's SR556 Takedown is another clever adaptation. It's a piston-driven AR-15 with a QD barrel feature. A small forward latch unlocks the barrel, at which point it will separate through a simple twist. The resulting package is extremely compact and will fit in a supplied case. An after-market .300 Blackout barrel is also available. Each barrel comes with its own front sight which (unlike most other AR types) is adjustable for elevation *and* windage. Each is first sighted in off its own front sight. Thanks to precision machining, a close zero can thus be maintained.

The addition of a receiver-mounted scope changes the landscape. Better plan on new zeros with switch-barrel designs and optics. If a different caliber is in the cards, I'd prefer a separate upper receiver, complete with its own scope. A swap is as simple as retracting two pins.

The .300 Blackout is gaining in popularity, largely because it will easily fit an AR-15. Beyond the limitations imposed by overall length, a cartridge's head diameter must be considered. The 5.56 and .300 Blackout share the same bolt dimensions, but most of the other calibers don't. The 6.8 SPC could be viewed as a ".270 Short," capable of extra punch. The case is larger in diameter, but it will run in an AR-15 with a bigger bolt face. Remington designed a very interesting .30-caliber alternative, the ".30 AR." It fits in a standard AR-15 and has a fatter case, but uses a rebated cartridge rim and larger bolt face. The .30 AR falls short of .308 power but does come fairly close—more in line with a .300 Savage. That's not too shabby, but for whatever reason, the Remington .30 AR really hasn't set the world on fire. Procurement of ammo will therefore be an issue. The fat-bodied and potent .450 Bushmaster shares the same rim but launches a .452 diameter bullet capable of smacking hogs, bear, or other tough customers at fairly close range. The .458 SOCOM is a similar idea that uses .458 bullets. Again, hopes for obtaining such ammo during tougher times will be less than favorable.

Such is not the case for the common 5.56mm NATO/.223 Remington. Ammunition abounds and a military 5.56mm chamber will digest either load.

CHAPTER 20

AR-15 AMMO OPTIONS

Earlier I mentioned the unsuitability of the 5.56mm/.223 for use on larger game. Lately, thanks in part to better bullets, people are pushing the envelope to hogs and deer. Some of the deer shot with these rifles are probably fairly small, weighing 100 pounds or less, dressed out. That helps reinforce claims of adequacy for whitetails. On the other hand, there are plenty of places where average weight is much larger. In Maine, a 90-pound deer would be a fawn. Moose roam statewide and some weigh half a ton. Black bear are common, but many are smaller than most non-hunters realize. Nevertheless, a 200 pound specimen is not unusual. It'll also come out the winner during any unarmed human combat.

When this Northern New England buck stepped out, the 7mm Magnum was suddenly not "too much gun." Dressed weight was 236 pounds. Live weight was probably closer to 300.

There are better (and safer) choices than the .223 for big game like this black bear. The .308 is adequate but a so-chambered AR will be large.

Bottom line: If a larger caliber (like a .308) is available, just go with it instead. If not, careful bullet selection will help improve performance of the smaller NATO cartridge. Much effort has gone into increasing the punch of our U.S. military 5.56mm ammunition. On the other hand, the .30/06 and .308 have been on solid ground for decades, indicating limits with the smaller caliber.

5.56 NATO/.223 REMINGTON LOADS

One consolation is that the smaller 5.56 rounds are somewhat more portable. Back in my Recon days, the basic load consisted of 15 magazines or nearly 300 rounds. Engagements were typically close-range, and terminal effects could be offset to some degree through sheer volume of fire. Ammunition was 55-grain FMJ, which could tumble after impact, but was unlikely to expand. Everybody talks about calibers when comparing stopping power, but few consider bullet construction. It makes a difference, but size matters too.

Performance: With most loads I'd rate big eastern coyotes as the upper limit for reliable one-shot stops. A really giant male will weigh around 50 pounds, but most are in the upper 30s. Still, like a determined human adversary, they're extremely tenacious. We had one heck of a time stopping coyotes in their tracks, even with expanding bullets. At night, in thick timber, they'll quickly disappear unless dropped on the spot. After much searching we found some that took perfect hits, confirming that shot placement wasn't the problem. More than once, we were tempted to move into .243 AR-10s. But patience prevailed and the .223 loads we're using are working. The secret involved use of tougher bullets, capable of producing both an entrance and exit wound. We'll look at some, shortly.

Big eastern coyotes are tough customers. They can cover ground after soaking up lead without the right .223 bullets. This average-size specimen piled up from one Federal 55 grain Ballistic Tip on a cold winter night. Note the IR unit atop the ATN NV scope.

On the other hand, the military is consigned to non-expanding, full-metal jacket projectiles. Penetration may increase but the wound channel will likely be narrower. It's true that the bullet may begin to tumble in flesh, but this trait is not guaranteed. In the bad old days I was thankful that our adversaries were not 200-pound individuals. Of late, the Mid-Eastern combat theatres have raised this specter, resulting in renewed efforts to improve terminal performance. Although 5.56mm bullet weights have increased, a large-scale switch to the shorter-barreled M-4 Carbine has decreased velocity, resulting in poor performance—especially beyond 200 yards. Even with a longer barrel, no matter how you slice it, the bullet is only .22-caliber. The heaviest bullets are still fairly light when compared to large calibers.

MORE POWER?

Within my circle, we don't have much .223/5.56 big game experience. Instead, everyone just switches to larger calibers. A .308 AR seems like the next logical choice, but most of them won't be very handy during long treks. This explains increasing interest in a few other AR-15 calibers which are now

Sporting Arms and Ammunition Manufacturers' Institute (SAAMI) listings. These domestically produced choices are loaded to SAAMI specifications, providing assurance of consistency. They seem like safer bets for bigger critters and may serve well as spare AR-15 uppers.

Magazine and action-length are limiting AR-15 factors. Shown L-R are a .223, 6.8 SPC, .300 Blackout, and 7.62x39 Russian.

6.8 SPC evolution: This "special purpose cartridge" is a product of the quest for a more effective round that will fit within the standard M-16/AR-15 platform. As good a caliber as the 6.8 SPC is, it doesn't share the luxury of a readily available brass source. Actually, there are several variants of this round, including the more recent 6.8 SPC II (loaded hotter and not for use in the earlier 6.8 SPC). The parent case is the .30 Remington, which is obscure and obsolete.

While some folks get standard AR magazines to work with a 6.8, others report feeding problems. In either case, capacity will be reduced. The LWRC 6.8 AR tackled the problem through use of proprietary magazines, with a matching lower-receiver well. A special, properly head-spaced bolt will also be needed, and some authorities claim its lugs are more susceptible to breakage.

On the other hand, the 6.8 "Special Purpose Cartridge" has a lot more punch than any 5.56mm, the reason it was developed. The actual caliber is .277, meaning it will handle bullets intended for the well-known .270 Winchester. The much smaller 6.8 case limits use to lighter projectiles, but bullet technology has come a long way. Most weighing 110–120 grains are suitable for deer or hogs. Muzzle-velocity will run around 2600 fps, providing a useful trajectory to 300 yards or thereabouts. One limiting factor is a requirement for relatively short and less streamlined bullets, needed to fit within the confines of an AR-15's action. On the other hand, the 6.8 should be a highly effective defensive cartridge. My son used his with good effect on Texas hogs. Barnes solid copper bullets will readily expand with excellent weight retention, for good penetration.

Lacking a large supply of expensive ammunition or components, any users are really at the mercy of a limited supply chain. At this point, the 6.8 seems like a possible flash in the pan. Another versatile newcomer may have stolen much of its thunder.

.300 Blackout: This cartridge is a hot new AR addition. In fact, the only necessary AR-15 modification is a new barrel. One of its virtues is the ability to launch true .30-caliber bullets at AK-47 velocities from a standard-sized AR-15. My 110-grain handloads average 2,350 fps or more from a 16-inch AR-15 upper. Many shooters will no doubt choose heavier 125-grain to 150-grain bullets. Another attraction is the capability to shoot suppressed subsonic loads that will function reliably through an AR-15. As it turns out, slow but very heavy bullets can develop enough pressure to cycle the action. My 220-grain load clocks 1,030 fps; just below the speed of sound. Without a sonic crack, it's extremely quiet when fired through a suppressor. The .300 Blackout can run off existing magazines with carefully chosen bullets. We'll take a closer look at this cartridge later.

7.62x39 Russian: Efforts have been made for quite some time to adapt this round to AR-15s. Results have been mixed for a number of reasons ranging from tolerances through taper. A .312-diameter, 123 grain bullet can achieve around 2,200 fps, which is quite similar to the newer Blackout round. Although I much prefer the latter, there are many shooters with large supplies of 7.62x39 ammo and AK magazines. Since they won't fit an AR's receiver, G.I. type magazines have been necessary; however, a few new hybrid AR/AK receivers have since materialized that will accept AK magazines. A different latching system is employed and like an AK-47, there is no provision for last shot lock-back. Of course, at this point you're into a dedicated lower AR receiver—unless you buy Windham Weaponry's version.

Subsonic .300 Blackout loads and a suppressor result in a quiet AR-15. The right heavy bullet/propellant combination generates adequate pressure to function the action.

6.5 Grendel: This cartridge makes a great hotrod, switch-top, AR-15 option. It uses a short fat case to launch 123-grain, .264-caliber bullets at up to 2,600 fps! Although not in the same league as a .260 Remington, such performance should handle deer out to 300 yards. Extended range is its main virtue, but this caliber should cover just about anything. Besides a different barrel, the 6.5 Grendel needs a 7.62x39 bolt. It will also achieve best function with purpose-built magazines. Like the 7.62x39 Russian and 6.8 SPC, a 6.5 Grendel conversion is best purchased as a complete package, complete with its own bolt carrier assembly and magazines. Alexander Arms is the source for this intriguing AR option. The ammunition, although harder to find, fills a real void in AR-15 performance.

More choices: Plenty of other cartridges have been adapted to the AR-15. We could print a list but here's the wrinkle: If times are hard will you bet on maintaining an adequate supply of specialist ammunition? I'd love to play with the .450 Bushmaster or .30 AR, both of which have much to offer; but availability is a problem, and so is cost. A logical alternative may be to stick with the standard and readily available .5.56mm/.223, focusing on the best bullet designs.

5.56 NATO/.223 REMINGTON FACTORS

As mentioned in the centerfire rifle section, both of these loads are close, but not identical. We'll need to understand their differences for, among other reasons, safety's sake.

Chambers and pressures: Boiling it all down, you can safely shoot .223 Remington rounds in a military 5.56mm chamber. The reverse is not guaranteed to be safe at all, owing to some dimensional differences with 5.56mm and slightly higher pressures. In a bolt-action, sticky bolt-lift is an indicator of a serious over-pressure situation. This won't be evident with a semi-auto, but other clues like chewed up rims or stuck brass should cause alarm. For this reason, many AR-15s are barreled with 5.56mm chambers. Look closely and you may see this designation stamped into the barrel. Surprisingly, it may not always guarantee a true NATO chamber.

Because a true 5.56 NATO chamber has a bit more slop, it may produce less than top-notch accuracy with premium .223 loads. Some builders use a hybrid "Wylde" chamber, which helps center the case-neck of a .223 for claimed accuracy improvement. Based on limited experience with a few so-chambered ARs, we agree. Out of the box, my lead instructor's Rock River 24"HB AR proceeded to punch a 1/4" 100-yard, 5-shot group with Hornady 55-grain TAP! Subsequent groups were a tad larger, but under 1/2." I had a second one on en route on short order, which shoots nearly as well (both are rifled 1x12). I'm just not sure how tolerant this design would be of surplus ammo or high-volume fire. If 1.5 MOA is adequate accuracy, and if the rifle will serve prominently in a defensive role, a NATO chamber makes a lot of sense.

Testing of Rock River's 24" HB AR-15s revealed impressive results. Short magazines permit a low and stable bench setup.

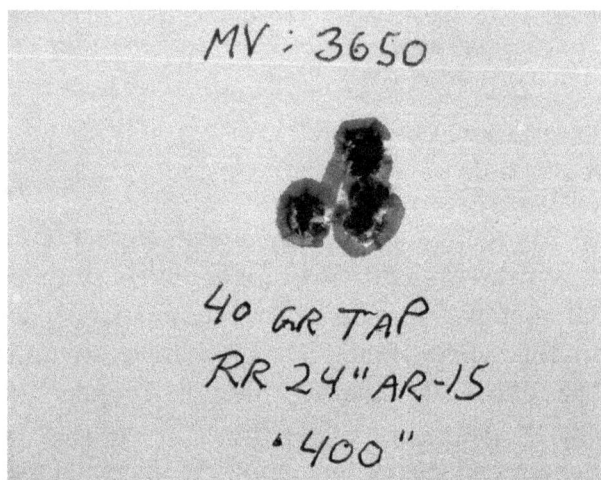

This 100-yard five-shot group was fired from a HB 24" Rock River 1x12 barrel. The Wylde Chamber isn't hype.

Rifling factors: For many shooters, the finer points of rifling science are likely of little concern. An off-the-shelf .30/06 will probably have a 1x10 barrel. A .308 may use a 1x12 twist. These numbers refer to the distance in inches necessary for the bullet to spin one complete revolution. In other words, the .308 bullet will rotate 360 degrees during each 12 inches of travel through the barrel. In general, bullets of a given caliber that are heavier or longer need more stabilization, imparted by a faster twist. In an effort to improve the long-range performance of the 5.56mm, heavier bullets were developed. The earlier 1x14 M-16 barrels were optimum for 55-grain FMJ, but too slow for the subsequent 62-grain SS109 replacement. An evolution was the M855 "Green Tip." These bullets with steel penetrators and lead-free cores resulted in slightly longer projectiles. The heaviest and longest bullets resulted in adoption of much faster 1x7 rifling. A recent 77-grain MK 262 load needs the very fast twist to stabilize its bullet.

An understanding of the basics may prove helpful when selecting ammunition. Those shooters planning on use of heavier bullets should shop for faster ROTs. Our 24-inch Rock River heavy-barreled AR-15s are an example of the opposite requirement. They were special-ordered with slow 1x12 twists for use on thin-skinned varmints, shooting fragile 40–55 grain bullets. A faster and increasingly popular all-around twist is 1x9. The quicker 1x8 is also catching on. We have a fair amount of experience

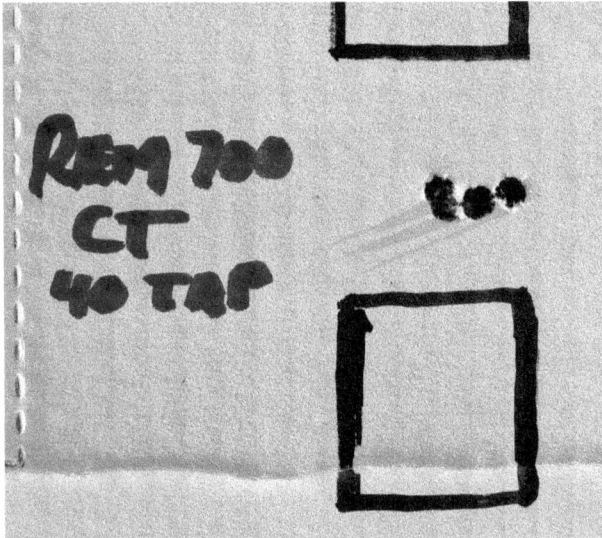

This respectable five-shot 100-yard .223 group was fired from a Remington M-700 Compact Tactical, rifled at 1x9. That twist-rate is a good AR-15 compromise.

with all and swear some black magic is involved. It makes sense to lean toward slower rates with light bullets and faster twists with heavyweights, but you'll never know for sure until you shoot them. A personal 18-inch AR-15 upper is rifled 1x8, but shoots Federal 55-grain Ballistic Tip with stunning sub-.375 MOA accuracy. My Remington Model 700 .223, Compact Tactical bolt-action has a fairly heavy, 20-inch fluted barrel with a 1x9 twist. Still, it shoots light 40–55 grain bullets very well, keeping up with an older 1x12 M-700. We fired a short but heavy 16" Rock River AR-15 with a very quick 1x7 twist and Wylde chamber. Surprisingly, it produced stunning 1/2 MOA groups with light 55-grain Hornady TAP.

One unanticipated outcome of firing over-stabilized bullets is disintegration. Especially with more lightly constructed projectiles, the possibility exists that they may unravel after minimal target contact. In fact, all though I haven't seen it with .223 rounds, I can recall a couple of instances where bullets never survived their 100-yard trip to a target. Centrifugal force literally ripped them apart in mid-air. Keyhole or sideways-bullet impacts are a sign of under-stabilization, which will typically be accompanied by poor accuracy. One might expect to see this when firing very heavy 75-grain bullets through slower twists like 1x12. I see the same effect with heavy .300 Blackout bullets, which get lobbed downrange at subsonic speed. Key-holing is sometimes evident with 220-grain bullets at 100-yards and beyond, despite a very fast 1x8 rifling twist. At closer range bullet holes are nice and round.

Unless you have a specific .223/5.56 load in mind which is either very light or unusually heavy, it may be safest to stick with rifling twists like 1x8, or 1x9.

AMMUNITION SELECTIONS

The very best AR-15s on the market won't perform without proper ammunition. The actual quality of the ammunition is a key part of the equation, and with prices creeping skyward, any bargain-priced rounds are increasingly attractive. Some may be surplus military of various origins, while others may be commercially reloaded. Dimensions may vary which, at best, could cause aggravating stoppages. Some less-often considered concerns involve brass thickness and primer hardness. Military cases tend to be thicker for better pressure resistance and improved function. Case volume will be less, which is a concern for handloaders. Less internal volume translates to higher chamber pressures with a given quantity of powder. A safe maximum load in a commercial .223 case may be dangerously over pressure in a 5.56mm brass. Those who never plan on reloading their own ammunition can still run into problems when firing loads assembled by others.

Commercial .223 Remington ammunition: These loads can be fired in a broad spectrum of firearm types beyond military designs. Consequently, top-shelf rounds will be precisely assembled using consistent components, designed to ignite within match grade actions. Primers may be a bit softer than mil-spec versions, which can introduce a problem in AR-15 rifles. Anyone who has extracted a live round may notice a small primer indentation that corresponds with the firing pin. It's typical of the AR design, which doesn't employ a spring-loaded system. When the mass of the bolt carrier seats the bolt head, inertia propels the pin forward, lightly contacting the cartridge's primer. Any live round bearing this small dimple has probably already been chambered at least once. Continue to re-chamber the same round and you run the risk of a very surprising discharge! Throw in a soft or high primer (maybe both), and it could happen anytime.

5.56x45mm NATO ammunition: Now we know why military ammo is built with harder primers. They're usually crimped into their pockets as well, for positive seating during violent, full-auto cycling. You can reload the stuff, but you'll need to swage out the small annular primer-pocket crimp. Several tools are made just for this purpose. For rough and tumble use in the harshest conditions, a mil-spec load and NATO chamber makes sense. Most such rounds will be loaded with FMJ bullets that will reliably feed, producing so-so accuracy and marginal terminal results. This so-called "ball ammo" will likely be the easiest to find, and it will also be a whole lot better than nothing. The 62-grain M855 "Green Tip" is a classic example that underwent much recent press after an attempt to ban it for civilian use. It bears the NATO symbol of a small cross in a circle.

RECOMMENDED 5.56/.223 LOADS

Disclaimer: I now operate in less rigorous conditions and can trade some tank-like durability for precision. Still, the prospect of a detonated primer remains. Even during sporting applications I avoid multiple chambering of the same round. After its third event I unload the magazine and then rotate it to the bottom. This practice has worked so far using a broad assortment of civilian loads. In fact, I don't shoot anything else. As for larger-scale firearms program operations, we stick with well-known brands. Of course, buying in large quantities helps reduce costs, but lacking that luxury, it's still worth spending a bit extra for ammunition of known quality.

This collection of .223 loads covers many needs. A 1x9 barrel should work in all but the heaviest load (but try it anyway).

Testing every load would be impractical; however, we have had good luck with the loads shown below. Conclusions are based upon a number of AR-15s, bolt guns, and other types. Your results may vary, so it's best to test a small batch before investing heavily. Then try to procure the same lot number. You can usually locate that on a box flap.

55 grain Federal FMJ ball #223AE: American Eagle seems to shoot 2 MOA or tighter, pretty much across the board, although we've seen a few rifles that beat 1.5 MOA. It's a good practice load and we burn it in large quantities. AE can be had in two flavors, one of which is primed to civilian .223 specifications (#223AE). The second, NATO-type uses mil-spec priming with a crimped primer pocket (#223AE-J). Either does well in a variety of twist rates.

40 grain Hornady TAP (now 40 grain V-Match #8325?): We've seen consistently good accuracy in all twists. Not many groups were under.5 MOA, but many were that size or only slightly larger (.625). A label on the box lists a MV of 3,800 fps, which seems to closely coincide out to 500 yards, using a Leupold VH reticle and 26" M-700 barrel. Our chronograph clocked 3,650 fps from a 24" Rock River AR-15. Regardless, this load is still flat-shooting medicine for light varmints. The polymer-tipped projectile is fairly frangible and lacks sufficient mass to anchor larger critters. On the other hand, its composite construction does result in a slightly longer bullet for its weight. My 1x12 HB AR will reliably punch five-shot, 1/2 MOA groups with 40 grain TAP, but we've seen a few good 1x9 barrels do nearly as well. The 40 TAP version is now discontinued, but the V-Match appears to be a very similar (if not identical) load.

With apologies for the graphic photo, this prairie dog illustrates the effects of .223 55-grain TAP at 250 yards.

55 grain Hornady TAP Urban #83276: This load is our overall accuracy champ, shooting well in nearly every circumstance. Most groups are somewhere around .5 MOA. Although heavier than the 40-grain version, it's still a frangible TAP bullet that won't reliably anchor our big male, hybrid wolf-coyotes. Anything smaller is in trouble, though. Like 40 grain TAP, low-angle strikes on hard ground seldom produce ricochets. The 55-grain load may have merit during close-quarter engagements where over-penetration is a concern. Our FBI ballistic gel tests confirmed its fragile construction. This load has evolved a bit. We're still running off the remnants of an older #83276.

Civilian #83278 iterations uses cases that are either black (or most recently) nickel-plated.

55 grain Federal/ Nosler Ballistic Tip #P223F or #T223F: This polymer-tipped bullet generally displays great accuracy in most rifling twists! I've shot lots of .5 MOA groups in ARs and bolt guns. A Wylde-chambered 1x8 AR reliably cuts 5-shot, .375 MOA groups! It also anchors big coyotes, and has performed satisfactorily in several defensive events that we're aware of. This makes sense since we shot it through the FBI testing protocols with satisfactory results. Using shorter 16" barrels, expansion is less, which increases penetration. We've used both product numbers interchangeably. P223 F is a civilian version with a prairie dog logo on the box. T223F is a "Tactical Tru" law enforcement product. Either is a good, general purpose choice.

55 grain Barnes VOR-TX Triple-Shock X Bullet #21520: We've seen varying accuracy results in 1x8,

9, & 12 twists. A Remington M-700 VSSF averaged .5 MOA from its 1x12 barrel. I have high terminal expectations, based upon experience with .30 Barnes TSX loads and other reports. With careful shooting, it should work on hogs or small deer. When shot through a recent FBI auto glass ballistic testing phase, the .223 TSX was the champ for weight retention and penetration. We weren't surprised. The bullet is solid copper, so jacket/core separations are eliminated. In tissue, four nasty petals peel outward without shedding mass. Our experience was based on Federal 's version, which used the same bullet. They no longer catalog this load, but the latest Barnes version should perform similarly.

60 grain Federal/ Nosler Partition #P223Q: We lack extensive testing data, but we have seen great results on big Kudjo-like coyotes. Accuracy has been good in several AR-15s, including a couple with 1x7 twists. The Partition design has been around longer than I have, and it is a well-proven, tough bullet, capable of good penetration. I'd use it on deer in a pinch, carefully choosing my shots. It also has defensive potential.

This alpha male was anchored by a Federal .223 /Nosler 60-grain Partition.

64 grain Winchester Ranger Bonded Solid Base RA556B: We received samples and shot them through the FBI protocols. The load looked like a real winner with good weight-retention and excellent penetration. For use in harsh conditions, the crimped, sealed primer and sealed bullet/case mouth offer extra reassurance. Since it's advertised with NATO brass, use in .223 Remington chambers may be ill-advised. However, for anyone with a 5.56mm barrel, this load is worth consideration!

75 grain Hornady TAP BTHP #80265: Long or heavy bullets generally need faster rifling twists for optimum stability. We had mediocre accuracy results in 1x9 and 1x12 twists, which is understandable. Still, we managed groups of around 1.25–1.5 MOA . I haven't yet tried it in a 1x7, or on any live targets. It's listed in deference to others, who report good performance where increased, but not excessive penetration is required. A friend fired one decisive shot to end a lethal LEO engagement. Hornady claims this load will penetrate less than many pistol bullets, which makes sense, given the HP design. Its heavier weight calls for fast rifling twists.

Another well-respected product-line worth exploring comes from Black Hills. They source bullets from a number of manufacturers, cherry-picking those best-suited for specific tasks. Unfortunately, we just don't have much personal range time with their products (yet). The same applies to Hornady's GMX loads, which use homogenous non-lead projectiles. Like the solid-copper Barnes TSX bullets, they'll no doubt offer great penetration and weight retention.

A short list of .223 loads: Larger-caliber uppers can condense a personal inventory of .223 ammo loads. Having chosen this route, heavy-for-caliber bullets are off my list. Three .223 choices cover my basic needs, using a common zero. Each one uses a 55-grain bullet:

<u>Training & plinking:</u> Federal 55-grain AE works just fine.

<u>General purpose:</u> For larger critters and defense, Federal 55 grain Ballistic Tip has proven accurate and deadly.

<u>Pure accuracy:</u> The choice is Hornady 55 grain TAP, which also performs well on many varmints.

I establish zero by shooting Federal 55-grain Ballistic Tips from 200 yards. The scope's friction-fitted scales are then set to "0."

This Lyman chamber-check gauge indicates an oversize .300 Blackout round. It should seat flush like the .223 load.

Being excessively picky, I also use 40 grain Hornady bullets for small varmints. However, due to increased velocity, a different zero is necessary. A small adhesive label inserted to the underside of the elevation cap reminds me of the necessary clicks. Just to be sure, the little label reads "40 Hndy: -6 clicks." The elevation scale will no longer be on "0" and the 1/4 MOA graduations will indicate this change.

Whatever load you settle on, check its overall length. I've run into a few that were just too long for standard AR-15 magazines. You'll want to be certain all is well before buying in quantity. Two other key factors are reliable function, and accuracy. Once these obstacles are overcome, try buying boxes from the same lot number. Purchasing them by the case will help.

Another good addition is a chamber-checking tool. I own a "Lyman Chamber-Checker," which is a well-machined aluminum block containing six SAAMI-minimum chambers in various calibers. Three of interest here are .223 Rem, .300 Blkt, and 7.62x39. In theory, any rounds that drop in until flush should fit a standard chamber. Some 5.56mm NATO loads may not fit, but those that I've tried have.

Note the absence of any steel-cased ammunition. We just don't have enough 5.56 experience with these cartridges. They're common AK fodder, but some shooters report AR issues. Steel-cased shooters should probably check their rifle's warranty first. One brand we'd consider is sold by Hornady as a lower-priced, non-reloadable alternative.

Chapter 21

AR SIGHTING SYSTEMS

Most AR shooters will benefit from some type of optical sight whether a dot or a more conventional scope. Nevertheless, especially with electronic aiming systems, a folding backup iron sight (BUIS) system is good insurance. With careful shopping, you can pick folding combinations that won't interfere with an optical image.

IRON SIGHTS

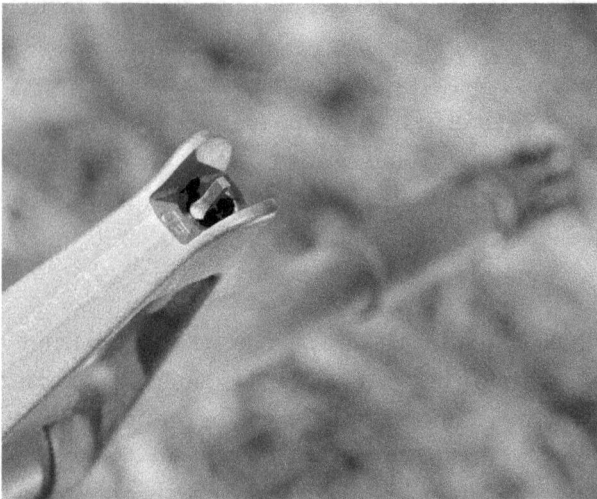

A close-up view of a G.I. front sight tower. The threaded post permits elevation adjustments. Reducing its height will raise the point of impact.

The carry handle equipped G.I. A-2 receiver sight is familiar to many veterans, and is preferred by some. Like the 40-L, it has two apertures. Note the windage reference scale.

The original G.I. front sight tower is far from dead. In fact, we specified that arrangement for our general purpose, patrol-type carbines. They're fairly high but also very simple integral gas-block/aiming units. When using dot sights or scopes with large fields-of-view, the tall front-sight housing will be plainly visible. The first inclination is to align the optical reticle with the top of the iron sight's post, but that's not necessary and our shooters quickly learn to tune them out. The G.I. front sight does serve one unanticipated benefit though. Since it's easy to cant a dot sight, the protective ears on the front sight tower can serve as a rough leveling reference. This trick can prevent windage errors during long-range shooting. For our semi-auto M-4 type carbines, we went with an A.R.M.S. 40-L, low-profile folding rear. The clamping nut is tethered to the sight's body with a fine steel cable to prevent loss. It's also fast to employ, co-witnessing with the optical sight and front post. Release of a simple catch will allow the aperture to pop upright under spring tension. To gain full elevation adjustment, you may need the .040" taller front sight post (the same one used with detachable carry handles). Two apertures are provided, one of which has a large CQB blade. Cost is around $110.

This folding A.R.M.S. 40-L is low enough to clear a Burris FFII 1.75-5 ocular bell. It also nests inside the QD lever on Warne rings.

If the small aperture is zeroed for 300-yards, the larger CQB blade should be on at around 200. Elevation adjustments are made using the threaded front sight. A clickable .75 MOA drum provides rear-sight windage. Always move the rear sight in the same direction you want your bullets to go. The front sight is the opposite (meaning you'd need to screw it in to pick up elevation). Open notches on the top of each blade are designed for 500–600 yard aiming. When folded down, the .610" height of a 40-L will permit it to tuck under the ocular bell of some scopes. It clears my 3x9 Leupold Compact Scope, which is mounted in Warne QD Rings. Up front, a folding Diamondhead unit is mounted to a free-floated forend. A crowning touch would be a Tritium front sight post for use during low-light conditions.

These are but a few examples of the many iron-sight arrangements now available. The latest trend belies that moniker, since some utilize polymer bodies. Magpul sells BUIS units within that category, and they are known for good products. We stayed with steel, due to our geographical location, having seen a number of "unbreakable" plastic parts snap during sub-zero temperatures.

DOT SIGHTS

It's been our experience that dot sights won't significantly improve accuracy over iron sights. But, they will certainly work better in the dark, and also seem to be much more intuitive. On moving targets, or during dynamic events, a well-designed dot sight is fast and simple to use. Directions:

#1: Put dot on target.

#2: Squeeze trigger.

The military has figured this out, explaining the proliferation of such devices in combat theatres. Although some civilian versions cost less than a hundred dollars, combat reliability won't come cheap. Besides expense, other factors worth considering include battery-life and availability. While we certainly haven't used every dot sight, we have played with several brands.

Aimpoint: Several different sights are in circulation. We've used a few, including the recently discontinued, military-issue Aimpoint Comp-ML2 that evolved to the "PRO" (Patrol Rifle Optic) during 2011. After a thorough testing period, we settled on the latter as a general-issue sight. The PRO uses a conventional 30mm tube. One immediate advantage of a tubular body is its ability to accept scope-type protective lens caps, two of which come standard. The lenses are also inset a bit, which helps keep them dry during inclement weather. One issue affecting zero at longer range is rifle cant. Without any crosshairs, it's quite possible to introduce a list to port or starboard. With a properly sighted-in rifle this problem will manifest through windage errors. Due to an AR's high sighting plane, it really doesn't take all that much (again, G.I. front sight ears can serve as a reference for a level hold). A rugged, QD ring-mount is included with each Pro. It mounts easily by hand, using a knurled over-torque knob. The height is correct for use on a Picatinny AR-15 flat top upper, and it will co-witness with iron sights. The 2 MOA dot is powered by a somewhat hard-to-find 3-volt Lithium battery. We feel this is a fair trade-off, considering its greatly improved 30,000 hour run-time! This figure is based on 70% illumination, and our original T&E unit has been switched to the "on" position for a couple of years. A rheostat on/off knob permits varying intensity levels, including four night vision and six daylight settings. We were told to leave it on, so that's what we do. Severe winter temperatures have had no effect on the dot, but just to be safe, we change out the batteries each January. The Aimpoint PRO is submersible up to 50 meters. Puddles are hopefully our limit, but since we often operate in bad weather, this rating is reassuring. These sights are compact but robust, weighing just under 12-ounces (with their mounts). All of our shooters have had positive comments. An Aimpoint PRO can be tracked down for a bit north of $430.

Aimpoints are rugged and reliable. They'll also co-witness well with many BUIS systems. The mounting system clears a folding 40-L sight.

Those willing to forgo the NV feature should look at the new Aimpoint Carbine Optic spin-off. The waterproof rating is 15 feet, and battery life is 10,000 hours. A nut replaces the PRO's QD knob, but cost is around $50 less.

We haven't used the Micro T-2, but that's just a matter of time. This tiny sight evolved from Aimpoint's T-1. Improvements include a rounder 2 MOA dot, shielded turrets, and lens caps. It's a rugged military-grade sight, priced accordingly at around $750.

EoTech: These innovative military-grade, waterproof sights are advertised as having a holographic, two-eyes-open, heads-up display. The image, which is adjustable for intensity, certainly does grab one's attention. With a TV-type screen,

field-of-view is great. Various reticle patterns are available including a popular central dot, which although fairly fine, is surrounded by a concentric ring for fast target acquisition. The hardest part may involve a final choice, with so many models

A small dot sight like Aimpoint's Micro T is the latest rage.

available. Besides reticle choices, rear or side-mounted controls, night vision settings, and different battery options are offered. We've used an AA-powered, NV-compatible unit for more than 10 years. It has an automatic shut-off feature, which helps prolong battery life. A night vision monocular can be mounted behind it for nocturnal operations, but the rear-mounted controls are then hard to access. Perusing the latest line, I'd forgo the AA battery advantage to gain some recent improvements. The Model EXPS3 offers water-proof construction, side-mounted controls, and more compact size. It runs on a #123 Lithium battery good for at least 500 hours, and the side-mounted compartment is easy to reach. It also has an AR-15/Picatinny QD mount. Several reticle patterns are offered and for those so inclined, separate magnifying optical units are available.

An Eotech, shown with an accessory magnifier. The BUIS rear is forgone here due to optical eye relief demands.

Leupold: Their "Prismatic" sight is relatively small, but boasts a 30mm tube. Its illuminated, circle & crosshair etched reticle is still plainly visible if the battery dies. It seems to works well for those with astigmatisms that sometimes

This Leupold Prismatic Sight has seen its share of action, but it's still ticking. Note the BUIS sight, just in case things go wrong.

blur illuminated dots. The included mount was properly designed for AR-15 use, and eye relief is generous; although not unlimited. While the Prismatic seems much more precise than the others, it does burn through batteries. Part of the problem is the pushbutton switch, which can be bumped on. With illumination adjusted to a lower setting it's easy to assume the diode if off in normal light—a situation that will eventually kill the battery. Spares will be needed, and they are the same 3-volt type used by Aimpoint (available from camera stores). The Prismatic won't accept a separate magnifier, but its strongest suite may be the clear, precise, and battery-independent crosshairs.

More recently, Leupold has developed a number of great-looking AR sights. Their "Leupold Carbine Optic" is small and rugged. Unlike some other units, its 1 MOA dot is surrounded by an uncluttered optical housing with a generous FOV. All of the LCO's controls are located below the display in a very tidy package. An interesting addition is the D-EVO 6x20 sight, which can mount behind the LCO. It sits low and won't obstruct the dot sight. Instead, the 6-power addition looks around it in an innovative sideways periscope arrangement. The dot sight can serve for fast, close-range engagements, and a slight head-shift downward will permit use of the 6-power optic. Both nest together, forming a very compact combination. The LCO costs around $1,000, and the D-EVO is $1,500. For significant cost, these Leupold units solve the vexing dilemma of a dot or scope.

Lucid Optics: We don't have any direct experience with this newer company. Still, Lucid seems to be gathering a following; probably because they specialize in unique and feature-laden products, sold for a fair price. Their HD7 dot sight is a prime example with its rugged aluminum housing, tethered turret caps, selectable reticles, limited lifetime warranty, and a street price of under $180. One AAA battery provides generous life from a cleverly located receptacle under the main body. This sight is designed for ARs, and a 2X screw-on magnifier is available (along with other accessories). The HD7 makes the list due to numerous good reviews.

Trijicon Reflex: These unique sights don't rely on batteries. Instead, their internal fiber optic system displays an aiming point which is powered either from ambient light, or an integral radioactive Tritium lamp. Several reticle choices are available, including chevrons, triangles, and dots of various sizes. We've used 4.5 and 6.5 MOA dot versions extensively with dependable results, during all sorts of severe conditions. Our Model RX01NSN units are equipped for AR-15 flat top mounting with a very strong base. Although the smaller 4.5 MOA versions permit a bit more precision at longer ranges, we have had good luck with 6.5 MOA dots out to 350 yards on steel humanoid silhouettes. The Reflex

Trijicon's non-electronic Reflex Sight is rugged and simple. This 6.5 MOA RX01 unit is a good match for its 9mm SMG host. It's not likely they'll be needed, but once again, a BUIS system is present.

Sights are simple and rugged units, if not altogether perfect. A quirk is that the dot may wash out under certain conditions, particularly if aiming into very bright outdoor light from a dimmer indoor environment. Also, if shooting toward the sun, some reticle flaring is possible. Rear-mounted night vision coupling is out since the dots are just too bright, but despite these faults, we like the Trijicons. They're really fast if shot with both eyes open, and battery failure is a non-issue. A newer version includes a battery assist (at a steeper price).

Trijicon's new "Miniature Rifle Optic" looks especially useful. Like the Aimpoint T-2, it's a very small dot sight, measuring only 2.6-inches lengthwise. The MRO employs shielded turret adjustments and is built like a tank.

Other Miniaturized dot sights: There appears to be a welcomed trend toward common batteries. Lithium AAs are a whole lot easier to find than some of the others. Paradoxically, dot sight miniaturization has also caught on. Ironically, many are now so small that even AAAs won't fit. These units are really tiny, resembling miniature 1980 TV sets.

You'll often see miniaturized dot sights mounted in offset positions, attached to conventional rifle scopes. They're popular with 3-gun shooters who switch between long and close-range targets while shooting on the move. The dot is employed as an auxiliary sighting system for the closest targets, where precision is subservient to speed. The shooter cants the rifle, bringing the miniature dot into view. The miniatures are also small enough to mount directly on pistol slides or revolvers. Some rifle shooters even use them as their primary rifle sights. Lately, everyone is jumping on the band-wagon with a proprietary model of varying quality. A comprehensive test would be an expensive and daunting challenge. Prices vary greatly, and you'll probably get what you pay for. For serious defensive use I'd consider spending more money. Some of the serious tactical contenders are sold by Trijicon, Leupold, etc. Most of my experience involves some Burris units. I have a FastFire mounted to an S&W .44 Magnum revolver. Another sits atop a Remington semi-auto .308 for fast shots in thick cover. My son has one on his 12 gauge Benelli M-4 shotgun, sighted in for slugs. It worked so well that I finally mounted one to a Beretta 12 Ga. turkey shotgun. All of these guns generate recoil and all four sights are still running. Of these Burris FastFires, their latest FF-III is the way to go. Like the FF-II, it's weather resistant, but it also has click stop adjustments, a rheostat dot, and doesn't require disassembly for battery changes (one CR-1632 3-volt). Cost is around $225 with a Picatinny mount. A Burris AR riser with protective wings is a useful extra. Having survived 3-inch magnum recoil, a FastFire should endure an AR-15.

The Burris FastFire III version has better zero adjustment and battery replacement features than early versions. Various mounts are sold, including this Picatinny design.

General comments: Ideally, these sights should be used with both eyes open. Besides quicker target pick-up and peripheral awareness, you can take advantage of the "Bindon Aiming Concept" - a useful trick that can overcome a front lens obstruction like snow or dirt. Our Aimpoint PROs come with a solid hinged front cover, which can also be forgotten. As it turns out, this feature is a great way to train on the Bindon technique. To see if it'll work for you, cover the muzzle-end of your lens with the cap (or some tape), and point the rifle normally toward a combat silhouette target from around 20 yards. Your dominant eye should still see the dot and your other eye will pick up the target. With a bit of practice, your brain will superimpose both images for emergency sighting. Some folks with vision issues seem to have difficulty with the process, but most others can figure it out in short order.

Dot sights are great for defensive or close-range hunting scenarios, either of which can involve low light. NV settings can enhance a system, and tactical-type shooters may even add a magnifier. As the name implies, these optical additions provide a way to incorporate magnification. Most are hinged and will swing aside for close-quarter dot use. Costs vary greatly and the best ones can tack on an extra $500. Given their extra mass, many shooters now gravitate toward compact, low-powered scopes with illuminated reticles.

AR SCOPE SYSTEMS

A flat top AR-15 is accommodating when it comes to scopes. Some people stick with the older carry handle design which, although simple, is not too optics-friendly. Yes, you can buy mounts that lock into a carry handle, but the resulting scoped package will be quite awkward. A solid cheek weld will be lost and bore offset will increase. The flat top design now dominates for good reason but, due to its straight-line action, both the barrel and stock are on the same plane. As a result, very high scope rings are usually required. Locating a sighting system well above the bore causes a condition called "offset." Assuming we zero for 100 yards, bullets will impact noticeably low at very close range. On a positive note, plenty of clearance exists for the mounting of larger-objective scopes.

AR Mounts: Standard "medium" or "high" rings

This AR has the original A-1 integral carry handle/sight system. The addition of a scope will result in a very high aiming system. Note the barrel-mounted bipod, which can change POI.

A detachable A-2 sight/carry handle assembly opened up all sorts of aiming options. The "Advanced Combat Optical Gunsight" (ACOG) eventually gained military ground.

will probably be too low for satisfactory mounting without riser bases. You can buy such adapters as one or two-piece units, and most will add an extra 0.5" of height the top of a flat top receiver. Although I've used them with success, I much prefer a simpler solution. There are some good one-piece integral base and ring units which clamp directly to a Picatinny rail receiver. Individual ring pairs are also sold that do the same thing. Some are secured with rugged fasteners, while others use QD levers. Costs can vary greatly, with some of the best tactical-grade systems going for hundreds of dollars. A serviceable mounting system can be had for around $100.

I have quite a bit of experience with Warne Quick Detach Ultra-High rings. They are secured by simple thumb levers, and will closely maintain zero during repeat attachments. Warne recommends the MSR height of 0.935" for AR flat tops and 1" scope tubes. The 30mm Ultra-High set is 0.850," and either is designed for optimum eye placement. Both dimensions indicate the height above a Picatinny rail, measured from the bottom of a scope tube. For me, these rings heights are about right. Some people grumble about their complexity during the initial assembly, which may be due to the manly sport of skipping directions. Sure, they're a bit more "fiddly" to set up, but they work well after that. My one gripe is their weight, which runs a bit over nine ounces. Warne has a new MSR Quick Detach set which nicely solves this problem, shaving off 1/4 pound per set. You can buy them with QD thumb levers or heavy-duty hex nuts (I went the QD route). Since all of these rings mount directly to a Picatinny receiver, plenty of latitude exists for optimum spacing. I mount the rear ring a bit forward to leave enough space for a backup rear sight. One thing to avoid is locating the forward ring on a forend slot, since slight flexing is possible.

The one-piece base and ring systems are also hugely popular. Some of these are sold with QD levers, while others bolt on. Most have a rakish forward ring slant, which eliminates forend mounting worries. Like the dual ring designs, you can often set them up with enough extra rearward space for a backup folding peep. We use Leupold units on our piston-driven .308 POF Designated Marksman ARs. I have a battle-scarred one-piece Rock River "Hi-Rise" unit that has traveled among numerous AR receivers. It's not the most graceful unit, but a pair of large slotted thumb-knobs provides secure mounting. Mine is a 1" version, which runs to the high side at 1.180" (also available as separate rings).

Warne new AR-specific MSR rings are lightweight but strong. This set has QD levers but a permanent version is offered.

AR scope mounting system heights can vary, depending upon the manufacturer. For many AR shooters, a.750" height is probably close to minimum. More height will probably be needed with a folding rear sight, but going too high can result in less stock and cheek contact. Adding a riser to the stock is another option, but don't forget about charge handle clearance!

AR Scopes: Regardless of the mounting choice, plenty of clearance should exist for giant bell scopes that are normally associated with strong magnification. I have a 4.5x14 Leupold on a 24" dedicated varmint AR upper, but for a general purpose rifle, that much glass is overkill. About the most magnification I'd want would be a 3x9. The older Leupold 3x9 Compact on my 18-inch upper seems well balanced, and usually remains on 3X. Of late, a large assortment of AR-15 specific scopes has appeared, many of which are lower-powered. Some have generous eye relief, which helps with

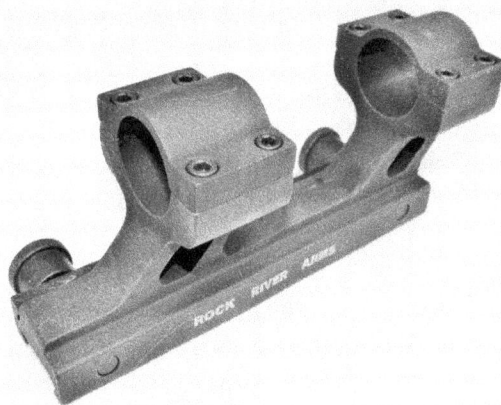

Rock River's one-piece base/ring set has little to go wrong. This unit has survived numerous bumps and dings.

an AR platform. Positioning the scope forward makes charge handle latch access easier. For those encountering some difficulty, after-market latches are available. All of my uppers are so equipped.

On their lowest settings, the 1x4s afford many of the same advantages realized with dot sights. In fact, some now have illuminated reticles, and on 1X, field-of-view is usually generous. The larger-diameter 30mm scope bodies permit greater range of adjustments and accommodate electronic circuits. The sport of Multi-Gun (three-gun) has greatly broadened the field, and because it's based on combat-type scenarios, the latest technologies extend nicely to our requirements. These include some capability to make long range hits, plus a quick transition for room-length targets. As we've noted, some shooters also attach an offset miniature dot sight for instant close-quarter selection. In the end, money talks and the price for a practical AR-15 won't be peanuts. Adding magazines and related gear jacks up the system cost, so a versatile scope selection may lower the final tab. Just about all of the major manufacturers now catalog lower-magnification multi-gun models that are perfect for our needs. Their reticles are often illuminated and graduated for holdover. Others employ calibrated turrets that match popular loads. Throw ring collars are common for fast magnification shifts.

Leupold's 3x9 Compact (now Ultralight 3-9x33) maintains a well-balanced AR package. The rings are Warne QDs. The forend is an older free-float quad-rail type. The BUIS folding front is part of the gas block.

Reticles: Each type has its followers:

Mil-Dots: This type of reticle is seen with increasing frequency. A true Mil-Dot subtends (covers) one meter at 1,000 meters. As such, it can be used to estimate range, using targets of known or approximate sizes. A dot 50% the height of a six-foot standing man would indicate an approximate range of 1,000 meters. Further uses involve hold-off for wind.

Ballistic aiming reticles: A number of manufacturers now list AR-specific scopes with interesting reticle designs. Depending on the caliber and load, one could zero normally and use the holdover marks for 200–600 yard shots. They make lots of sense when combined with a lower-power, illuminated scope.

Ballistic turrets: The latest vogue involves elevation drums calibrated for popular .223 loads. After initial sighting in, the shooter simply turns the dial to the number corresponding with the target's range. Cranking the turret up to "3" would allow dead-on aiming at 300 yards. This assumes wind is not a factor, which it normally is — especially with light .22-caliber bullets.

Which system is best? For a disciplined shooter willing to commit serious effort, the Mil-Dot arrangement is highly effective. But for the average shooter, on the fly, ballistic-aiming reticles are the easier bet. Used with a rangefinder, you paste the appropriate elevation line on the target and squeeze off a shot. Some designs now have windage marks that correspond with full-value 10 & 20 mph crosswinds. As mentioned in the Rifle Section, it's best to locate a spot where you can stretch out the distance for a test fire. Don't be surprised if see some discrepancies. These can be noted on a small, weapon-mounted label.

Some of these scopes now have first focal plane reticles which, unlike more common second focal plane designs, maintain ballistic-aiming usefulness throughout their magnification range. The reticle will appear larger as the magnification increases on a first-plane scope but the relationship of target to hold-points will remain unchanged.

Most domestic sporting scopes use a second-plane system, whereby the reticle appears the same regardless of the power setting. The problem is, when calibrated hold-point marks are introduced, the values will change as magnification decreases. In other words, second-plane designs only work at specific settings, which are typically the maximum; however, on a fighting system, a large field-of-view is important to help pick up targets. The scope is normally best left on a lower setting but, with second-plane designs, the ballistic-reticles won't properly calibrate. This explains the move to first-plane systems on tactical scopes.

SCOPE CHOICES

The latest optical developments have included higher magnification ratios. Leupold's Mark 6 provides a very useful times-six variable, running from one up to six-power. The Mark 8 provides a corresponding increase and would be hard to beat, but comes at substantial cost. Other manufacturers are now jumping on the 1x8 bandwagon. It's an ideal magnification range, but one that requires considerable engineering. Many of us will settle for a lower-priced compromise.

Leupold scopes: A series of practical AR choices exist. Costs run from downright expensive to fairly affordable:

Leupold Mark 8 CQBSS 1.1x8: At nearly $3,000, this scope is well beyond the reach of most shooters. Its oddball 34mm main tube provides great strength and increased adjustments. Several first-plane reticle choices are available, and just about every good feature possible to incorporate into a tactical scope resides within this model.

Leupold Mark 6, M6C1, 1x6: Falling a step below the Mark 8, many features are preserved. Its $1,000 saving will result in a slight magnification reduction although, at around two grand, it's not exactly bargain priced.

Leupold Mark 4 MR/T 1.5x5: "MR" stands for mid-range and the "T" means tactical. Two versions are available; either an illuminated M-2 30mm option, or smaller non-illuminated one-inch tube. The latter is cheaper, running around $800. Both have an SPR reticle with some interesting features. It combines a fast circle with hold-points that work with popular 5.56 and 7.62mm loads. We spent another $300 for M-2 variants, gaining a good all-around compromise with plenty of great features.

Leupold VX-R Patrol 1.25x4: For a bit less magnification and cost, one can still have an illuminated scope. A 30mm tube accommodates the circuitry, which has a very useful "Motion Sensor Technology" feature. After five minutes of inactivity, the MST shuts off the illumination to preserve CR-2032 battery life. Moving the rifle will activate the sensor to re-power the crosshairs. The degree of illumination is adjustable and the MST will return it to the last setting. The SPR reticle is still visible if the power gives out. Cost is a bit below $600.

Leupold's Mark 4 MR/T 1.5-5x30mm is a winner. This M-2 illuminated version sits in a Leupold 30mm mount. The rifle is a POF.

Leupold VX-R Hog 1.25x4: Add 3.5 ounces, a 30mm tube, and another $300 to get a beefier but illuminated version of the more basic VX Hog. It's sort of a hybrid Patrol/Hog model.

Leupold VX Hog 1x4: Although designed for feral pigs, this light-weight, rugged scope provides a generous field-of-view. It should serve well for those seeking a smaller package at an affordable price. At its highest 4x setting, the circle reticle provides holdover points. The one-inch tube is non-illuminated, but trims the weight to only 8-ounces. A lightweight scope can prove invaluable once AR accessories are installed. For around $230, it's a pretty good deal.

It's worth taking some time to carefully peruse these models (and others) online. If considering a ballistic-aiming reticle, note its focal plane location. The lower-priced VX series are second-plane designs that only coincide with published values on maximum settings.

Other brands: A number of firms have rallied to the AR-15 with intriguing optics. As mentioned previously, to meet growing speed-competition needs many such scopes trend toward lower magnifications with larger FOVs. Enlarged power rings permit rapid magnification changes for engagements of from just a few feet out to 400 yards. Reticles are designed for fast target acquisition and trajectory compensation. Not too coincidentally, these characteristics translate well to practical field conditions. The scopes with illuminated reticles usually have 30mm main-tubes.

Burris: The company has directed much attention to the growing AR market, as evidenced by their MTAC-30 line. This illuminated 2nd FP "Ballistic Close Quarter" reticles matches longer-range 5.56 trajectories, while permitting fast close-quarter use. The 1x4 and 1.5x6 models offer a great balance of features and size. An MTAC/FastFire dot sight package is also offered for multi-gun shooters. An intriguing new Burris is their XTR II 1-8x24. Although it has a 34mm tube, the lack of an objective bell results in a fairly compact profile. Both 1st and 2nd FFP illuminated-reticle versions are offered. The larger tube and tactical-grade construction account for a weight of 24.4 ounces, but its features could cover just about any AR use from CQB to long range targets. This versatility comes at a price, which is nearly $1,200.

Bushnell: This long-standing firm hasn't been sitting idly on the sidelines. Bushnell has gone heavily into the tactical market with a series of long-range and AR scopes. Some are geared toward three gun (multi-gun) competition, with features equally useful for all AR owners. Besides a number of interesting choices in the $250 range, Bushnell sells a higher-priced "Elite Tactical" series of scopes. A pair of 1st and 2nd FP 1-6.5 30mm models are listed, along with a 1st FP 1-8.5x24 SMRS. Cost start at around $1,000. A pair of less expensive and lighter-weight, straight-tubed "Designated Marksman" scopes are sold in 1-4 and 1-6. They have 30mm tubes with illuminated reticles, and costs start at around $270.

Tactical scopes are in, but this basic 1.75-5 Burris Fullfield has served admirably on a number of ARs. Its heavy German reticle is fast and effective in low light. FOV on 1.75X is huge.

Nightforce: Built to survive in all foreseeable conditions, these scopes continue to hold a pricey but well-deserved edge. Some knowledgeable shooters consider a Nightforce the gold standard for tactical use. A lower magnification model will constitute one heck of a great choice. Costs begin near the upper end of some competitive brands, yet these scopes continue to sell.

Nikon: Among their diverse line of optics, Nikon is solidly into AR-specific scopes, many of which are reasonably priced. The P-223 1.5-4.5x20mm is a good example, selling for under $200. Like many other AR-oriented Nikons, it has tactical-type turrets and a BDC reticle. Nikon's "Spot-On" ballistic match program adds a whole new level of versatility to their BDC reticles, and it's worth spending some time in their website.

Trijicon: Their "Advanced Combat Optic Gunsight" scopes are often seen on military M-16s. The ACOGs are built to tough, military-grade specifications, and have well-earned reputations for dependability. Many versions are offered, including compact, lower magnification scopes meant for use in harm's way. Several illuminated reticle patterns are also offered with Tritium/fiber optic elements that eliminate the need for batteries. Costs start at around $1,000.

Trijicon's ACOG spawned a military aiming revolution, along with a number of similar-looking knock-offs.

Vortex: This brand is rapidly gathering steam for good reasons. Their innovative 1x6 "Strike Eagle" scope is geared toward AR-15s. Its 30mm body contains a second focal plane, illuminated reticle. On its lowest magnification this scope serves well as a dot sight. On 6X, its interesting ballistic reticle offers long-range potential. The elevation holdover grid is etched and remains useable without battery power. A spare battery inside the windage cap is a clever and reassuring touch. So far, mine has proven to be an exceptional deal at its listed $330 price.

Others: Truthfully, a decent 1x4 will work, and some can be had for around $200. One thing worth looking for is generous eye relief, which comes in handy on an AR-15. It's hard to access the charging handle when an ocular bell is too far rearward. For most AR shooters, an eye relief of four inches or more will locate the scope ahead of the latch, or at least close to that point. Lower-magnification scopes often have smaller-diameter ocular bells with adequate clearance for folding backup peeps, and use of QD rings will support a BUIS alternative. While the true QD mounts are nice, the one-piece AR-15 specific mount & base designs will also do a decent job. Some are attached with slotted nuts that can be tightened with a quarter. If field removal is ever necessary, a coin or key could save the day.

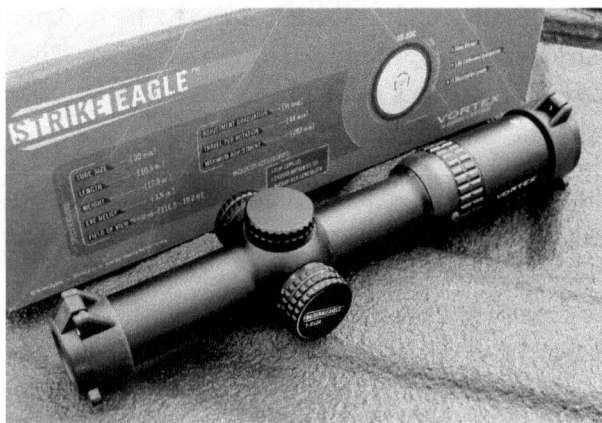

The Vortex 1-6x Strike Eagle is a feature-rich AR scope, sold for a fair price.

Some AR shooters may want higher magnification scopes. The trade-offs will typically be a smaller field-of-view and a larger package, more susceptible to damage in the field. Besides a bigger and more costly optic, other possibilities include two scopes in QD rings; or a different scoped upper.

CHAPTER 22

CHOOSING AN AR-15

For many AR owners, defense plays a critical role. As such, a shorter and more maneuverable rifle will be advantageous. One problem is the myriad number of manufacturers. Sticking with the theme of known products, I'll reserve comments to just a few. Configuration is also important, and what follows is a composite DI rifle, very similar to our agency patrol-carbine. Of course, an AR can be tweaked, or entirely reconfigured to suit individual tastes.

SOME KEY AR-15 FEATURES

For starters, why not stick with mil-spec (military specification) offerings? The greatest odds of procuring spare parts will thus be assured. A good starting point is the serial-numbered lower receiver. Besides serving as a foundation, it can host additional non-SN uppers.

Lower receiver: The mil-spec, small-pin version will provide the greatest versatility should a spare upper be entertained. Colt used "large pin" civilian market receivers, supposedly to help dissuade use of full-auto parts. Just about everyone else went with the mil-spec diameters. These "pins" refer to the forward take-down hinge pin, plus the hammer and trigger pivots. The differences are:

- Front take-down pin: Small 0.250   Large 0.315

- Trigger & hammer pins: Small 0.154   Large 0.170

We're hearing that Colt receivers made between 1991 and 2009 use the larger diameter pins. If you have a Colt, be sure to check prior to ordering parts. This also applies to triggers, since Colt has used a sear-block modification to hinder installation of auto-sear components.

Trigger: The G.I. version may suffice, but it is fairly heavy. There are many other choices offering vast improvements. Some are truly match grade, which doesn't mean they'll survive heavy-duty abuse. I'm happy with my Rock River trigger after firing many rounds. That said, it hasn't undergone protracted rough treatment. The Geissele unit is supposedly tough and dependable, explaining its popularity among three-gun and tactical shooters. Their site has information pertaining to Colt sear-block issues. There are other good triggers as well.

Pistol grip: One with a storage compartment is handy. Among the many beyond G.I. types, Tango Down and Magpul come to mind. They provide a nice spot for extra batteries, which many accessories require. I always have a spare pair of Lithium 123s stowed inside the waterproof compartment of my Tango Down gripped, night vision AR.

Buffer tube (and buffer): An aluminum tube threads into the rear of an AR's receiver, housing its large recoil spring and buffer. During cycling, the bolt carrier assembly reciprocates within the tube, driven by a spring. It also serves as the mounting point for AR stock assembles. Three main types exist. The rifle tube is longest. The carbine-length assembly uses a shorter tube, buffer, and spring. Its tube also has an integral rib which serves to guide a telescoping stock. A pistol variant lacks the rib, precluding the use of a collapsible stock (mounting one to an AR pistol would turn it into an NFA short-barreled rifle, requiring a $200 stamp). Furthermore, two carbine tube diameters are available in mil-spec and commercial forms:

- Mil-Spec 1. 148" tube: This version is machined from a solid forging. The actual tube portion is machined down from the thicker 1.185' threaded section, and is considered stronger. It'll probably have a flat 90-degree rear end.

- Commercial 1.168" tube: This type is made from an extrusion, and its threaded section has a bit less metal. It may also have an angled rear surface that can cause fitting issues with some stocks.

Either carbine tube will fit a standard AR receiver. When switching to an after-market stock, a mil-spec version won't slip on to a commercial tube. A commercial-diameter stock will slide onto a mil-spec tube but it will fit poorly. Some sling-attachment points are also tube-specific. The actual buffer plays a key role in reliable function. Different weights are offered to provide inertial resistance. A standard carbine buffer weighs 3-ounces, but several other heavier versions are also sold. The standard carbine system makes a good starting point.

Stock: Here we have many options running the full gamut of complexity. I still don't mind the solid, rifle-type G.I. units, which are simple and dependable. The original A-1 version was fairly short, so the A-2 version was lengthened a tad. These stocks are secured to the rear of a rifle-length buffer tube by the upper buttplate screw (a short spacer slips inside the tunnel of an A-2 stock). Both

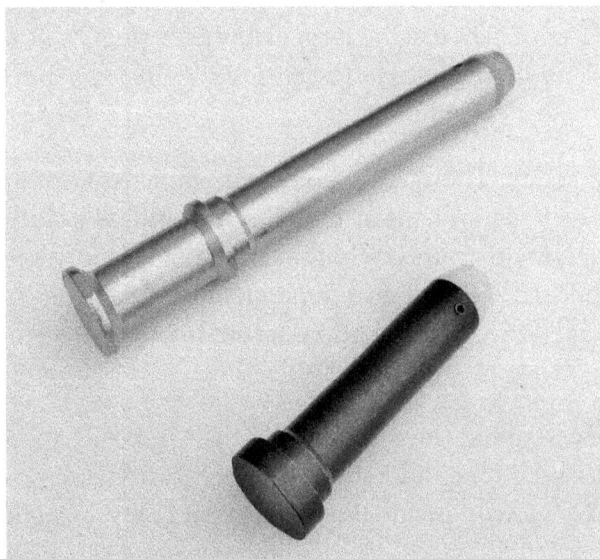

Rifle and carbine buffers are available in several weights. This carbine version is a heavier type to delay unlocking.

have a built-in storage compartment located in the buttplate, which is a handy spot to stow a G.I. cleaning kit, spare batteries, or other gadgets. The short-length stock is still a good pick for smaller-statured shooters, and either will fit a standard receiver. If you do remove one, be careful not to lose the small captive receiver pin detent spring! I have a skeleton/tubular Ace rifle-length stock, which has a foam covered comb. I clipped off its steel sling loop and ground small flats into the supporting stud. The result was a handy connection for QD swivels.

Lately, collapsible (or telescoping) units are popular for lots of good reasons, including an adjustable length of pull. Squeezing a lever retracts a locking stud for lateral travel. Once released, the stud can engage one of several corresponding

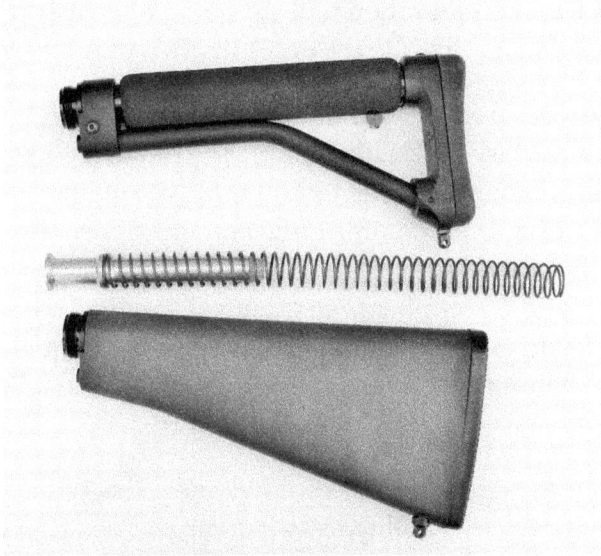

The AR furniture shown here includes Magpul's ACS stock, pistol grip, and trigger guard.

An Ace (top) stock is shown above an A-2 solid unit. Either require a rifle-length buffer tube assembly.

sockets bored into the rib on a carbine buffer tube. Of the many available, Magpul sells some interesting units. Their stocks, unlike several others, aren't wobbly. The basic MOE version works just fine, but you can buy models with extra locking features and storage compartments. The ACS is among my favorites. Inside the box, you'll find good directions along with a buffer tube fit guide. Versions are sold to fit either type.

The short AR pistols are designed to be used without any stock. Due to their recent popularity, a few attempts have been made to offer a "stock" of sorts, which will comply with NFA requirements. The "Stabilizing Brace" is an odd accoutrement that wraps around a shooter's forearm. It superficially resembles a collapsible carbine stock, and soon caught the attention of BATF. Following a period of confusion, the brace is now permissible. Although ergonomically poor, it is possible to place one against a shoulder. Any shooters doing so are immediately on rocky ground. As presented to BATF, the brace was "designed" as a support for non-shouldered shooting. Its housing wrapped a shooter's forearm to minimize wobbles. In other words, legality involves the "designed" wordage. Placing the rear of the brace against a shoulder constitutes a non-designed use, thus moving it into NFA/SBR classification. The addition of a shorter eye relief rifle scope only makes things worse. A dot sight is okay but, if an AR is used as a true pistol, practical accuracy will suffer for most.

I'd much rather go with a shoulder-mounted carbine. Looking at the big picture, a telescoping-stocked lower and 16-inch upper become a practical all-around alternative.

Upper receiver: The Vietnam era AR-15 employed an integral carry handle with a receiver sight. Shooters jumped through hoops trying to mount scopes to their carry handles, resulting in excessively high arrangements. Fortunately, flat top receivers have now become the norm. The

This A-2 sighted AR "pistol" is on legal ground in many locales, but short of specialized uses, its practicality is another matter.

handle is gone, replaced by a mil-spec Picatinny rail. This configuration will support a huge assortment of optical sights, many of which are correctly adapted to provide the necessary height.

The original M-16 was also designed around a gas system optimized for its 20-inch barrel. A shorter carbine variant appeared next, paving the way for the military M-4. Either employs a handy 16-inch barrel better suited for vehicle-borne warfare. A correspondingly shorter forend is fitted, and the gas tube is also shorter. Because pressure enters the tube closer to the chamber, the bolt unlocks sooner. The result can be accelerated extractor and locking lug wear. A mid-length design helps alleviate the problem by moving the gas-block forward a bit. My 18-inch upper is so designed, and its longer forend covers the additional gas tube length. These changes are all good from a function point-of-view, but do limit availability of replacement parts. Bottom line: The shorter, 16-inch system still works, providing a compact and handy package.

Some 14-inch uppers are sold with permanently attached muzzle devices. They meet the 16-inch legal minimum while offering a slightly shorter package, but the ability to switch muzzle devices is lost. If a suppressor is ever in the cards, it will need some means for attachment, making a threaded 16-inch barrel the better choice.

There are even shorter variants, which is where things get dicey. Attaching a 7", 10.5", or other such upper to a standard AR lower will result in a "Short-Barreled Rifle" (SBR). At that point, it'll be in NFA territory, requiring a $200 SBR stamp. Pressure dynamics will also be altered due to shorter gas systems. The AR "pistols" circumvent SBR requirements by combining short-barreled uppers with non-stocked AR lower receivers.

This SBR variant employs a G.I. style telescoping stock. It's an NFA item for more than one reason as evidenced by the safety/selector switch. One more thing: It's loud!

As for the actual upper receiver, some inexpensive ARs are sold minus standard features. Three that sometimes get sacrificed for cost savings are a dust cover, forward assist, and brass deflection lug. Left-handed shooters will want the latter, which was added to redirect hot brass away from faces and shirts. I routinely use a forward assist, and a dust cover just makes sense for real world use. An upper receiver hosts a number of other components. Shown below is a generalized list based on the standard DI system, but there are even spin-offs within this category. Monolithic uppers are a fairly recent idea whereby the upper receiver and forend become one piece (Aero Precision sells such a design). Most others will include the following:

Bolt carrier & bolt: The bolt carrier is a massive steel cylinder. Its front end houses the separate, rotating bolt. A common problem we've seen involves the bolt key coming loose. This is the part that mounts atop the bolt carrier with two cap screws and encircles the gas tube. As mentioned previously, the screws need adequate torque and staking to prevent gas leakage. The separate bolt requires correct head spacing for safe firing, meaning it isn't an interchangeable part. For this reason, I maintain dedicated carrier and bolt assemblies for each personal upper receiver. A few good spare parts are a firing pin, retaining pin, gas rings, and extractor assembly. Some shooters obsess over alignment of the rings to maintain pressure. Since each has a small gap, staggering their alignment makes sense. It can't hurt, but you'll probably get function either way.

Forend: This part is often a one or two-piece sleeve that encircles the barrel and gas tube. Lots of

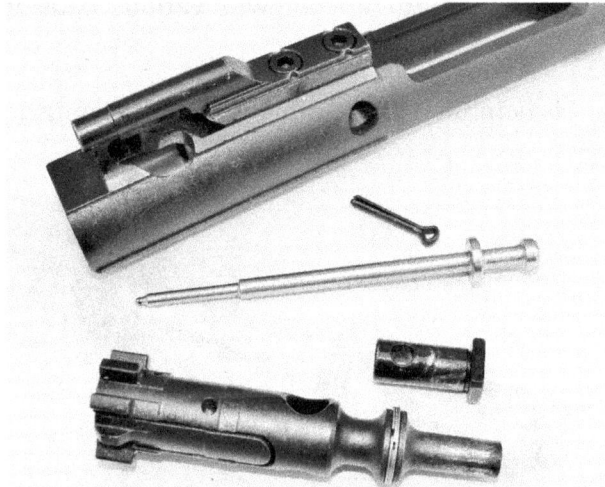

The firing pin is captured by the cotter pin. After its removal, the cam can be rotated and pulled out to free the bolt. A separate pin contains the bolt's extractor. Two heavily staked screws secure the gas key to the bolt carrier.

Since each bolt is head-spaced to a particular barrel, switching one could be unsafe. The spring-loaded ejector and extractor are visible in its face.

great new systems are on the market, including many streamlined tubular designs with removable rails. By comparison, my older four-sided integral rail unit was cumbersome and sharp-edged. It was replaced by a Diamondhead free-float model, which is drilled and tapped for separate accessory rail pieces (available in different lengths). A free-floated forend will likely improve accuracy because it is isolated from barrel contact. A further benefit is that hand, sling, or bipod pressure won't change zero. However, an older two piece design may make sense for those with a front sight tower (its flange captures the front ends). Although somewhat difficult to remove, both halves can be separated in the field. We specified this type for our patrol carbines. Once again, they're Diamondhead forends with Picatinny rail sections, which provide serviceable if not match grade accuracy.

Barrel: Standard G.I. barrels have long had chrome-plated bores for corrosion protection. Although possibly a bit less accurate than an un-plated, true match barrel, the extra insurance is probably a fair trade. A stainless barrel is another option and one that I prefer. A threaded muzzle will accommodate a muzzle device. The heaviest AR-15 barrels are dedicated varminters, which are normally un-threaded, un-plated, often stainless, and built for supreme accuracy. Many are 20 or 24-inch types, but since even a 16" HB is weighty, lighter-profile barrels make sense. A 16" M-4 barrel has largely supplanted the original 20" version, at some ballistic expense. Still, for a practical, all-around AR-15, a 16–18" medium-weight barrel is good. As for rifling, a 1x9 or 1x8 should cover most bases.

Gas block: This part acts as a collar, surrounding the barrel's gas port. It also supports the gas tube's forward end, and the original design included an integral G.I. front sight tower. With the popularity of flat top receivers, today's trend is toward lower gas blocks. Some have short Picatinny tops, capable of mounting detachable front sights. Others feature folding sights. I have a few low-profile units which are strictly gas tube supports that fit inside today's long forend tubes. Folding front sights can be mounted to these forends, in heights matching backup rear sights. With all types, proper block and barrel-port indexing is crucial for reliable function. A recent idea is an adjustable unit, capable of metering gas volume. This permits tuning of pressure for optimum function with various loads or suppressors.

Muzzle device: Where legal, some sort of threaded unit is helpful, if for no other reason than muzzle

YHM's suppressor version of the Phantom is threaded for QD mounting. The sharp fingers are carbon-scrapers to cut internal can fouling.

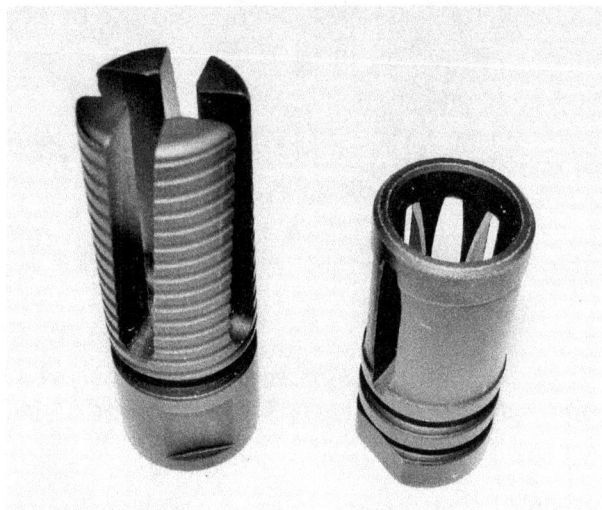

The Smith Vortex (L) will actually self-tighten with use. The G.I. A-2 cage is better than nothing for flash reduction. When correctly installed, its solid bottom will minimize flying debris if shot from prone.

protection. The standard AR-15 thread pattern is 1/2x28, and many different devices are available. Some are muzzle brakes, geared toward recoil reduction. Others cut down on flash. The Smith, Phantom, or Surefire certainly minimize the latter issue, but even the old G.I cage is better than nothing. We specified Smith Vortex units for our patrol carbines (they'll also accept a Smith Industries suppressor). We also run some Yankee Hill Machine (YHM) units with suppressors. The forward sections include a Phantom flash hider. From prone, some devices will kick up dust or grass. The G.I. unit is has no port underneath to help minimize this problem. My pet heavy-barreled AR has a bare, unthreaded muzzle for maximum accuracy. In some locals, this type of muzzle is required, so check before buying.

Charge handle: The original G.I. version will do, but it can be a bit hard to access underneath the ocular bell of a scope. Several after-market models exist with larger latch levers, including some neat ambidextrous designs. The more extreme examples are best avoided since they'll catch on lots of items. I have a few Badgers with moderate extensions, but our patrol carbines use basic G.I. latches.

Magazines: The most reliable AR-15 on the planet won't run with poor magazines. We had an armory full of 10-year old Bushmasters that gradually developed stoppages. Naturally, blame was first assigned to the rifles, but in retrospect, it occurred to us that many of our heavily-used magazines were at least that old. We contacted the Connecticut firm of Mags LLC and soon had a pile of new aluminum, curved 20-rounders, which immediately solved our problems. We've also had great luck with Brownell's magazines. We're told that some of the polymer types are also good, but just don't have as much in-depth experience with them. Part of the reason is that we operate in extreme cold where breakage could be an issue. We've seen a number of supposedly indestructible polymer parts fail after sub-zero exposure. We have shot Magpuls and Lancers on a limited basis with satisfactory results.

We maintain a separate inventory of training magazines, reserved exclusively for range use. They all

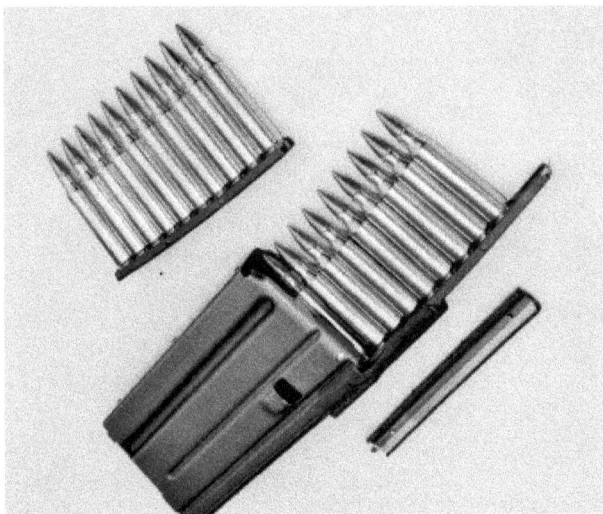

An older 20-round G.I. magazine shown with stripper clips. Slipping on the supplied adapter permits rapid recharging in 10-round increments.

hit the ground when empty, so on a gravel range (with rain or ice thrown in), they take a beating. Our duty magazines are first proven during live fire, and then reserved for service use. With either batch we avoid anything other than the most minimal lubrication, which just attracts dirt. Most 30-round designs work fine, but because our troops wear lots of other gear (including pistols), the smaller 20-round versions get us by.

Sights: The options are abundant. Unlike the original M-16 fielded during the 1960s, so many different systems now exist that they warrant a separate chapter. Through careful shopping we can procure a rifle capable of accepting numerous options. Not too coincidentally, all of the forthcoming contenders will be flat top designs.

A FEW CONTENDERS

There are many manufacturers from which to choose—too many to list here. While plenty of them no doubt build first-rate products, we just haven't had the luxury of wringing them all out. Prices run all over the map, from less than $700 up into the thousands. Until recently, the lower-cost ARs were stripped of common features like dust covers, brass deflectors, and forward assists. Thanks to a crowded and completive market, that situation has changed. Standard features can now be preserved without breaking the bank.

One brand we have high confidence in is a relative newcomer, backed up by highly experienced builders...

Windham Weaponry CDI: For those with some AR history, Bushmaster will be a familiar brand. We dealt extensively with that firm and used their rifles for many years. Eventually, Bushmaster was sold and moved out of Maine, but the plant and most of the crew remained behind. Before long, black rifles once again began rolling out the same doors, this time under the "Windham Weaponry" banner. With plenty of motivation and lots of experience, the Windham staff is building very good rifles. We've been through the plant and seen the process, including reject parts with nearly undetectable flaws. After putting some of their rifles through the wringer, we made a wholesale agency switch to new AR-15s, configured as "patrol carbines." Ours are similar, but not identical, to the well-thought-out WW CDI model.

- Upper receiver: Flat top, M-4 type.

- Lower receiver: Dual-sided markings (good for ambi safety installs).

- Stock: Magpul MOE 6-position, collapsible.

- Pistol grip: Magpul with storage compartment.

- Barrel: 16" M-4 profile with 1x9 twist and 5.56mm chamber.

- Muzzle device: Smith Enterprises flash hider.

- Forend: Diamondhead free-float with detachable, accessory rail sections.

- Sights: Diamondhead flip-up front & rear irons.

- Weight: Approximately 7 pounds.

- Length: Approximately 32–36 inches.

- Price (2016): $1,680, including one 30-round magazine and hard case.

This WW carbine was assembled to agency specs. Since it served as a prototype, the Magpul grip and trigger guard are absent here. The sight is a reliable Aimpoint PRO.

Numerous WW versions are available. A film-dipped finish has transformed this one into northern predator medicine.

It's a business-like package with a transferable life-time warranty. Odds are it'll run just fine, but if it doesn't, the people in Windham, Maine will hook you up. They also sell more basic versions of the CDI for much less money.

Windham Weaponry's MCS is shown here in 7.62x39 Russian. Note the different well assembly capable of accepting AK magazines. The barrel release system is visible on the forend.

Interchangeable magazine wells are part of the ACS design. They slide downward onto forward receiver rails. This kit offers 5.56, .300 Blackout, and 7.62x39 capabilities. A separate bolt assembly is required for the Russian round.

MCS system: Some buyers may be interested in WW's new DI, "Multi-Caliber System." Two-caliber upper kits cost around $1,000, and will mount to any standard lower. Sliding a retainer in the forearm frees up a pair of locking arms for barrel exchange:

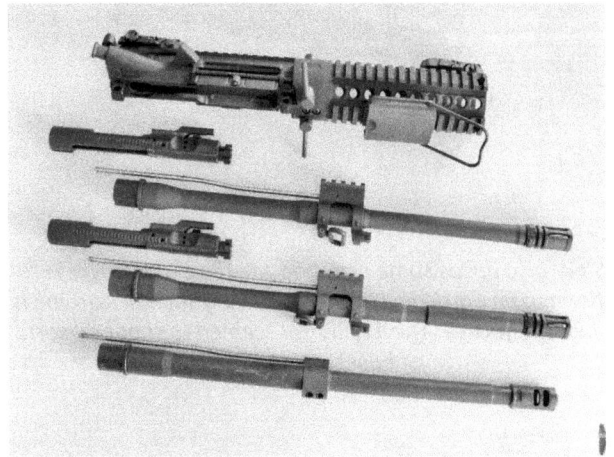

With the MCS release disengaged, two detent arms can be swung outward for easy barrel exchange. Note their captive gas tube assemblies.

- The MCS-1 upper receiver kit comes with a modified upper, plus two barrels for 5.56 NATO (.223) and .300 Blackout. Both share the same bolt and will run off of common magazines. Each upper has its own gas tube, and its block has a Picatinny rail section that will accept a front sight (the forend is also fully railed).

- The 5.56/7.62x39 MCS-2 kit contains two bolt carrier assemblies and a modified 7.62x39 magazine that will fit a standard AR-15 lower.

- The MCS-3 kit is for .300 Blackout and 7.62x39.

Complete rifle systems are also sold in various caliber-combinations. They employ easily interchangeable magazine wells, and the 7.62x39 module accepts true AK-47 magazines. The 9mm version takes Colt SMG magazines. A four-caliber package is sold in a hard shell case for $2,971.

Smith & Wesson: We have a long-standing relationship with S&W, and we have used a number of their AR-15 carbines without complaint. The Model 15-T or 15-TS carbines look like very interesting choices. Both have Picatinny forends but are lightweight offerings. The "T" is rifled 1x8, and the "TS" utilizes a quicker 1x7 good for heavy 5.56/.223 loads. The one I shot still cut two-inch groups with 55-grain bullets at 200 yards. Another intriguing model is chambered for the .300 Blackout (more on that caliber later). A larger AR-10 type .308 is fairly manageable due to its light-profile barrel.

A prospective AR-15 buyer on a budget could do a whole lot worse than S&W's latest "Sport II." All of the basic features are there, including a forward assist, dust cover, and Magpul rear sight. It's very close to a military M-4 Carbine, with a front sight tower and two-piece G.I. forend. The 16-inch barrel is rifled with an ammo-tolerant 1x9 twist. The Sport II looks like a good all-around choice as is, but it will readily accommodate future upgrades. The best part is its $739 list price! You could match it up with a rimfire S&W M&P 22 Sport for an extra $499, gaining an affordable .22 LR trainer. Street pricing would likely keep the two-gun set below $1,200.

Rock River: Among the many offerings, check out their 18-inch R-3 three-gun model. You get a

S&W also builds some high-end AR-15 versions. The Surefire muzzle flash device on this "Viking Tactics" carbine is highly effective. The 1x7 barrel seemed to shoot all sorts of bullet weights well.

.75 MOA accuracy guarantee thanks to its Wylde chamber. The 1x8 twist will handle a broad range of bullet weights and the R-3 is just a cool-looking rifle. The Delta Mid-Length is a bit shorter, but uses a NATO chamber. Among their latest products are true, mirror-image left-handed versions. A new 7.62x39 AR-15 is also interesting. Its receiver has been modified to work with AK-47 magazines, thus solving function issues. All of the Rock River rifles we've shot were well-built and extremely accurate. The product line is extensive and the pricing is fair.

DPMS: We've shot them off and on for many years and the firm is well-established. Like the others, DPMS has a fairly extensive product line. A stainless-barreled upper on hand here shoots 1/3 MOA 5-shot groups, which may not be an accident. Their "GII" .308 is especially intriguing because much work has gone into scaling down the rifle. Size-wise, it falls somewhere between an AR-10 and AR-15. Dual ejectors and other improvements are all for the good, making the GII an interesting candidate for those in search of 7.62 NATO performance. The AP4 and MOE versions are laid out similarly to a 5.56 M-4, and weigh only 7 1/4 pounds.

Patriot Ordnance Factory: Here's a piston gun for

Another view of Rock River's HB rifle. Absolute AR accuracy is often obtained with a bare muzzle and tighter chamber (in this case a Wylde). The gas block has a Picatinny top. A handy bolt block/safety flag is sitting on the bench.

the list. We have a few 20-inch .308s for designated marksman roles. They are real Cadillac rifles with a number of substantive features from stem to stern. While testing a 6.8 SPC, ejection was fairly anemic. Then, we remembered the adjustable gas-metering system. Voila — problem solved. In other words, latitude is available for different loads or the pressure dynamics associated with suppressors. POF also came out with an improved "E-2 chamber." It ducts gas flow to improve ejection, thereby saving wear and tear associated with many piston-driven designs. A 5.56mm version is available on the smaller AR-15 platform and new DI variants have even appeared. The new Renegade 5.56 has a nine-position "Dictator" gas block for fine-tuning of gas pressure. The most novel POF of all has got to be their "ReVolt," which is actually a manually-operated bolt-action designed to thwart onerous AR restrictions. Regardless of the type, you'll know you're looking at a quality rifle when you hold a POF.

This heavy-duty POF .308 piston gun is equipped for designated marksman duty. Look closely through the forend slots and the reciprocating operating rod can be seen. At first glance it resembles a gas tube.

POF .308 development: The whole premise of this AR-15-weighted section is based on the premise that an AR-10 is overly large. Well, this assumption may soon be out the window. Leave it to POF to break new ground with an AR-15 scaled .308! Putting it mildly, this is a *huge* development! Their piston-driven "USA Revolution" is advertised as the lightest .308, period. When placed side-by-side with an AR-15, the only noticeable .308 difference is a larger magazine well. The reduction is largely possible through the use of an AR-15 sized bolt-carrier in the Revolution. Initial press focuses on an SBR version weighing just over six pounds. Hopefully, a 16-inch model will also be offered as well but, in any case, we'll need to wait until the fall of 2016. Price is projected to be around $2,500.

More 308: Meanwhile, all of the above companies sell AR-10 type rifles. If you'd just as soon skip the smaller AR-15 cartridge choices, a .308 makes a whole lot of sense. Although weights have come down, it's still worth handling any prospective AR-10 candidates before placing an order.

Other AR manufacturers? As I've said, shooting everything out there would be nigh onto impossible. The company that started it all is Armalite, and they're still in business. So is Colt, Barrett, BCM, Bushmaster, Daniel Defense, FNH, LaRue, LMT, LWRC, Knight's Armament, Midwest Industries, Mossberg, Nordic, Noveske, Ruger, Sig, Stag, and YHM — just to name a few. Hats off to anyone who has tested every brand!

Chapter 23

MORE AR POSSIBILITIES

As we've discussed, the AR-15 is true transformer. With a personalized 5.56 mm rifle on hand, you may want to entertain other options. Perils to your marriage or savings account aside, a small-pin receiver will allow some interesting additions!

NFA TERRITORY

We looked at silencers in Section 1. Interest has mushroomed and a rise in short-barreled rifles has accompanied this craze. Threading a suppressor on to even a 16-inch barrel will result in an unwieldy package, so an SBR upper is a whole lot more manageable. The trouble is, since ownership of either item requires a $200 Federal NFA stamp, both items greatly escalate the cost.

Suppressors & short-barreled rifles: One way around the 16-inch minimum is an SBR with a *permanently* built-in suppressor. As long as this combination exceeds 16-inches, one $200 stamp will suffice. This concept is catching on, driven in part by .300 Blackout interest. A non-removable suppressor body on a 10-inch barrel can do the trick, but such a combination won't be cheap since extra engineering is necessary. Besides a shortened gas tube (and altered pressure), forward disassembly of the silencer is required for cleaning. Still, it's a neat concept—especially in the efficient .300 Blkt chambering.

Since each state has separate statutes, it's best to check before getting overly aroused by the prospect of low-DB escapades. In my home state, suppressor ownership is legal, and hunting is now possible with a special permit. Of course, BATF controls the federal level.

Even if you're good-to-go on all fronts, physics can't be ignored. Any supersonic projectile will have a distinctive crack, and action types have an effect. Semi-autos tend to be noisier and their function can be affected by pressure dynamics. Gas ports, buffers, and barrel lengths all come into play. We recently took a hard look at several suppressed AR-15 options. Our interest was based on three likely outcomes resulting from discharge of rifle rounds inside a steel and concrete environment:

1. Everyone in close proximity will be blind.

2. Everyone will also be deaf.

3. Bullets, or chunks of bullets, will fly in all directions.

We considered a suppressed pistol-caliber, short-barreled sub-machinegun variant, chambered for 9mm Luger. The idea was to fire frangible bullets, which disintegrate upon contact with hard surfaces. One problem involved AR function with pistol rounds. Instead of gas operation, a simple blow-back design is used. It's not unlike a rimfire design, relying on a careful balance of recoil and bolt mass for reliable function. A weighted bolt carrier serves to delay unlocking until the bullet exits the barrel. Addition of a suppressor, combined with lighter non-lead projectiles, can affect reliability. While these issues can be overcome through action tuning, consistent ammunition is important.

A buzz-gun is a tightly controlled NFA item. This suppressed SBR 9mm SMG utilizes a blow-back system with a weighted bolt carrier. Reliable all-weather function can require some tuning.

After much testing, we switched gears and returned to the 5.56mm. The guys from Windham Weaponry and Smith Enterprises showed up with an 11.5" WW AR-15, equipped with a Smith Enterprises "Vortex" flash hider. Besides effectively mitigating flash, the Vortex also accepts the same firm's suppressor. The short barrel resulted in a still-manageable overall length and a fairly quiet AR-15. We judged the report similar to an un-suppressed .22 Magnum, and flash was non-existent. It's far from silent, but certainly much less concussive. Recent 5.56 mm frangible-bullet developments can minimize ricochet concerns.

Minus a "can," such short 5.56 barrels are *extremely* loud. They can also emit a huge muzzle flash without a good muzzle device. Ballistic performance will also suffer. Minus a suppressor, a non-NFA 16-inch overall barrel length probably makes more sense.

ALTERNATE CENTERFIRE UPPERS

To realize the full potential of a suppressor, subsonic ammunition is required. This is problematic due to semi-auto pressure parameters. During a recent conversation, the question of subsonic .223 rounds came up. Trouble is, the low projectile weight won't provide enough resistance to generate adequate AR gas pressure. It would probably just make more sense to shoot one of the new .22 LR subsonic loads. Nevertheless, the popularity of the AR platform and corresponding rise in suppressor interest has sparked efforts to find practical subsonic solutions. One that began as a tailor-made cartridge eventually assumed a life of its own.

.300 Blackout: At this point it's probably safe to assume that this cartridge is more than a fad. I've seen Remington ammo in Walmart, and a number of AR manufacturers have jumped on the Blackout bandwagon. You can buy either a whole .300 Blackout rifle, or just an upper receiver. I wouldn't consider this somewhat oddball, but an increasingly popular caliber as a sole AR choice. On the other hand, 5.56mm owners could easily pick up a spare .300 BLKT upper to gain .30-caliber punch. Pop those two receiver pins and you're in business.

A .300 Blackout AR becomes a modern day .30/30 of sorts with supersonic loads. It's light and handy with minimal recoil. Reduced-capacity magazines keep it legal in many locales.

A switch to heavy subsonic .300 Blkt loads will permit quiet shooting with a suppressor. Bear in mind a significantly different zero will be necessary.

That's the route I chose, mainly because the whole concept seemed too good to resist. During the last big AR frenzy I picked up a 16" .300 Blackout barrel, rifled with a typically fast 1x8 twist. All of the other necessary parts from the bolt through the magazine were standard 5.56 types. Using this collection of AR-15 pieces, I connected with a well-known AR-15 manufacturer for assembly of a prototype upper. The project almost seemed too simple, although we wound up scratching our heads after realizing no headspace gauges or proof loads were on hand. In the end, I just brought the upper home and popped it on a lower receiver. The first step was to chamber some dummy rounds. This was a few years ago, before the .300 Blkt caught on in a big way. Fortunately, I had reloading equipment and the Internet. It didn't take long to track down the SAAMI specifications. A set of .300 Blackout dies was already on hand. So was a good assortment of .30-caliber bullets, powder, and primers. One thing missing was .300 Blackout brass, but with lots of fired .223 brass available, the crisis was over.

How can this be? The answer is simple: Ammo can be created from shortened 5.56 (or .223) brass. After cutting off the cases directly below the shoulder, they are simply run into a .300 BLKT re-sizing die. A final trim will bring them down to SAAMI length. The result is a rather odd-looking little cartridge with a .30-caliber neck and small shoulder. Before long, I had a batch of experimental ammo ready to test. A few dummy rounds fed and extracted normally so it was time to make some noise. Although it was a bit convoluted, the whole project went smoothly. I will say that I *hate* making Blackout brass from .223 cases. The independence is nice, but it's a time consuming process. Of course, commercial or re-formed 5.56 brass is now available, in addition to loaded rounds.

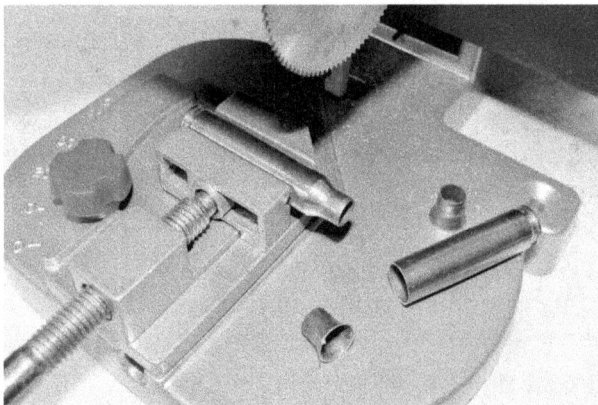

.300 Blackout forming: A fired .223 case is cut off just below the shoulder. Afterward, it can be run through a .300 Blkt sizing die in a reloading press.

Technically, the .300 Blackout is a 7.62x35, and with .308-diameter bullets of 110–125 grains, ballistics are similar to the 7.62x39 Russian. In a

The newly formed .300 Blkt case is then trimmed to SAA-MI-specified length, chamfered, and de-burred. A "Little Crow" trimmer is handy for mass production.

After forming stages are completed, .300 Blkt cases can be primed, charged, and loaded per normal procedures.

16-inch barrel, the .300 Blkt will develop just under 2,300 fps, firing 115-grain bullets. My 110 solid-copper Barnes TAC-X handload safely achieves 2,400 fps. I zero this ultra-sleek bullet at 200 yards, and at 100 yards POI is less than two inches high. Unlike the Russian round, the .300 Blkt will generally function reliably through a standard AR—with no special bolt face being necessary either. Most standard AR magazines will also work, although some dedicated .300 types have recently appeared to accommodate longer, heavier subsonic bullets. With the right bullets, the .300 Blackout has enough "thump" to use on deer or hogs.

Some readers will recall the older .300 Whisper, which is the same idea. It used very heavy bullets loaded just below the speed of sound, and was based on Remington's .221 Fireball; a shorter case with the same .223 head diameter. Either .300 round is short enough to fit in an M-16 magazine. Add a very heavy 190–220 grain .308-diameter bullet and sufficient gas pressure can be developed to cycle that action. When fired suppressed at subsonic velocities through a suppressor, these loads are *really* quiet. Quicker-twist rifling (1x8 or 1x7) is needed to help stabilize the unusually heavy bullets.

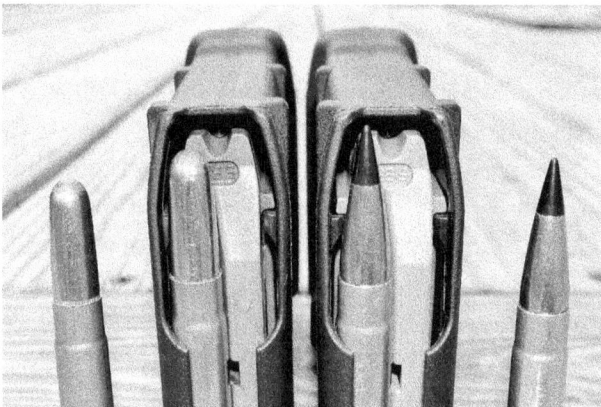
Two .300 Blackout iterations: Blunt subsonic s (220-grain Hornady RN), and sleek supersonics (Barnes 110 TAC-TX). The TX can be loaded to the same overall length as a .223 cartridge for optimum function in AR-15 magazines.

Seizing on the concept, Advanced Armament Corporation (AAC) saw a marketing opportunity. Two hot products are anything AR-15 related, and suppressors. As a manufacturer of both, by resurrecting the Whisper with some very minor changes, the Blackout came into being. It's now a SAAMI listing, but supposedly, either cartridge can be fired interchangeably (Hornady's boxes are labeled .300 Whisper). AAC and Remington have corporate connections, explaining the availability of factory-loaded .300 Blackout ammunition. Pressures are compatible with the AR-15 system, either

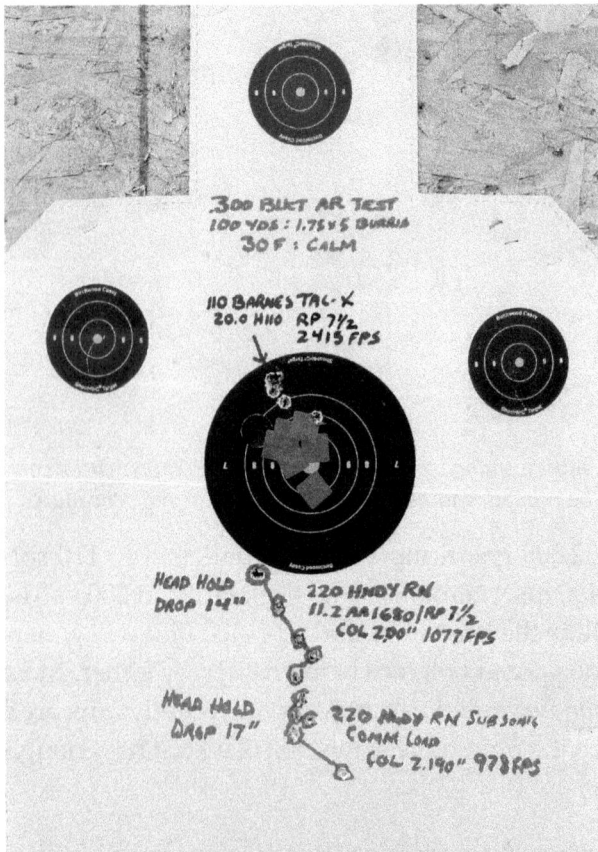

This .300 Blackout target illustrates the effect of velocity on drop. The supersonic group resulted from a center hold on the same bull. Short of a major zero change, the subsonics would've struck underneath the target. Groups were captured by aiming at the IPSC head.

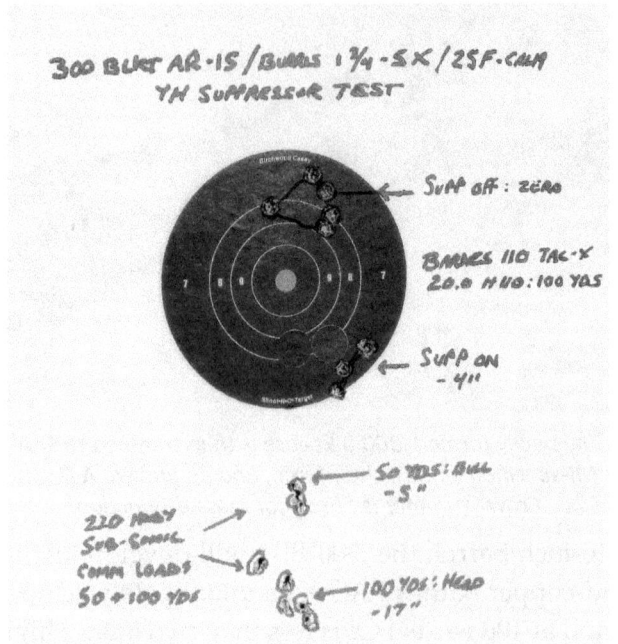

One zero and different results: Addition of a suppressor shifted 100-yard supersonic loads 4" low. The can stayed on for both subsonic groups. The 50-yard series hit 5" low. The 100-yard group was lobbed in by aiming at the head of the IPSC Target backer. Variables affect POI!

suppressed or un-suppressed — something that is actually no small feat.

Back to SBRs, the Daniel Defense ISR-300 kills two birds with one stone. The "integral suppressed rifle" has a permanently attached silencer, which is fixed to a short 10-inch barrel. The resulting combination affords a legal length exceeding 16 inches. In other words, it's not a federally classified short-barreled rifle, so a $200 SBR stamp is not required. The suppressor will still require the $200 fee, but at least you save 50%. At around $3,200, the ISR isn't cheap, but then again, the suppressor is part of the package. You'll probably spend somewhere around a grand for one as a separate device.

When firing suppressed supersonic bullets, the .300 Blackout's report will be more on the order of a .22 LR CCI Stinger — clearly detectable. On the other hand, heavy subsonic loads will be so quiet that the mechanical function of the action is audible. The very heavy bullets, traveling below the speed of sound, result in a loopy trajectory best limited to close range. Fortunately, specially calibrated .300 Blackout scopes have appeared from major manufacturers like Nikon and Leupold. Reticles are calibrated for both super and subsonic projectiles. Interestingly, the subsonic 100-yard elevation line is very close to the supersonic 400-yard grid. One thing to keep in mind is that windage could vary between loads. Although I don't have that problem, subsonic 220 grain bullets strike *well* below my crosshairs at 100 yards. The exact amount depends on the supersonic zero and subsonic load's velocity. Being a handloader presents opportunities to experiment. Besides function and accuracy, consistent subsonic velocity is necessary. The deviations shown below are based on a 110-grain bullet with 2,350 fps MV, zeroed 1.5" high at 100 yards.

A 220 RN with a 1,030 fps average MV will remain safely below the sound barrier, lobbing 220-grain bullets 12 1/2 -inches under POA. I can squeak it up to 1,055 fps and reduce drop to 11 1/2 inches, but temperature introduces subsonic variables. Cold, dense air is less forgiving, so inevitable velocity variations can occasionally cross the sonic-crack threshold. A commercial version with a 1,000 fps MV is comfortably quiet at all temperatures, but strikes 14 inches low. Obviously, velocity plays a critical role here. Bullet expansion is another concern, and so is function, which may require some tuning. Gas port location (pistol-length vs carbine) and diameter affect pressure. Cycling or lock-back can also be dependent on buffer/spring combinations.

If we take the subsonic aspect off the table, the .300 Blackout still has useful attributes. With the right supersonic bullets it could become a 200-yard deer cartridge. I settled on a Barnes 110-grain TAC-TX handload, in part because this solid-copper bullet is very sleek, and designed to approximate 5.56 overall cartridge lengths. The slender profile aligns well with many magazine ribs, providing a good fit. Accuracy is great with 3-shot groups approaching one MOA. When zeroed at 200 yards, they form nice 100-yard clusters 1.75" above the crosshairs. Recoil is nil, permitting fast repeat shots. I do have some reservations about its use on very large deer, but based on other Barnes TSX results, I know it won't unravel. Factory-loaded ammo is also available from Barnes.

Although it's a fascinating AR alternative, the odds of finding a useful .300 Blackout stash during a societal crash remain slim. However, plenty of 5.56mm and .223 brass is kicking around for handloaders. Worst case, it's easy to pop the two take-down pins and swap the .300 upper for a trusty 5.56 unit.

A downside to owning both calibers is the possi-

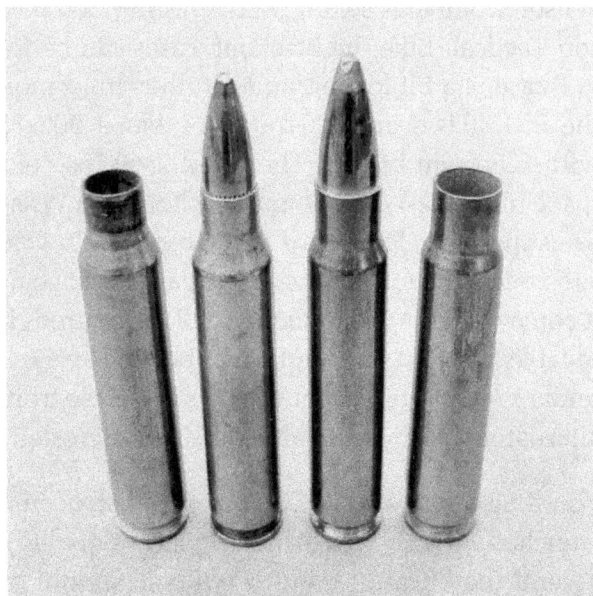

The innovative .25-45 Sharps is just a necked-up .223 (shown for comparison). Velocity approaches 3,000 fps with 87 grain bullets and recoil is nil. Complete uppers are available but ammo isn't widespread. A cartridge management system would be imperative!

For safety's sake it's a good idea to have a distinctive .300 Blackout identification system, which should include both rifles and magazines.

bility of mixing them up. Discharge of a .300 Blackout round in a .223 chamber would be catastrophic. Distinctive dust covers and magazines help. I like the "300 BLACKOUT" logo etched into the dust cover of my AR. I feed it with 10-round Magpul magazines, which can be purchased with tan coloring. Magpul sells a 5-round limiter for game law restrictions.

Other calibers: Among the most popular caliber conversions, the 6.8 SPC remains a viable upper receiver option; however, standard AR-15 magazines can be balky, and their capacity will be reduced.

The same applies to the 6.5 Grendel—an excellent concept for those willing to procure a stash of dedicate magazines. Its big advantage is a quantum leap in long-range performance, combined with adequate terminal effects on larger game—achievements that are no small feat!

A 7.62x39 Russian upper makes the most sense for those sitting on a large supply of ammo. A substantial quantity of 5.56x39 Russian also appeared in the U.S., so among others, S&W produced uppers chambered for this round. Some of the Russian cartridges employ steel cases, which can be problematic in precise ARs. One of the newest dedicated 7.62x39 AR rifles may be the best bet. For starters, it will be designed specifically with this cartridge. CMMG's MK47 Mutant is such an example. Among its function enhancing modifications, the Mutant's is specifically built to accommodate AK-47 magazines. Since they're a global commodity, this may be a fair trade for lack of a last-shot hold-open feature. Receiver pin-spacing is different, but the price seems reasonable at around $1,400. Rock River sells a similar AR line as their LAR-47 series, with a number of attractive models starting at around $1,270. Of course, the modular Windham Weaponry design is another possibility.

Wilson Combat is selling an interesting .300 Blackout/7.62x39 Russian alternative; their .300x40 Wilson Tactical. Like the Blackout, cases can be formed from shortened 5.56 brass. However, the .300 WT case is a bit longer, and can thus hold more powder. Using a 110-grain bullet for comparison, the .300x40 is nearly 200 fps faster than a .300x35 Blackout. It can also exceed 110-grain Blackout MV with 125-grain bullets. The listed 2460 fps velocity trounces 123-grain 7.62 Russian by almost 150 fps. Unlike the Whisper and Blackout, the Wilson Tactical .300 rendition was designed primarily to fire supersonic loads. For this reason, a slower 1x12 twist barrel is cataloged (the WT can also fire subsonic bullets, but a faster 1x8 barrel will be needed). At $1300, an upper isn't cheap. Then again, if it comes from Wilson, quality will be assured. Use of Lancer L-5 magazines will supposedly permit reliable function at a slight sacrifice in capacity. Of course, the proprietary nature of this load also limits availability. Ammunition is available from Wilson. It seems like a great general purpose AR-15 alternative for those handloaders not interested in suppressors.

You'll also see .458 SOCOM uppers listed on Wilson's site. A 300-grain .458-caliber bullet can be launched at 1,800 fps, providing legendary .45/70 performance from an AR-15. An upper requires several modifications, but it will still mount on a standard lower. Although an extra-power buffer spring is recommended, the swap is simple enough (keep it with the upper to jog your memory). Despite its radical design, the .458 will supposedly run with Lancer L5 AWM 5.56 magazine. A 20-rounder will hold nine rounds. This caliber is serious medicine which should handle just about any North American animal, transforming an AR-15 in ways never imagined. Other manufacturers, including Rock River, also sell .458 SOCOM versions. Like me, Wilson appears to be a big fan of Barnes solid-copper projectiles. They load 110 and 300-grain versions in .300 WT and the SOCOM. You'll be hard-pressed to find tougher bullets.

The .450 Bushmaster is a similar idea that uses pistol-diameter .452-caliber bullets instead of .458 rifle types. As developed with Hornady, the slightly smaller bore permitted use of their pointed SST 250-grain Flex-tips. These accurate and streamlined bullets easily afford 200-yard capability, and handloaders sometimes substitute .45 Long Colt or .460 S&W bullets. Standard AR magazines work, although capacity will be greatly reduced. A 20-rounder will hold nine .450 BM cartridges, which is actually a formidable payload. The 250 SST will do nearly 2,200 fps from a 16-inch barrel, and Bushmaster uppers will drop right on to a standard AR lower. When it first came out, a few Bushmaster guys took samples to Texas and said it was absolute hell on hogs. I believe 'em! An upper runs around $670 and my wallet pocket is duct taped shut.

Pistol calibers: Several companies sell upper receivers as well as complete rifles. Most often the caliber is 9mm Luger, although .40 S&W and .45 ACP uppers (among others) have been made. Unlike a standard AR-15, the pistol-caliber variants are generally blow-back operated. Instead of a gas tube, a one-piece bolt/bolt carrier unit imparts sufficient mass to delay unlocking. It's simpler and a bit easier to clean. Special magazines are necessary, which won't fit a standard AR-15 mag well. The fix involves either an adapter/insert, or modified lower receiver. Magazine capacity in 9mm is normally 30 rounds or more, but the last few load hard! Since a special 9mm hammer will probably be necessary, a switch-top conversion becomes less practical.

Why bother with a pistol-caliber AR-15 at all? As originally conceived by Colt, it made a handy SMG package, running with a short 10.5" barrel and Uzi-type magazines. The addition of a suppressor resulted in a very quiet package, good for close-in places. Controllability on full-auto fire is quite good. The telescoping stock permits fairly accurate shots in semi-auto mode and velocity improves somewhat thanks to a longer barrel. As I mentioned, we looked into frangible bullets for use indoors where ricochets were a hazard. The lighter, sintered-copper projectiles created less recoil, which was further influenced by suppressor dynamics. Bolt-mass needed adjustment and things got complicated, temperature concerns aside.

Still, for some people, a simpler non-select-fire pistol-caliber carbine may have value. We once inventoried a semi-automatic 9mm Colt with a 16-inch barrel, which ran reliably and was fun to shoot. Recoil and noise were minimal, making the package a viable alternative for some home defense scenarios. That extra 12 inches of barrel length may add enough velocity to change the terminal dynamics of pistol bullets, with a likely effect being increased expansion. A tougher projectile may be advised to prevent jacket and core separation. The newest bonded bullets or solid-copper slugs seem perfect for carbine use. In the former category, weights beginning at 124 grains would be a good starting point. The all-brass bullets run lighter but act like heavier projectiles. Although the Cor-Bon DPX and Barnes TAC-XP only weigh 115 grains, full weight-retention is likely, along with dramatic expansion. One big concern is reliable function, which calls for actual shooting. Once a good load is chosen, equivalent-weight FMJ can be fired during practice. This will hopefully result in a fairly close zero.

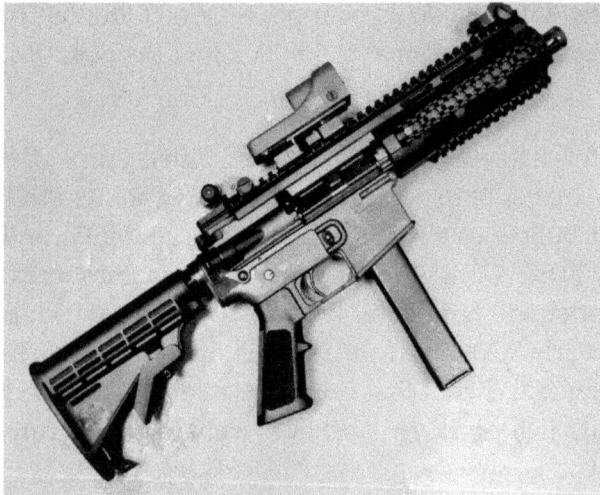

Trijicon's Reflex dot sight provides very useful accuracy from this short 9mm SMG, right out to 100 yards.

On pistol-caliber carbines, a dot sight will suffice. Ranges will be closer and a large field-of-view, free from eye relief issues, will nicely support multiple users. We use a 50-yard zero, but find a 9mm AR-15 to be quite useful right out to 100 yards. Accuracy may be surprisingly good and 9mm FMJ will work on small game without waking up the entire neighborhood.

Add a 9mm handgun and you'll enjoy the same utility recognized during the late 1800s. Of course, back then the combination consisted of a six-gun and lever-action chambered for a common cartridge like .38/40 or .44/40. Today's .40 S&W is actually similar to the .38/40, right down to bullet diameter. Today it's possible to buy a .40 S&W or .45 ACP AR variant.

The 9mm is now so popular that several well-known manufacturers catalog AR variants. Some use dedicated receivers with magazine wells cut for 9mm magazines. Most employ double-column, high capacity stick versions, but several versions now accept popular pistol magazines. Wilson Combat just released one heck of a 9mm AR designed specifically for this cartridge. A blow-back design can be hard on an AR, so the Wilson has been beefed up in critical areas. Versions are available that accept Glock, S&W M&P, and Beretta magazines. Unlike some other types, the Wilsons lock back on the last shot. Sig's new MPX is another great looking 9mm that uses proprietary magazines. A good share of the 9mm carbine market is probably related to home defense, and ammo cost is likely a driving force.

AR-15 .22 RIMFIRE OPTIONS

The latest trend involves dedicated AR-15 rimfire knock-offs, but the concept began years ago with special drop-in .22 LR AR-15 adapter kits. Regardless of the type, they all use simple blow-back designs, which don't utilize a gas tube. They were covered in the *Rimfire Rifles* edition, as follows.

Conversion kits: The .22 rimfire kits are clever adaptations that replace a standard AR bolt carrier assembly. The assembly was (is) typically a two-piece affair, consisting of a breech face/chamber insert, and separate spring-loaded bolt. The bolt reciprocates behind the chamber adapter, guided by connecting rails. The chamber-insert is shaped like a .223 round, but bored for a .22 long rifle cartridge. A special rimfire magazine is part of a kit.

These conversion units permit the use of high-speed, .22 LR ammunition in a standard centerfire AR-15. The latter's bore diameter is a tad larger than the former's, which sometimes results in so-so accuracy. At anything beyond point-blank range, zero will change as well. Lead-fouling in gas tubes has been another reported problem. Despite some faults, the conversion kits remain in production, their principle attribute being affordability. Prices run from $150-$250 and rimfire ammo is cheaper—when you can find it.

CMMG Unit: Cabela's (among other retailers) sells them for $220, including a 26-round magazine. You pop the rear take-down pin, withdraw the standard AR-15 bolt carrier, and drop in the equivalent rimfire parts. It's quick and easy. The rifle's bolt-catch won't work in the normal fashion, although it will lock back on the last shot. Instead, a very high magazine follower juts upward to capture the bolt. The magazine has small plastic pads which serve as fitting spacers to minimize slop when seated. If initially tight, the pads are carefully trimmed until a workable fit occurs. CMMG cautions against use of Remington .22 ammo and recommends bargain-priced Federal 36-grain HPS sold in 550-round bulk packs. All things including pricing considered, that's a very good happenstance. Frequent cleaning is recommended, followed by discharge of a few full-strength .223 rounds to help blow fouling out of the gas tube. Leaving the .22 unit in place overnight is not recommended, since fouling can begin to fuse the adapter to the chamber.

A rimfire kit is a clever adaptation of the AR design. The blow-back bolt reciprocates on a carrier chassis. Its special .22 LR magazine fits a standard AR-15 lower.

CMMG's .22 LR upper is mounted to a .223 AR-15 lower receiver by simply pulling two pins. The shorter magazine is a 10-shot S&W version.

Dedicated rimfire uppers: The next evolution involved complete upper receivers. They generally use true .22 LR barrels which lack gas systems and incorporate some sort of conversion kit. Like the simpler drop-in kits, you still use your centerfire lower receiver, meaning the trigger will be familiar. Accuracy is likely to improve and most of the concerns associated with the kits become a non-issue. With a pre-mounted aiming system, one can pull the two receiver pins, install the dedicated .22 upper, and commence firing. Since you're buying half of a rifle, cost will be higher, running somewhere around $450-$500. That's not too far from a complete .22 LR AR-15. However, like an adapter kit, it's a non-serial numbered part that can be mail-ordered. Nordic Components sells an interesting looking example.

Complete rimfire ARs: AR-15 clones eventually appeared, and some were really just cosmetic rep-

The controls on S&W's M&P rimfire will be very familiar to anyone versed on an AR-15/M-16 system.

resentations of conventional models; but when S&W introduced their AR-22 rimfire rifle, a new chapter dawned. It was covered in the *Rimfire Rifles* edition, as follows.

S&W's AR-22: This stand-alone rifle is mostly plastic, but shares some common AR-15 parts. Operation is identical to a standard AR-15, and price is fairly reasonable. I snapped one up shortly after its introduction. An immediate revelation as a long-time AR-15 shooter was that running the S&W .22 was old hat. This early model had an unthreaded, plain barrel which, unfortunately, didn't shoot worth beans. With garden-variety high-speed ammo it averaged only around two inches at 25 yards. It hit the road and I waited a while for S&W to sort things out. The following year I stumbled upon a used but like-new MOE version, factory-equipped with MagPul's collapsible stock, pistol grip and iron sights. This one had a 50% stoppage rate from stove pipe failures to eject. Another trip to the internet revealed a simple solution involving a minor ejector adjustment. I'm betting the previous owner bent it during cleaning. The fix was easy and it now runs like a Swiss watch. Incidentally, both S&W rifles reliably digested Federal 36 grain bulk-pack HPs.

The latest S&W shoots twice as well as the first. The economical Federal HPs cut five-shot groups of around an inch at 25 yards, which is acceptable plinker-grade performance. Federal Gold Medal Target does much better, putting 5 shots into just over one inch at 50 yards – not too shabby! During initial accuracy testing I discovered the supplied 25-round magazine was too long for benchrest

S&W's M&P 15-22, shown with 10 and 25-shot magazines. The shorter type is handy from a bench.

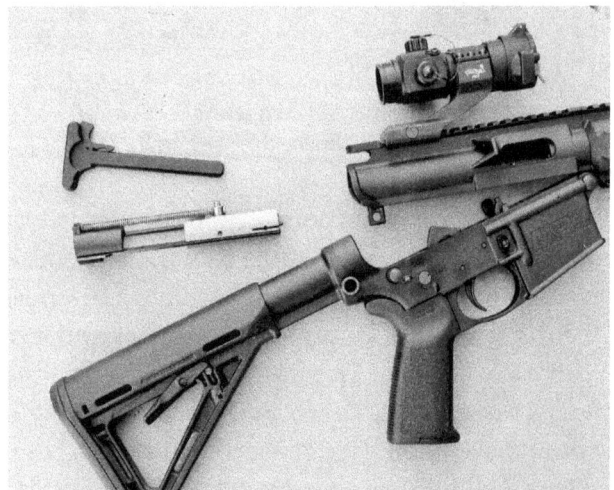

The rimfire S&W version is easy to service. The socket behind the rear pin on this MOE version accepts a push-button QD sling swivel.

The easily separated receiver halves will stow in a relatively small space. The dot sight is an inexpensive Walther that has seen plenty of use.

work. Shooting off sandbags, it hit the bench. A 10-round magazine was ordered, which fixed the problem nicely. The longer magazines take some getting used to during loading, due to the large stack of rimmed cartridges. S&W incorporates a side-button, which helps control the follower. You need to hold your mouth just right, but with some practice, you can properly line them up.

My latest AR-22 has a mil-spec 1/2x28 threaded muzzle and A-2 flash hider, making it a good candidate for a suppressor. Many, but not all, parts will interchange with AR-15 components. Stocks, pistol grips, and triggers are supposedly common, but the receiver halves are intentionally different. Disassembly is, however, fairly similar. Both push-pins are there and cleaning is a breeze. Pushing the rear pin allows the receiver halves to separate. The charging handle (plastic) and bolt assembly are withdrawn just like an AR-15, but the rimfire lacks a gas system, and is much easier to maintain. Push the front pin and you have a true, take-down rifle.

The supplied sights are fine, but are now stored in the S&W box. For serious accuracy testing, I used a Burris 1.75x5 scope on a Rock River AR-15 one-piece base. It was later switched out for an inexpensive but useful Walther dot sight that seems just about perfect on this rifle. The forend/quad-rails provide plenty of mounting points. A Safariland RLS light slips right on providing 24/7 critter control capabilities. Here's one thing to consider, though: A high sighting system makes close range hits difficult. Rounds will strike noticeably low by an error equivalent to the distance between bore and sight centerlines. For small game hunting this can be a problem. On the other hand, it's lots of fun to

S&W's M&P 15-22 on the bench for accuracy testing. The scope and mount were plucked off an AR-15 for this phase.

Accuracy from the S&W was useful if not spectacular. It pays to try different types, as evidenced by Federal Gold Medal Target. A subsequent 50-yard test did nearly as well.

shoot! As for the heavy trigger, a modest $10 investment to Brownells resulted in the arrival of a J.P. Trigger Spring Kit (the springs are reduced-power and painted yellow). Voila, a half-way decent pull was instantly achieved, with no degradation of function! It took a while to sort things out with the S&W, but for me, it was well worth the aggravation. I'd rate the S&W AR-22 as a rifle worth owning. It's both a trainer and a plinker, which may also help put meat in the pot.

Note: S&W recently made a few upgrades to the design, including a sleek new forend. Several other versions are available, including tricked-out Performance Center models.

Nordic Components: We've used their well-built extended shotgun magazine extensions, but a series of ARs have just appeared. Among them is an interesting .22LR version that just seems "right." It's made from aluminum, comes with a Vortex dot sight, and runs off of Black Dog .22 magazines. The true AR construction no doubt accounts for its listed $900 price. Of course, you do get a Strikefire II sight.

Which .22 system is best for you? Well, maybe, none of them. It's an additional expense no matter which type you choose, so it may represent extra icing on an already-expensive cake. Still, a .22 rim-fire of some sort is worth owning, and you could base an entire rifle system exclusively on the AR platform.

Even though a basic adapter kit is the least expensive route, I'd be inclined to skip it if for no other reason than the need for re-zeroing. That requires extra ammo, not to mention the accuracy and fouling issues. Although an entirely separate .22 LR upper will double your cost, these problems cease to exist. However, you may still be aggravated by the inability to latch the bolt rearward without a magazine inserted. You may also encounter enough stoppages to turn the air blue. I'd be inclined to do lots of internet surfing prior to choosing a unit. Because an AR upper is not a firearm, you can legally have one shipped directly to your address. I was leaning in that direction until S&W came out with their AR-15 clone.

A rimfire AR ready for action with lots of ammo and a light. Note the two scope base riser-blocks, a solution for repeatable QD ring mounting on softer plastic receivers.

I think a complete .22 AR-15 is the best bet, if for no other reason than convenience. An S&W is only a bit more money than an upper receiver although, as a complete firearm, it is subject to purchase requirements. After fooling with a cranky conversion .22 upper, the S&W is a welcome respite. Prior to a recent high-speed rifle training course, I broke it out for some practice. Did it make a difference? You bet! Believing in the adage "train as you fight," it's nice to gain the identical function of a true centerfire counterpart. Sure, the weight is different, but many common accessories can be added, ranging from pistol grips to lights. Mine is always ready for action, sporting a forend-mounted light.

COMPATIBLE AR-15 AIMING SYSTEMS

Regardless of the caliber choice, you'll probably want an optical sight of some sort. Because we were equipping multiple agency users, we went with Aimpoint Patrol Optic dot sights. This choice solved most individual zero or eye relief issues, and permitted location of the dot sights well-forward of our folding rear sights. Enough room also existed to locate an NVD behind the Aimpoint, which has several NV settings. The configuration is strictly defensive and we're not planning on potting our supper with them.

Aimpoint's Patrol Optic leaves lots of reserve rail space for BUIS or NVDs. The factory-supplied lens caps and tethered turret caps are nice touches.

Sig's new "Romeo" dot sight is another compact option. The BUIS rear is reassuring.

For a good all-around rifle, consider a low-power variable scope. Keep it on the lowest setting and you'll gain the large FOV seen with dot sights. For longer-range shots you can always crank up its power setting. A package like the WW CDI and Leupold 1x4 would be pretty darned useful. If possible, try to physically check for ocular-bell clearance with a backup rear sight. The 30mm tubes will have a bit less room, owing to their larger diameters.

Rimfire ARs could benefit from either aiming system. Among others, Nikon sells a nice rimfire 2x7 scope. A lower-priced dot sight wouldn't be a bad choice either. The S&W .22 has a polymer receiver that seems a bit too soft for repeatable zeroes, using QD rings. With this rifle it's probably one sighting system or the other.

Pistol-caliber ARs seems like naturals for dot sights. They're really 100-yard setups at best, so long-range precision is out.

Shooters seeking precision AR capabilities can always add a specialized upper. When coupled with a higher magnification scope, true varmint rifle performance will be possible. Switching out an upper is a breeze thanks to those two receiver pins. Another possibility is a compromise AR with a 20-inch barrel and 2 1/2-10X (or similar) scope.

Vortex's PST 2.5-10x32 FFP Viper is an option for those seeking a do-all scope. It can handle any long-range AR demands but has a large FOV on 2.5X.

CHAPTER 24

AR ACCESSORIES

Because the AR-15 is such a unique system, one can spend a small fortune on a series of related gadgets and tools. To keep things simple, let's just focus on a few. Those flush with cash could no doubt locate lots of extra goodies but, in either case, the Brownell's website is worth a look. You'll find a number of interesting trinkets, as well as these basics.

AR-15 reference material: Several good publications exist, including the military Technical Manuals (TMs). They make a good reference and will also help you understand all aspects of the system. Besides a manual, you'll also want a supply of essential cleaning gear and parts. A publication worth owning is Jeff Zimba's *"Evolution of the Black Rifle."* It's much more comprehensive than this short section and will help steer you toward lots of handy items.

Cleaning rod guide: Assuming you already have some cleaning gear, an AR-specific receiver guide is worth owning. Most are just an insert that replaces the bolt carrier assembly. Drop one in and you'll ensure concentric passes of your rod through the barrel while cleaning from breech-to-muzzle. Mine is a simple design made out of Delran plastic, but it actually works as well as a more elaborate unit in our armory.

Chamber brush: The recessed area to the rear of the chamber is relieved for locking-lug engagement, and it's a nuisance to access for cleaning. Some special tools are available, but the simple G.I. unit will do. It has a bronze brush matching the chamber, followed by an integral, larger-diameter, stainless brush section. After threading onto a pistol-length rod, a few twists will do the job. A clean chamber is necessary for reliable function and this accessory is inexpensive insurance.

Pipe cleaners: They're flexible and small in diameter, so you can slide them through a bolt head's firing pin channel. They'll also feed through the gas key and into the bolt carrier. Pipe cleaners or cotton swabs also come in handy for the areas adjacent to the gas tube and receiver. Make sure pieces don't get lodged within the bolt key tube or firing pin channel.

Spare parts: Any firearm has a "life" and the AR system is no exception. Regular maintenance will go a long way toward prolonging your rifle's longevity, but things can fail. Sustained firing produces heat, which can be a contributing factor. A modest collection of spare parts can be purchased, ranging from gas rings through a firing pin.

For extra insurance, when a break down on the fly would be disastrous, a spare bolt carrier assembly may be worthwhile. Better yet would be a complete bolt carrier/bolt assembly. Just pull out the offending original and drop in the replacement. This somewhat expensive solution won't be fully appreciated until needed, but it should solve anything from a loose bolt key or broken firing pin to a damaged extractor. If going this route, make sure the replacement bolt will properly head-space with the barrel. Any gunsmith with a set of head-space gauges should be able to check.

Remembering Murphy's Law, spare pin and spring kits are worthwhile. Chrome silicon springs cost more but provide much longer life. Interestingly, although experienced shooters recognize that pistol recoil springs need periodic replacement, the same mindset is seldom extended to shoulder-fired arms. With an AR system, the analogous buffer spring can be changed after 3,000 rounds. In fact, an extra buffer and spring won't break the bank. Just make sure you buy the correct type, whether carbine or rifle. To help prolong spring life, don't store your AR with the bolt locked open. Hammer spring tension can be relieved by dry-firing, *after making sure the rifle is unloaded!*

A full-blown armorer's kit would be excessive, but some tools are helpful. A lower receiver block is helpful with a vise. An upper receiver block is useful as well. A 2-Unique wrench is nestled beside it.

Tools: An armorer's wrench will perform several distinct tasks. It can also get you into trouble (hence the manual). AR owners with carbine-length buffer tubes will appreciate a means to re-tighten the castellated retaining nut. A good clue that it's loose will be some rotation of the stock assembly. Additional slots in the wrench fit things like the flats on most muzzle devices, etc. An armorer's wrench is fairly large, but mine will fit inside a G.I. ammo can if turned kitty-corner. That container also serves as a repository for other AR-15 widgets.

A Maine company, 2-Unique LLC, sells a nice line of handy AR-15 tools which are first-rate products (their forend tools are worth a look). Gerber came out with an irresistible "Short Stack AR-15 Multi-tool" which will fit inside some pistol grips. This $45 device could really save the day in light of its many functions. Gerber describes it as "the answer to your cleaning and maintenance needs" for good reason! It can handle some of the same chores as an armorer's wrench thanks to its folding design. It also has a built-in sight adjustment tool.

A G.I.-type sight adjustment tool is also handy. The AR-15's front sight is used for elevation adjustments. Even many of the after-market front sight units actually employ a G.I. front sight post, which has a flange with four detent notches spaced 90 degrees apart. Depressing the detent catch permits the threaded sight post to be rotated downward or upward until a zero has been achieved. Although a bullet tip will work, you really need to hold your mouth just right. A better bet is the simple, purpose-built tool. It's small and inexpensive.

Backup iron sights: Depending on how your AR is configured, a BUIS alternative may be worth a look. As noted in the previous chapters, our agency's dot sight carbines are BUIS equipped. Make sure enough rail space exists to accommodate a rear sight, which will also need adequate clearance if used with a scope. Correct front and rear heights are also necessary. Some users prefer combinations that will co-witness through the center of a dot sight when deployed. Others would rather see them through the lower third of their optic. If your life depends on a BUIS system, don't skimp on cost. We're happy with our ARMS 40-Ls, but there are plenty of other good choices.

Assault case: A good, solid hard case offers maximum protection, but soft-sided, AR-specific cases are also handy. We use different lengths, matched to corresponding uppers. They all have side-mounted magazine pouches, durable carry straps, and loops for convenient hanging. Besides spare magazines, a larger zippered side pocket will accept a Harris Bipod or other goodies. The result is a handy grab & go package that can be slung across a shoulder. I don't permanently store a rifle in a case, but it's easy enough to toss one in on short notice. The cases we've used bear "Brownell's" or "Blackhawk" labels. Others (like the "discrete carry" types) offer similar features while looking less sinister. Since one of my cases contains .300 Blackout rounds, it has a piece of orange surveyor's tape tied to the handle, along with a distinctive logo.

An "assault case" provides a handy grab & go package, with compartments for magazines and other items. Save the one-piece rod for a workbench and use a bore guide. Ranger plate extensions work well with shorter magazines stored in pouches.

AR-15 magazines, including (top row L-R): 30-rd P-Mag, 30 Rd Lancer (with steel lips), 20 Rd Brownells (with Ranger Plate), and 20-Rd G.I. type. Bottom: 10-rd P-Mag (with 5-rd adapter), and 5-rd MWG.

Magazines: While extras are good, reliable magazines are essential! Many of us will accumulate a collection of different types, in varying condition. Magazines with high use or questionable lineage will probably impede reliability. I personally have no interest in any holding more than 30 rounds, and actually prefer the more compact 20-rounders.

In order to comply with our state's hunting laws, a few 5-round magazines are also on hand. As it turns out, they're also useful for benchrest shooting. Although made out of plastic, I like the ultra-short MWGs. Unlike some other types that are modified 20-rounders, the thermo-molded 5-shot jobs are distinctly different. They're also very quiet which helps during nocturnal coyote operations. Magpul sells a Polymer 10-shot magazine that is nearly as compact. A 5-shot limiter is easy to insert thanks to its removable floor plate. I use these for easy .300 Blackout identification and a friend goes a step further, buying earth-colored versions.

As for 20-round types, we've had good luck using either curved aluminum Brownell's; or Mags LLC brands. Ranger plates provide an extra purchase for withdrawal from tactical vest pouches. Some people also use these small add-ons as an impromptu rest from prone. I often worry about stoppages although the practice does seem to work with low-mileage magazines. As mentioned previously, we maintain a separate stash of range magazines. There are probably plenty of good AR magazine brands, including the latest Gen-3 Magpuls and Lancers. Test each one for secure engagement, feeding, and lock-back.

Magazine pouch or bail-out bag: For casual AR shooting, I often use the pockets sewn onto an assault-type case. Afield, the shortest 5-shot types will drop inside a pants pocket. One reason I like 20-round magazines is that they carry well on a belt-mounted pouch. We've had good luck with a double Blackhawk version, which has fairly secure Velcro belt-retaining loops. Nowadays, just about everyone is into 30-round types, and most pouches are sized for their greater length. Make sure your magazines are compatible with the chosen pouch. If not, a magazine add-on like the Ranger Plate can improve access.

A brass catcher can rescue exotic cases during range sessions. This Caldwell unit has snagged precious .300 Blackout brass for future reloading.

Caldwell's QD unit easily slips over a provided mount. The bag assembly is captured by two small detents.

Grab & go bags are another option. They resemble a small pack with a series of magazine compartments. Midway USA sells one that holds six 30-round AR magazines. It has a shoulder strap for rapid deployment, and cost is around $25.

Sling: The AR system provides plenty of options for attachment devices and actual sling types. We've been running an inventory of single-point slings that connect to a buffer tube loop directly behind the lower receiver. The slings are attached to our operators' vests, and will snap onto various shoulder-fired weapons via a rugged QD hook. This system permits great versatility; however, for general purpose use, I'd rather have a two-point hook-up design. The rifle will be less likely to flop around on the go, and muzzle control will improve. Some types will actually facilitate either option. Among the many choices, Viking Tactics and Vickers units are worth a look. Shooters with railed forends

This Blackhawk double-magazine pouch is sized for 20-round types. The single-point sling hooks to a QD loop behind the receiver.

can choose among clamp-on hook-up systems. A QD stud is available for solid A-2 buttstocks. It replaces the rear G.I. loop and is captured by the lower buttplate screw. Magpul's telescoping ACS has sockets for a plug-in QD sling stud. Their simpler units are slotted to accept a simple sling.

Rail sections: A free-floated forearm is now common and many are now streamlined. Integral full-length cheese-grater rails have evolved to detachable Picatinny sections. Several mounting methods are in use, but they all accomplish the same thing. Most of my rails are shorter sections which are attached sparingly. I always keep a few extras on hand, but it doesn't take much rail space for most uses. The most common accessories are probably lights and/or vertical grips, sling-mounts, and bipods. A forend full of rails adds bulk and has lots of sharp edges, in which case plastic rail covers are useful.

Lights (and maybe lasers): A defensive AR cries out for a light and it should come as no surprise that many types are available. Prices vary greatly, as do their mounting systems. The output will often be expressed in lumens, with more being brighter. Some sort of momentary switch is advisable to prevent becoming a constant-on target. I'm sure I could do better, but I manage just fine with an issued, general purpose Safariland RLS. Its pivoting mount will easily slip over most Picatinny-type pistol or rifle rails. It will then pivot 90-degrees, snapping into place on a Picatinny rail. Output is a fairly modest 90 Lumens, and the tail button is positive. I leave one on the left side of an AR's forend, where the switch is readily accessible with my support-hand thumb. A second RLS migrates between other firearms as needed.

A popular two-for-one adaptation is one in a vertical forend grip, which some users prefer for more positive purchase. Crimson Trace is well known for pistol laser grips. They just broke new ground with a dedicated AR design. Their "LINQ" system employs a wireless combination light and laser

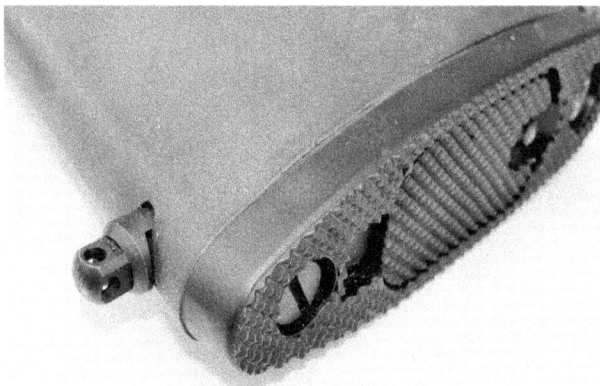

This aftermarket QD sling swivel stud replaces a standard solid-stock G.I. loop.

Several sling options are possible here. Besides double receiver loops, the slotted Magpul stock has been modified with a QD stud after drilling one hole.

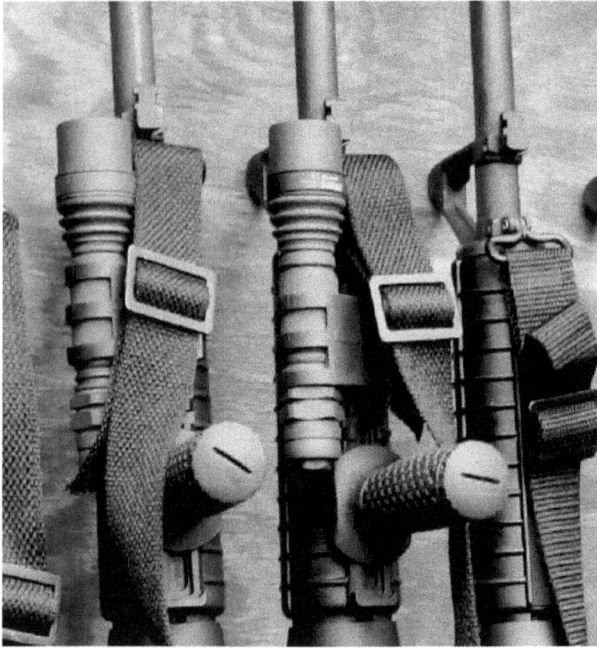

Lacking a Picatinny system, adapters will permit use of accessories on standard G.I. forends.

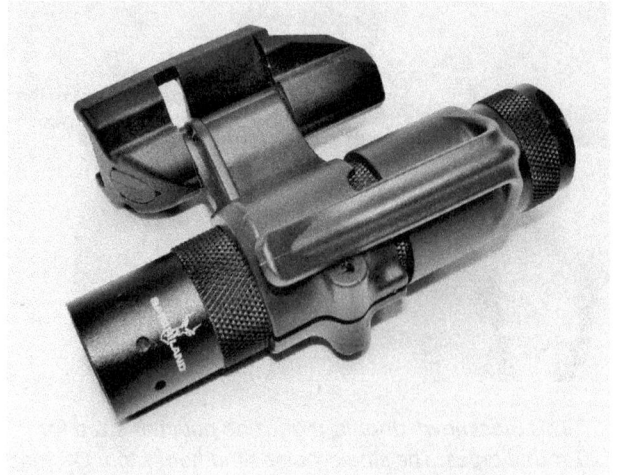

Safariland's "Rapid Light System" will quickly mount to numerous rail-equipped firearms. It also has a belt hook.

unit, which is mounted to the forend. A special AR pistol grip then provides activation in a manner similar to Bluetooth technology. It's a brilliant idea in more than one way! The absence of wires and finger pads is especially welcome (I avoid them entirely). The LINQ may be the perfect solution for home defense.

LaserMax has a clever new light that seems perfect or AR-15s. The 140-Lumen "Manta-Ray" is lightweight and flat. It simply snaps on to a Picatinny rail section, making it a useful option for shooters with multiple firearms. A built-in pressure pad will activate this light, but an accessory pad is available.

Some lights put out nearly enough light to weld with. The effects against an opponent are debilitating, going beyond some other uses such as navigation and identification. When it comes to the latter, muzzle discipline is closely connected, so training is advised!

Bipod mount: One thing I quickly learned was that my favorite Harris units wouldn't properly mount to a slender forend. Its connector engaged the QD stud, but the support pads remained afloat. A short Picatinny rail section solved this problem, in concert with a small bipod adapter. The adapter is easily secured with a retractable button, but there are many different types. Tactical-type bipods have also blossomed for use with

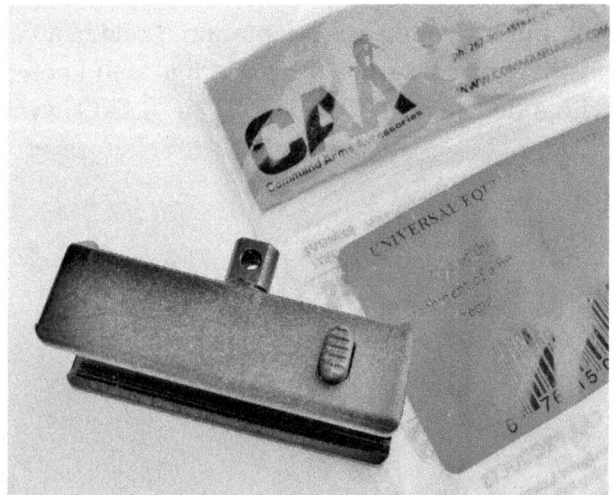

This simple CAA bipod adapter will slide over the end of a rail section after depressing a spring-loaded button. Others clamp over rails via set screws.

rails. All of the designs need a free-floated forend to isolate the effects of extra upward pressure. The inexpensive barrel-mounted adapters may seem like a simple solution, but they won't work well.

Don't run amuck: It's easy to get carried away with AR accessories. They are easy to mount and abundant, providing nearly irresistible gadget attractions. We've noticed that, by the second day of our basic rifle school, many have disappeared. They not only add weight and bulk, but may also loosen up or just fall off. From behind the firing line, the last event is nearly priceless. Fortunately, training provides a good equipment shake down. The casualties are mostly bruised egos and lightened wallets. The KISS principle is worth remembering!

Rails invite accessories like vertical forend grips, lights, and lasers. These items will add extra weight, further affecting overall handling.

CHAPTER 25

USEFUL AR TIPS

The first and last things you'll see in this brief chapter are recommendations for formal training. Meanwhile, here are a few AR-related thoughts to whet your appetite. The list is far from all-inclusive, so save your pennies for a school. Don't forget at least one AR-specific manual either.

RELIABILITY

A properly built AR-15 should run reliably with good magazines, quality ammunition, *and proper lubrication.* We sometimes train in extreme cold, which can serve as a good proving ground. A marginal rifle will sometimes reveal itself through stoppages in temperatures of 10 F or lower (a freezer can accomplish the same thing). Note that the wrong lubes can cause stoppages when they stiffen up. If that condition is suspected, degrease the action and try Liberty Lube CLP.

Reliability test: Try shooting at least a few rounds with a loose grip (or better yet, the rifle un-mounted). Shoot the last shot separately, checking for lock-back. This test should be performed using each magazine.

Number your magazines: As often as not, stoppages can be traced to a bum magazine. Numbering each one is a way to identify the culprit. You can insert each empty magazine into your disassembled lower receiver while watching for bolt stop and follower engagement. Not every combination is compatible.

Load 18 rounds: This applies to G.I. type 20-rounders, which generally run better when not topped off. You can check them by pushing down on the cartridges. Enough space should remain to accept a couple more. Most 30-rounders will run when full.

OPERATION

These tips can keep you in the game by avoiding the loudest sound in the world – "click!" Some pistol shooters will be familiar with a press-check, whereby a chambered round is partially exposed through slight slide retraction. Having a loaded chamber is reassuring at times, but when it comes to the AR, we use a different technique.

Chamber check: Before inserting a magazine note the position of its top cartridge. Assuming it's sitting high and right, remove the magazine after chambering a round. The top round should now be high and left. This trick is especially useful in the dark since it will work by feel.

Tug your magazine: Give it a good yank after locking into the rifle. Sooner or later one will pop out.

This step can save a "click" or lost magazine, either of which would be disastrous in a fight. It's just extra insurance worth doing when time permits.

Don't ride the bolt: When you chamber a round, pull the charge handle fully rearward and just let go. That way the bolt carrier assembly will have plenty of oomph to fully chamber the cartridge. That's how the rifle functions anyway (during emergency reloads you can hit the bolt release).

Use the forward assist: It'll serve as extra insurance after chambering a round. If the bolt is slightly out of battery the rifle won't fire (considering the amount of pressure generated upon discharge, this "problem" is actually a blessing).

Close the dust cover: This is another good habit that will help keep the action dirt free. It'll pop open on its own anytime you fire a shot or open the bolt.

Latch the charge handle: If you don't ride the bolt forward, the handle should latch on its own. If you baby the release, the charge handle may remain afloat. It can then rap you in the nose upon firing to serve as an excellent training incentive!

Learn sear reset: Many shooters spank a trigger or do a half-baked squeeze. To improve control, hold the trigger fully rearward after the shot breaks. Then, ease it forward until you feel a distinct click. At that point, stop and begin another deliberate compression of the trigger. Sooner or later the next shot will happen. When it does, repeat this process. It takes some getting used to, but this reset trick will greatly improve your shooting.

Sense lock-back: Discharge of an AR round creates much moving mass, so with practice you should be able to sense the absence of the bolt carrier's forward momentum upon lock-back. At that point it's time to reload! This trick works well in the dark and beats a blank look in any light.

PRECAUTIONS

Remove the ammo supply *prior* to unloading the chamber! This practice is essential when clearing any firearm. Sounds simple, right? Trouble is, people still manage to get it backwards.

Clearance: Two rare occurrences involve discharged rounds that detonated either by getting tangled up in an action, or after being dropped. So, when extracting a live round, don't try to catch it. Instead, go down on a knee to shorten its fall. Don't recover the live round until the rifle has been cleared.

Cocking-indicator/safety position: You can't apply the safety unless the hammer is cocked, a quirk that can prove useful at times.

Drop cautions and carry modes: A cocked AR hammer can fail with the safety on, so a hard blow can cause a discharge. During routine operations, a common "carry condition" consists of an empty chamber with the rifle "on safe" and a loaded magazine locked in. FYI, a hard butt strike can inadvertently chamber a round through inertial bolt carrier movement. If in doubt, check!

Short rounds, primer indents, and ammo segregation: A cartridge undergoes a fairly violent journey from the magazine to the chamber. Besides the previously described light firing pin contact, a bullet *could* be shoved further inside the case neck. A double-feed can cause the same situation, dangerously elevating pressure if the round is fired. It's worth checking any previously chambered cartridges for both conditions. Any multi-caliber users should also ID their ammo. A well-known manufacturer has a demolished 5.56 AR that tried to digest a .300 Blackout round. No doubt there are others.

The light strike on the center primer indicates previous AR-15 chambering. Repeating that process several times could set it off.

Ejected brass cautions: Fired cases are energetic and hot! You don't want one lodged between your shooting glasses and face, so a hat with a visor is recommended. Likewise, a hot case inside a shirt can be pretty exciting. Dress accordingly to prevent a bout of dangerous break dancing—and manage that muzzle!

Sight height & bullet strikes: It's all too easy to drill a bullet into an adjacent object. We see this often during on-range cover stages. The sight/bore offset is greater than most other rifles, so although your target is visible through the sights, the barrel may be pointed elsewhere. Besides flying bullet fragments, some unplanned body work could be necessary after shooting over the hood of a vehicle.

Bore obstructions: The rifle should be cleared and inspected after any unusual event. A lodged bullet in a barrel would cause a catastrophic failure upon discharge of another, but snow or twigs can create a similar situation. Some flash hiders and brakes can act like scoops, too. If an AR is immersed it'll need to be drained prior to firing. The rear of the buffer tube has a drain hole for this reason. Muzzle-down carries are popular nowadays, but some of us live in snow country. Passage through a shoveled walkway invites a bore obstruction with a muzzle-down sling carry. A muzzle-up technique solves the snow problem, but it isn't great in rain. Absent a case, little plastic muzzle caps are available for A-2 flash hiders. Like electrical tape, they'll blow off through air pressure.

Sling issues: Single-point slings will cause a rifle to dangle muzzle-down. Much attention will be necessary to avoid sweeping feet, or making ground contact. None of the other systems are perfect, so muzzle discipline should always be a priority. Most rifle dismounts require extra attention to avoid sweeping others.

OTHER TIPS

Telescoping stocks: They can be instantly adjusted to accommodate different users, clothing layers, or positions. A simple adjustment is often all it takes to correct a scope eye relief problem. Living well above the Mason Dixon Line, I usually perform an initial AR setup in thick winter clothing. This setting will locate most telescoping stocks two stops inward of full extension. The next outward stop works for warm-weather garb, while the longest setting is good from prone. Others will probably prefer longer adjustments, but some users may share a rifle. If so, a color-coded mark or two on a buffer tube can indicate personalized settings.

Lubrication: The amount will depend on conditions, but in general, an AR likes some oil. The bolt carrier parts and bearing surfaces will show you where it's needed, but keep the chamber dry or excess bolt-thrust and pressures could result. Flammable solvents in gas tubes are also capable of unpleasant results.

Stoppages: The Army teaches an immediate-action solution called SPORTS, which stands for:

- SLAP the magazine to make sure it's seated.

- PULL the charge handle sharply rearward, which will hopefully clear the offending round.

- OBSERVE the chamber for further actions.

- RETURN the bolt to chamber a new round.

- TAP the forward assist.

- SQUEEZE or shoot.

These steps won't fix every stoppage and some can be challenging, so…

Riot helmets are probably out but training helps. This line will be firing from behind the short barricades next. Their close examination will reveal powder burns and bullet strikes.

Get some training: Since a small amount of knowledge is a dangerous thing, an investment in training is strongly advised! It's what we don't know that can get us in trouble.

Effective defensive use of an AR-15 requires many of the same skill sets common to semi-auto pistols. Since many AR owners also own pistols, an in-depth handgun training course makes a nice first step. From there, rifle training becomes a logical progression. There's also a good chance that immediate transition-to-handgun drills will be included in the program.

CHAPTER 26

THE AR-15: SUMMARY

The AR system may not be perfect, but it does provide a number of advantages. As we've seen, today's rifles offer mounting points for all sorts of accessories. The inherent modularity of an AR-15 also permits easy reconfiguration to meet nearly any requirement. Its size and weight are manageable. Its substantial firepower is controllable, reloads can happen quickly, and a large supply of ammo can be carried on foot. Toolless disassembly permits maintenance on the fly, and spare parts remain abundant. The same is true for ammunition and magazines.

Of course, we've barely scratched the surface. Shooters considering acquisition of an AR-15 will find no shortage of information, and it's worth doing homework before jumping in with both feet. Besides Jeff Zimba's *"Evolution of the Black Rifle,"* there are a number of AR-specific publications. Although the Internet has its share of BS, it remains another great source. AR15.Com will link you everywhere. Brownell's has an online "gun builder" feature that will let you switch out lowers, upper, and parts. Just about all of the manufacturers have interesting sites.

The big question is: Do you actually need an AR? From the perspective of a sportsman, I view the black rifle as an ancillary system. My ARs augment a stable of time-tested high power rifles, covering specialized outdoor and occupational requirements. Shooters less into hunting will probably focus on defense, in which case a black rifle makes perfect sense. Of course, this assumes no onerous restrictions exist to muddy the water. If not, one well-appointed 16 or 18-inch flat top 5.56 AR-15 could cover just about *all* shoulder-fired needs.

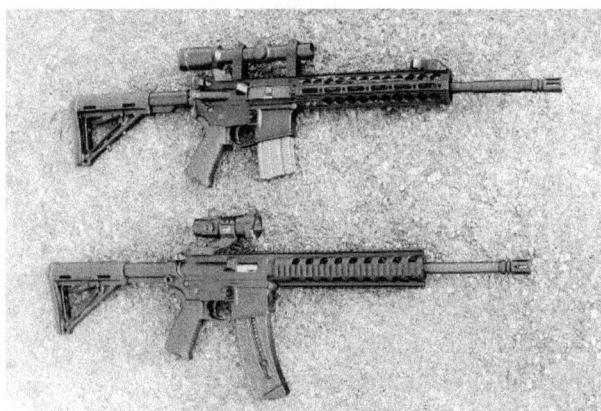

Lots of potential exist with this centerfire/rimfire system. The adjustable stocks can accommodate different users, and recoil is nil with either. The .22 is a great trainer, plinker, and small game tool. The .300 Blackout is adequate for deer or hogs. Suppressor capability exists as well.

It could also serve as a solid foundation for future growth. If extra punch was called for, there's always the .300 Blackout option. It's an easy addition since both calibers will run off the same supply of magazines. A suppressor becomes another intriguing possibility.

Progressing through a systems-based approach, a separate S&W AR-22 rifle would fill the rimfire niche without breaking the bank. You'd then have a darned useful 3-caliber AR system capable of handling tin cans, intruders, and deer. With telescoping stocks they will even adjust to multiple users.

Any future long-range itch could be scratched with a 6.5 Grendel upper. Yes, it's more of a specialty option, but two pins would put you back on solid 5.56 footing.

Or, you could just buy a basic AR-15 and call it good. Wasn't that easy?

ADDENDUM

CENTERFIRE RIFLES: A BUYER'S AND SHOOTER'S GUIDE

CLOSING THOUGHTS

This edition has explored two different, but not dissimilar paths.

The first path wound through a maze of conventional rifles from bolt-actions through lever guns and self-loaders. Some have been in production for a century or more, and many are still in service. Even today, a classic rifle has undeniable charm, extending well beyond its utility.

The second path explored the rapidly expanding universe of black rifles, driven by legions of new devotees. Fears of restrictive legislation account for much of this growth, but the technical aspects offer further intrigue. AR possibilities are endless and the "wow" factor is there. Some prospective owners may have little-to-no experience with traditional firearms of any sort.

Which route do we take? Maybe it's time for a reality check…

As mentioned in *Survival Guns*, we (the firearms training cadre) occasionally run a graphic demonstration, which serves as an education for the participants of an 800-round, week-long, basic pistol school. Somewhere near the conclusion of this program everyone is feeling cocky, so we like to pit one shoulder-fired shooter against two good semi-auto pistol graduates. The students are allowed to elect their pistol team, which will then compete against a solo cadre member. The shoulder-fired weapon is most often a 12 Ga. pump shotgun, but a .357 lever gun is sometimes thrown in.

Each side faces off against an identical 5-target array, located from 12-15 yards away. One extra centrally-located "stop plate" ends the event, only after a team's first five plates are down. In other words, the first "team" to clean all six wins. The remaining trainees serve as judges to determine the winner. Is it fair?

19th century technology which, in the hands of a good Cowboy Action shooter, could trounce most modern systems. Winchester's Model 1873 can spit out a whole lot of lead!

Well, at best, a single lever gun shooter will have 10 rounds to work with. Between both pistol-shooters, somewhere around 36 shots will be available. The contest begins on a whistle, and is followed by a whole lot of noise. Surprise: 19th Century technology usually beats the Tactical Tupperware crew, hands down. Despite significant recoil, a pump-shotgun is even more illustrative of shoulder-fired effect. A very good handgun team *may* score an occasional win, but that outcome will be less likely as the range increases. At some point the rifle will emerge as the undisputed victor, which is exactly the point.

We carry a handgun because it's expedient to do so. A shotgun remains the better close-quarter choice, but a well-chosen rifle provides extended reach and punch. Of course, there's always a kicker. Here it is: The simultaneous addition of all three arms would incur substantial expense; not counting the various other items constituting true "system costs." Those starting from scratch will have to pick and choose. A shotgun makes a darned good starting point, not overly encumbered by extra equipment requirements.

Conversely, a rifle can quickly decimate a bank account. Scopes, mounts, rangefinders, bipods, and other gear can quickly jack up the cost. The types of rifles shown in Section 1 might help, but if we come down with AR fever, sometimes referred to as "Black Rifle Disease," all bets are off.

Many of us will need a reality check, driven by funds. Some who suffered through both Sections may find themselves back where they started, gazing inside the family gun cabinet. As we've seen, Grandpa's Winchester can still make an effective lead dispenser in the hands of a skilled user. The average deer hunter is not likely to have a small fortune tied up in black rifles, and let's face it, dead is dead. With the right bullet, a .30/30, .308, or 30/06 will certainly cause most living things to assume ambient temperature. For someone with limited resources, it might just make more sense to grab Ol' Betsy than invest in a completely new system. Find a shotgun if you can and save for a handgun. Go that route and a more elaborate rifle can wait until later.

Our decisions may further depend upon localized restrictions. As we've seen, a "modern sporting rifle" is not much different from Uncle Joe's old wood-stocked Remington Woodsmaster. Either is a magazine-fed, gas-operated rifle requiring separate pulls of its trigger, but good luck beating that into the heads of politicians or media types. Those spared from the inherent evils of pistol grips and black stocks needn't feel defeated. A ten-shot magazine can be fitted to a Remington auto-loader, as well as several bolt-action types. A slide-action rifle will work, and may also match up nicely with your shotgun.

Similar function is desirable. Factor common operation in when shopping and you'll come out ahead of pure glitz. The high-end items are nice, but they won't guarantee success. Odds of survival are better for a well-trained user of mediocre equipment than the other way around. Even with unlimited resources, practicality still counts. KISS is good and Murphy's Law is real.

A good school is hard to beat, and might just save your hide. Gun handling skills require the utmost attention, and the wrong practice will just reinforce imperfect techniques. We don't know what we don't know, so *quality* training is important. There are a number of great firearms academies throughout the United States, many of which are geared toward newer shooters. Course duration varies, as does ammo consumption. Factoring in travel, accommodations, food, gear, and tuition, the cost won't be cheap; but then again, you'll generally get what you pay for. If you go light on equipment you might just recoup costs otherwise blown on the wrong items. You'll also gain a life-altering experience, and one more memorable than most vacations.

Lastly, membership in The National Rifle Association is strongly recommended. Without this organization many of the firearms we just examined would almost certainly be banned. The NRA is also a good informational source for a number of topics including ranges and training. An annual membership is reasonable and includes extra perks.

GLOSSARY & QUICK REFERENCE GUIDE

Jargon of any kind can be confusing and shooters are often guilty of spitting out their unfair share. A couple of good handgun-related examples are IWB and OWB holsters. Those who aren't regular gun rag subscribers may not know they stand for "inside-the waist-band" and "outside-the-waist-band" designs. The rifle realm is probably worse, as evidenced by terminology scattered throughout this book. Instead of an alphabetical reference system, a topic-related progression follows. This approach might help connect a few dots.

TARGET AND ACCURACY TERMINOLOGY

Some of the target-related acronyms (like MOA or POI) can slow down the comprehension process in a hurry. A few of the terms (such as come-ups) are confusing as well.

Come-ups: Scope turret elevation adjustments applied using clicks and/or a graduated reference scale.

Elevation: Vertical aiming adjustments applied to compensate for trajectory. Among the numerous factors, a few "environmental" ones include altitude, barometric pressure, and temperature. These are not to be confused with extreme up or down angles that introduce further gravity-based compensations.

Flier: An errant shot, often revealed as an aggravating deviation from a shot group. If only somebody could invent a hole-eraser…

Group: A series of carefully fired shots, recorded to assess accuracy. A series of five shots is typically the benchmark for precision rifles, and three shot groups are a common sporting rifle standard. Measurements are taken from the centers of the furthest shots.

MOA: Minute Of Angle is an angular measurement which actually measures 1.047 inches at 100 yards. As such, an "MOA rifle" should be mechanically capable of shooting 1" groups at 100 yards, 5" clusters at 500 yards, etc. Most accuracy testing results are based on 100-yard groups.

POA: Point of aim indicates an aiming point. It may be different from a target's center to allow for the effects of zero, trajectory, or wind. With a 200-yard zero, using a .308 rifle, our POA might be 2 MOA (2") low at 100 yards. The lower POA should produce a centered hit.

POI: Point of impact, for targeting purposes, indicates the deviation of projectile impacts from point of aim. In the above example, without that -2 MOA correction, our 100-yard POI would be 2" high.

Windage: Aiming corrections (POA) applied for horizontal sighting discrepancies, or the effects of wind on a bullet's path. Kentucky Windage refers to allowance for an incorrect zero. Wind hold-offs are used to compensate for projectile drifts caused by wind. POA at longer ranges may be expressed in MOAs. A sniper will often have a spotter who bases MOA wind calls on environmental cues.

Zero-distance: The range at which our rifle is "sighted in" for a dead-on hold. At other ranges an adjusted point of aim will be needed.

OPTICS

Although this information is covered in the scope chapters, it might come in handy as a quick reference when scanning catalogs or surfing the 'net.

3-9x40 (example): We're looking at a variable-magnification scope with a 3 to 9X range. Its front (objective) lens is 40mm in diameter—maybe. Sometimes this number is based on the housing instead of the lens. Still, it'll serve as a guide.

Eye relief: The distance from the rear (ocular) lens of an optical device to a user's eye, where a full image is visible. This will occur with many scopes at around 3-4 inches, allowing for recoil protection. Binoculars and spotting scopes will have much shorter ERs. Pistol and scout scopes are often advertised as EER models with extended eye reliefs.

Exit Pupil: The shaft of light emitted by an ocular lens, which displays a magnified image for user of scopes, binoculars, etc. Dividing the objective lens diameter by a scope's magnification will indicate its exit pupil size. A 40mm objective and 5X magnification will result in an 8mm exit pupil. Since most human pupils won't dilate beyond 7mm, this is useful low-light combination (but only with good lenses).

FFP (1st FP): A scope design in which the reticle's size accompanies magnification shifts. First focal plane scopes were more popular in Europe, but they are finding favor with long-range and tactical shooters who use trajectory-compensating reticles. Values remain constant throughout the magnification range, but the actual reticle is harder to see on the lowest settings.

FOV: Field of view, a measurement most often expressed in feet, indicating the linear distance visible through an optical device. A scope with a 34' FOV would have an image matching two stakes set 34 feet apart at 100 yards (some European manufacturers list degrees instead).

IR: An Infrared light source, normally projected through a special illuminator, in a spectrum not visible to the human eye. It may also stand for "illuminated reticle" on scopes so equipped.

Multi-Gun (or Three-Gun): A formalized combat-shooting completion involving use of handguns, shotguns, and rifles. It's referenced here because of strong influence on AR-15s and optics.

NVD (or NV): Night vision device or instrument, often used with IR during extreme darkness.

Objective Lens: This term refers to a scope's front lens. Its diameter is expressed in millimeters (like

40 or 50mm), and some higher-magnification bell-housings may also include a P/A feature. Lower magnification models can get away with smaller objectives. Some are even straight-tubed 20MM types.

Ocular Lens: A scope's rear lens, within the ocular housing. Most have some sort of individualized focus feature which could be fine-threaded, or a newer fast-focus type.

P/A: When a scope's reticle and focal point coincide, precise alignment is possible. Distance extremes can introduce aiming errors known as parallax. A <u>parallax-adjustable</u> scope provides a means for corrections through a graduated knob or front bell, typically displaying yardages.

Picatinny Rail: The military mounting system, which uses precisely specified dimensions that accommodate scope rings, lights, lasers, and other accessories.

QD System: A <u>quick disconnect</u> design for easy dismounting of scope rings, sling swivels, etc.

Reticle: The crosshairs or dot within a scope used for aiming. Scope reticles are normally mounted within a separate interior housing, to permit adjustments via turret contacts. A "ballistic reticle" will display a series of additional reference points for trajectory compensations.

RFP (2nd FP): Scopes from the more common American <u>second focal plane</u> design present a consistent reticle image throughout their magnification range. In low light, the reticle will be easier to see, but those with ballistic reticles will only calibrate as intended on their maximum magnifications.

RIFLE BASICS

The following is just a short list of endless terminology. I'm no doubt guilty of throwing some around, so here goes...

Bedding: The interface of a rifle's action and stock. Precise fit is necessary for maximum accuracy. Glass bedding is a trick used to create a form-fitting "bed" between an action and its stock. Some synthetics employ a molded-in aluminum V-block to accomplish this purpose.

Bolt shroud: An assembly on the rear of bolt that captures the striker. This part is common to bolt-actions, and further serves to redirect gas in the event of a pierced primer. Look closely around the forward receiver and you'll also see a small hole designed to vent excess pressure.

Bore: The center of a barrel through which a bullet passes. Its smoothness and dimensions can affect accuracy or fouling.

Breech: The rear end of a barrel and its adjacent locking surfaces.

Carbine: A generic, shorter-barreled rifle of compact size. For our purposes, it will also have a finished barrel at least 16-inches long to meet federal requirements (see SBR). An AR will more than likely have a telescoping stock that can adjust LOP.

CF: <u>Controlled-feed</u>, describing a Mauser-type bolt design whereby cartridge rims are captured by an extractor as they emerge from the magazine.

Chamber: The rear area of a barrel precisely dimensioned to accept a cartridge. The "chambering" of a barrel is typically stamped to its exterior.

Crown: The muzzle surface that contacts the bore. It's often recessed, affording some protection from accuracy-robbing nicks or dings.

DI: A gas-operated <u>direct impingement</u> design (like the AR-15/M-16) directs gas rearward from a port within the barrel through a tube. The pressure then impinges upon a reciprocating bolt for positive function.

DM: A <u>detachable magazine</u>, most often easily removed.

Floor plate: The bottom plate that covers many bolt-action magazines. Hinged floor plates permit cartridges to be removed without running them through the action.

Follower: The spring-loaded magazine part that pushes or lifts cartridges.

Fouling: An accumulation of carbon or copper deposits which, in a barrel, can lead to deteriorating accuracy if not removed.

Gas-operation: Rifles within this category harness high-pressure propellant gas to cycle semi-automatic (or self-loading) actions. Many full-auto firearms work in the same manner, the difference being that the latter type will continue to fire as long as the trigger is depressed.

Headspace: A carefully controlled chamber dimension, limiting breech face clearance for safe containment of pressure. Some cartridges, like a .30/30, headspace on their rims. Other "belted magnums," like .300 Winchester Magnum, headspace off an annular belt, just forward of the base. Rimless, non-belted, necked rifle cartridges (.223, .308, etc.) develop headspace through proper fit between their shoulders and breech face. In all cases, fit is critical for containment of pressure!

Leade: A tapered transitional area between a chamber and the rifling, which helps guide a bullet into the bore. This area is subject to erosion from the full effects of heat and pressure. It's usually the first spot in a bore to suffer.

LOP: <u>Length Of Pull</u>, the distance from a trigger to the rear of a stock (i.e. 13 1/2" LOP). This dimension can affect fit and scope eye relief.

Piston-type: This gas-operated variant substitutes a reciprocating rod for a gas tube. Pressure is still ducted through a barrel-port, but it remains within that area, driving a connecting rod that bears upon the bolt.

Rifling: The spiral cuts machined into a barrel's bore, which engrave and stabilize a bullet. The "lands" are the high surfaces separating "grooves."

ROT: The <u>rate-of-twist</u> of a barrel's rifling. A 1x12 twist will spin a bullet 360 degrees with 12-inches of passage through a section of rifling. Heavier or longer bullets generally require faster twists in order to develop adequate stability. Shorter or lighter bullets can tolerate a slower ROT. A 1x12 is fairly common for many middle-of-the-road .308 Winchester loads.

Striker: A heavy, spring-loaded firing pin, used in bolt-action designs, instead of a hammer. The striker is cocked by manipulation of the bolt. Most do so upon opening.

AMMUNITION ABCs

Some are sprinkled throughout the book, but others (like JHP) can appear on the end-flap of an ammo box. It's worth learning a few basics before hitting a sporting goods isle. If ever in doubt, don't even try chambering a cartridge, let alone shoot it! *Survival Guns* has more information on this subject.

AP: The military uses special <u>armor piercing</u> bullets. They occasionally show up in gun shows or collections. Most have a very hard insert made out of dense metal like tungsten. U.S. types can be identified by a black tip (not to be confused with some sporting rounds that use polymer nose sections). They'll be hell on any metal targets and are much more likely to ricochet.

BC: <u>Ballistic coefficient;</u> a numerical assignment of a bullet's aerodynamic efficiency, based on mass and profile. A higher BC indicates less "drag." A BT can help. A RN bullet will have such a low BC that a BT is… pointless!

Berdan-primed: A European design in which part of the ignition system is integral with the cartridge case. Some of this stuff may be corrosive. Manufacturers of steel or aluminum-cased cartridges employ Berdan priming to discourage reloading. These materials lack the elasticity for safe resizing. The U.S. built loads from Hornady, CCI, or Winchester are non-corrosive.

Boat-tail (BT): A streamlined rifle bullet design with a tapered rear section that helps reduce turbulence for better long-range accuracy. A somewhat flatter trajectory is another byproduct, useful beyond 350 -400 yards.

Boxer-primed: Conventional U.S.-type reloadable priming design, with a cartridge-case pocket and central flash-hole. Primers are self-contained metallic cups. Fired primers can be "de-primed" and replaced with new ones. New U.S. ammo should be non-corrosive but old rounds (and some imports) could use mercuric priming.

Cannelure: A knurled band that encircles some bullets to improve cartridge-case crimping. Most lever-action bullet types have cannelures to prevent bullet push-back in spring-loaded tubular magazines. The same design improves feeding with military bullets in other fast-cycling actions.

Chronograph: An instrument used to "see" bullets and record their velocities. Useful hint: Don't shoot it.

Dies: The cartridge forming and bullet-seating tooling used to reload ammunition, in conjunction with a reloading press. A sizing die squeezes a fired brass cartridge case back to its original dimensions. A seating die is then used to secure a bullet to the case.

FMJ: A bullet design where the lead core is clad in a <u>Full Metal Jacket</u>, and not designed to expand upon impact. Many are Spitzer types for good long-range performance. Military rifle bullets are so designed.

FPS: A projectile's velocity, expressed in <u>feet-per-second</u> (3000 fps).

Frangible: A specialty type of bullet, designed to disintegrate upon impact with hard surfaces, in order to minimize ricochet hazards. The core is often sintered-copper and polymer mix, clad with copper plating.

Ft lbs: <u>Foot-pounds</u> is an expression of projectile energy, relating to its mass and velocity. What it won't factor in is the design of a bullet. Some states require a 1000 ft lb minimum for cartridges used on bigger game like elk. They'll more than likely also prohibit use of FMJs.

Head Stamp: Most cartridges have identifying marks on their bases. U.S. civilian head stamps indicate the caliber and maker (30-06 Sprg RP). Military cartridges (and some foreign types) are another matter. They may be stamped with arsenal abbreviations (LC for Lake City), and year of manufacture.

JHP (or HP): A <u>jacketed hollow-point</u> bullet design, with a nose-cavity for rapid expansion. Many (but not all) are varmint loads. The solid-copper Barnes TSX is another type of HP, which lacks a jacket due to its homogenous composition. Its small nose-cavity is intended to initiate expansion through a controlled progression.

JSP: A <u>jacketed soft-point</u> bullet design with an exposed lead tip to initiate expansion. It could be a RN type, or a modified Spitzer.

Meplat: The forward-facing end of a bullet, which could be miniscule or pronounced, depending on its design.

MV: <u>Muzzle velocity</u>, usually recorded 15 feet beyond a muzzle, to minimize the effects of blast on a chronograph.

Non-corrosive: Nowadays, non-corrosive priming mixes are standard throughout the U.S., but that wasn't always true. The original mercuric compounds explain why many older barrels are pitted, due to lack of prompt attention after firing. There are still corrosive-primed surplus rounds in circulation, including some imported types. If in doubt, clean the barrel thoroughly after firing, or better yet, buy something else.

Ogive: The curved section of a bullet extending from its shank to the ogive. A pointed bullet has a sharper ogive, but all types need sufficient parallel surfaces for rifling engagement.

RN: A bullet of <u>round nose</u> design. A blunt tip is needed with tubular magazines to prevent the detonation of adjacent primers during recoil. That's why the classic lever gun cartridges use them. These bullets have larger meplats.

SAAMI: The <u>Sporting Arms And Manufacturing Institute</u> is an industry body that provides consistent standards for the manufacturing of American sporting firearms and ammunition. Using a cartridge as an example, upon its acceptance by SAAMI, a set of dimensional drawings will be published to govern tolerances. Such a load is a safer bet than some obscure surplus imports.

Spitzer: A pointed-type rifle bullet commonly used in vertical-magazine, centerfire rifles like a Mauser 98; M-16; or many sporting rifles. Spitzers have tiny meplats to help overcome aerodynamic drag. Some of the hunting types may even have a small polymer nose-cone.

Tracers: Just as their name suggests, these bullets emit a burning trail to help military forces "walk in" rounds on a target. They'll also start fires! The flammable element is ignited upon cartridge ignition and acts very much like a sparkler, so a good barrel is probably much better off without them. Military tracers have red bullet tips. Of course, so do some sporting bullets with polymer tips. Look closely and you can tell the difference. Another clue is a military head stamp.

VLD: A typically heavy-for-caliber, <u>very low drag</u>, streamlined projectile with a high BC, intended for shooting at extreme ranges.

LEGAL-ESE

When we research the more exotic aspects of firearms and extras, all sorts of head-scratching acronyms appear. It's worth getting to know them, even if you won't be buying a tricked-out firearm. Note the FFL process.

BATF (ATF): The <u>Bureau of Alcohol, Tobacco, Firearms, and Explosives</u> which regulates FFLs, SOT holders, NFA items, and other firearms. Airguns and muzzleloaders are out of the federal loop and can be ordered by mail if no local restrictions exist.

FFL: <u>Federal Firearms License</u>, held by firearms dealers (non-NFA). A gun shop is a typical FFL example. We can also buy a firearm through the Internet, but it will need to be shipped to an FFL holder in the purchaser's state of residence. From there a Form 4473 must be completed. The dealer will next contact ATF for a NICS check (National Instant Check System). Upon clearance of the NICS process, the buyer (transferee) can assume ownership of the firearm. A transfer fee ($25-$50) is commonly part of the deal, and covers an FFL-holder's efforts. Check your local laws before proceeding.

Firearm: A "firearm" will have serial-numbered part, which is usually its receiver. Purchase of a serial-numbered AR lower will require the Form 4473 and NICs process. Uppers aren't numbered and can be purchased like scopes or boots. The same applies for accessory barrels used on T/C or CVA single-shot rifles. Some are offered as muzzleloaders but, since their frames can also accept centerfire barrels, an FFL purchasing process is required. For this reason manufacturers sometimes offer an entirely different muzzleloader-dedicated frame and barrel design, for sale through the large sporting emporiums.

NFA: <u>National Firearms Act</u>, which regulates the sale and transfer of silencers, SBRs, etc.

SBR: A "<u>Short-Barreled Rifle</u>" has a shoulder-stock and barrel less than 16-inches in length. As such, it requires a special $200 federal stamp and permitting process.

Select-fire: This term describes firearms which can be fired in semi-automatic or full-auto modes. The latter is tightly regulated as an NFA firearm which, like SBRs and silencers, is subject to special permits and fees. Some firearms are strictly full-auto, but either constitutes a machinegun.

SOT: <u>Special Occupational Tax</u> status for dealers and manufacturers of NFA items. Purchasers of SBRs and suppressors will need to use an SOT Dealer.

Suppressor: Another word for a silencer. Like an SBR, ownership is legal through the federal permit process. The actual device is serial-numbered in the same way as a firearm, and must be registered to its legal owner.

OTHER *SURVIVAL GUNS* TITLES

If you purchase a gun safe and attempt to fill it up in one fell swoop, you'll be hemorrhaging dollar bills. To keep things manageable, why not adopt an incremental approach? That's exactly what's been done with the succession of firearms manuals. You can focus on just one system and chip away until the essentials have been procured. The old saying, "a little knowledge is a dangerous thing" certainly holds true with firearms. Accordingly, each book serves as a source for in-depth knowledge pertinent to a specific system. Furthermore, each is geared toward survival-based roles and the core principles espoused in *Survival Guns: A Beginner's guide*.

SURVIVAL GUNS FIREARMS PUBLICATIONS IN PRINT

Survival Guns: A Beginner's Guide: This book is the first in the series, and serves as a guide to help build a Prepper-based firearm battery. It starts with a gun safe, to which firearms and accessories can be added, with a planned process. To help make the best choices, some key underlying principles are defined. From there, procurement of several "essential systems" can commence. A baseline inventory of a shotgun, two rifles and a handgun serve as cornerstones. Further additions include some interesting specialty firearms and accessories. The firearms on the "essentials list," as well as many other types, are more thoroughly covered in firearms-specific editions. In each, the various models, ammunition and accessories are closely examined. While *Survival Guns* is written for beginners, those familiar with firearms should find topics of value.

Shotguns: A Comprehensive Guide: Would you like a bird gun, riot gun, and high powered rifle all rolled into one single gun? Where's the trade-off on recoil and performance? What shells work best with different chokes? This publication covers just about everything related to shotguns. Technical aspects are explored including the different types of guns, gauges, shells, chokes, shot sizes and ballistics. Accessories are examined, along with training tips and other useful information. The human factor is addressed with methods to accommodate smaller-statured shooters. Putting it all together, you'll not only have serious defensive capabilities, but also a means for the harvesting of both small game and very large animals. This shotgun edition shows you the way.

Rimfire Rifles: A Buyer's And Shooter's Guide: As a prepper, you've probably stashed emergency rations. Well, your food stores won't last forever, and don't forget, they could also be lost. So, like it or not, some form of subsistence hunting just might be in the cards. In that case, the *right* tools will essential. Noise could be a concern, so for those who understand its full capabilities, a rimfire rifle could be the perfect choice. Put the right load in the right rifle, and the loudest sound heard will be a bullet striking its target. The key is an understanding of the entire rimfire system, from firearms through calibers, and the many cartridge options. Since not every combination will work, knowledge is our key to success (and a full belly). Solid shooting ability counts as well, and a rimfire rifle is the perfect practice tool. Throw in a dash of defensive value, and we have a system worth a close look. That's what this book is all about.

Air Rifles: A Buyer's And Shooter's Guide: Did you know you can mail-order airguns in most locales? Unlike conventional firearms, they aren't federally regulated. They'll also get you into some tight places that would be strictly off-limits to any powder-burning guns. The latest air-powered technologies are a quantum leap beyond a common BB gun, offering real quality and impressive performance. How about a rifle that runs on high-pressure air, combining effortless operation with multiple shots? These "pre-charged" types can be filled from a scuba tank or special pump. Accuracy is phenomenal and so is power, yet noise is typically less than most silenced firearms. And again, no special BATF permits are necessary. Some of these air-powered rifles can even be purchased as big-bore versions in .45 and .50-caliber. Others run independently from highly compressed springs, or gas-strut type technologies. The *Air Rifles* edition provides the knowledge you'll need to fully exploit their capabilities. A wide range of ammunition and power-plants are explored, along with their advantages and limitations. Scopes and other sighting systems are detailed, as are useful accessories. The airgun edition is your source for non-firearm technologies, from plinking and training through hunting.

FUTURE PREPSMART FIREARM PUBLICATIONS

Handguns: A Buyer's And Shooter's Guide: You can shoot yourself with the wrong combination of pistol, holster and clothing, so which ones are dangerous? You may understand the fundamentals of shooting, but how do they apply to handguns? Are you interested in a 1911 pistol? If so, did you know you can create your own multi-caliber pistol off a single frame? What about other types? Which loads are your best defensive choices? This publication thoroughly covers handguns from different models, through practical calibers, holsters and accessories. You'll see some interesting alternatives to six-shot revolvers, and the latest high-capacity pistols. The smaller guns are covered, too. Practical revolver and pistol skills are detailed, along with recommended practice regimens. The handgun edition rolls all of this information into one source for safe and effective handling.

www.ingramcontent.com/pod-product-compliance
Lightning Source LLC
Chambersburg PA
CBHW081406270326
41931CB00016B/3398